THE MICHIGAN ECONOMY:

ITS POTENTIALS AND ITS PROBLEMS

The Michigan Economy

Its Potentials and Its Problems

BY

William Haber
The University of Michigan

AND

Eugene C. McKean and Harold C. Taylor
The W. E. Upjohn Institute for Employment Research

WITH CONTRIBUTIONS BY

Harvey E. Brazer, *The University of Michigan*
Fantus Factory Locating Service, Chicago
Daniel H. Kruger, *Michigan State University*
Henry C. Thole, *the Institute*

1959

PUBLISHED BY

The W. E. Upjohn Institute for Employment Research
709 South Westnedge Avenue
Kalamazoo, Michigan

Printed in the United States of America

Foreword and Acknowledgments

MANY PERSONS in the state of Michigan have been concerned with the need for a study of the Michigan economy, and their concern has been mounting in intensity for a good many years. It is desirable to recount the indebtedness of the authors of this report to some of the persons and groups that have long been interested in the economic problems of the state.

Professor Haber has been interested in the labor and employment problems of the state of Michigan for nearly three decades. That interest was expressed, for example, in a short study of the Michigan economy which was included in his report, *How Much Does It Cost?*, prepared for the Michigan Employment Security Commission in 1951. His belief that the need for a more intensive study of the Michigan economy had become acute led to his proposal, in the early spring of 1958, that such a study be carried on under his direction and under the auspices of the W. E. Upjohn Institute for Employment Research.

The entire program and objective of the Institute are such that Professor Haber's proposal was received with enthusiasm. Moreover, the Institute had had specific reasons to develop a high degree of interest in such a study. Dr. Taylor had been chairman, since August, 1956, of the Advisory Committee on Industrial Expansion Research of the Michigan Department of Economic Development. For nearly two years, that committee had been laying plans for studies of the Michigan economy, and had carried on some pilot studies related to the subject. Members of this committee were Dean Lloyd E. Fitzgerald of the College of Commerce and Finance, University of Detroit; Dean Walter C. Folley of the School of Business Administration, Wayne State University; Dean Russell A. Stevenson of the School of Business Administration, University of Michigan; and Dean Herman J. Wyngarden of the College of Business and Public Service, Michigan State University, who was later succeeded by Dean Alfred L. Seelye.

This committee was aided at all times by the directors of the bureaus of business research at the four universities. Dr. Paul A. Herbert, Chief of the Research Division of the Michigan Department of Economic Development, served as secretary to the committee. Dr. Wilbur R. Thompson, Assistant Professor of Economics at Wayne State University, was engaged as staff director for the committee. The work of the committee resulted in two reports.

One was a *Proposal for A Research Project Entitled, "Forecasting State Economic Development (with Special Reference to Michigan),"* which was presented to the Economic Development Commission in November, 1958. The other was a book by Professor Thompson and Professor John M. Mattila, entitled, *An Econometric Model of Postwar State Industrial Development.* The book is now being published by Wayne State University Press. The authors of the present report are much indebted to all those who participated in these committee activities which, among other things, indicated several areas in which detailed research was urgently needed.

The authors accept responsibility for all statements made in the study. They are grateful for the counsel and criticism of many persons in government, labor, universities, and industry. All or most of the manuscript has been read by Dr. Paul A. Herbert; Dr. Paul W. McCracken, Professor of Business Conditions, School of Business Administration, University of Michigan; Samuel C. Stearn, Chief, Labor Market Analysis Section, Research and Statistics Division, Michigan Employment Security Commission; John R. Stewart, Director of Research, Greater Detroit Board of Commerce; and Nat Weinberg, Director of Special Projects and Economic Analysis Department, and Woodrow L. Ginsburg, Director of the Research and Engineering Department, UAW. The opening chapter, "What's Ahead for Michigan?" which contains a summary and conclusions, has also been read and criticized by Walter H. Blucher, Executive Director, Southeastern Michigan Metropolitan Community Research Corporation; Dr. Harvey E. Brazer, Associate Professor of Economics and Research Associate, Institute of Public Administration, University of Michigan; William M. Day, President, Michigan Bell Telephone Company and Commission Chairman, Michigan Department of Economic Development; Dr. George Katona, Program Director, Survey Research Center, University of Michigan; H. F. Lange, Vice President and Treasurer, Michigan Bell Telephone Company; and Dr. Rensis Likert, Director, Institute of Social Research, University of Michigan.

Special thanks are due to Mr. Stearn and to Norman Barcus, Director of Research, Michigan Employment Security Commission, both of whom gave counsel and assistance to the authors on many occasions while this study was in progress.

The authors are indebted also to those who have prepared special studies or reports for this volume. These include Dr.

Brazer; Fantus Factory Locating Service; Dr. Daniel H. Kruger, Coordinator, Labor and Industrial Relations Center, Michigan State University; Dr. Edwin Grossnickle, Professor of General Business, School of Business, Western Michigan University; and Henry C. Thole, Industrial Project Director, the W. E. Upjohn Institute for Employment Research. In addition, Dr. Kruger helped with the editing of several chapters of the manuscript; Professor Walter W. Waring of Kalamazoo College participated in the editorial work on most of the manuscript; and Carleton W. Collin of Station WKZO, Kalamazoo, did considerable work in preparing the statistical tables included in the study.

Although considerable time and effort have been expended in preparing this study of the Michigan economy, the report must be regarded as exploratory rather than as definitive. On many important issues, the authors have been able to do little more than to demonstrate the need for further study, and to spell out the directions in which such further study ought to proceed. To provide a definitive study of the Michigan economy will require many times as much effort as has gone into the present report.

It is hoped that this report will help the people of Michigan to secure a better understanding of the economic problems of their state. Even more, however, it is hoped that the study will stimulate the interest of the citizens of the state in carrying on further studies and in pursuing the lines of action which the authors believe are urgently needed. The authors hope that the Committee on Michigan's Economic Future will be in a position to spearhead further study and action, and they hope that this report will provide the committee with a useful starting point for its work.

> The W. E. Upjohn Institute
> for Employment Research

September, 1959

The W. E. Upjohn Institute
for Employment Research

THE INSTITUTE, a privately sponsored nonprofit research organization located in Kalamazoo, Michigan, was established on July 1, 1945. It is an activity of the W. E. Upjohn Unemployment Trustee Corporation, which was formed in 1932 to administer a fund set aside by the late Dr. W. E. Upjohn for the purpose of carrying on "research into the causes and effects of unemployment and measures for the alleviation of unemployment."

Contents

Appendix Chapters

Tables

xiii

Appendix Tables

xiv

PART I

SUMMARY

What's Ahead for Michigan?*

Introduction

WHAT IS LIFE going to be like in Michigan during the next five, ten, or fifteen years? How big will the state be? How prosperous will it be? Will business and industry flourish? Will there be jobs for all who wish to work, and at wages which provide a standard of living equal to or better than is available in other states? Will the state be looked upon as a bright spot in the nation, or as a problem area? What problems shall we face? Can we know about them now, and can we do something about solving them?

Such questions as these are of interest to the people of any state at any time. Certainly they are of interest to the people of Michigan. Indeed, the people of Michigan may be especially concerned with the answers to such questions. Our unemployment rate was higher than that of the nation during the 1958 recession, and it remained higher during the period of national recovery which was taking place during 1959. We find that our state government is in financial difficulties. We hear it said that the "climate for business" is poor in Michigan. Such charges come not only from various factions within the state, but are reported also in the public press all over the nation. We Michiganders have had reason to do a rather special amount of soul-searching with respect to the economic destiny of our state.

Many of the answers we need in order to plot our course effectively in the years ahead are simply not available without much careful economic research followed by a great deal of thoughtful appraisal. Still, some answers can be given; and at least a clear enough picture of the state and its economic problems can be presented so that people will know what questions to ask and what answers to seek. In the following pages the problems of the state's

---

* This chapter is less than a complete summary of the book, in that it does not review systematically each major topic covered in the book as a whole. In another sense, this chapter is more than a summary. It attempts to present issues and points of view relating to Michigan's economic problems, whether those issues have been covered adequately by our own research or not. Thus, we hope that this chapter will be helpful to the citizens of Michigan, not only as a report of research completed and an outline of what needs to be done, but also as a more general guide to their own thinking about the future of the state.

3

economic future will be outlined as well as can be done on the basis of existing information.

We may say at the outset that prolonged and substantial unemployment has been one of the major factors leading the people of Michigan to be concerned about the future. The state reached, in 1953, a total nonfarm employment of 2,694,000, a number which has not been equaled yet in any year since 1953. Thus, although we had a very good year in 1955 because of the high demand for automobiles, one can say that our employment troubles really started after the peak year of 1953. In 1956 and 1957, when the nation as a whole was enjoying a high degree of prosperity, Michigan had 6.5 and 6.8 percent of its labor force unemployed; and we moved from there to the crushing year of 1958 when our unemployment rose to 406,000, or 13.5 percent of the labor force. Even in the late spring of 1959, with recovery from the recession practically completed in the nation as a whole, it appeared that Michigan needed about 140,000 jobs to reduce unemployment to frictional levels, and about 400,000 jobs to achieve the same proportion of full employment labor force participation as characterized the nation as a whole.

This is one of the major problems which has stimulated interest in the question of Michigan's economic destiny. The present report is concerned with that problem as well as with the other factors that must be considered in appraising the future of the state.

Long-Run Prospects for the Nation

IN THE YEARS TO COME, some states will markedly outpace the nation in economic progress and prosperity, while others will lag substantially behind. Even so, the destiny of the nation certainly establishes a range within which the destinies of the individual states will lie. In appraising the future of our state, we may start, therefore, with a look at what seems to be in store for the nation as a whole.

Except for the possibility of another World War (in which case, all bets are off), seldom in history have men been as excited about the potentialities of their future as we in the United States are today. A few years ago a sober scientific study stated that in many ways our progress during the first fifty years of this century was greater than progress in all the previous history of mankind. We have good reason to hope that this remarkable pace of scientific and technological development can be maintained and even accelerated. If the pace is maintained, the standard of living of Americans in the years ahead will improve dramatically.

This general conclusion is reached in objective studies carried on by the Committee for Economic Development (1958), the National Planning Association (1958), and the Joint Committee on the Economic Report (1959). Similar conclusions are stated in the Rockefeller Report on the U. S. Economy (1958). *Fortune* carried an article in its issue of November, 1955, entitled, "Productivity: The Great Age of 3%." Assuming that we can maintain a three percent annual increase in productivity, the authors point out that spendable income per average family, which was $4,400 in 1955, could rise (in constant dollars) to $8,000 by 1980, and $15,000 by the year 2000. And this would be done even with a work-week dropping to 35 hours by 1980.

Going along with this encouraging rise which is expected in the standard of living, a continued upsurge in population is anticipated. The continuation of high levels of birth rates in the years since World War II has amazed the experts, and has led to several upward revisions in the estimates of populations to be expected in the future. No one can tell what birth rates will actually prevail, and the nation's population in 1970 may range from a low of 202.5 million to a high of 219.5 million. Even the lowest of these will represent a substantial increase. From a population of 174.1 million in 1958, this would be an increase of 28.4 million or 16 percent. The increase may run as high as 45.4 million.

To add 28 to 45 million people in a scant period of twelve years and to provide all of them with a substantially better standard of living than that which we enjoy today is quite an assignment; but it is not an impractical dream and it is one which most students believe the nation can achieve.

What does all this mean to the people of Michigan? Not that the problems of our state will be solved automatically, nor even that they will be solved easily. But it does mean that, if we tackle our problems with vigor, we can be encouraged to know that a great surge of national prosperity is adding its weight to our efforts.

Michigan Since 1940: A Story of Growth

THE EMPLOYMENT PROBLEMS of the state of Michigan strike us with special force because they have followed a period of truly remarkable growth. Let us look briefly at the history of the state since

1940. We shall see that Michigan was one of the busiest states in the nation through 1953; that signs of trouble were clearly developing from 1953 through 1957; and that our need to re-examine our economic destiny was brought forcibly to our attention by our experiences during the recession of 1958.

Michigan and the Manufacturing Belt

Neither the past nor the future of our state can be very well understood unless we look at its place in the geography and in the industrial life of the nation. The facts should be of interest to every citizen.

A remarkably large proportion of the productive power of the nation is concentrated in a fairly narrow strip extending roughly from New York and Boston on the east to Chicago and St. Louis on the west. This strip is usually referred to as the "manufacturing belt." It comprises portions of several additional states, but generally the industrialized portions of the three Middle Atlantic States of New Jersey, New York, and Pennsylvania, and of the five East North Central States of Illinois, Indiana, Michigan, Ohio, and Wisconsin. Concentrated in the manufacturing belt, which accounts for only eight percent of the land area of the nation, are over two-fifths of its people, over half of its income, and about two-thirds of its manufacturing employment. The very existence of this heavily concentrated manufacturing belt lends strength to its further growth; for it provides either the raw materials or the markets or both for a vast proportion of those businesses which are looking for a location for additional manufacturing facilities. During the six-year period, 1951-1956, well over half of all of the nation's expenditures for new manufacturing plant and equipment were made in this general area. It will be quite some time before increasing manufacturing expenditures in most areas of the south and southwest will constitute a competitive threat to the area.

Partly as a cause of this industrial concentration and partly as a result of it, a tremendous proportion of the nation's railroad facilities are concentrated along the east-west lines between New England and New York on the east and Chicago and St. Louis on the west. Moreover, the recently developed four-lane super-highways have come into being first along exactly these same east-west channels of trade, so that the advantages of the manufacturing belt come to be continually enhanced.

To a large degree, Michigan is allied with this entire group of industrial states. We are even more closely associated, however, with the five East North Central States which include Ohio, Indiana, Illinois, Michigan, and Wisconsin. Let us look briefly at the industrial power of this region. With about 20 percent of the nation's population, the region produces 50 percent of the entire nation's nonelectrical machinery; 44 percent of its transportation equipment; 42 percent of its fabricated metal products; 41 percent of its primary metals; 41 percent of its rubber products; 38 percent of its electrical machinery; and 32 percent of its furniture and fixtures. Such an industrial concentration offers an attractive array of suppliers and customers which must appeal to many firms which are seeking a location.

Population

In mid-1958, there were almost 7.9 million persons living in Michigan. In comparison with the growth of other states in the Middle Atlantic and East North Central regions, the growth of population in Michigan has been conspicuous. In percentage terms, the growth of Michigan from 1950 to 1958 was substantially higher than that of any of the other seven states. Indeed, in sheer numbers added, the growth of Michigan during that period was greater than the growth of any other state in the union except California, Texas, and Florida. Nor was this growth a fluke of the past few years. During the decade from 1940 to 1950, Michigan's percentage growth was also well above the growth of any of the other seven states. In numerical terms the population growth of Michigan was exceeded only by growth in California, Texas, and New York.

In-Migration

Because of high birth rates, nearly every state in the union has shown some sort of population increase in recent years. But in addition to birth rates, states gain or lose population as a result of net migration from one state to another. Some of the facts about net migration serve to dramatize the extent to which Michigan has seemed attractive to persons moving from other states. During the years from 1950 to 1956, Michigan gained 484,000 people by net in-migration, a number larger than that gained by any other state in the union except Florida and California. Next below us was our sister state of Ohio. During that period all states of the East North Central region gained population by virtue of net in-migration; but

7

in-migration to Michigan was 40 percent of in-migration to the whole region.

During those same years there was net migration *out of* every one of the New England States except Connecticut, while in Pennsylvania the net out-migration was so great as to be exceeded only by net out-migration from each of three southern states.

Not all of the above relationships held true during the decade from 1940 to 1950, but net migration to Michigan was again very heavy (nearly 400,000), and was exceeded only by migration to Florida and California. During that decade, all of the Middle Atlantic and East North Central states except Wisconsin and Pennsylvania gained population by net migration.

The population growth of Michigan during the past couple of decades has indeed been remarkable; and that growth apparently was continuing at substantial rates even through 1958, despite the fact that signs of economic trouble had already begun to appear. And to the growth of population we may now add two other interesting signs of economic vigor within the state.

Capital Expenditures in Michigan

One is the story of capital investment — investment in new plant and equipment. Capital expenditure data reported in the Census of Manufactures and in the intercensal Annual Survey of Manufactures show that over one billion dollars of new plant and equipment were put in place in Michigan during 1956 alone. Part of these expenditures represent, of course, replacement of existing plant and equipment.

During the four years, 1953-1956 inclusive, capital expenditures in Michigan were accounting for from 9 to 11 percent of all capital expenditures being made throughout the whole country. Moreover, during this period, Michigan's share of all capital expenditures was larger, for the most part, than it was during such earlier years as 1939 and 1947. Thus, it appears that Michigan's basic industrial foundation was being reasonably well sustained through 1956, although capital expenditures did drop substantially as the recession began to affect the state in 1957. A state that for several years was accounting for almost one-tenth of the nation's new plant and equipment can be assumed to have considerable industrial vitality.

Michigan's record on capital expenditures during the years 1953 through 1956 was very good in comparison with outlays made in its neighbor states. Michigan and Ohio were the two leading states in terms of state shares of national capital expenditures. Since Ohio is a larger state than Michigan (both in population and in manufacturing employment), Michigan appears to have fared somewhat better than Ohio through 1956. Data relating to these observations appear in the following table.

Area	Percent of Total Capital Expenditures			
	1956	1955	1954	1953
United States............................	100.0	100.0	100.0	100.0
East North Central region................	33.3	32.4	33.3	32.8
Ohio.....................................	9.4	8.3	9.4	9.1
Indiana..................................	5.2	5.5	3.7	5.3
Illinois..................................	7.3	6.8	7.0	7.5
MICHIGAN...............................	9.0	9.8	10.9	8.8
Wisconsin...............................	2.0	2.1	2.1	2.1

The East North Central States as a group provided the market for one-third of the nation's new plant and equipment during these four years. The attention that has been given to industrial growth in other sections of the country should not obscure the fact that the East North Central States have been laying the foundation, through substantial outlays for plant and equipment, for their continued industrial pre-eminence.

Number of Manufacturing Establishments

There is some interesting information on this topic with respect to the number of manufacturing establishments covered under the old-age and survivors insurance program. These data reveal that Michigan had 10,914 manufacturing establishments in 1949, and 12,355 in 1956, for a net gain of over 1,400 new manufacturing establishments, an increase of 13.2 percent. It is interesting to compare this increase in the number of manufacturing establishments in Michigan with the experience of the United States and the other East North Central States. By comparison with Michigan's increase of 13.2 percent, the United States as a whole increased by 4.3 percent and the East North Central States by 5.0 percent. Michigan's percentage increase was two-and-a-half times as great as the percentage increase in the East North Central States as a whole. The increase in Ohio was 7.6 percent; in Indiana, 5.3 percent; in Wisconsin, 1.5 percent; while in Illinois there was an actual loss in the number of manufacturing establishments, a loss of one-half of one percent. Thus, the gain in Michigan was greater than the gain in any of the other East North Central States, and was almost twice as great in percentage terms as the increase in the next ranking state of Ohio.

Additional data for industry groups for the period 1953-1956 point up the fact that the over-all record of growth of manufacturing establishments is a result of gains and losses in the various component industries of both the durable and the nondurable sectors. This pattern differs from the record on employment which, as discussed later, shows that all of the durable industry groups reported a job loss from 1953 to 1957, while most of the nondurable groups reported a modest job gain. Data on plant gains and losses from 1953 to 1956 follow:

Industry Group	Number of Plants Added or Lost
Durables	
Lumber and wood products	− 69
Fabricated metal products	+154
Machinery (nonelectrical)	− 53
Electrical machinery	+ 33
Other transportation equipment	+ 42
Nondurables	
Textile mill products and apparel	− 24
Printing, publishing, and allied products	+ 75
Chemicals, petroleum, and coal products	+ 22
Rubber products	+ 18

Operating records of the Michigan Department of Economic Development present an encouraging picture for 1958. They suggest a net gain of over 200 new plants or plant additions in Michigan in that year. Plant gains (264) were more than four times as great as plant losses (57).

The Michigan Department of Economic Development data show that expansions by existing companies and newly started plants were both more numerous than plant move-ins. Certainly, it would have been desirable for more outside plants to have located in Michigan. But the data suggest that Michigan's highly industrialized economic structure provides substantial impetus for its own continued expansion. Such a tendency is more encouraging than if the state were heavily dependent on move-ins from other states to assure its continued industrial growth.

These figures have to be reconciled with the fact that during recent years our over-all employment opportunities have declined, despite the fact that the evidence seems to be suggesting that we are strong in the number of new plant openings. The story seems to be that we have lost ground in automotive employment and with respect to other larger establishments — those of 500 employees and over — and have made up our plant inventory by virtue of a larger number of smaller-sized plants. The situation is shown in the following table, which is based on manufacturing establishments under the old-age and survivors insurance program.

Employee-size Class	Number of Manufacturing Establishments [a]		Percent Distribution		Percent Change in Number
	1956	1953	1956	1953	1953-1956
All Classes...................	12,355	12,069	100.0	100.0	2.4
0-7 employees.............	5,504	5,477	44.6	45.3	.5
8-49 employees...........	4,594	4,265	37.2	35.3	7.7
50-249 employees..........	1,632	1,672	13.2	13.9	−2.4
250-499 employees.........	312	298	2.5	2.5	4.7
500 employees & over........	313	357	2.5	3.0	−12.3

Source: *U.S. Department of Commerce and U.S. Department of Health, Education and Welfare, County Business Patterns, First Quarter 1953 and First Quarter 1956, Part I, Table 2.*

[a] *Based on "reporting units." "Virtually all of the reporting units shown for manufacturing industries represent single establishments." Data are as of the first quarter of the calendar year. Each establishment had at least one employee during part of the calendar quarter.*

While these data on increases in the number of manufacturing establishments do not present an unqualified picture of industrial growth, the figures do lend encouragement to the belief that the spirit of enterprise still flourishes in the state of Michigan.

Michigan's Employment Problem

WE HAVE SEEN that, on the whole, the years since 1940 have been years of remarkable growth for the state of Michigan, and that, in some important respects, there were no signs of let-up through 1956 or later. Thus, capital expenditures in the state were conspicuously high as recently as 1956; and population growth was continuing at a substantial rate even in the recession year of 1958.

But in 1953 Michigan reached a level of employment which, despite the continued growth of population, we have not yet regained. Severe losses of employment were sustained between 1953 and 1957, even though the latter year was a generally prosperous one for the nation as a whole. In some respects, we can secure a clearer picture of Michigan's problems by examining our experience from 1953 to 1957 than by moving at once to the recession year of 1958.

Retarded Growth, 1953 to 1957

In 1953, Michigan was a prosperous state in a prosperous nation. All lines of business and industry were flourishing; and, in addition, Michigan was especially busy with Korean-defense production and with production of automobiles to meet ever-pressing pent-up demands. The state's labor force expanded abnormally; there was perhaps over-employment. Nearly 42 percent of the state's entire population were at work, whereas a figure of 38.5 percent is often considered to be a reasonable goal for full employment. By 1957, only 35.5 percent of the state's people were at work, while in the generally prosperous nation as a whole the percentage was at a comfortable 38.6.

Our losses during the four-year period were mainly losses of manufacuring jobs. Of these, losses of defense jobs were substantial. There is no industrial classification of "defense jobs," of course; these jobs are carried under the usual classifications of transportation equipment, electrical machinery, fabricated metals, and so on. Estimates suggest, however, that Michigan's losses of defense work after 1953 may have amounted to 125,000 to 150,000 jobs — a significant part of our total job loss.

But let us look now at the loss of jobs in the state in terms of the usual industrial classifications. In all manufacturing activity, our state lost at least 180,000 jobs in the four years, 1953-1957, including the loss of defense work. The nation lost manufacturing jobs in that period, too — 456,000 jobs. But it is significant to note that the job loss in Michigan was nearly two-fifths of the loss in the entire nation! The major sources of decline in the number of Michigan manufacturing jobs are shown in the following table.

Industry	Employment		Loss
	1953	1957	
Motor vehicles and equipment	503,000	395,000	108,000
Other transportation equip.	33,000	13,000	20,000
Nonelectrical machinery	165,000	149,000	16,000
Fabricated metal products	121,000	107,000	14,000
Primary metal products	87,000	77,000	10,000

All of these reductions, it will be noted, are in durable goods manufacturing. Of all other durable goods manufacturing industries not shown in the above table, not one registered a gain in Michigan during this four-year period. In the above table, the tremendous importance of the automotive job loss to the state is made clear. (The national job loss in that industry during the same four years was 143,000.)

But what happened to nondurables manufacturing jobs during this period?[1] In total, we picked up a scant 4,000 jobs in the state in this entire sector, moving from 185,000 to 189,000 jobs in the four years. During that same period the nation as a whole had lost 172,000 nondurables jobs, chiefly because of a substantial drop in textiles.

We have examined Michigan's experience in manufacturing, both durables and nondurables. We must now consider the whole field of nonmanufacturing nonagricultural employment.[2] It is in this area that the nation as a whole made spectacular gains during the four years, 1953 to 1957, registering a net increase of over 2.9 million jobs. This was far more than enough to offset the nation's losses in manufacturing, so that there was a very good level of prosperity and over-all employment. Unfortunately, it is not clear just what happened in Michigan. In the nonmanufacturing sector, Bureau of Labor Statistics data suggest that Michigan's gains, percentagewise, were about as good as those in the nation as a whole; while Michigan Employment Security Commission data suggest that our performance fell far short of that of the nation. If we use the MESC data, we conclude that Michigan's gain in the nonmanufacturing sector amounted to about 49,000 jobs.

According to the Bureau of Labor Statistics data, the only ones which can be used to compare our state with the region and the nation, Michigan's rate of increase in *nonfactory* employment during 1953-1957 exceeded that of Ohio, Indiana, and Illinois. Only Wisconsin, which has about half the population of Michigan, showed a larger percentage gain in this category.

The increases were: Wisconsin, 12.6 percent; Michigan, 9.5 percent; entire United States, 9.1 percent; Ohio, 8.1 percent; Indiana and Illinois, 7.2 percent each.

Although Michigan experienced the second largest percentage gain in its region in this category of employment, fewer than 18 out

1 Food and kindred products; textiles and apparel; paper and allied products; printing, publishing, and allied industries; chemical, petroleum, and coal products; and other nondurable goods manufacturing.

2 Mining; contract construction; transportation and public utilities; wholesale and retail trade; finance, insurance and real estate; service and miscellaneous industries; and government.

of 100 of this state's residents had nonfactory jobs in 1957. This was the lowest proportion in the region. Next above Michigan was Indiana with just 18 nonfactory employees for every 100 persons in the state. The highest proportion (23) was in Illinois.

Trends in total employment for the state also do not compare favorably with those of surrounding states. When factory and non-factory jobs are lumped together, BLS data show that Michigan experienced a decline of more than three percent over the four-year period, 1953-1957. Indiana lost almost one percent, while Ohio increased almost two percent, Illinois close to three percent, and Wisconsin better than five percent. Over-all, the East North Central States added less than one percent to nonagricultural employment, while the nation as a whole averaged a five percent gain.

In any case, it must be concluded that Michigan's employment experience, 1953-1957, was markedly at variance with the experience of the nation. The nation, though suffering a loss of manufacturing jobs, gained, in the over-all, nearly 2.5 million jobs, so that the year of 1957 was on the whole a year of national prosperity. Michigan, by contrast, suffered a net loss of jobs that may have run in the neighborhood of 130,000. Our crushing loss of 180,000 manufacturing jobs was two-fifths of the loss sustained in the entire nation; and well over half of that loss was in automotive employment. Mixed into the figures showing losses by industrial classifications is a substantial loss of about 125,000 to 150,000 jobs occasioned by our decline in defense work following the Korean period. Michigan's problems were indeed upon us before the recession of 1958.

The Recession of 1958

Although trouble was already brewing in Michigan before the recession, it became evident to all in that year. Affecting all business in the nation to some degree, unemployment was especially severe in Michigan, where it rose to a total of 406,000, or 13.5 percent of the labor force. Unemployment was especially conspicuous in the motor vehicles and equipment industry, in which the number of Michigan jobs dropped from 395,000 in 1957 to 293,000 in 1958, a loss of 102,000 jobs. Moreover — and of telling significance — Michigan's loss during the one-year period, 1957-1958, was two-thirds of the entire nation's employment loss in that industry.

By May, 1959, national recovery was well under way, with unemployment below the five percent level. Michigan was improving also; but the unemployment rate for Detroit was still 9.8 percent, which was about double the national rate; and the rate for the state as a whole was 8.3 percent, which was still much too high for comfort.

Labor Force Participation in Michigan

With 240,000 persons unemployed in the state in May, 1959, our difficulties might not seem to be overwhelming. But there is reason to fear that our problem is considerably greater than that figure would suggest. As is well known, the counting of "unemployed" persons is tricky. An unemployed person is one who is not working but who *is seeking work*. When work gets too hard to find, during a recession, many persons give up the search and are no longer counted as unemployed. In the spring of 1959, only about 33.5 percent of the state's people were at work. This should be compared with the figure of 38.5 percent which may be regarded as normal during a period of full employment. If we are short by 5 percent, and with a population of perhaps 8 million in mid-1959, we might need 400,000 additional jobs to bring the state back to a proper condition of full employment.

There may be some who doubt whether 38.5 percent is a proper measure of full employment. It is, however, a figure which Michigan exceeded in many years prior to 1954, and it is a figure which has been equaled in the nation many times in the past half-century, exclusive of war and depression periods. To assume that we can settle for a lesser goal may be wishful thinking.

Recent Income Trends

The importance of maintaining a high proportion of employed persons in Michigan's total population is emphasized by recent income trends in this state. As population has increased and job opportunities have remained stable, income per person in Michigan has declined relative to the rest of the region and the nation as a whole.

Income per person in this state was very substantially above the national average in 1953, and somewhat above the average for its neighboring states, including Illinois, Indiana, Ohio and Wisconsin. But by 1957, Michigan's income per person was slightly below the average for its region and only moderately above that for the entire nation:

Year	Income per Person		
	United States	East North Central Region	Michigan
1953............................	$1,788	$2,050	$2,120
1957............................	2,027	2,214	2,141

Undoubtedly, when income figures for 1958 are released, they will show a further decline in average income for the state, both in actual amount and in comparison with regional and national levels. However, the recent decline in income per person does not necessarily portend a continuing loss of Michigan's relative income position. Michigan's position, relative to that of the region and of the nation, has fallen and risen in the past; it is reasonable to assume that it will rise again if and when we can attain fairly full employment in the state.

Reasons for the State's Employment Problem

BY IMPLICATION, we have already said a good deal about the reasons for the severe employment problems of the state of Michigan, but we must now state these reasons in orderly fashion.

Our "Industry-Mix"

First of all, Michigan has nearly always been a "feast-or-famine" state, and the reasons are found in the kinds of industrial activity that are carried on in the state. For example, manufacturing employment tends to fluctuate more widely than nonmanufacturing employment; and in Michigan the percentage of total nonfarm employment which is in manufacturing is third largest of all the states. Moreover, employment in the manufacture of durable goods fluctuates much more widely than employment in the manufacture of nondurable goods; and Michigan has a larger percentage of its manufacturing employment in durable goods than does any other state. Finally, a state in which manufacturing activity is heavily concentrated in any one industry group tends to be seriously affected by ups and downs in that particular industry. Except for Oregon's concentration in the forest products industry, and North Carolina's concentration in textiles, Michigan's concentration in the motor vehicles and equipment industry is the most conspicuous example of industrial concentration in the nation. As recently as 1955, that industry accounted for nearly a fifth of all wage and salary workers in the state, and for 40 percent of all manufacturing employment in the state.

These special characteristics of Michigan explain why unemployment in our state almost always makes the headlines during periods of recession. Our fluctuations are explainable in terms of the fluctuating nature of the activities that happen to be carried on in the state. It should have occasioned no surprise that unemployment in Michigan made the headlines during 1958; and it should be no surprise to us to learn that unemployment may remain somewhat more severe for a somewhat longer period of time in Michigan than in the nation as a whole. But of course there is more to the story than this. Why did we drop so very low in our employment level during 1958? Moreover, the state has always bounced back after previous recessionary periods and has gone on to full employment and to new peaks of economic activity. Why is there some fear that we may not bounce back this time?

Shifts in Defense Procurement

As has already been noted, there has been a dramatic shift in the nature of defense production, away from wheeled vehicles, in which Michigan dominates the field, and toward aircraft, electronics, and missiles. We have referred to Michigan's estimated loss of 125,000 to 150,000 defense jobs in the period since 1953. In the fast-growing aircraft and electronics industries, Michigan has made little headway. The aircraft, aircraft engine, and aircraft equipment (not elsewhere classified) industries in the nation altogether employed over 800,000 people in 1954; but Michigan's employment in these industries was less than 20,000. The radios and related products industry (which takes in most of what is generally called the electronics industry) employed 294,000 people in 1954, of whom only 4,700 were employed in Michigan — actually fewer than were employed in the state in 1947. Our state — a conspicuous producer of military equipment during World War II and during the Korean period — has come to play a minor role in the defense business.

Decentralization of the Automobile Industry

A third factor in explaining Michigan's difficulty is the gradual decentralization of the automobile industry. Actually, such decentralization has been going on for a long time. Michigan hit its peak as the automobile center of the world during the 30's, when the state accounted for over 60 percent of all automotive employment. Since then, our share has been gradually reduced to the point where in 1958 Michigan had about 47 percent of the nation's employment in this industry. Such decentralization was dictated largely by market considerations. With the large volume of automobiles being produced during the past decade, and in view of the fact that these cars are purchased by people all over the country, producing them all in one state or in one region would be manifestly impractical.

Michigan would have felt the impact of this gradual decentralization long ago, had it not been for the sharp increase in the number of cars and trucks produced to meet pent-up demands in the years following World War II. Production reached a peak of over 9 million vehicles in 1955, so that Michigan's losses in percentage terms up to that time were more than offset by increases in production levels. But, as is well known, automotive production dropped very severely in 1958, to only 60 percent of the production of the peak year of 1955. Michigan employment in the motor vehicles and equipment industry dropped from highs of 503,000 in 1953 and 467,000 in 1955 to the lowly average of 293,000 in 1958.

These factors explain why Michigan employment dropped so low in 1958. There was the recession itself, which affected all lines of activity to some degree. The very heavy concentration of durable goods manufacturing in Michigan, which makes our state highly sensitive to ups and downs in the economy, was an especially important factor. There was also the dramatic drop in automotive production, from the spectacularly high year of 1955 to the disastrously low year of 1958. And, as if to aggravate the impact of all these forces, there was the shift in the nature of defense procurement and there was the gradual decentralization of the automobile industry.

The last two of these — the shift in defense requirements and the gradual decentralization of the automotive industry — are among the major reasons for our fear that the number of jobs in Michigan may not easily or quickly return to the levels needed in order to maintain full employment. But there is a third reason for that fear: the rapid rate at which efficiency-increasing capital investments have been made in recent years. To that subject we must now turn our attention.

Efficiency-Increasing Capital Investments

Beginning as soon after World War II as the construction materials situation permitted, the automotive industry began to invest huge sums of money in new plant and equipment. Well over half of this new investment has been made in Michigan. In the single year of 1956, the industry invested over a billion dollars, almost half of it in the state of Michigan.

New plant and equipment are more efficient than old plant and equipment. More product can be put out with fewer workers. The cumulative effect of these large investments is now beginning to make itself felt, in the number of cars that can be produced with a given number of employees. Such improvements usually show up more dramatically after a "shakedown" period, such as occurred in the 1958 recession. The net result of all this is that it may be many years before the automotive industry will employ as many workers as it did in the previous peak. In the years ahead, production levels may occasionally run as high as 10 million cars and trucks per year; but it is believed by some observers that the industry could turn out such a volume with no more workers than were employed in the peak production year of 1955 when nine million units were produced.

Efficiency-improving investments in Michigan have by no means been confined to the automotive industry. Although about half a billion dollars were spent by that industry in 1956, other industries also invested half a billion in the state in that year. And, as we observed earlier, Michigan has been conspicuously high among the states in capital outlays in other recent years. We must note also that in Michigan an unusually high proportion of capital outlays tends to go into equipment rather than into plant. Equipment tends to be labor-saving, while plant tends to be job-providing. Michigan's industry tends to be of the mass-production, high-profit, and high-wage type. Such industries have the means to make efficiency-improving equipment purchases, and they have strong motivation to hold their total labor costs in line.

Efficiency-improving investments, which include changes often referred to as "automation," are in evidence everywhere in the nation. They have occurred in almost every industry. Broadly speaking, we must view these efficiency-increasing investments with enthusiasm, not with distrust or fear. Such improvements make possible the eight-hour day and the five-day week, and the great increase in our standard of living that is expected in the years to come. But these developments do bring dislocations and problems, and, at the moment, Michigan has its share of the problems.

19

This factor, along with the others we have discussed, leads to doubt as to whether Michigan may soon be able to re-absorb its large pool of unemployed workers.

Future Population and the Need for More Jobs

WE SEE that in the spring of 1959 Michigan needed about 140,000 jobs to reduce unemployment to frictional levels, and about 400,-000 jobs to achieve the same proportion of full employment labor force participation as characterized the nation as a whole. Even if the shortage should be temporarily obscured by a high quarter or two of automotive activity in the near future, it remains as a persistent problem in our state's economy. And what of the future? Michigan has for many years been one of the fastest-growing states in the nation. Will such growth continue? If it does, either Michigan will have to develop job opportunities at rates that now seem very unlikely, or we shall be plagued with unemployment problems of continuing severity.

To a degree, there is something almost inexorable about the directions of population growth. For many years, movements in the United States have been from south to north, from east to west, from rural areas to urban centers. All of these trends have contributed to the growth of the state of Michigan. For well over a century, except for the period, 1890-1910, Michigan has grown at a more rapid rate than the nation as a whole. Such long-term trends can and do change, of course; but they seldom change abruptly, over such a short span as the time between now and 1970.

Based on our past history and on various expectations of population growth in the nation as a whole, the 1970 population of Michigan can be estimated anywhere from a low of 9.4 million to a high of nearly eleven million. Let us assume a reasonably conservative figure of 9.9 million and look at the number of jobs required for that population. If we assume that 38.5 percent of the people should be working under conditions of full employment, then we should have about 3.8 million jobs available in 1970. With the number of job-holders at about 2.7 million in May, 1959, this means that we would have to develop 1.1 million new jobs in about eleven years, or an average of about 100,000 per year. Since we are now short of full employment by 400,000 jobs, we have considerable "catching up" to do; and thus both the short-run and the long-run future present a strong challenge.

It is time now to add a word of caution, which at the same time offers some consolation. Conceivably, job prospects may not be as gloomy as they appear. It is easy to over-react with pessimism when things look bad. Moreover, most forecasters have had quite a record, especially in the postwar years, of underestimating the degree of national prosperity that lay ahead of us. At the close of World War II, it was generally assumed that we would have considerable unemployment during the transition from war to peace, and much was written on the subject of how to manage that transition. As late as 1949, prolonged unemployment was being viewed as the major problem of the 1950's. The phrases of "stagnation" and "the mature economy" were still being heard. Not many students foresaw the fabulous developments in population, productivity, and prosperity that have actually characterized most of the present decade. Thus, although we cannot perceive the manner in which Michigan's economy may move forward, new and unforeseen developments may occur which will cause the state to maintain its position in the ranks of the prosperous and rapidly growing states.

We may hope that such happy developments will occur. Unfortunately, the facts as they appear at present give us no right to count on any automatic solutions to the problems of our state. The facts call, rather, for a serious appraisal of our economic problems, and for a sober and diligent effort to solve those problems. In that effort, there will be a need for the understanding and support of all citizens of the state.

Michigan's Assets and Liabilities

THE LONG-RUN NEED to develop new job opportunities in the state is, as we have noted, a task of sobering proportions. We can hardly hope to accomplish the task without considering carefully the attractiveness of Michigan as a place in which to do business. In order to understand the economic problems of the state, we must take a look at Michigan through the eyes of a prospective manufacturer who is considering various locations in which to start a manufacturing operation. The matter is going to get a bit complicated, but we have no alternative if we want to understand our state and the problems of its economic future.

There is a rather standard list of the factors that are taken into account by manufacturers in selecting a location. The list consists of the following: production materials, labor, sites, industrial fuel, transportation facilities, markets, distribution facilities, power, water, living conditions, laws and regulations, tax structure, and weather. We shall have something to say about several of these later.

It is immediately apparent that these factors take on their fullest meaning only when they are considered in terms of the needs of a specific industry or firm. What, for example, is the firm going to transport, by what specific carriers, and to what markets? Thus, these factors must be looked at as they affect each of the kinds of industries for which Michigan might be suitable.

Moreover, some of these factors affect directly the costs of operating in a given locality (labor costs, transportation, taxes, utilities), while others are more intangible (living conditions, laws and regulations, climate). In seeking a location, the manufacturer normally establishes first the general region of the country in which he needs to have a factory. For some firms this region can be pinpointed rather closely, while for others the range of possible choices may be very wide. Then he selects a sizable number of communities which might be suitable. Next, he determines what his operating costs would be in each of these communities. Finally, he looks at the intangible factors — living conditions, the general "spirit" of the communities, their school systems, their public services and facilities, their cultural advantages, the efficiency of local government, and particularly, the availability of the sort of services that such governments usually provide. These intangibles may greatly influence his decision, but he has to give substantial and perhaps primary weight to his costs of operation.[3] Let us, then, appraise the assets and the liabilities of the state of Michigan.

---

3 An analysis of operating costs of a typical hypothetical company in a few selected cities in Michigan and nearby states was made. It was hoped that the information would shed light on the differences in operating costs from one state to another. Intensive study of the data has revealed that the cities that happened to be chosen for the study are seriously unrepresentative and not comparable. The three lowest-cost cities, for example, proved to have so little employment in the industry involved in the study (metal stamping, coating, and engraving) that the hypothetical company could not possibly secure enough skilled labor within those communities, and to have recruited labor from other communities would have raised costs and invalidated the comparison. Two of the highest-cost cities proved to have wage costs which are demonstrably far above typical wage costs in the state in which they are located. Moreover, even within the range of city sizes included in the study, cost differences appeared to be much more closely related to city size than to the state within which each was located. Thus, the results of this study cannot be used in this summary chapter as illustrative of inter-state differences in operating costs, without involved qualifying explanations. To be meaningful for that purpose, such a study would need to cover a much larger number of communities, and the comparability of the communities chosen would have to be ascertained through exhaustive preliminary investigation. See Appendix D for a discussion of this study.

22

Markets

PERHAPS THE GREATEST SINGLE ASSET possessed by the state of Michigan is its position in that part of the country which has developed the most concentrated markets in the nation. From the standpoint of consumer markets, we may note that the $16.7 billion of personal income received by Michigan residents in 1957 was exceeded in only five other states. The East North Central States receive almost one-fourth of the nation's personal income and account for over one-fifth of the nation's retail trade.

As a market for manufactured goods which are sold to other manufacturers, the attractiveness of the East North Central States, including Michigan, should prove irresistible to many manufacturers seeking a location for their plants. These states carry on nearly a third of the total manufacturing activity of the nation, including half of its nonelectrical machinery and 44 percent of its transportation equipment. And these same activities produce the *materials* needed by other manufacturers; for it has been estimated that four-fifths of the industries in the United States utilize materials that have already been processed by other industries. The very industrial might of Michigan and its neighboring states provides in itself the most powerful impetus for its further growth.

Labor

EVERYTHING that is known about the factors that influence decisions concerning industrial location suggests that the "labor factor" is of high importance. Let us appraise the state of Michigan with respect to several aspects of this factor.

Labor Availability

From the standpoint of sheer numbers of workers available, the very fact of a substantial labor surplus gives Michigan a present advantage which the state has seldom had in the past two decades. We must not, of course, overstate this advantage. The unemployed are by no means a cross-section of the state's labor force. Many are "hard-core" unemployed; many others will need re-training before they are likely to qualify for available jobs. It may be surprising to some to learn that, even in some labor-surplus areas of the state during 1959, active recruiting efforts had to be carried on in order to bring in, from outside, employees who could qualify for the available jobs. Even so, the pool of available workers offers some attractiveness not present in areas where the labor market is tight.

The Michigan labor force is generally acknowledged to be, by comparison with available labor in less-industrialized areas, a factory-oriented, production-minded, well-educated, civic-minded, stable group. Although skilled labor is not in over-supply, either in Michigan or anywhere else, the number of skilled factory people in Michigan is an attraction to a manufacturer who is seeking a location for new operations. In fact, the character of the Michigan labor supply and our favorable position in the nation's industrial markets are probably the state's two most noteworthy assets for continued industrial growth. It must be recognized that we share these two advantages with many of the other states of the manufacturing belt. We cannot claim special superiority over our neighboring states in either.

Unionization

Inasmuch as industrial managements and labor unions have sharp differences of opinion on many matters affecting the conduct of a business, there can be no argument that industrial managers will be less attracted, *other things equal,* to an area in which union membership is high and in which unions are aggressive. Degree of unionization alone may, of course, be an inadequate measure. The nature of the unions, their sense of responsibility, their co-operativeness or their militancy, are also important. The degree of unionization (as a percent of nonagricultural employment) in Michigan was 43.3 in 1953, the last year for which information is available. This figure was exceeded in Washington (53.3), in Montana (47.0), and in West Virginia (44.1). The Michigan figure was higher than in the nearby states of Indiana (40.0), Illinois (39.7), Wisconsin (38.3), and Ohio (38.0). While this factor would be regarded as a disadvantage by manufacturers, we must observe that the degree of unionization in the nearby states is not markedly lower than in Michigan.

Wages

Information on wage levels is not as good as one could wish. What is really needed is a good comparison of wage levels in various locations, within states and among states, industry by industry and job by job. Such information is scarce. Even so, such studies as there are seem to indicate quite consistently that Michigan is a relatively high-wage state. Detroit usually emerges in such studies as one of the highest-wage cities in the nation. Average weekly earnings of production workers in manufacturing in Michigan are the highest in the nation. In 1958, average weekly earnings of production workers in Michigan were $99.29 as compared with $83.58 for the United States. Michigan also led the nation in 1956 and 1957. Relatively high wage rates would affect the experience of business and industry in the years ahead unless unit costs were reduced through higher productivity.

Perhaps it will be useful to look for a moment at some of the factors that have brought about Michigan's high wage level. Undoubtedly, the most important explanation is economic, that is, the high demand for labor in this area. In addition to that, union pressures have also been a factor. Since the prime objective of labor unions is to raise wage levels, we must assume that their efforts have met with some success.

Another reason for the relatively high wage structure in Michigan stems from the fact that the manufacturing sector of the state's economy is composed of industries using large numbers of skilled and semi-skilled workers. In 1957, roughly 45 percent of the working population were in the skilled and semi-skilled classifications as compared with 34 percent for the entire nation.

Still another reason for the high level of earnings of workers in Michigan is that 80 percent of the employees in manufacturing are employed in high wage-paying industries, e.g., motor vehicles, primary and fabricated metals, machinery, and chemicals.

Let us turn to the economic influences that have been at work. We have pointed out that the work pace in Michigan, from 1940 through at least 1953, was at sizzling levels. The competition for workers was intense. During World War II and again during the Korean period, there were large-scale efforts to recruit workers to Michigan from other areas of the country, especially from the South. In all such efforts to get people from elsewhere and to outbid the competition, wages are the primary attraction. In fact, in our free market economy, price has always been the major mechanism by which scarce resources are transferred from one economic activity to another; and this goes for the re-allocation of labor resources as well as for any other. Thus, it appears to have been inevitable that wages would rise in Michigan to a point which would permit the busy manufacturers of this state to get out the work. Incidentally, such studies as we have indicate that, in general, business and industry grow more rapidly in high-wage areas than in low-wage areas. This is obviously not because industry is seeking a high-wage location, but merely because wages tend to go up in the places where industrial growth and economic opportunity are expanding rapidly.

Another factor was involved in raising Michigan's wage levels. During much of the period from 1940 through 1953, the prime objective of Michigan's manufacturers was to get the work out as rapidly as possible, sometimes without too much regard to cost. During World War II this was certainly the objective. It was the objective during the Korean conflict. It was the objective of the motor vehicles and equipment industry when it resumed automobile production in 1946. Most of us can remember very well our impatience at having to wait so long for a car during the late 40's, and we remember that we were much more interested in getting one as quickly as possible than in the price we were going to have to pay for it. In such an atmosphere as this, manufacturers have to buy time with dollars. They use labor in uneconomical quantities and at uneconomical rates of pay.

But all this is now past. There are available workers in Detroit and in some other areas of the state, so that the competition for help among manufacturers is less intense. Manufacturing facilities in general are improving, and in some lines are ample and excellent, so that the manufacturers can keep up with demand and at the same time give proper attention to the matter of costs. In this situation, the economic factors suggest that, in the months and years ahead, wages are likely to rise more rapidly in those areas of the country in which expansion is proceeding at a pace which puts pressure on the supply of available labor, and which thus reduces differentials.

Productivity

The Michigan worker's contribution to the productive process in 1954 and 1956 was higher than that of the U.S. worker, either per production worker or per man-hour worked. However, Michigan's favorable record may stem largely from the fact that the state's manufacturing economy is largely composed of industries in which the value added by manufacture is high. Moreover, the efficiency of plant and equipment can vary so much from industry to industry or from place to place that meaningful productivity comparisons are very difficult to secure. There are many claims that Michigan workers are not as productive as those of some other areas. The statistical support for such claims is hard to find. This is therefore an area which needs intensive study.

Stability

Michigan compares favorably with other industrial states with regard to work stoppages. On the average, only about one-fourth of one percent or less of estimated working time was lost each year through strikes for the period 1955-1957, a figure which is in line with the experience of other industrial states.

The quit rate in Michigan's manufacturing industries compares favorably with that for the United States in each year of the period 1955-1958. Even in 1955, a year of high employment in the state, the United States' average monthly quit rate was 1.6 per hundred workers as compared with 1.5 for Michigan. In the subsequent years Michigan's record was much better. The average in 1956 was 1.6 for the United States and 1.0 for Michigan. For 1957 the United States had an annual average of 1.4 while Michigan had an 0.8 average. On a month-by-month basis, the United States rate was double that of Michigan in 1958. This relative stability of the Michigan work force undoubtedly has a salutary effect on training costs.

Workmen's Compensation

The cost of workmen's compensation in Michigan compares favorably with rates in other states. In many instances the rate is lower for certain industries in Michigan than in other states. This is especially noteworthy since the benefits to injured workers tend to be higher than those in other states in the midwest and in New York.

A study of average manual rates for 45 occupational classifications for the years 1950-1956 shows Michigan to have ranked only 11th in costs among 16 leading industrial states in six out of the seven years involved.

While the benefits of the Michigan Act are somewhat higher than in other states in the region, the cost to employers, as measured by the average manual rate, compares favorably with that in other states. Therefore, in terms of costs, the Act does not appear to place Michigan employers at a disadvantage.

Unemployment Compensation

During the seven-year period, 1950-1956, the United States rate of employers' contributions for unemployment insurance was higher than that of Michigan in four of these years. However, when Michigan is compared with other states in the East North Central region, we find that the average contribution rate of employers in the state was the highest for six of these years. This may be partially explained by the industrial composition of the state, with its emphasis on durable goods. With the greater volatility of employment in Michigan, unemployment insurance costs are necessarily greater. In addition, benefits are higher in Michigan than in many other states.

Water

MICHIGAN'S ABUNDANT WATER resources, like our favorable market position, are often taken for granted without full realization of their potential value. Our water resource potential is not intermediate among the states but stands at the very top. Our primary water supply (excess of precipitation over transpiration and evaporation) is fairly good in comparison with the rest of the country; stream flow is stable for the most part; and the state's geological base is such as to provide large reservoirs of ground water. And the fresh waters of the Great Lakes are no more than 85 miles distant from any point in the state.

The increasing importance of water supply in plant location is suggested by the following statement made by the President's Materials Policy Commission:

> Water supply has always had a significant effect on industrial location, but until recently most of this influence was exerted in an indirect manner. By 1975 water supply may be the most important factor affecting industrial location.

No detailed explanation is necessary as to why the water factor is expected to become so important. A number of sections of the country have already experienced difficulty in providing enough water to cope with substantial population and industrial growth. Some areas are subject to considerable variation in the adequacy of their water supplies.

Referring to the rapid population growth in the Southwest, a recent press release of a demographic research agency states: "The Bureau's Director, Robert C. Cook, predicted that some of these localities might be forced to take steps to restrict the number of new residents, and more especially of new industries in some communities." Elsewhere in the release it is stated that: "In 1957, an estimated one in every four Americans felt the water shortage in some manner...."

And — contrary to our common beliefs — water shortages are anticipated even in parts of the general region in which Michigan is located. Serious problems are predicted as early as 1970 in large parts of Ohio, Indiana, and Kentucky. These problems in our neighboring states should in no way be viewed with pleasure by Michiganders; our future cannot really be made brighter by the existence of problems in other states. But the abundance of our Michigan water supply is certainly a source of attractiveness to industry, a source which will grow in importance in the years to come.

Transportation

IT CAN HARDLY BE DOUBTED that transportation facilities represent one of the most important keys to the industrial future of Michigan, and that their development cannot be left to chance. A glance at a map will show that the Lower Peninsula is "blocked" on the east by Lake Huron and on the west by Lake Michigan. In many ways, the lakes are an asset to Michigan, of course; but certainly not from the standpoint of land transportation. We are a bit off the beaten path of east-west rail lines and of the most heavily travelled east-west highways.

The east-west "ridge" of highest market penetration at lowest cost has been computed. It runs from New York City westward through such cities as Harrisburg, Cleveland, and Toledo, and on west through South Bend, Indiana, and Decatur, Illinois. Thus, the low-cost ridge is substantially south of many Michigan cities. The Indiana Toll Road is 41 miles south of Kalamazoo, and 90 miles south of Grand Rapids. The most heavily used east-west rail lines are south of the Indiana Toll Road, passing through such Indiana cities as Elkhart and Fort Wayne.

The "beaten path" tends to become ever more used. It is no accident that the Indiana Toll Road is already in use — permitting travel without a traffic light from Chicago to New York and to many other eastern cities — while a four-lane development of U.S. 12 through Michigan industrial cities is still several years in the future. Good feeder lines from Michigan cities to the Indiana Toll Road are yet to come. These highway needs — so important to industry — are evident even to the casual motorist. Not so evident but equally serious to industry are problems of rail, air, and water transportation.

We must not conclude that Michigan's transportation outlook is in any way overwhelming. For example, many Ohio and Indiana cities are just as far south of the low-cost transportation ridge as Michigan's major cities are north of it. Not all industrial development has taken place, or will take place, precisely along that ridge. Our highway system will continue to improve considerably during the next few years. And we may have considerable advantage from the St. Lawrence Seaway. Even so, continuous aggressive attention to transportation problems must be high on the priority list of those persons and groups charged with responsibility for Michigan's industrial future. To aid such groups, a research outline has been prepared for the present study by Fantus Factory Locating Service. This outline should form the basis for hard study and effective action.

Taxation

OUR MAJOR CONCERN in this report is to consider Michigan from the standpoint of its likely industrial growth, and to appraise it in terms of its attractiveness for additional manufacturing activity. We shall make no attempt, therefore, to consider the entire complicated subject of state and local taxation, important and interesting though that subject certainly is. Some comments on the subject, however, may give the reader a useful frame of reference from which to consider the question of taxes as they relate to industrial location.

As a result of some excellent studies of Michigan's tax structure which have recently been made, and as a result of the keen present interest in Michigan's fiscal problems, the citizens of the state are beginning to get an unusually good opportunity to comprehend their tax problems.

If we choose to measure relative tax loads merely by dividing total tax receipts by population, Michigan ranks among the "high" tax states. In this sense it ranked, in 1957, twelfth among the 48 states. But its $181 in state and local taxes per person was exceeded by higher figures in all three of the rapidly growing states bordering upon the Pacific Ocean, as well as in such states as Colorado, Connecticut, Massachusetts, and New York.

Furthermore, in Illinois and New Jersey, frequently cited as "low" tax states, total state-local tax receipts, at $179 and $174 per person, respectively, were not appreciably lower than they were in Michigan. This result is achieved because comparatively low state taxes in Illinois and New Jersey are accompanied by very much higher levels of local tax collections than are found in Michigan.

If we examine the data over a period of years, moreover, we find that differences among the states in state and local tax receipts per person have tended to narrow markedly. The states in which tax receipts increased most between 1953 and 1957 were generally those which ranked lowest in 1953. All states are being subjected to increasing demands for public services, so that differences in the levels at which these services are furnished are declining and are bound to continue to decline, just as differences in income levels, standards of private consumption, and so forth, are narrowing. Thus, if a state is judged to be a "high" or a "low" tax state in terms of its state-local tax receipts per person, there is every likelihood that current rankings are going to be found to be ephemeral.

If we employ an alternative measure of general tax level, namely, state-local tax receipts as a *percentage* of personal income received in the state — a measure that may be regarded as one that more meaningfully measures gross tax "burdens" — Michigan ranked thirty-first among the 48 states.

Michigan, in these terms, can hardly be classified as a high-tax state. Moreover, the state of Michigan is not "out on a limb" with respect to the kinds of expenditures that might be associated with a "welfare state." Our expenditures for public welfare in per capita terms rank us thirty-fourth among the states. The states in which state and local taxes tend to cut most severely into the personal income of their citizens tend to be the sparsely populated, low-income, rural states. For example, North Dakota is first, Mississippi is second, and South Dakota is third in this respect.

Let us see how Michigan compares with other states in the manufacturing belt. As we indicated above, in terms of the percentage of personal income which is taken by state and local tax revenues, Michigan ranks thirty-first among the states. Among the other eleven states which may be considered to comprise this heavily industrialized area, only three had higher rankings than Michigan — Wisconsin (11), New York (22), and Massachusetts (23).

All of the others of these states take a smaller proportion of personal income in taxes than does Michigan as shown by the following ranks:

Pennsylvania 38   Connecticut 42
Rhode Island 39   Indiana 44
Illinois 40   New Jersey 45
Maryland 41   Ohio 47

Among other industrialized states, California and North Carolina also take a somewhat larger slice of personal income than does Michigan, with rankings of 17 and 29, respectively. But in general these figures point to Michigan as ranking on the high side among industrial states in the share of income taken by state and local taxes.

Responsible studies have shown that variations in such factors as income, urbanization, and density of population are closely associated with differences in state-local expenditures per person, accounting for some 70 percent of such difference. Hence, a state in which industrial growth is bringing with it increases in income, urbanization, and, necessarily, population density, is very likely to be one in which tax collections per person will be rising more or less commensurately. The movement into an area of new industry, whatever the existing level of taxation may be, is bound to raise that level.

Taxes are always a burden when we are paying them, but they do purchase governmental facilities and services which we need or want; and we must therefore consider whether we are satisfied with what we are getting for our tax money.

Let us compare Michigan with California, the large industrialized state which takes the highest percentage tax bite, and with Ohio, the industrialized state which takes the lowest percentage tax bite. Where does the money go? The answer is in the following table.

State Rank According to Per Capita Amounts of Expenditures for Selected Functions, Selected States

Function	California	Rank Michigan	Ohio
Higher education	12	1	35
Local schools	1	11	19
Highways	29	28	30
Public welfare	7	34	24
Health and hospitals	7	6	28

32

These results are revealing, and they deserve the sober consideration of all of the state's citizens. Note that on educational expenditures, we seem to share the spotlight with California. We spend more, relatively speaking, on higher education, whereas California spends relatively more on local schools. Ohio is pretty far down the line on both classifications of educational expenditures.*

On highway expenditures, all three states appear to be rather comparable.

On public welfare expenditures, Michigan ranks well below either of the other two states. This is the very function in which Michigan has occasionally been "accused" of being out on a limb. Whether our actual ranking of 34th for expenditures in this area is something for the state to be proud of or ashamed of is a matter for the citizens to decide.

On expenditures for health and hospitals, Michigan and California appear to be about comparable, whereas Ohio is far down the list.

How does it all stack up? Today as we look at our state from the standpoint of a manufacturer seeking a low-cost location, we find ourselves noting that taxes in Michigan are substantially higher than they are, for example, in Ohio. Tomorrow, however, as we think of our state as a place in which to live, we may be gratified to see that we have given outstanding attention to our needs for higher education, local schools, and health and hospitals. There is no formula which can tell us on which day our thinking might be more correct. However, sooner or later the population in our neighboring states is going to demand services on a par with those in Michigan, and the longer their construction is delayed, the more they will cost and the greater will be their tax impact.

All this is by way of background for some searching questions which we Michiganders need to ask ourselves with respect to taxes and their influence on the attractiveness of our state for industry. For some of these questions, research has provided at least partial answers. For others, additional research is needed. For still others, the answers depend mainly on our philosophies—on what we want.

First, are state and local taxes in Michigan *too high?* We have noted that they are somewhat higher than in the other states of the manufacturing belt. Even so, are they too high? To answer the question, we must ask ourselves whether our state and local governments are providing us with facilities and services which we would be willing to do without. Only by having fewer facilities and serv-

* See *Concluding Note* at the end of this chapter for additional comments on educational expenditures.

33

ices can we have lower taxes.[4] Let us look again at where our tax money goes in Michigan. Education accounts for 40 percent; highways, 18 percent; health and hospitals, 9 percent; public welfare, 6 percent; sewers and other sanitation, 3 percent. These items add up to 76 percent of our total state and local general expenditures. Where shall we cut? For those who may have paused at the item of public welfare, we should reiterate that in per capita expenditures for this item Michigan ranks 34th among the states. We cannot answer for the people of Michigan the question as to whether they have more or less governmental service than they wish; but it is important to note that these decisions are constantly being made by the people themselves, through their elected representatives on school boards, township boards, city councils, and county boards, and in the legislature of the state.

Second, if we in Michigan were to cut back our levels of governmental services, and therefore our taxes, in the hope of attracting more industry to the state, would we actually do so? Industry is interested in lower taxes, *other things equal*. This can be taken for granted. But many firms, though not all, are also interested in operating in good communities — communities with good schools, streets, parks, police and fire protection, and so on. Would Michigan communities gain industrial firms — or at least the kinds of industrial firms which would be an asset to the community — by cutting down on such facilities and services? Again, we cannot answer, and there are no data that shed light on the question. The best answers we can get will be those that grow out of the thoughtful deliberation of our civic and governmental leaders, at both state and local levels. We may hazard a guess, however, that the people of Michigan and of its communities should continue to approve such governmental services as they want to have and believe they can afford, rather than to be influenced by the remote and uncertain question as to how their tax levels may affect the growth of business and industry.

But there is another question — and the most important one that we shall raise with respect to taxation — that needs to be considered. Taxes must be paid either by individuals or by business and industry. Although we have suggested that perhaps there is not a great deal that can be done about our general level of taxes in

---

4 Improving the efficiency of governmental operations is another possibility. We may assume that inefficiencies exist in any operation, be it a school, a municipality, or a factory. It would probably be a mistake, however, to assume that efficiencies can be improved to a degree which would make any substantial difference in tax levels.

Michigan, it would be a far cry to assume that all is therefore well with respect to our taxation of business in Michigan. Are we, in Michigan and its communities, saddling industry with an undue *proportion* of the tax load? For example, if total taxes in some Michigan community are, say, ten percent higher than those in a comparable community in another state, the level of services in the Michigan community may be sufficiently better so that good industrial firms will be willing to pay the ten percent difference. But if the tax burden *on industry* in the Michigan community is 30 or 40 percent above the burden in the other community, the decision may be quite different. We need very much to examine our present taxes, at both state and local levels, both in principle and in practice, to determine whether we are burdening industry disproportionately for the good level of government facilities and services which we have in Michigan. We need also to examine all new tax proposals carefully, in order to determine whether they place burdens on industry which are out of line with the burdens placed on industry in other states. On this whole matter, accurate information is not easily obtained; but such information is extremely important to have.

Finally, we must observe that there has been a good deal of controversy as to whether the whole question of state and local taxes has a significant bearing on industrial location. Without reviewing the controversy in detail, we may say that the weight of evidence suggests that in many cases taxes should not be a major consideration. The most important objective for many firms is to be close to customers on the one hand or close to suppliers and raw materials on the other. Related to both of these is the adequacy of transportation facilities. Another major consideration is the availability of labor, and such related matters as wages, skills, and stability. By comparison with these considerations, tax levels are usually much less important.

Even so, it may happen that the major requirements of a firm can be met equally well in several alternative locations, so that final decisions may hinge on the sum total of a number of secondary matters, including taxes. Moreover, there are too many stories to dismiss lightly, concerning individual Michigan firms which have apparently found substantial tax advantages in operating in other states. Such instances should be investigated thoroughly, to see what lessons we can learn from the experiences of these firms. We may find that certain *types of firms* are taxed unduly in Michigan;

or that certain *specific taxes* are particularly irritating and unfair to business firms; or that some specific Michigan *communities* have tax burdens far above the state-wide averages.

In general, evidence as to the differentials in business taxes, at various locations within and among states, is not now available with sufficient reliability to warrant the suggestion that these differences have, in fact, been measured precisely. While we may thus doubt the validity of the actual *size* of the inter-state tax differentials suggested by some of the comparative studies that have been conducted elsewhere, there is good reason to believe that taxes paid by business firms in Michigan are somewhat higher than they are in Illinois, Indiana, and Ohio, states in which there is no major business tax comparable to Michigan's Business Activities Tax or Annual Corporate Privilege Fee, the income taxes of New York or Wisconsin, or the income and franchise taxes of Pennsylvania.

All in all, the tax treatment of industry in Michigan needs much additional study.

Financial Inducements to New Business[5]

WE HAVE NOW LOOKED at some of the major industrial location factors and we have considered especially those in which Michigan has considerable attractiveness for new industry and those in which Michigan may have special problems. There are some other matters affecting the industrial future of the state of Michigan to which we must now turn our attention. One of these is the question as to whether Michigan should be offering financial inducements of one sort or another to new firms which we wish to attract. Let us consider first the ways in which such financial inducements are customarily offered, and then consider the extent to which such inducements ought to be made more widely available in Michigan.

At the community level, there are throughout the United States about 1,800 local organizations known as "industrial development corporations," "industrial development foundations," and so on. These organizations have funds at their disposal which have been subscribed by individuals and businesses in the community for the specific purposes of improving the community and of providing additional jobs. Such organizations are generally prepared to offer

---

5 The facts and points of view presented in this section are drawn from a manuscript by Harold T. Smith, "Equity and Loan Capital for New and Expanding Small Business." This manuscript is to be published by the W. E. Upjohn Institute for Employment Research.

industrial sites and plant facilities for lease or sale and to extend financial and other assistance to incoming as well as to established industry. These organizations range from a few well-established ones such as the widely known Louisville Industrial Foundation which has served Louisville well since 1918 in bringing new industries into the community and in salvaging existing ones, to literally hundreds of tiny organizations in some very small communities.

A second avenue of financial assistance to new business is the state-wide development credit corporation. These corporations are quite similar to the community organizations referred to above, except that they are organized to serve communities throughout the entire state. They are privately owned and privately financed, and their funds come chiefly from banks in their area of operations, each of which agrees to contribute a portion of the needed funds at very low rates of interest. The first state-wide development credit corporation was chartered in Maine as the Development Credit Corporation of Maine in 1949 and it began operations in 1950. Similar corporations were chartered in the remaining New England states by the middle of 1953 and in New York, North Carolina, Kansas, and Wisconsin during 1955. Since then, enabling acts have been passed in eight other states including Michigan, but progress in setting up corporations in these states is in various stages. Only seven corporations, in New England and New York, have actually made loans to industry. It is known that there is active interest in the formation of such corporations in at least 17 additional states.

Finally, there is a third type of corporation known as the state industrial development *authority*. This authority is an arm of the state government, with funds originating at least in part from public sources at its disposal, organized to foster the industrial development of the state. The Pennsylvania Industrial Development Authority is the most widely known of these organizations. Created in 1956, it is authorized to make public funds available to the non-profit community development corporations for financing industrial firms in distressed areas. Authorities similar to the Pennsylvania one exist in Kentucky, Mississippi, and Arkansas, and such organizations are under consideration in the states of West Virginia and Florida. One has been proposed in the Michigan legislature.

In considering all three of these types of institutions, we must note two important characteristics. First of all, such organizations have developed largely in distressed areas, in which economic opportunities were dwindling or had never existed in sufficient quantity to provide the people of the area with a good standard of living. A second characteristic is that with few exceptions they have been nonprofit organizations. Capital for these organizations has been provided by citizens, by banks, or by the state itself, in order to build up the economic vigor of the communities. Those who put up the money have expected to benefit, if at all, only indirectly through the improvement of general business conditions in the communities involved.

Before considering the applicability of these institutions in Michigan we must interrupt the story in order to refer to one additional type of organization. In 1958 there was passed by the Congress the Small Business Investment Act which provided for the establishment of small business investment companies throughout the nation. The small business investment companies, it must be noted, were intended by the Congress to provide new and improved sources for the financing of small business in general, and they were not designed specifically to serve the needs of communities or states which were in economic distress. Even so, the small business investment companies may well provide an additional source of funds through which the needs of distressed areas and states can be met.

Leaving out the possible role of the small business investment companies, let us return to our consideration of the three kinds of financing institutions previously described. We have noted that none of these has so far been adopted very widely in the more rapidly growing and more prosperous states. What the future may hold in this respect is not clear; but it is at least uncertain whether such devices are likely to flourish in the fast-growing and prosperous states. There is perhaps no point in such states attempting to outbid each other for additional population and industry, when in many cases they are already having difficulty in absorbing the growth that has come to them. In Michigan, such organizations have not so far been conspicuous. In 1958 there were 79 community industrial development corporations in the state. Enabling legislation has been passed to provide for the establishment of state-wide development credit corporations, but so far no move has been made to set up such corporations. Finally, a state-wide development authority, empowered to make use of public funds for industrial expansion, has been proposed in the legislature but no act has been passed. If, as we suspect, Michigan may now be faced with difficult economic problems, the time is ripe for all of these devices for providing financial inducements to new industry to be given very serious consideration.

From an entirely different viewpoint, these financing devices merit consideration in Michigan whether we have problems of distress or not. Many of the eastern institutions, although started to meet distress conditions, have found themselves increasingly useful in assisting with the expansion of already-existing promising local businesses. Perhaps in every community there are firms with good ideas and good management, but without sufficient capital to operate at their most efficient level. To seek out and to help such firms would be a real contribution to the economic health of the community. Efforts to do so commend themselves to the civic leaders of every community in the state.

The "Climate for Industry"

THE TERM, "climate for industry," has been used to mean so many different things that it has become little more than a slogan. Discussion of most of the matters related to it could proceed in a more constructive atmosphere if the term were dropped from our vocabulary.

The term usually refers to the businessman's interpretation of the costs of doing business in Michigan, including the political and economic issues related to the labor-management conflict. Thus, it includes the degree of unionization itself, together with the strength and aggressiveness of Michigan unions and their possible influence on labor costs. It includes also the businessman's interpretation of the political influence of organized labor, an interpretation which poses a constant question in his mind as to what future legislation may be enacted which he may consider contrary to his interests. In addition, the term includes actual legislation as viewed by the businessman — the nature and level of state and local taxation, the nature and costs of unemployment insurance, the costs of workmen's compensation, and so on. It includes the businessman's view of court decisions, jury awards in accident cases, and other actions of the judiciary branch of government. And finally, it includes the businessman's conception as to whether public officials are friendly or hostile to business.

We have noted that the term, "climate for industry," or "business climate," views these matters from the standpoint of business. If the phrase, "climate for unions," or "climate for the workingman," had been coined, the state's characteristics might be appraised from different points of view. What the people of Michigan really want, of course, is a proper "climate for the general good of all," if we could but know how to achieve that climate.

What is basically involved, then, is the conflict between "liberals" and "conservatives," together with the very important political and legislative manifestations of that conflict. Let us look somewhat further at these issues.

First, Michigan has all the ingredients of a headline-maker in this respect. Wherever we find large, powerful, and successful companies, we are apt to find large, powerful, and successful unions. Moreover, in any state where labor and management groups are so large and influential, political lines are bound to be drawn sharply on matters that relate to their points of view. On all counts, Michigan is notable.

On the other hand, it should be clear that these issues are not confined to Michigan. Almost every industrialized state is concerned with these matters. One has but to examine the situation in New York, Pennsylvania and Massachusetts—to mention the more obvious — to recognize that our state is not unique in this respect. These states, among others, also claim that their costs of doing business are more unfavorable than elsewhere.

Under such conditions, it can be taken for granted that every business group will utilize all available strategems to improve its position. For example, managements will surely wish to disperse their operations, so as to ensure, if possible, that no single labor dispute can cripple their production. In choosing locations, they will prefer, when possible, to locate where their vulnerability to aggressive union efforts is reduced; where taxes are as low as is consistent with their other locational objectives; and where their fears of unfavorable legislative actions are minimized. Some management spokesmen in Michigan have stated that these considerations are among their criteria in choosing plant locations. Such assertions should occasion no surprise; the surprise would be if it were *not* so. On the other hand, managements must also consider such powerful locational factors as proximity to customers and suppliers, transportation to their markets, labor availability, and similar factors. No location has all the advantages a manufacturer wishes and none of the disadvantages. The continued growth of Michigan suggests that, on balance, Michigan locations must often have been chosen, even if with some reluctance, in preference to others. Moreover, unions can be expected to counter management's dispersal tactics by attempting to organize plants wherever they are located, so that success in "running away from labor problems" may be short-lived.

And "escape" from relatively higher taxes may be only a temporary solution; for it can be documented that as communities become more industrialized and grow in population, their outlays for community services, schools, and other publicly provided functions are bound to rise. Still, if the temporary escape results in lower taxes for a firm for a decade or more, the escape is bound to be attractive to some firms.

To be sure, many people believe that the emphasis on business climate and on the relative cost of doing business in Michigan is exaggerated. This may be so; but whether right or wrong, the "image" of Michigan in the eyes of business management has come to be an unfavorable image. These beliefs or perceptions which are widely held by the business community have unquestionably influenced its behavior. The real task is to get to the bottom of these perceptions — to determine as far as possible what causes them, whether they are fact or fiction, and to create a more favorable image. To contribute to a better understanding, we must search diligently in several areas. We wish to propose four lines of study and action which we believe have constructive possibilities.

Study of Reasons for Plant Locations

Despite the great amount that has been written on the subject of plant location, and despite the comments that are made from time to time by firms indicating their reasons for choosing a particular location, remarkably little systematic information is available concerning the factors which, on the whole, do actually determine plant locations. In the absence of carefully collected information, the people of Michigan — or any other state — are bound to have difficulty in determining the true value of their assets as well as the true magnitude of their problems.

The plain fact is that we do not know how important the business climate may be — whether judged by tax differences, by labor-management conflicts, or by the liberal-conservative conflict and its political manifestations — as a factor influencing industrial location. In the nature of things, there is no count of the number of plants which have moved out of Michigan because in the opinion of their managements the atmosphere of the state was unsympathetic. Likewise, there is no count of the number of firms which might have moved to Michigan and did not; nor of the number whose reason for not locating in Michigan was the presumed or actual politico-economic complexion of the state.

It is not easy to devise an objective research study which would shed light on these matters. The answers could easily represent only an expression of political views or prejudices. It would be desirable, however, to attempt a careful inquiry designed to elicit, from the managements of a large number of firms which have built new plants in one or another of the East North Central States, the reasons for each management's choice of location. Such a study would shed light on the relative importance of all of the major industrial location factors, including the importance of the labor-management factor and its political ramifications. The value of such a study would be considerable, not only to Michigan but to other states as well.

Study of the Conditions of Doing Business in Michigan

There have been allegations that the Michigan tax structure is unfavorable to the growth of business enterprise. We have already called attention to the importance of a careful study of that matter. But there have been allegations also that the unemployment insurance law of Michigan thwarts the growth of business; that court decisions of various sorts have deterred business growth; and that in numerous other ways conditions in the state are not conducive to maximum economic development. These allegations have appeared chiefly in the context of political debate; and, while much good information does emerge in the course of political debate, the atmosphere does not lend itself to an orderly accumulation of facts, to a calm appraisal, and to the achievement of impartial conclusions. There needs badly to be drawn up a "bill of particulars" as to those matters which are believed to be thwarting our economic growth, and there needs to be a careful study and a sober weighing of the facts.

Such a study need not be — and must not be — conceived as a vehicle for the propagation of pro-business or pro-union viewpoints. Maximum economic development of the state is to the benefit of all. Not labor unions, nor consumers, nor anyone else, can look hopefully to the unsuccessful business as a source of good profits, good wages, good products, or lower prices. The general welfare, and the welfare of every group in the state, depend on the encouragement of economic growth. A calm appraisal of our success or failure in achieving that objective in Michigan is urgent.

Passage of "The Economic Growth Act of 1960"

The example of the national *Employment Act of 1946* encourages us to propose a similar development in the state of Michigan. We suggest a different name for the Michigan Act, for the reason that employment is but one of several economic objectives which are now being recognized as necessary goals of the national Act. We shall review very briefly the important characteristics of such an Act in the state of Michigan.

The Act itself, like the national Act, would be a short affirmation of the intent of the state government to concern itself with the sound economic growth of the state. It would provide for a Governor's Council of Economic Advisers. It would require the Governor to deliver to the legislature an annual report on the economic situation of the state. Finally, it would set up a Joint Committee of the House and Senate on the Economic Report. The Joint Committee would be provided with its own staff. The Committee would consider the Governor's Economic Report, would conduct its own hearings, would direct its staff to provide such additional information as it wished, and would then consider needed legislation in the light of all available information.

Passage of an "Economic Growth Act of 1960" is recommended for the consideration of the people of Michigan and of their elected officials in the state government.

Improvement of the Michigan Reputation

During the past year or two the reputation of the state of Michigan has suffered grievously. Articles referring to our "fiscal mess," describing us as a "welfare state," purporting to show "why industry shuns Michigan," and so on, have appeared in the public press of the nation with disturbing frequency. Perhaps all factions in the state — both those who believe that the conditions of doing business in Michigan are generally good and those who do not—could agree in acknowledging that the reputation of the state has suffered seriously. It is to be hoped that all leaders in the state, regardless of faction or political affiliation, can join in making the improvement of the Michigan reputation a prime objective.

The Fiscal Problems of the State

THE FISCAL PROBLEMS of the state of Michigan have been among the most widely publicized evidences of its economic troubles. The people of the state have come to recognize that many other states have similar problems, so that the so-called "fiscal mess" is not peculiar to our state. Even so, there is no disposition to minimize the problem as it confronts us in Michigan.

The fiscal difficulties of the state have sprung from many causes. We have noted, for example, that few other states in the nation have experienced such explosive population pressures in the last two decades as has Michigan. These pressures have inevitably brought to the state and its communities an unusual share of needs for public facilities and services, and therefore an unusual share of financial problems. Some of the financial problems of the state date back to the thirties, when the people wrote into the Constitution the fifteen-mill limitation on local taxes. This action by the voters made it inevitable that, sooner or later, the communities of the state would find themselves in financial difficulties. Some years later, in an attempt to bail the communities out of the problems caused by the earlier mistake, the voters passed the sales tax diversion amendment, and thereby made it certain that, sooner or later, the state government would be in financial trouble.

Constitutional revision is obviously a "must" for the state of Michigan, as a necessary first step toward permanent improvement of the fiscal situation of the state and its communities. New patterns of state and local financial interrelationships are needed, as well as new decisions concerning the kinds of taxes that may be used to secure revenues to meet state and local needs. While constitutional revision can hardly solve all of our state and local financial problems, it provides an absolutely necessary starting point, and it will lay a foundation upon which other constructive actions can be built.

Growth and Stabilization of Existing Firms

IT IS GENERALLY RECOGNIZED that the economic forces which lead to growth or decline of certain industries, as well as the forces which cause violent cyclical fluctuations in certain industries, are usually pervasive of the whole economy, and are substantially outside the control of the individual firm. It would be a mistake, however, to assume that the individual firm is completely at the mercy of forces beyond its control. Intelligent and imaginative management is, of course, a major creative factor accounting for our economic progress. Such creative management can fruitfully be brought to bear on the economic problems we have been considering as problems of the state of Michigan. Although these are the economic problems of the state, they are even more directly and intimately the problems of the business enterprises which make up the economy of the state.

The continued growth of business firms in the state, for example, is not solely dependent upon continued growth in the demand for their present line of products. Many of the successful firms of today have little in common, except their name, with the company that existed under that name twenty-five years ago. The profitability of many companies stems from products not even known a decade ago. Every industry runs the danger of obsolescence. And many communities have serious economic problems because of dead or dying industries. With aggressive innovation on the part of our existing industries, Michigan need not become a state of declining industrial importance.

Even the problem of cyclical fluctuation may not be completely beyond the control of the existing firm. The automobile industry's sales and credit policies, for example, exert a preponderant influence upon the economic life of the state. Easy credit and intensive sales campaigns at a time when sales are generally good tend to boost the industry's production to "excessive" peaks and to draw more workers into the area than are necessary for normal operations. Undoubtedly, some of this occurred in 1953 and 1955. The automobile industry in 1955, for example, marketed a far greater number of automobiles than could be marketed on a year-by-year basis. Thus, it borrowed business in 1955 which might otherwise have developed in 1956, 1957, and 1958. While we cannot presume to say that the industry itself could have succeeded in leveling out automobile purchases over those years, it does have a serious responsibility to consider how its policies of expansion affect the economic life of the community. Any success that it can achieve in the future will surely be a substantial contribution to the economy of the state of Michigan and even to that of the nation.

In the 30's and even in the 40's, there was a great deal of interest in the subject of reducing business fluctuations through the efforts of individual firms. While no miracles are to be expected from such efforts, perhaps now is the time to re-kindle interest in the subject on the part of the Michigan business community.

The Problems of the Currently Unemployed

WE HAVE NOTED ELSEWHERE that the unemployed persons of the state do not represent a cross-section of the state's labor force.

There is urgent need for special studies — both at the state level and in communities where unemployment is severe — of the unemployed people, as a basis for appropriate action. Perhaps some of these people should be induced to go elsewhere, to some area where jobs are more plentiful. Perhaps some can be retrained for jobs which may now be available. No doubt some, though counted as unemployed, are in reality unemployable except during periods of severe labor shortage. For these persons, some solution to their difficulties other than a job in private industry must be sought.

In the effort to meet the problems of the unemployed, full utilization should be made of the counseling, vocational guidance and other facilities of the local offices of the Michigan Employment Security Commission.

What Industries Are Most Likely to Spark the Future Growth of Michigan?

WE HAVE NOTED the remarkable growth of the state of Michigan during the years from 1940 to 1953 and perhaps to 1955, and the great extent to which this growth was brought about by Michigan's predominance in the production of the wheeled vehicle. Both in production for civilian use and in production for military purposes, this industry was the mainstay of the Michigan economy. We have noted also that, beginning in 1953 or 1955, the pace of the wheeled-vehicle industry began to slow down somewhat. When coupled with decentralization of manufacture and assembly, we have been forced to conclude that the industry will not provide the necessary support that Michigan needs in the future for its continued growth. We must look elsewhere for the additional industries that may provide growth in this state in the years to come; and the search for appropriate industries to spark that further growth is one of the major research needs of the state at the present time.

This search should not be confined to manufacturing industries, although these have been our major focus in the present report. There may be possibilities in such areas as finance, insurance, mail-order firms, tourism, and others. In fact, diversification has often been mentioned as an important objective in itself for the state of Michigan.

Research-oriented industries are among the nation's most promising developments. While Massachusetts and California are leading the procession at the present time, Michigan has good potentials for growth. Our universities have a strong research orientation.

The establishment of the Institute of Science and Technology at the University of Michigan in Ann Arbor and the strong research programs there and in other institutions of higher education in the state should provide an attraction for industrial organizations built around the research function. This impetus is already under way with the expansion or establishment of research facilities in the state announced by such firms as Michigan Chemical Corporation, Wyandotte Chemicals Corporation, W. L. Badger Associates, the Upjohn Company, Parke, Davis and Company, and Bendix Systems Division.

In addition to the types of industries mentioned above, the search for appropriate industries for the state can proceed in several different ways. The most basic procedure is to take each major industrial activity in the United States which might possibly be suitable for location in Michigan and to consider the suitability of Michigan for that industry in terms of every single one of the basic industrial location factors.

One illustration will show the kinds of conclusions that might be reached in such studies. This example is from a speech by Mr. Bert Cremers, entitled, "The Future of the Chemical Industry in the Great Lakes States." Mr. Cremers' conclusion is as follows:

> Forecasting the future of the chemical industry in the U.S. is a pretty large order for any one man, even with years of sales and administrative experience in one segment of the industry. Regional products constitute a massive product mix affected by internal and external forces — each product with its own market future. By such limitations and using the usual background assumptions of one and one-half percent population growth, a 3 percent annual growth in gross national product and continuation of the cold war, I have arrived at a forecast through 1965. It is my belief after reviewing all of these factors, that the Great Lakes States will continue to experience annual increases in chemical production in the order of 100 to 150 million dollars of value added by manufacture.
>
> Despite some of the real natural advantages enjoyed by the Great Lakes States, such as an abundant supply of fresh water (a scarce commodity in some areas), low-cost water transportation, vast resources of limestone and salt, the Great Lakes States' share in the national market for chemicals will decline. This decline is attributed primarily to population shifts, industry decentralization and a trend to greater importance for petroleum chemicals.

This study embraced the entire East North Central region, whereas we should have to have studies oriented specifically toward Michigan. It considers, of course, but one of the large number of industries that should be investigated with reference to their potential future in Michigan.

As a concluding part of each such study, it would be necessary to make cost analyses showing the extent to which typical firms in the industry under consideration could compete successfully from Michigan locations with similar firms located in other suitable states.

Another approach to the problem of pinpointing industries which are most likely to expand successfully in Michigan is to analyze the growth industries of the United States in order to see which ones have already shown some potential strength in the state of Michigan. Illustrative of this approach is an analysis prepared especially for this study by Henry C. Thole, of the W. E. Upjohn Institute for Employment Research, with assistance from Dr. Edwin Grossnickle, Western Michigan University Professor of General Business. They have analyzed the latest available data on growth industries which cover the period 1947-1954. Let us review some of their findings.

Among the twenty-five largest growth industries in the East North Central region for the period 1947-1954, there were 22 in which Michigan's gain or loss from its share—based on Michigan's population as a percentage of that of the East North Central States — was 600 or more workers. Michigan gained more than its share of added jobs in 16 of these 22 industries. But three of the industries in which Michigan did not perform as well as its neighboring states were very important—aircraft engines, aircraft equipment (not elsewhere classified), and radios and related products. While Michigan did show a substantial employment gain in the aircraft parts and equipment field, its rate of growth was not equal to that of the region. In only two of the more important growth industries did Michigan experience actual job losses. These were radios and related products and the plating and polishing industry.

Michigan has shown up best in machinery (except electrical) and fabricated metals industries. The strong showing by Michigan in these industries suggests favorable location factors for firms in such industries.

Other growth industries in which Michigan has compared as well as other areas and which should continue to show healthy growth are paper and allied products, chemicals, instruments and related products, and printing and publishing industries.

Although Michigan has not done as well as other areas in aircraft and missile parts industries, their good growth prospects plus the need for accurate machining to close tolerances for many of the parts required by these industries suggest that Michigan may be able to secure a larger share of this business than it has in the past, even though most prime contractors for such business are located in the eastern, western, and southwestern parts of the country.

While Michigan has kept pace with the East North Central region and the nation in nearly all growth industries examined in this study, absolute gains in employment have been small. The largest absolute gains in employment have been in special tools and dies, and metalworking machinery attachments, in which employment increased by 17,000 workers for the period 1947-1954. Significant gains have occurred also in aircraft parts and equipment (not elsewhere classified) (9,500 jobs) and aircraft engines (7,400 jobs). During this same period the motor vehicles industry declined by nearly 24,000 jobs, and the gray-iron foundries industry declined by more than 14,000 jobs. Other significant employment declines were experienced by heating and cooking equipment (5,800 jobs) and metal stampings (3,300 jobs). Thus, many small increases in growth industries in Michigan have not been sufficient to offset losses in motor vehicles and other "nongrowth" industries and still maintain over-all growth rates comparing favorably to the East North Central region and the nation.

Finally, in searching for suitable industries to assure the growth of Michigan, it should be helpful to try to look beyond the industries that are already among us and growing, and to try to peer into the more dim and distant future. For example, we are apparently within sight now of further declines or perhaps the virtual elimination of rail passenger transportation. What kind of change is this going to bring about in the relative desirability of various industrial locations? As another example, we can already foresee that some day the use of atomic power for the production of electricity will be common. This development will wipe out the cost of coal as a factor in the location of a good many kinds of industrial processing. How much and what kind of effect will this have on the relative desirability of various industrial locations? As a third example, is a practical process in sight for making fresh water out of sea water? If so, the process will lift the industrial ceiling set by short water supplies which now exist in some parts of the Southwest and far West. How much of an effect will this have on the relative desirability of various industrial locations?

All along the developing front of technology, we could take a look at what is in the offing and attempt to estimate what effects it may have on Michigan during the next fifteen to twenty-five years. Obviously, anything that can be learned along these lines is not going to be discernible by any study of industrial location factors or by any study of past historical trends. It is a line of investigation quite separable from the others. Such studies as this should not be considered in any way to be idle daydreaming. Many of the industries of prominence today were dreamed of and foreseen long before they became forces in the economic life of our day. Some of the developments of the next quarter century are already, if not on drawing boards, in the brains of our scientists. We should profit from knowing about them.

By the use of all suitable procedures, we must determine what industries may set Michigan again on the course of progress. Armed with such information, we shall perhaps find it easy to attract to Michigan those industries whose most profitable future is really linked to our own.

Community Action

THIS ENTIRE REPORT, since it has been devoted to the economic problems of the state, has had little to say about action or study at the community level. The fact is, however, that the economic health of the communities of the state probably lies more in their own hands than it lies in the hands of any or all of the agencies of the state as a whole. While we cannot attempt here to enumerate all of the responsibilities of local communities, we can point up some of those which bear most directly on the objective of economic development.

High on the list comes the provision of community services. While we have not studied this matter directly, we believe it could be documented that Michigan's communities are, on the whole, attractive to industry in this respect. Continued diligent attention should be given to the provision of good schools, good highways and streets, good parking facilities, good police and fire protection, and other community services.

Local tax problems are of special concern and importance. We are unwilling to suggest that Michigan's communities should reduce the *over-all level* of their taxes by reducing their level of services in the hope of attracting industry. But the *kinds* of taxes, and the *relative impact* of taxes on industry, merit sober consideration.

The property tax presents serious problems concerning the relative assessment of industrial property and concerning the uniformity of assessment in general. Moreover, the property tax alone cannot bear the burden of rising local needs for facilities and services, and it must be supplemented by additional sources of revenue.

Zoning for industry is of the utmost importance. Industrial firms are reluctant to choose a plant site and then attempt to get it rezoned for their use. Such attempts nearly always arouse community conflicts. Land which should be put to industrial use should be properly zoned in advance of a specific need for the site.

A spirit of cooperativeness on the part of local governments in making such facilities as sewer and water available to new industries is indispensable. To an increasing extent, communities are developing "industrial parks," in which sites and facilities for industry are made available in advance of need. Local financing of industrial plants is important, including local industrial development corporations.

As far as aggressive efforts to attract new industry are concerned, the attitude of Michigan communities will no doubt vary. In those communities which are faced with serious problems of unemployment, aggressive efforts may be strongly favored. In others, the emphasis will be on selective and orderly development, rather than on an increase in the rate of growth.

That the Detroit area is crucial to the state is clear. It has over half of the people in the state and over half of the unemployment. Without reviewing Detroit efforts in detail, we may note that much attention is being given to its problems, including the recent formation of the Southeastern Michigan Metropolitan Community Research Corporation.

An Industrial Development Point of View for the State of Michigan

THERE ARE SOME persons who seem to value population growth for its own sake, perhaps with the mistaken notion that bigger necessarily means better. There also are some, though not many, who profit directly from population growth. But there are others who view growth with some misgiving. They see, correctly, that the rapid growth of Michigan has brought problems more rapidly than benefits—problems of schools, hospitals, parking, streets and highways, high taxes, state and local debt, and so on. These persons may well wonder if all the efforts we have been discussing — efforts to help Michigan grow — are even in the right direction. Is there a state economic objective with which all citizens could agree? Let us try to formulate one.

First of all, it is admittedly difficult to see why the prosperous states of the manufacturing belt should get into a competitive race, trying to out-bid each other for every new factory that is seeking a location. These states already contain two-fifths of the nation's people and two-thirds of its manufacturing. Their people might on one day gloat over the acquisition of a new factory, and on the next day wring their hands over their parking problems and a proposed bond issue for a new school building. Why anyone should wish to foster additional growth in these already large and rapidly growing areas is not easy to see.

In this sense, Michiganders should view the beginnings of industrial growth in the South, for example, with enthusiasm rather than with misgivings. An improvement of the economic opportunities of the people in the southern states is bound to be a net gain to themselves, to Michigan, and to the nation as a whole.

Why, then, should we be concerned at this time to encourage the economic growth of Michigan? There are two reasons. First, we in Michigan must make sure that the rate of growth in the future will be adequate to provide work for our present and our growing population. We must emphasize that in-migration *will continue* — though perhaps not at the high rates of the past two decades — to Michigan and the other industrialized states. The southern states have been experiencing out-migration at substantial rates for many years; and the rate of industrialization of those states, though encouraging, is far short of enough to take care of their growing populations. Many people will come to the North, even if economic opportunities are not very good, because they will feel that they are bettering themselves somewhat by doing so. Moreover, movement from the farms to the cities will continue; and this, too, adds to the number of jobs that will be required in the factories and offices of the state. The conclusion of all this is that Michigan's industrial job-seeking population is *going to grow,* and that considerable effort is going to be required if we are to provide suitable job opportunities for those of our people who wish to work.

But there is a second reason why we should be concerned about Michigan as a place in which to do business. It has nothing, basically, to do with population pressures as such. That reason is that it is to the advantage of Michigan, and indeed of the whole nation, for us to do our share of the nation's work as efficiently as possible. If we have transportation problems, for example, difficulties which impede the free flow of goods and services, then we should solve them. If there is any basis for the charge that our tax structure thwarts the maximum development of profitable businesses and therefore of well-paying job opportunities, then we should correct it. In taking an aggressive stand toward the solution of our problems, we are in no sense "competing" with other states; we should be glad to see all of the other states solve their problems, too. The whole forecast of a bright future for Americans depends on the assumption that, as individuals, business firms, communities, and states, and as a nation, we shall continue to solve our economic problems with reasonable success.

A Program of Action and Study

PERHAPS IT WILL SERVE as a summary of the ground we have covered in this report if we list in orderly fashion the things that should be done in order to advance the economic growth of the state of Michigan. Each item to be listed involves some combination of things to do and things to learn. In some cases, there is much to learn before we shall know exactly what to do; but there is perhaps no item in which action has to wait entirely on the development of further knowledge.

1. Industrial promotion. While many persons doubt whether industrial promotion efforts have been effective in other states, it seems to us desirable that such efforts be stepped up in Michigan: determine what staff the Department of Economic Development needs in order to carry on its industrial contact work effectively, and provide whatever additions are necessary. Undertake a program of institutional advertising of Michigan as a site for industrial location.

2. The Michigan reputation. Guard zealously the good name of the state. Stop undermining its reputation by exaggerating its problems and minimizing its virtues. We have short-changed the state long enough.

3. "The Economic Growth Act of 1960." Affirm the intent of the state government to concern itself with the economic growth of the state, by passage of "The Economic Growth Act of 1960." Implement the Act by creating a State Council of Economic

Advisers; by requiring the Governor to deliver an annual Economic Report to the legislature; and by establishing a Joint Committee of the House and Senate on the Economic Report, with a staff to assist the committee.

4. *Constitutional revision.* Undertake at once a thorough revision of the Michigan Constitution, as an essential first step in alleviating the fiscal difficulties of the state and its communities.

5. *Most suitable industries.* Initiate a full-scale research effort to determine the industries for which Michigan is best suited. Correct with special care such problems as Michigan may have in meeting the locational needs of those best-suited industries. Pinpoint promotional efforts toward expanding firms in those industries. One of many criteria of selection will be the choice of industries which will serve to diversify the economy of the state.

Knowing that some of the most promising industrial growth will occur in research-oriented, technology-centered new products, encourage the development of research facilities, both in universities and in industrial firms, and, in all possible ways, attract scientific talent to the state.

Give special attention to a study of the potentialities of the tourist industry. While this industry will have little to do with growth in the industrialized southern half of the Lower Peninsula, it would be very helpful in improving the economic status of the remainder of the state.

6. *Growth and stabilization of existing firms.* Encourage existing firms to "keep pace with the times," to invest in innovation, so that their growth will not depend solely on presently existing product lines. Re-kindle interest in the possibilities of stabilization efforts on the part of individual firms. Reduce in all possible ways our character as a "feast-or-famine" state.

7. *Reasons for plant movements.* Undertake a study of manufacturing plants that have actually located in Michigan and in nearby states, in order to determine the reasons for their choice of location. While the truth is difficult to ascertain in such situations, this study should shed light on the relative importance of various factors in influencing locational decisions, and on the factors that have actually brought plants to Michigan as well as to specified other states. This study will help Michigan assess the relative importance of her assets or the relative seriousness of her problems. It will aid, too, in pinpointing the kinds of firms for which Michigan is an attractive location.

8. Transportation. Undertake an all-out study and action program designed to bring Michigan's transportation system up to a condition of complete adequacy. There should be a Committee on Transportation to carry the responsibility for this program. The outline prepared by Fantus Factory Locating Service for our study of the Michigan economy provides a starting point for the work of the Committee on Transportation.

9. Water. Set up an exploratory committee to consider what is needed in order to capitalize on Michigan's industrial attractiveness from the standpoint of water. The work of this committee should be fully coordinated with the Michigan Water Resources Commission. Water, though not a conspicuous factor at the present time, will be of increasing industrial importance in the future. Its potentials should not be overlooked.

10. Conditions of doing business in Michigan. Undertake a thorough, patient, objective study of the actual conditions of doing business in Michigan, as compared with the conditions of doing business in other states.

11. Taxes. Undertake a thorough study of taxes as they affect business costs in Michigan and in other states. This is really a substudy under point (10) but is lifted out for special attention because of the importance given to this item by many people in business and industry.

12. Financial inducements. Give earnest consideration to the possibility that Michigan needs to establish financial inducements to attract industry, especially in areas where unemployment is prolonged and severe. Serious consideration needs to be given to the establishment of area-wide or state-wide development credit corporations. Consideration also needs to be given to the establishment of a state-wide authority similar to the Pennsylvania Industrial Development Authority. The possible usefulness of small business investment companies as an aid in these efforts should be investigated.

13. Community action. Encourage the communities of the state to consider their problems of economic development seriously, and to take steps, where necessary, to attract sufficient industrial growth so that they may provide full employment for all of their residents who wish to work. Alert communities can do a great many things to encourage and promote the orderly growth of industry and of jobs; and it may be that a state-wide agency can do much to assist the communities of the state in these efforts. The Department of

Economic Development could appropriately carry on this function.

14. The present unemployed. Undertake careful studies of the unemployed people themselves. Consider such possibilities as encouraging them to seek jobs elsewhere. Provide opportunities for retraining, counseling, and guidance toward new job possibilities. Give special thought to the problems of those persons who may be largely unemployable.

Program Implementation

THE CHAPTERS in the body of this report outline the problems and the areas of research which should be developed. The preceding program items suggest many activities and approaches which can be undertaken with little delay. In the opinion of the authors of this report, a responsible official agency of the state government, combining in its membership leaders of management, labor, and the general community, is essential to spearhead the research and activities herein outlined. The Committee on Michigan's Economic Future (COMEF) may be such an agency. Under its auspices, a research organization guided by several key committees representative of the appropriate interests of the state can begin to function. Such committees may include the following:

1. Committee on Industrial Promotion
2. Committee on Suitable Industries
3. Committee on Transportation
4. Committee on Water Resources
5. Committee on Conditions of Doing Business in Michigan
6. Committee on Business Taxation
7. Committee on Financial Inducements to Business
8. Committee on Community Development
9. Committee on Problems of the Unemployed.

It is believed that the above organization of committees under COMEF could work effectively toward implementation of most of the recommendations we have outlined above. There could also be a Committee on Growth and Stabilization in Existing Firms, if this topic is judged to be a fruitful area for concentrated effort. None of the above committees could easily handle the recommendations concerning "The Economic Growth Act of 1960" and Constitutional revision. Possibly a general Committee on Government might take care of these two topics if COMEF wishes to pursue them.

The authors of this report hope that their work will arouse the interest of all citizens of the state in working toward the solution of the economic problems of Michigan, and that that interest will be evidenced by enthusiastic support of the activities of COMEF as it undertakes the difficult assignments which are required in the accomplishment of its mission.

CONCLUDING NOTE

THIS CHAPTER ON "What's Ahead for Michigan?" was published as a separate booklet in September, 1959; and, in order to avoid the confusion which would result from publishing two versions of the chapter, we have left it substantially as it was at that time. This choice requires us to make a few explanatory comments.

First, additional data relating to the state of Michigan have become available since this chapter was prepared. Such data have been incorporated in the body of this report, even though they are not set forth in this chapter.

Second, we have been reminded that the Michigan Department of Economic Development already has a very active program to assist the communities of the state in working toward their economic and industrial development. The wording of our Recommendation 13 (page 55) seemed, unfortunately, to imply that the Department has no such program in operation at this time; whereas it was our intent, rather, to endorse this program and to encourage the expansion of such activities.

Third, we have been urged to remind the people of the state that the relative state rankings on various types of public expenditure — which we reported in our discussion of taxation — do not provide a complete guide as to the amounts of money that we may need to spend in Michigan for those functions. For example, we reported that Michigan stands first in expenditures for higher education, whereas Ohio ranks thirty-fifth. But it is important to note that in Michigan about three-fourths of all college students attend public colleges and universities, whereas in Ohio only a little over half of all college students attend the public institutions. In some of the important industrial states, the percentages are even lower: in New York, 32.5; in New Jersey, 23.2; and in Pennsylvania, 13.8. These figures are averages, 1949-1955, and are taken from issues of the *Biennial Survey of Education in the United States,* published by the U. S. Department of Health, Education, and Welfare.

Additional data demonstrate that Michigan has ranked far behind seven competing states (those of the East North Central and Middle Atlantic regions) in total expenditures for higher education by *private* institutions. The conclusion of all this is that Michiganders may not be paying more *in total* for higher education than are the residents of other states; but merely that our expenditures in Michigan are concentrated in the public institutions more than in private institutions.

It is worth noting also that the commonly quoted data on per capita expenditures for higher education include student fees such as dormitory and meal charges and athletic fees, and grants for contract research. Thus, the amounts quoted are far beyond the sums actually appropriated by the state legislatures. While such items are included in the expenditure levels of all states, Michigan received unusually large grants, for example, for contract research, from industries and from agencies of the federal government. Thus, state rankings of total expenditures may be a rather inaccurate measure of the actual cost of higher education to the tax-paying public in one state versus another.

There may well be similar qualifying information with respect to relative state expenditures for highways, welfare, health and hospitals, and other types of public services and facilities. We urge the people of this state, and their governmental leaders, to seek full information as a guide in determining the level of expenditures which we in Michigan need to achieve in order to accomplish our own chosen objectives.

PART II

THE PROBLEM AND ITS ORIGINS

Chapter I

Michigan's Employment Problem

DURING THE PAST year or two, Michigan has become increasingly concerned about the problem of unemployment. The immediate cause for concern was, of course, the very serious amount of unemployment prevailing in the state during the recession of 1958. It was a year in which national unemployment rose to almost seven percent of the labor force, the highest level in the postwar period, and in which Michigan's rate of unemployment was twice as great as that of the nation. Not in a quarter of a century had unemployment been so much more serious in Michigan than in the country as a whole.

Of course, there are always persons without jobs in every free-functioning economy. However, public attention focuses on the problem when unemployment rises to such a high proportion of the available labor force that harmful side-effects develop, affecting workers, business, and government. All of these groups were affected by the high level of unemployment prevailing in Michigan in 1958 — in loss of jobs and in reduced earnings, in curtailed business sales, and in larger governmental expenditures for relief clients.

But the concern of the people of Michigan exceeded that occasioned by the 1958 recession alone. Would prosperity return to the state with the return of prosperity to the nation? Or have we developed a deeper and more pervasive problem? There has been reason to suspect that we do have deeper problems; and this suspicion has intensified the preoccupation of the citizens and of their leaders with the economic destiny of the state.

It is the purpose of this report to examine all facets of the problem. What are the facts? How bad are they? How did the state get into trouble? What must it do to get out? In this introductory chapter, we shall present a few of the dramatic facts about the recent development of unemployment as a problem in our state. They will suggest that there is, indeed, cause for concern.

To a degree, the relatively severe unemployment in Michigan

during 1958 should not have been surprising. Michigan's employment history has long had "feast or famine" characteristics. When slumps develop in the nation, Michigan tends to be affected more severely than the country as a whole, with a consequent higher unemployment rate. In periods of general prosperity, on the other hand, economic activity in Michigan tends to rise more rapidly than that in the national economy. The most important single reason for this is that in Michigan there is a concentration of durable goods industries, which are characterized by wide variations in production levels during periods of boom or recession. These tendencies are illustrated by the following data, which show the percentage of the labor force unemployed in the United States and in Michigan for the years 1949 through 1958.

Year	Percent Unemployed	
	United States[a]	Michigan
1949	5.5	7.3
1950	5.0	4.0
1951	3.0	4.0
1952	3.1	4.1
1953	2.9	2.7
1954	5.6	7.1
1955	4.4	3.7
1956	4.2	6.5
1957	4.3	6.8
1958	6.8	13.5

Source: United States: U. S. Bureau of the Census. Data from various issues of Annual Report on the Labor Force (Series P-50), and from Economic Indicators, March, 1959, p. 11. Michigan: Table I of this report.

[a] Data from 1952 to date on "new definition" basis. These data run from 0.3 to 0.6 percentage points higher than data on "old definition" basis formerly shown by the Bureau of the Census for these years.

From these data, it can be seen that in the recession years of 1949 and 1954, as well as in 1958, Michigan's unemployment problem was considerably more severe than the nation's as a whole. On the other hand, in the high-level years of 1953 and 1955, unemployment in Michigan was somewhat below national levels. It is clear that the fluctuation of employment in Michigan is greater than in the nation, especially on the downturns.

Systematic information is not available to show how Michigan fared in earlier years. Estimates made in the mid-thirties for the early years of that decade suggest, however, that unemployment in Michigan was especially severe at that time. It is estimated that up to 45 percent of all nonfarm workers were unemployed in Michigan in 1933, as compared with 33 percent in the nation at large.[1] One indication of the drastic drop in employment in the state during that period of the Great Depression is the decline in manufacturing employment from 599,000 in 1929 to 336,000 in 1932 — a decline of 44 percent.[2]

But if unemployment in Michigan is usually severe during recession periods, what is there in the present situation that seems to be particularly alarming? Should our employment not recover as quickly and as fully from this recession as from those in the past? First, it must be noted that Michigan's experience in 1958 was worse than it had been in previous postwar recessions. Our rate of unemployment in 1958 was twice as great as the rate in the nation; whereas in 1949 and in 1954 our rate of unemployment had been less than 50 percent greater than in the nation. But another fact also stands out in the data. Michigan's unemployment problem had already begun to develop well in advance of the national recession. Our state was experiencing substantial unemployment even in 1956 and 1957, amounting to 6.5 and 6.8 percent of the labor force in those two years. Our experience is in sharp contrast to that of the country as a whole, which enjoyed a high level of economic activity both in 1956 and in 1957.

A look at the employment data given in Table 1 reveals, in fact, that the number of jobs in Michigan has been trending downward ever since the Korean defense-production peak in 1953. Whether one looks at total employment, at jobs held by wage and salary earners, or only at persons holding manufacturing jobs, the trend in Michigan remains the same — a defense-period peak of job holders in 1953, a substantial drop during the recession year of 1954, appreciable recovery during 1955, and a decline again in 1956 and 1957. In the nation, the number of jobs was increasing through 1957. Nonfarm employment for the country rose by almost three and a half million jobs from 1953 to 1957. It is true that the number of manufacturing jobs in the nation fell also between 1953 and 1957, but the drop was but a few hundred thousand. Everything seems to suggest that the state of Michigan has had a problem of unemployment which has perhaps been developing ever since 1953.

Let us turn for a moment from the data on unemployment to some information on per capita income, which is another measure

---

[1] William Haber, *How Much Does It Cost?* (Michigan Employment Security Commission, 1951), Table XXXI, p. 181. The data cited were taken from W. Haber and P. Stanchfield, *The Problem of Economic Insecurity in Michigan,* 1936, pp. 21-22.
[2] *Ibid.,* p. 304.

Table 1
Michigan Labor Force and Employment Trends
1949-1958

(Numbers in thousands)

Year	Total Labor Force[a]	Unemployment		Employment						
		Number	Percent of labor force	Total	Farm	Nonfarm				
						Total	Wage and salary workers			Other[b]
							Total	Mfg.	Nonmfg.	
1949	2,614	190	7.3	2,416	176	2,240	2,020	976	1,044	220
1950	2,685	108	4.0	2,555	174	2,381	2,160	1,070	1,090	221
1951	2,773	112	4.0	2,658	169	2,489	2,267	1,122	1,145	222
1952	2,790	115	4.1	2,666	167	2,499	2,275	1,104	1,171	224
1953	2,941	79	2.7	2,858	164	2,694	2,466	1,230	1,236	228
1954	2,928	208	7.1	2,718	162	2,556	2,325	1,075	1,250	231
1955	2,916	108	3.7	2,805	159	2,646	2,413	1,155	1,258	233
1956	2,934	190	6.5	2,741	157	2,584	2,349	1,074	1,275	235
1957	2,933	199	6.8	2,731	155	2,576	2,335	1,050	1,285	241
1958[c]	2,993	406	13.5	2,573	153	2,420	2,177	883	1,294	243

Source: Michigan Employment Security Commission. For 1949-1957, *Michigan's Labor Market,* January, 1958, p. 8. For 1958, data (revised basis) were made available to the Institute prior to their publication in *Michigan's Labor Market.*

a *Includes workers involved in labor disputes. Latter not included in Unemployment or in Employment.*
b *Includes proprietors and self-employed, domestic workers, and unpaid family workers.*
c *Data for 1958 not entirely comparable with earlier years.*

of the level of economic well-being of the citizens of the state. The following data show per capita personal income for the United States, the East North Central States, and Michigan, for the years 1953 through 1957, the period of job decline in Michigan.

| Year | Per Capita Personal Income | | |
	United States	East North Central States[a]	Michigan
1953	$1,788	$2,050	$2,120
1954	1,770	1,961	1,982
1955	1,866	2,083	2,146
1956	1,975	2,194	2,191
1957	2,043	2,238	2,192

Source: Table 18 of this report.
  [a] In addition to Michigan, includes Ohio, Indiana, Illinois and Wisconsin.

Michigan's loss of position is apparent from these income data. In 1953, per capita personal income in Michigan was very substantially above that of the nation as a whole and somewhat greater than the average of the East North Central States. By 1957, our per capita income was somewhat below the average of the East North Central States, and only moderately above that of the nation as a whole.

The year 1953 — the Korean defense-production peak — was, of course, a year of especially high levels of employment and income in Michigan; and some decline in Michigan's income position, compared with that of the nation and of nearby states, could have been expected after 1953. However, between 1955 and 1957, per capita income in Michigan advanced only slightly, while it was still rising appreciably both in the nation and in the East North Central States. These data are again symptomatic of economic problems that seem to have developed in the state of Michigan prior to the 1958 recession.

What are some of the causes of these troubles which had begun to plague the state of Michigan even before the 1958 recession accentuated the problem? Several possible explanations will be explored in the chapters that follow.

Much of the problem originates in the automotive industry, the state's most important employer of labor. Automotive employment in Michigan dropped a drastic 100,000 from 1953 to 1957, and 70,000 of these jobs were dropped in the crucial span, 1955 to 1957. A substantial portion of the drop in automotive employment can be attributed to the lag in the new car market after 1955. In addition, however, decentralization of automotive operations away from Michigan and technological improvements, including automation, have been advanced as important factors explaining the drop in automotive employment in Michigan.

Another fact of some importance was the shift in the nature of the national defense effort in the years following the Korean build-up of 1953. Whereas that build-up had emphasized the wheeled vehicle in which Michigan production facilities were pre-eminent, later defense efforts have emphasized the fields of aircraft, missiles, and electronics, in each of which Michigan's development has lagged substantially behind that of some other states.

Finally, a loss of Michigan plants and employment to other states has been suggested by some as contributing significantly to Michigan's current unemployment problem. Such losses, and the failure of more industrial companies to locate in Michigan, have been attributed to such factors as higher taxes, higher wage rates, and lower productivity in Michigan as compared with other industrial states. In connection with this view, the statement is often made that a generally unfavorable business climate prevails in Michigan. The pros and cons of this belief will be examined in later chapters.

*   *   *

A rather gloomy picture of Michigan's recent employment situation has been sketched in this introductory chapter. It is evident that the situation is serious enough to warrant concern on the part of all of those who are interested in the economic future of the state.

Chapter II

Population and Labor Force Trends

MICHIGAN'S POPULATION has been growing at a rapid rate in recent years. This chapter is intended to provide some quantitative estimate of the amount of that growth, not only with regard to population but also with regard to labor force — that is, the working population. Numerical information on these trends is helpful as a basis for the discussion of employment trends that follows later in this study.

Michigan's Rapidly Growing Population

MICHIGAN HAS BEEN experiencing a period of very rapid population growth during the 1950's. Table 2 indicates that in July, 1958, the state's population, as estimated by the Bureau of the Census, amounted to almost 7.9 million persons. Comparison reveals 1.5 million more persons living in Michigan in 1958 than in 1950 — a gain of almost 25 percent in eight years. This is a very substantial rate of growth. It means adding to Michigan's population base during this eight-year period a number of persons equal to the 1950 population of two of the New England states — Maine and New Hampshire.

Moreover, as Table 2 shows, Michigan has been a rapidly growing state over a long period of time. Starting with the decade ending in 1890, the state's population has increased from 15 to 30 percent during each 10-year period except for the depression decade of the thirties.

Michigan and the Nation

Michigan is growing, and has grown, at a more rapid pace than has the nation generally. For the period 1950-1958, Michigan's rate of growth (23.5 percent) was half again as high as the rate (15.0 percent) recorded for the country at large. If we take a longer view, Michigan's population has increased each decade since 1850 more rapidly than that of the nation generally, except for the two decades between 1890 and 1910.

Table 2
Population Increase, United States, East North Central States, and Michigan, by Decade

1850-1958

(Numbers in thousands)

Year[a]	Total Population			Percentage Increase			Percent of United States Total in—	
	Continental United States	East North Central States[b]	Michigan	Continental United States	East North Central States[b]	Michigan	East North Central States[b]	Michigan
1850	23,191.9	4,523.3	397.7	...	...	...	19.5	1.7
1860	31,443.3	6,926.9	749.1	35.6	53.1	88.4	22.0	2.4
1870	38,558.4	9,124.5	1,184.1	22.6	31.7	58.1	23.7	3.1
1880	50,155.8	11,206.7	1,636.9	30.1	22.8	38.2	22.3	3.3
1890	62,947.7	13,478.3	2,093.9	25.5	20.3	27.9	21.4	3.3
1900	75,994.6	15,985.6	2,421.0	20.7	18.6	15.6	21.0	3.2
1910	91,972.3	18,250.6	2,810.2	21.0	14.2	16.1	19.8	3.1
1920	105,710.6	21,475.5	3,668.4	14.9	17.7	30.5	20.3	3.5
1930	122,775.0	25,297.2	4,842.3	16.1	17.8	32.0	20.6	3.9
1940	131,669.3	26,626.3	5,256.1	7.2	5.3	8.5	20.2	4.0
1950	150,697.4	30,399.4	6,371.8	14.5	14.2	21.2	20.2	4.2
1958[c]	173,260.0	35,618.0	7,866.0	15.0	17.2	23.5	20.6	4.5

Source: Bureau of the Census, 1950 Census of Population, Vol. II, Pt. 1, pp. 1-8 and 1-9, and Current Population Reports, Series P-25, No. 189, November 13, 1958.

a Month in which census was taken varies. For 1930, 1940, and 1950, data are as of April 1.

b Includes Ohio, Indiana, Illinois, Michigan, and Wisconsin.

c Provisional estimates as of July 1. Excludes armed forces stationed overseas. Data for states include persons n the armed forces stationed in state.

Michigan's greater-than-national growth in population is reflected in a gradual, but irregular, increase over the years in the share of the nation's population found within its borders. In 1958, the people of Michigan accounted for 4.5 percent of the nation's total population, as compared with 3.2 percent in 1900.

Michigan and the East North Central States

We have noted that Michigan has been growing at a faster rate than has the country at large. How does Michigan compare in population growth with its neighbor states in the East North Central region — Ohio, Indiana, Illinois, and Wisconsin?

Table 2 discloses that during only one period since 1850 (the 20 years, 1890-1910) did the population of Michigan fail to increase more rapidly than that of the East North Central States as a group. Since 1950, Michigan's population has increased by 23.5 percent, as compared with about 17 percent for the East North Central States. The share of the East North Central region in the nation's population has fluctuated around 20 percent since 1910, while Michigan's share has been increasing.

Michigan's growth in population has been more rapid than that of its neighboring states, considered both individually and collectively. (See Appendix Table I.) Within the region, the percentage of population growth in Michigan (23.5 percent) from 1950 to 1958 was well above those for the next ranking states, Ohio and Indiana, 17.6 and 16.4 percent, respectively. There have been, however, some years since 1950 when population growth proceeded at a more rapid rate in other states.

Michigan and Other Rapidly Growing States

Table 3 lists the states that have enjoyed a larger-than-national rate of population increase since 1950. As indicated, Michigan ranks tenth among the states in rate of growth. In view of the state's generally rapid growth in recent years, a ranking this low may seem somewhat surprising.

However, if one looks at the states ranked higher than Michigan in the listing, the reason for Michigan's relatively low standing becomes clear. With one exception (California), all of the states experiencing a higher percentage increase in population growth since 1950 have smaller population in absolute terms. A relatively modest actual growth results in a substantial percentage growth for most of these states.

On the other hand, one may note that several of the nation's

Table 3

Percentage Increase in Population for States Having Percentage Increases Greater than National Average

1950-58

(Numbers in thousands)

State	Total Population[a]			Percentage Increase	
	1950	1957	1958	1950-1958	1957-1958
United States......................	*150,697.4*	*170,293.0*	*173,260.0*	*15.0*	*1.7*
Nevada...........................	160.1	262.0	267.0	66.7	1.9
Florida...........................	2,771.3	4,209.0	4,442.0	60.3	5.5
Arizona..........................	749.6	1,078.0	1,140.0	52.1	5.8
Delaware.........................	318.1	434.0	454.0	42.7	4.6
California........................	10,586.2	13,879.0	14,337.0	35.4	3.3
Colorado.........................	1,325.1	1,663.0	1,711.0	29.1	2.9
Maryland.........................	2,343.0	2,895.0	2,956.0	26.2	2.1
Utah.............................	688.9	840.0	865.0	25.5	3.0
New Mexico......................	681.2	813.0	842.0	23.6	3.6
MICHIGAN.......................	6,371.8	7,705.0	7,866.0	23.5	2.1
Texas............................	7,711.2	9,175.0	9,377.0	21.6	2.2
New Jersey.......................	4,835.3	5,617.0	5,749.0	18.9	2.4
Virginia..........................	3,318.7	3,828.0	3,935.0	18.6	2.8
Ohio.............................	7,946.6	9,206.0	9,345.0	17.6	1.5
Oregon...........................	1,521.3	1,743.0	1,773.0	16.6	1.7
Indiana...........................	3,934.2	4,507.0	4,581.0	16.4	1.6
Washington.......................	2,379.0	2,725.0	2,769.0	16.4	1.6
Montana..........................	591.0	671.0	688.0	16.4	2.5
Louisiana.........................	2,683.5	3,066.0	3,110.0	15.9	1.4
Connecticut.......................	2,007.3	2,269.0	2,316.0	15.4	2.1

Source: Bureau of the Census, *Current Population Reports,* Series P-25, No. 189, November 13, 1958.

a Excludes armed forces overseas. Data for states include persons in the armed forces stationed in the state. Data for 1950 are from the 1950 Census of Population taken as of April 1. Data for 1957 and 1958 are as of July 1. Data for 1958 are provisional.

larger states (those having a population of 4 million or more in 1958 — New York, Pennsylvania, Massachusetts, Illinois, Missouri, and North Carolina) do not appear on this list of states which are growing more rapidly than the nation as a whole. Thus, if we compare Michigan with states of comparable size, Michigan shows up more favorably. Only two of the larger states — California and Florida — have grown at a more rapid rate than Michigan during the last eight years. And Florida's fast-growing population is still not much more than half of Michigan's.

The preceding discussion has been in terms of rates of growth. Let us now look briefly at how Michigan's actual population gain from 1950 to 1958 (1.5 million persons) stacks up against such gains in other states. The following figures show that Michigan ranked fourth during this period in actual population increase. Even so, population gain in Michigan was only slightly under that recorded in Florida and Texas, the second and third states in actual increase.

State	Population Increase (millions)
California	3.75
Florida	1.67
Texas	1.67
Michigan	1.49

From all of these data, it is clear that during the 1950's Michigan has been one of the nation's most rapidly growing states.

Population Growth within Michigan

Now that we have compared Michigan's population growth with that of other states, we shall consider the differences in growth rates inside Michigan. The following data indicate that the Detroit Metropolitan Area (Wayne, Oakland, and Macomb counties) is growing more rapidly than outstate Michigan. Population growth in the Detroit area in recent years has been proceeding about half again as fast as in the rest of the state. From 1950 to 1957, Detroit population grew by 27 percent, that of the balance of the state by 18 percent. The data also indicate that almost half of the state's population is concentrated in this three-county area. The greater growth rate in this region since 1950 suggests that the Detroit area could account for over half of the state's population within a relatively short period.

Area	1957 Population[a] (thousands)	Percentage Increase 1950-1957	Percentage Increase 1956-1957
Michigan	7,803	22.5	3.8
Detroit Metropolitan Area	3,833	27.1	4.7
Wayne County	2,844	16.8	2.9
Oakland County	637	60.9	8.6
Macomb County	352	90.5	14.1
Outstate Michigan	3,970	18.3	3.0

Source: Michigan Population Estimates by Counties: July 1, 1956, and July 1, 1957 (Lansing: Michigan Economic Development Department, February 1958 and August 1958). Based on estimates released by Statistical Methods Section, Michigan Department of Health.

[a] As of July 1. These estimates are based on Bureau of the Census estimates for Michigan that have been superseded by revised Census estimates.

It should be noted, however, that more recent population estimates made in the Detroit area itself do not show as rapid a growth for the area as do the estimates just cited, which are based on Census estimates for Michigan. Estimates released by the Detroit Metropolitan Area Regional Planning Commission suggest a population of 3,840,000 persons in the three-county area on July 1, 1958.[1] This is about the same level shown in the text data for the area for July, 1957.

In any event, it is clear that about half of the state's population will be concentrated in the metropolitan area of Detroit for some years ahead.

The Importance of In-Migration

Michigan, like other fast-growing states, obviously has been drawing a large number of persons from other states in recent years. Data do not appear to be available to indicate the importance of net migration in Michigan through 1958. However, the Bureau of the Census has estimated the components of civilian population growth for the period 1950-1956.[2] According to this estimate, Michigan civilian population grew by 1.2 million persons between April, 1950, and July, 1956. This increase reflects natural increase (excess of births over deaths) of 773,000, net civilian migration into the state of 484,000, and net "loss" into the armed forces of 53,000.

There are several ways to highlight the importance of these 484,000 in-migrants who came to Michigan during the six-year period. They accounted for two-fifths of the state's growth from 1950 to 1956. They added almost eight percent to the number of people who had been living in Michigan in 1950. They accounted for over 40 percent of the total net migration (1,129,000 persons) into the East North Central region during these six years. On a net basis, only California and Florida exceeded Michigan during this period in the number of persons moving into the state.[3]

Michigan's industrial expansion as a war production center during the 1940's also drew many persons into the state during that decade. Apart from natural increase, the civilian population of the state grew by almost 400,000 from 1940 to 1950 as a

---

[1] *Population and Occupied Dwelling Units in the Detroit Region,* September, 1958, Foreword.

[2] *Current Population Reports — Population Estimates,* Series P-25, No. 165, November 4, 1957, Table 5.

[3] Both of these states had substantially more net move-ins than Michigan. Net migration into California during the period amounted to 1.7 million persons, and into Florida, almost 800,000 persons.

result of net migration into the state.[4] These move-ins accounted for over one-third of the total increase of 1.1 million persons in the state's civilian population during the ten-year period. Again during this decade, only California and Florida added more persons through in-migration to their population base (civilian) than Michigan.

Other data point to net migration into the state as an important factor in Michigan's steady population increase during earlier decades also. The following data indicate the importance of both interstate migration and foreign immigration in the state's growth from 1900 to 1940.

| Decade | Percent of Total Population Increase from — | |
	Interstate Migration	Foreign Immigration
1900-1910	18.8	13.9
1910-1920	32.9	15.2
1920-1930	43.7	10.4
1930-1940	1.1	− 3.2

Source: William Haber, How Much Does It Cost? (Michigan Employment Security Commission, 1951), Table II, p. 131. The data were based on A. H. Hawley, The Population of Michigan 1840 to 1960 (University of Michigan, 1949), p. 12.

It is apparent that net migration into Michigan was a substantial factor in the state's growth during the three decades ending in 1930. Foreign immigrants were also settling in the state in appreciable numbers during the period. Further, it should be noted that the severity of the depression in Michigan during the thirties brought to a halt — temporarily — the inflow of persons from outside the borders of the state.

Over the years, then, the population of Michigan has grown significantly more than that of the nation because of the large number of persons who have moved into the state. In spite of periods of substantial unemployment, job opportunities in the state generally have been so abundant and so lucrative that persons from other states have moved to Michigan year after year.

Michigan's Labor Force

IN VIEW OF the substantial, and fairly steady, growth of Michigan's population decade after decade, one would expect that the state's labor force — defined very simply as those employed plus those

---

[4] Bureau of the Census, Current Population Reports — Population Estimates, Series P-25, No. 47, March 9, 1951, Table 4.

73

unemployed but seeking work — would show a similar pattern of growth. For the most part, such an expectation is confirmed by available statistics.

Labor Force Growth in Michigan

Appendix Table II indicates that during each decade since 1910 the labor force increased more rapidly in Michigan than in the United States generally and in the East North Central States as a group. Except for the depression thirties, the rate of increase of the work force in Michigan was substantially greater than that in the nation and the region. For the fifty-year period 1900-1950, Michigan's working population increased by about 180 percent as against about 110 percent in the East North Central region and the country at large.

However, a look at labor force growth since 1950 discloses a somewhat different, and perhaps unexpected, pattern of growth. As shown by the following information, Michigan's work force in recent years has grown at a rate only one-third greater than that of the country as a whole in spite of the fact that, as we pointed out earlier, Bureau of the Census estimates indicate that Michigan's population has been growing half again as fast as that of the nation during the 1950's.

| Year | Civilian Labor Force (thousands) | |
	United States	Michigan
1950	63,099	2,685
1958	68,647	2,993
Percent increase	8.8	11.5

Source: Table 4 of this report.

Let us look more closely at the record during the period since 1950, as shown in Table 4. Nationally, the number of persons in the civilian labor force declined somewhat from 1950 to 1951, reflecting the build-up of the armed forces. However, in each year thereafter the nation's civilian labor force increased. In Michigan, the labor force moved upward through 1953, reaching 2.94 million persons in that year. However, during the next five years, the state's work force failed to expand significantly. By 1958, the labor force was somewhat larger, averaging about 3 million workers for the year. Thus, the relatively stationary level of the labor force in Michigan for the years 1953-1958 inclusive explains the relatively limited percentage increase noted for the whole period, 1950 to 1958.

Table 4

Percentage of Population in Labor Force, United States and Michigan

1950-1958

(Numbers in thousands)

Year	United States					Michigan				
	Population[a]		Civilian labor force			Population[a]		Labor force		
				Percent of—					Percent of—	
	Total[b]	Civilian	Number[c]	Total population	Civilian population	Total[d]	Civilian	Number	Total population	Civilian population
1950......	151,234	150,202	63,099	41.7	42.0	6,421	6,411	2,685	41.8	41.9
1951......	153,384	151,082	62,884	41.0	41.6	6,510	6,489	2,773	42.6	42.7
1952......	155,761	153,366	62,966	40.4	41.1	6,664	6,642	2,790	41.9	42.0
1953......	158,313	156,046	63,815	40.3	40.9	6,860	6,845	2,941	42.9	43.0
1954......	161,191	159,086	64,468	40.0	40.5	7,126	7,112	2,928	41.1	41.2
1955......	164,303	162,307	65,848	40.1	40.6	7,358	7,343	2,916	39.6	39.7
1956......	167,261	165,341	67,530	40.4	40.8	7,571	7,555	2,934	38.8	38.8
1957......	170,293	168,368	67,946	39.9	40.4	7,705	7,691	2,933	38.1	38.1
1958......	173,260	171,433	68,647	39.6	40.0	7,866	7,850	e2,993	38.0	38.1

Source: Population: Bureau of the Census, *Current Population Reports,* Series P-25, No. 165, Tables 2 and 3; No. 186, Table 1; and No. 189, p. 3.

Labor force, United States: Bureau of the Census, *Annual Report on the Labor Force—1957,* Series P-50, No. 85, p. 3, and *Economic Indicators,* April, 1959, p. 11.

Labor force, Michigan: For 1950-1957, *Michigan's Labor Market,* January, 1958, p. 8. The labor force estimate for 1958 (revised basis) was made available to the Institute prior to its publication in *Michigan's Labor Market.*

a **As** of July 1.
b *Continental United States. Includes armed forces stationed in this country.*
c *Data for 1952 and subsequent years on* "New definition" *basis.*
d *Includes armed forces stationed in the state.*
e *Revised basis, not entirely comparable with preceding years.*

Another way to compare developments in Michigan with those in the nation at large is to look at the labor force participation rates that emerge from the data.[5] The percentage of the population found in the labor force in 1950 both in the United States and in Michigan was at a relatively high level — around 42 percent. In the nation at large, the percentage moved down to a 40-41 percent level in 1952 and has remained at that general level since. In Michigan, however, the labor force participation rate moved up to a Korean-defense period high of 43 percent in 1953, declined to a more normal 40 percent level by 1955, and by 1957 and 1958 moved down to 38 percent.

These figures indicate, then, that Michigan's labor force has expanded very little since 1953. This, in turn, has resulted in a steadily diminishing proportion of the state's population participating in the work force. By 1958, only about 38 percent of the state's population was in the labor force as compared with around 40 percent in the nation generally.

Causes of Labor Force Stability

It is unusual that Michigan's work force has not been increasing in size during these last few years. The Research and Statistics Division of the Michigan Employment Security Commission suggests that the situation may be explained largely in terms of the recent decline in job opportunities.[6]

As a result of the Korean-related defense boom in Michigan in 1953, the number of persons in the work force that year increased by 150,000 over 1952 levels. This increase was almost as large as that for the three preceding years combined. The demand for workers to meet defense production requirements resulted in intense labor recruiting activity on the part of employers, especially in the Detroit area. Some employers were reported to have been hoarding workers during this period, placing additional stress on the labor supply. Many persons normally not in the work force took jobs — larger-than-customary numbers of women, older work-

---

[5] The labor force participation rate is the percentage of the total population that is found in the labor force. A better basis for computing labor force participation rates is provided by relating the labor force to the population aged 18-64, or to the population 14 years old and over, since these latter groups are the segments of the population from which the labor force is normally drawn. The conclusions drawn in this section, however, are not affected by the age grouping base chosen for the computation of participation rates.

[6] The remarks in this section are based on informal discussion with staff members of the Division. The data cited in this section can be found in Tables 1 and 4.

ers, and young people. Workers came to Michigan from other states in large numbers.

As the peak production activity of 1953 gave way to the recession year of 1954, job opportunities declined. The number of manufacturing jobs dropped by 150,000 from 1953 to 1954. As available jobs diminished, marginal workers withdrew. Some workers from other states returned home. These withdrawals tended to offset new entrants into the labor force from the growth of the population.

By 1955, as already noted, the state's labor force represented about 40 percent of the population — a level frequently assumed to be something of a normal relationship. The stability of the size of the labor force since 1955 — and the consequent decline in the labor force participation rate — reflects a continued lack of job opportunities. As noted in the preceding chapter, Michigan suffered substantial unemployment, in contrast to the nation generally, in 1956 and 1957. The scarcity of job openings since 1955 has kept out of the labor market many persons who normally would be seeking work.

Apart from the failure of job opportunities to match population growth in the past few years, other factors may contribute to the relatively low labor force participation rate suggested for Michigan by data on the labor force and population. The Bureau of the Census may be overestimating the increase in the state's population. Perhaps, because of decreased job opportunities, migration into the state has not been as important during the past few years as the Bureau has assumed in its estimates.[7] It is also possible that there has been some growth in the state's labor force that is not reflected in the data released by the Michigan Employment Security Commission. (Staff members responsible for these data state, however, that they believe their statistics are realistic.) If either of these explanations has any validity, it would mean that the state's labor force participation rate is actually higher than that suggested by current data.

Implications

For the past several years Michigan has had a relatively low proportion of its population in the state's work force, and this may

---

[7] Some indication of this is the fact that the Bureau's estimate for Michigan for July 1, 1957, as given in Series P-25, No. 186, dated October 27, 1958, runs 100,000 under the estimate given for the same date in Series P-25, No. 168, dated December 9, 1957.

carry unfavorable implications for the state. If the situation were to continue, it could mean, for the short run, a relatively lower level of per capita income (as compared with earlier periods). Over the longer run, the state's population growth could become less rapid if job opportunities were to continue to be insufficient to maintain a more-or-less normal relationship between the work force and population. At any rate, the data cited in this chapter concerning the recent failure of the work force to grow in accordance with the increase in population highlights one aspect of Michigan's employment problem.

Chapter III

Recent Employment Trends in Michigan

IN THIS CHAPTER, we shall look at the decline in Michigan employment since 1953. In what industries has this decline been concentrated? How does the recent level of factory jobs compare
with those of earlier periods? How does Michigan's decline in job
opportunities compare with what has been happening in the neighboring Great Lakes states? To what extent is Michigan's employment problem confined to the Detroit area? How many lost jobs
can be attributed to the automobile industry? How important have
defense jobs been in the state's economy in recent years? These
are some of the questions for which answers will be sought in this
chapter.

For the most part, our discussion will center around the period
1953-1957, the period of job decline in Michigan in the face of
national prosperity (except for 1954). At several points in our
analysis, however, we shall refer specifically to developments during the recession year of 1958. In a few other cases, we shall take
a look at longer run data so that our conclusions will not be
influenced solely by short-run developments.

The analysis will also center primarily around changes in the
number of wage and salary workers who account for the great
bulk of employment in Michigan (See Table 1). Our discussion
will thus generally omit consideration of farm employment and
employment of a group comprised of the self-employed, domestic
workers, and unpaid family workers.

Trends in Total Employment

IN CHAPTER I we noted that in most types of employment in Michigan the recent trend was the same — a peak in the defense year of
1953, abrupt decline in 1954, some recovery in 1955, and decline
again in the following two years. This was true for total employment, nonfarm employment, total wage and salary employment,
and factory employment. The one exception to this pattern of

gradual decline since 1953 was the nonmanufacturing industries group. Jobs in these industries — construction, wholesale and retail trade, services, finance, government, mining, transportation, and public utilities — increased by about 50,000 during the period 1953-1957 while factory employment declined by 180,000 employees.[1] Thus, on the basis of these data, Michigan may have lost about 130,000 jobs from 1953 to 1957. The record indicates also that the state's recent employment problem originates primarily in the manufacturing sector of the state's economy.

Michigan and Nearby States

The following data (Bureau of Labor Statistics) provide a comparison of the change in the total number of employees (factory and nonfactory) in Michigan from 1953 to 1957 with that in other states in the region.

Area	Employees in Nonagricultural Establishments (In thousands)		
	1957	1953	Percent change
United States	52,162	49,681	5.0
East North Central region	11,605	11,497	.9
Ohio	3,163	3,110	1.7
Indiana	1,415	1,427	—.8
Illinois	3,498	3,411	2.6
MICHIGAN	2,376	2,456	—3.3
Wisconsin	1,154	1,094	5.5

Source: Appendix Table IV.

From these data, the relative seriousness of Michigan's recent employment problem is apparent. From 1953 to 1957, the num-

---

1 See Table 1. A considerably larger increase in the number of employees in nonmanufacturing establishments is reported by the Bureau of Labor Statistics (See Appendix Table III). If one accepts the BLS figures (rather than the Michigan Employment Security Commission data on wage and salary workers shown in Table 1), then the peak employment year in Michigan would be 1955 rather than 1953. Also, the loss of jobs in the state from 1953 to 1957 would be about 75,000 rather than the 130,000 mentioned in the text.

The discrepancy between the MESC series on wage and salary workers and the BLS series on employees in nonagricultural establishments (essentially the same series) poses a problem in analysis of recent employment trends. In general, we shall use MESC data when we examine Michigan as an entity. We shall use BLS or other data when comparison with other states is desirable or when comparison of figures over a longer period of time is in order. (The MESC data cover the period 1949 to date; the BLS data extend back to 1939.)

In referring to these figures, one should bear in mind that there are differences in industrial classification between the two sets of data. It should also be noted that the MESC data provide information not only on wage and salary employment but also on farm employment, and on the self-employed, domestics, and unpaid family workers. The BLS data are confined to employees.

Beginning with 1959, the MESC and the BLS have integrated their reporting systems so that hereafter the two agencies will issue identical monthly and annual figures on wage and salary employment in Michigan. These 1959 data for Michigan are not comparable with those issued by MESC for years prior to 1958 except for the figure on total wage and salary employment. Detailed MESC data for 1958 are available for Michigan on both the revised and the unrevised basis.

ber of employees in the state's nonagricultural establishments dropped by over three percent. Although three of the four years were generally prosperous and Michigan's population continued to grow rapidly, the number of jobs declined. Of the other states in the region, only Indiana experienced a decline in total employment, but this was less than one percent. The other three states showed an increase. Nationally, the number of nonfarm employees was five percent greater in 1957 than in 1953.

These data make clear also that what was happening in Michigan was contrary to what was happening in the other Great Lakes states and in the country at large.[2]

Detroit and Outstate Michigan

As might be expected, Michigan's employment problem has affected Detroit much more severely than the rest of the state. As indicated below, total nonfarm employment in the Detroit area declined from 1953 to 1957 by about seven percent. Outstate Michigan experienced a decline of about one and a half percent. Detroit lost 100,000 jobs of the total state loss of 118,000 nonfarm jobs during these four years.

Year	Total Nonfarm Employment[a] (thousands)		Total Wage and Salary Workers (thousands)	
	Detroit Area	Outstate Michigan	Detroit Area	Outstate Michigan
1953	1,508	1,186	1,393	1,073
1957	1,408	1,168	1,286	1,049
Percent decline	6.6	1.5	7.7	2.2

Source: Appendix Table V.

[a]Includes self-employed, domestics, and unpaid family workers in addition to wage and salary workers.

Even though outstate Michigan lost relatively few jobs after 1953, its employment position in 1957 could hardly be described as good. In the face of continued population growth and in comparison with the increase in the number of jobs elsewhere, the fact that nonfarm employment in the area outside Detroit declined by "only" 18,000 jobs during the four years is not especially encouraging information.

The Record since 1950

The data cited thus far highlight the decline in job opportunities in Michigan since 1953. But, as has been noted, jobs were at an

---

2 In this report, the term "Great Lakes states" refers to the East North Central States. In other usages, the term sometimes covers all of the states that touch on the Great Lakes.

especially high level in the state in 1953 because of the Korean-defense production boom. Less than three percent of the state's workers were unemployed. Perhaps the employment problem is overstated by comparing a peak employment year such as 1953 with 1957.

However, comparison over a longer span of years also tells a story of inadequate job opportunities for the people of Michigan in recent years. Table 1 indicates that there were 2.56 million persons working at farm and nonfarm jobs in the state in 1950. By 1957, this number had increased to 2.73 million, or a gain of about 7 percent. But, in the meantime, Michigan's population had increased by 20 percent.[3] An increase in employment of 7 percent was by no means adequate to care for the job needs of a population increase of 20 percent; so that, as indicated in Table 1, in 1957 there were about 200,000 unemployed workers in Michigan. And, if job prospects had been better, undoubtedly more persons would have been looking for work.

Thus, the record since 1950 provides another indication that the loss of jobs from 1953 to 1957 was not merely a more-or-less normal decline from extraordinarily high employment levels. It was a decline severe enough to reduce job opportunities well below levels needed to meet the job requirements of a rapidly growing population.

Trends in Manufacturing Employment

Concentration of Employment in Durables

Manufacturing in Michigan is characterized by a high degree of concentration in durable goods manufacturing (autos, furniture, household appliances, industrial machinery, etc.). Appendix Table VI indicates the extent to which these durable goods industries dominate the state's manufacturing economy. During the nine-year period 1949-1957, durables accounted for from 82 to 85 percent of all manufacturing employment in the state. In the three-county area comprising Metropolitan Detroit, the percentages run somewhat higher (86-89); in outstate Michigan, somewhat lower, on the average (76-80). In the country at large, jobs in the durables field provided only 59 percent of all factory jobs in 1957.[4]

---

3 Based on civilian population in Michigan in 1950 and 1957 as shown in Table 4. Data for both years are as of July 1.
4 Bureau of Labor Statistics, *Employment and Earnings — Annual Supplement Issue,* July, 1958, p. 84.

In many respects, durable goods industries are of great value to the industrial structure of any state or locality. They have a high-value product, generally enjoy favorable earnings, and typically pay high wage rates to their employees. A state with a high proportion of durables employment usually enjoys a high per capita income.

There is, however, a price to pay for a substantial reliance upon these heavy industries because they are particularly sensitive to the business cycle. As the economy moves downward, durable goods suffer a greater contraction of their market than do nondurable goods. Consumers — whether industrial, business, or household — take advantage of the long life that is built into durable goods and make long use of the existing stock of goods. After a sustained period of industrial expansion, substantial satisfaction of the industrial demand for capital equipment may result in a tapering off of orders for new plant and equipment. This in itself may start a downswing in the economy. In any event, the amplitude and the duration of the swings in economic activity is greater in durables than in nondurables. Therefore, Michigan, because of its heavy dependence on durable goods industries, is especially vulnerable to business fluctuations.

When the data in Table 5 are examined, the contrast in the experience of the durable and nondurable groups in Michigan since 1953 is seen to be striking. Employment in durables fell by over 15 percent during the four-year span while the number of jobholders in the nondurables group increased slightly. Every industry in the durables field experienced a drop from the Korean-period peak in 1953. These data point up dramatically the impact of recent economic changes on the durable goods industries in Michigan.

Experience in Michigan during this period differed somewhat from that of the nation. Both in Michigan and in the country at large, employment in durables dropped sharply in 1954, but turned upward substantially during the recovery year of 1955. In Michigan, as is apparent in Table 5, jobs in the heavy industries resumed their decline after 1955. In the country as a whole, durables employment continued at high levels during 1956 and 1957, on the average.[5] Jobs in the durables sector declined sharply in both areas during 1958.

---

5 *Ibid.*

Table 5

Percent Change in Wage and Salary Workers in Manufacturing in Michigan, by Industry

1953-1957

(Numbers in thousands)

Manufacturing Industry	Number of Wage and Salary Workers					Percent Change, 1953-1957
	1957	1956	1955	1954	1953	
All manufacturing industries.............	*1,050*	*1,074*	*1,155*	*1,075*	*1,230*	*– 14.6*
Durable goods industries.................	*861*	*886*	*968*	*893*	*1,045*	*– 17.6*
Lumber & wood products..............	14	15	15	16	18	−22.2
Furniture.............................	22	22	22	21	24	− 8.3
Metal industries	184	189	209	186	208	−11.5
Primary metal products..............	77	81	86	76	87	−11.5
Fabricated metal products...........	107	108	123	110	121	−11.6
Machinery (nonelectrical)..............	149	158	148	147	165	− 9.7
Electrical machinery...................	35	37	39	34	36	− 2.8
Transportation equipment..............	408	418	483	438	536	−23.9
Motor vehicles & equipment........	395	404	467	417	503	−21.5
Other transportation equipment......	13	14	16	21	33	−60.6
Other durable goods manufacturing....	49	47	52	51	58	−15.5
Nondurable goods industries.............	*189*	*188*	*187*	*182*	*185*	*2.2*
Food & kindred products..............	55	55	53	52	53	3.8
Textiles & apparel.....................	14	12	13	12	13	7.7
Paper & allied products...............	28	29	31	30	30	− 6.7
Printing, publ., & allied industries......	28	28	28	28	27	3.7
Chemical, petroleum, & coal products..	46	45	42	43	43	7.0
Other nondurable goods manufacturing	18	19	20	17	19	− 5.3

Source: Michigan Employment Security Commission, *Michigan's Labor Market,* January, 1958, p. 8.

From Table 6, the impact of heavy concentration in durable goods production can be noted also in the labor markets within the state. The data are for 1956, a year in which the nation was enjoying high-level economic activity, but in which Michigan was experiencing a sharp increase in the number of persons without jobs. Kalamazoo and Battle Creek, it will be seen, had the lowest percentage of factory workers engaged in producing durable goods, with percentages of 41 and 60, respectively. These two communities also had the lowest unemployment rates, 2.1 and 3.6 percent. In other words, the two localities in which nondurable industries were relatively more important than elsewhere suffered least from unemployment in 1956. Reference to data for 1957 and 1958 discloses the same situation.

All these data suggest that Michigan's unemployment problems will be severe during economic declines as long as the state's

Table 6

Percent of All Manufacturing Employees Engaged in Durable Goods Industries and Percent Unemployment, Individual Michigan Labor Markets

1956

(Numbers in thousands)

Labor Market	Wage and Salary Workers in Manufacturing			Unemployment	
	All manu-facturing industries	Durable goods		Number unem-ployed	Percent of total labor force
		Number	Percent of all mfg.		
Michigan^a............................	*1,074.0*	*886.0*	*82.5*	*190.0*	*6.5*
Detroit Metropolitan Area^b..............	590.0	511.0	86.6	120.0	7.9
Battle Creek...........................	23.2	13.8	59.5	2.0	3.6
Bay City..............................	11.4	9.6	84.2	2.1	6.1
Benton Harbor........................	22.6	18.0	79.6	2.2	4.2
Flint.................................	79.9	76.7	96.0	9.4	6.2
Grand Rapids.........................	53.4	41.7	78.1	6.1	4.4
Jackson..............................	17.1	13.8	80.7	2.0	4.2
Kalamazoo...........................	26.9	11.1	41.3	1.3	2.1
Lansing..............................	28.1	25.9	92.2	4.6	5.4
Muskegon............................	28.3	25.8	91.2	3.7	6.4
Port Huron...........................	9.7	7.4	76.3	2.5	7.4
Saginaw..............................	26.0	23.2	89.2	3.3	4.7
Upper Peninsula......................	18.3	11.4	62.3	6.3	6.3

Source: Michigan's Labor Market, January, 1957, p. 9.

a *Includes smaller labor markets not shown in table.*
b *Wayne, Oakland ,and Macomb counties.*

manufacturing economy is predominantly composed of the durable goods industries.

Decline Since 1953 by Industry

What manufacturing industries of the state have been hardest hit in the decline of employment since 1953? Enough has been suggested already, both in this study and elsewhere, to pinpoint the automotive industry as a primary area of decline.[6] During this four-year span, employment in the industry dropped by over 100,000 workers, well over half of the total decline of 180,000

---

6 As indicated in Table 5, data on the automotive industry are carried under the category "Motor vehicles and equipment." This category includes not only the production, or assembly, of cars and trucks, but also the manufacture of major automotive components. Throughout this report, the terms "automobile industry," "automotive industry," and "the motor vehicles and equipment industry" will be used interchangeably, when reference is made to the industry as a whole.

employees in all manufacturing taken together (Table 5). Although the percentage decline in jobs (21.5) in the automotive industry is not the largest one shown, it is the largest for any sizable industry.

Two other industry groups — the metal industries and non-electrical machinery — had, by 1957, dropped about 10 percent of the work forces they were using in 1953. A 60 percent loss in employment during the period is indicated for "other transportation equipment" (aircraft and parts, ships and boats, railroad equipment, etc.), a relatively small industry group in the state.

As noted earlier, every industry group in the durables sector experienced a loss of jobs during this four-year period. On the other hand, the number of employees in several of the nondurable industry groups increased modestly during this period.

While a substantial share of the decline in factory jobs since 1953 occurred in the automotive industry, it is important to bear in mind that other industry groups also declined. Some of these industry groups, particularly the metals industries, are tied in closely with the automotive industry and with other industries in the transportation equipment group.

Michigan and Nearby States

As was true when we looked at employees in all nonagricultural establishments, Michigan makes the poorest showing when its factory employment in recent years is compared with that of other states in the region. As indicated below, there was a drop of 16 percent — or about 200,000 jobs — in the state's manufacturing employment during the period 1953-1957.[7] While all states in the region suffered a decline, the Michigan experience was the

Area	Employment in Manufacturing Establishments (In thousands)		
	1957	1953	Percent change
United States	16,782	17,238	−2.6
East North Central region	**4,687**	**5,116**	−8.4
Ohio	1,340	1,424	−5.9
Indiana	607	673	−9.8
Illinois	1,260	1,324	−4.8
MICHIGAN	1,026	1,222	−16.0
Wisconsin	454	473	−4.0

Source: Appendix Table VII.

7. It should be noted that the loss of 200,000 factory jobs mentioned here is based on BLS data. As noted earlier, MESC data show a decline of 180,000 industrial jobs during this period.

most severe. Indiana saw about ten percent of its industrial jobs evaporate. Ohio lost nearly six percent, Illinois about five percent, and Wisconsin, four percent. The national decline was small, something under three percent.

Thus it is clear that Michigan's loss of factory employment during these years was not an isolated phenomenon. Rather, it appears that all these industrial states shared in the boom production that accompanied the Korean-defense period and that all shared in the subsequent decline in factory jobs. Michigan's factory employment problem is more easily understood against this background.

The Long-Range View

The data above relate Michigan's recent factory employment situation to a larger geographic environment. Let us now take a longer look at manufacturing employment in Michigan to see how recent job levels compare with Michigan's long-term experience.

The data in Table 7 show the proportion of the population that has worked in factories in the United States and in states in the East North Central region during the measurable past. Population provides a desirable base against which to measure employment in that it is a standard common denominator for all areas. By use of this measurement, differences between states in actual size of population and in their differing rates of population growth are recognized.[8]

The data reveal that during the last 30 years between 14 and 15 percent of the state's population, on the average, have been working as factory employees. Such a relatively high percentage points up the strong industrial character of Michigan over the years. Considerable variation by year can be noted. In the depths of the Great Depression, only seven out of every 100 persons in Michigan were employed in factories. During the peak years of war production (1943 and 1944), one out of every five civilians in the state was contributing to the war effort by working in a factory. During the Korean-defense peak of 1953, nearly 18 percent of the people of Michigan were working in manufacturing. The percentage has declined since 1953. However, as recently as 1955, a peak automotive year, about 16 out of every 100 Michigan residents held

---

8 As noted in a footnote to the table, civilian population is used as the population base for the period 1940-1957. One could, of course, use total population. Reasons can be advanced for using either population base. In any event, the last average shown in Table 7 removes much of the special effects of the war years.

Table 7

Percent of Population Working as Manufacturing Employees, United States, East North Central States, and Michigan[a]

Selected periods, 1919-1957

Year	United States	East North Central States					
		All	Ohio	Indiana	Illinois	MICHIGAN	Wisconsin
1919	10.1	...	...	...	...	...	...
1920	9.9	...	...	...	...	...	...
1921	7.5	...	...	...	...	...	...
1922	8.2	...	...	...	...	...	...
1923	9.1	...	...	...	...	...	...
1924	8.3	...	...	...	...	...	...
1925	8.4	...	...	...	...	...	...
1926	8.5	...	...	...	...	...	...
1927	8.3	...	...	...	...	...	...
1928	8.1	...	...	...	...	...	...
1929	8.7	...	...	...	...	12.5	...
1930	7.6	...	...	...	...	9.5	...
1931	6.5	...	...	...	...	8.6	...
1932	5.4	...	...	...	...	7.0	...
1933	5.8	...	...	...	...	7.8	...
1934	6.6	...	...	...	...	11.0	...
1935	7.0	...	...	...	...	12.2	...
1936	7.5	...	...	...	...	13.4	...
1937	8.2	...	...	...	...	14.8	...
1938	7.1	...	...	...	...	10.1	...
1939	7.7	10.5	11.1	10.3	10.1	12.1	8.2
1940	8.2	11.4	11.9	11.1	10.8	13.5	8.8
1941	9.9	13.8	14.7	13.6	12.8	16.0	10.6
1942	11.5	15.4	17.0	15.4	14.0	17.3	12.5
1943	13.6	18.7	20.0	18.7	16.7	22.2	15.0
1944	13.5	18.6	19.4	18.3	17.2	21.6	15.4
1945	12.0	16.5	17.4	15.9	15.8	17.7	14.5
1946	10.4	14.7	15.6	13.5	14.4	16.0	12.7
1947	10.7	15.5	16.2	14.6	14.9	17.2	13.3
1948	10.6	15.1	15.7	14.3	14.3	17.1	13.2
1949	9.6	13.7	14.1	13.0	13.1	15.5	11.9
1950	10.0	14.6	15.0	14.5	13.6	16.6	12.4
1951	10.7	15.5	16.5	15.2	14.4	17.1	13.5
1952	10.7	15.3	16.5	15.1	14.2	16.5	13.5
1953	11.0	16.0	16.7	16.3	14.8	17.9	13.4
1954	10.1	13.9	14.5	14.7	13.3	14.9	12.0
1955	10.2	14.4	15.0	14.3	13.6	15.9	12.2
1956	10.2	14.1	15.1	13.9	13.7	14.3	12.2
1957	10.0	13.4	14.6	13.5	13.1	13.3	11.8
Average-1919-57	9.2	...	...	...	...	...	...
Average-1929-57	9.3	...	...	...	...	14.5	...
Average-1939-57	10.6	14.8	15.6	14.5	13.9	16.5	12.5
Average-1939-57, excluding war years[b]	9.9	14.0	14.8	13.6	13.3	15.4	12.0

factory jobs. For the more recent years of 1956 and 1957, the percentages were slightly over 14 and 13, respectively.[9]

When Michigan is compared with other states in the Great Lakes region we see that in 1955 the Michigan percentage rate was still the highest. By 1957, the proportion of the state's population working as factory employees trailed behind that of Ohio and Indiana. When the record for the period 1939 through 1957 is examined, it is apparent that the gain in percentage rate for Michigan is smaller than for the other states. If the comparison is made for 1939 to 1955, Michigan is on a par with its neighbors. These data suggest that the loss of Michigan's factory jobs became a critical problem for the state after 1955, even though the problem began developing after the 1953 peak in industrial jobs.

The data for the United States show that, for the last 40 years, about nine out of every 100 persons in the country have, on the average, held factory jobs. In the postwar years, the figure has been about 10 percent. Since there have been references to the relative decline of manufacturing employment, the stability of the percentage of persons holding factory jobs may be surprising. As the population of the country has increased, manufacturing jobs have increased accordingly. Even with technological advances and increased consumer expenditures for services, the percentage has remained fairly stable. Over the long run, the adverse impact of technological gains on job opportunities has been offset by growth factors in the nation's industrial economy.

The Decline in Defense Employment

There have been several references in this study to defense produc-

---

9 On the basis of the 883,000 manufacturing jobs in Michigan in 1958 (Table 1), the percentage for the year was slightly above 11 percent. This was the lowest percentage recorded in the state since the recession year of 1938 when the percentage was 10.1. Such a low relationship of factory jobs to population reflects the impact of the 1958 recession on an already depressed manufacturing situation in the state. By May of 1959, the percentage appeared to have risen to about 12 percent or somewhat above.

Source: Population—
    Bureau of the Census, *Current Population Reports—Population Estimates*, Series P-25, Nos. 72, 139, 165 and 186.
    Manufacturing employees—
    United States: Bureau of Labor Statistics, *Employment and Earnings—Annual Supplement Issue*, July, 1958, p. 1.
    East North Central States, 1939-1957: *Ibid*, p. 101, and *State Employment, 1939-1956*, May, 1957, various pages.
    Michigan, 1929-1938: William Haber, *How Much Does It Cost?* (Michigan Employment Security Commission, 1951), p. 304.

a *Population data are for civilian population after 1939. Average percentages shown are straight arithmetic averages*
b *War years excluded are 1941-1945 inclusive and 1953.*

tion during the Korean period and to its impact on employment in the state. The decline in manufacturing employment in Michigan appears to be related, in large part, to the tapering off of defense work in the state. There is, however, no direct way to measure defense-related employment. Outside of "ordnance" (Standard Industrial Classification 19) there is no defense industry as such. Rather, contracts go to companies making varied products — automobiles, aircraft, electronic components, metal products, etc. Defense production forms a part of the output of a number of industries, and therefore it is difficult to determine the number of jobs associated with defense production within a company or industry.

The Michigan Employment Security Commission has made rough estimates of defense-related factory jobs in Michigan since 1951. The data in Table 8, under the caption "Engaged in defense work," show dramatically the importance of defense jobs in Michigan's manufacturing economy in 1952 and 1953. They averaged 185,000 and 200,000 jobs, respectively, during those two years. The monthly data upon which Table 8 is based indicate that over 200,000 workers were engaged on defense jobs each month from October, 1952, through July, 1953. Peak defense employment was reached in March, 1953 when some 220,000 jobs were based on government defense orders. During 1952 and 1953, about one of every six factory employees in Michigan was involved in defense work. By 1956 and 1957, the ratio had dropped to around one in every 20 workers.

From the data, one can see the tremendous importance of defense work in the state in 1952 and 1953. These figures also indicate that total factory employment has fallen as defense jobs have diminished in number. The loss of over 90,000 defense-related jobs during the recession year of 1954 accounted for well over half of the total drop (some 150,000 jobs) in factory employment that occurred during that year. Similarly, from 1953 to 1957, the number of all persons working in factories declined by 180,000 while the number of those working in defense jobs declined by almost 150,000. Most of this loss of defense employment had occurred by 1955. During 1956, loss of jobs in the automotive industry gave Michigan's manufacturing economy additional downward impetus.

Rough as the data may be, they point out dramatically that the substantial loss of defense work in the state since 1953 accounts

Table 8

All Wage and Salary Workers in Manufacturing and Defense Workers, Michigan, Detroit, and Outstate Michigan
1952-1957

(Numbers in thousands)

| Year | Wage and Salary Workers in Manufacturing | | | | | | | Defense Workers as Percent of All Manufacturing Workers | | |
| | Total | | | Engaged in defense work | | | | | | |
	Michigan	Detroit	Outstate Michigan	Michigan	Detroit	Outstate Michigan		Michigan	Detroit	Outstate Michigan
1952	1,104.0	646.0	458.0	184.7	105.1	79.6		16.7	16.3	17.4
1953	1,230.0	727.0	503.0	198.7	116.0	82.7		16.2	16.0	16.4
1954	1,075.0	604.0	471.0	105.8	59.6	46.2		9.8	9.9	9.8
1955	1,155.0	652.0	503.0	71.0	42.1	28.9		6.1	6.5	5.7
1956	1,074.0	590.0	484.0	61.2	39.8	21.4		5.7	6.7	4.4
1957	1,050.0	587.0	463.0	52.4	33.2	19.2		5.0	5.7	4.1

Source: Michigan Employment Security Commission.

All manufacturing workers: *Michigan's Labor Market,* January, 1958, p. 8, and *Detroit Labor Market Letter,* January, 1958, p. 7.

Defense workers: Unpublished Commission estimates.

for a good share of Michigan's recent employment problem. Undoubtedly a substantial share of the drop in jobs in the automotive industry, especially from 1953 to 1954, reflects a concurrent decline in defense-related production.

Trends in Nonmanufacturing Employment

WE HAVE DEVOTED considerable space to the deterioration of manufacturing employment in the state after 1953. Earlier, however, we did note briefly the fact that jobs in nonmanufacturing establishments had increased steadily after 1953. At this point, we shall examine Michigan's growth in this area in comparison with what was happening elsewhere and with what had happened during earlier years.

Michigan and Nearby States

In view of the somewhat cheerless findings on the Michigan job situation up to now, the picture shown by the data on nonfactory jobs is encouraging. Between 1953 and 1957, as indicated below, there was an increase in the state of about 115,000 persons working in stores, shops, public utilities, on construction jobs, for governmental agencies and the like, a gain of over nine percent.[10] Without this substantial increase in nonindustrial jobs, Michigan would have been confronted with a much more grave employment problem in 1957.

Area	Employees in Nonmanufacturing Establishments (In thousands)		
	1957	1953	Percent change
United States..........................	35,380	32,443	9.1
East North Central region..............	**6,919**	**6,382**	**8.4**
Ohio.................................	1,823	1,686	8.1
Indiana..............................	808	754	7.2
Illinois..............................	2,238	2,087	7.2
MICHIGAN..........................	1,351	1,234	9.5
Wisconsin...........................	699	621	12.6

Source: Appendix Table III.

---

10 It will be noted that these figures, which are from the Bureau of Labor Statistics, give a job increase substantially larger than figures released by the Michigan Employment Security Commission. At the beginning of the chapter, MESC figures were quoted that suggested an increase of only about 50,000 nonmanufacturing employees during the four-year span. If one uses the MESC data, the conclusions in this section must be toned down somewhat.

Most of the difference between the BLS and MESC nonmanufacturing data is traceable to government employment. During the 1953-1957 period, different sampling techniques were used by the BLS and MESC. Other definitional differences also existed. For example, BLS data included temporary postal employees but MESC data did not. BLS data included employees in government manufacturing operations in "government" but MESC data included these workers in manufacturing.

On a percentage change basis, Michigan's experience compared favorably with that of the United States as a whole. The state did better than the region generally in increasing nonfactory employment. Wisconsin, with a gain of 12.6 percent, was the only state to exceed Michigan. Thus, although industrial jobs in the state were declining in numbers after 1953, Michigan's rate of gain in nonmanufacturing employment during these years compared favorably with that of its sister states in the region. However, as indicated in a succeeding section, the additional jobs in the nonfactory area were not quite sufficient to keep pace with Michigan's fast-growing population.

Increase by Industry Since 1953

In what areas of activity did these new jobs in Michigan arise? Were they concentrated in a few areas, or were they dispersed? The following data show the areas of growth and decline.

Industry Group	Employees in Michigan Nonmanufacturing Establishments (In thousands)		
	1957	1953	Percent change
All nonmanufacturing industries........	**1,350.5**	**1,233.5**	**9.5**
Mining.................................	16.6	17.8	—6.7
Contract construction.................	109.5	106.3	3.0
Transportation and public utilities.....	151.2	150.1	.7
Wholesale and retail trade............	475.1	453.6	4.7
Finance, insurance, and real estate...	75.9	65.7	15.5
Service and miscellaneous industries..	248.1	207.2	19.7
Government..........................	274.1	232.8	17.7

Source: Bureau of Labor Statistics, *Employment and Earnings* — *Annual Supplement Issue*, July, 1958, pp. 98-106.

From the data above we see that three industry groupings — finance, insurance, and real estate; service and miscellaneous industries; and government — accounted for 92,000 new jobs or about 80 percent of the total increase. Employment in each of these groups increased from 15 to 20 percent during the four years after 1953. There was an increase of about five percent or 20,000 new jobs in wholesale and retail trade. Only mining, a relatively unimportant industry in the state, was providing fewer jobs in 1957 than in 1953.

In several respects, job trends in nonmanufacturing industries in Michigan after 1953 were similar to those taking place elsewhere in the Great Lakes region, as shown by the following data.

Industry Group	Percentage Change in Nonmanufacturing Employees, 1953-1957					
	All	Ohio	Indiana	Illinois	MICHIGAN	Wisconsin
All nonmanufacturing industries...........	8.4	8.1	7.2	7.2	9.5	12.6
Mining................	−10.4	−3.5	−13.7	−16.6	−6.7	......
Contract construction.	12.7	7.6	17.0	22.9	3.0	10.3
Transportation and public utilities.......	−2.9	−5.5	−6.3	−1.5	.7	−2.9
Wholesale and retail trade.................	6.7	9.0	6.6	3.6	4.7	14.2
Finance, insurance, and real estate......	13.4	15.1	19.1	8.9	15.5	18.4
Service and miscellaneous industries...	15.6	14.5	11.3	14.2	19.7	19.8
Government...........	11.7	10.2	9.2	9.6	17.7	13.0

Source: Bureau of Labor Statistics, Employment and Earnings — Annual Supplement Issue, July, 1958, pp. 98-106.

These data indicate that the decline in mining in Michigan was part of a general regional trend. There was also a general decline in the number of jobs available in the transportation and utilities fields, although Michigan's volume of jobs in these industry lines remained steady rather than declining.

Jobs in finance, in the service industries, and in government increased at appreciable rates in all of these states during these four years. Michigan experienced more rapid rates of growth in all three of these areas than did the region generally. This was especially true of governmental employment. Here the rate of gain was about half again as high in Michigan as in the region as a whole.

The state lagged far behind the region in the rate of expansion of construction jobs after 1953, the respective percentage gains being 3.0 and 12.7. The rate of gain in Michigan in job opportunities in the wholesale and retail trade fields — the state's largest nonfactory industry group — was also well under regional experience. Investigation of the relatively limited rate of expansion in these two nonfactory lines would seem to be in order to determine whether or not these lags were as serious as the data by themselves suggest.

The Long-Range View

Table 9 shows employees in nonmanufacturing establishments (based on BLS data) as a percent of the population for the period 1939-1957. Examining the data for 1953, we see that 18 out of every 100 persons in Michigan were working at nonfactory jobs.

Table 9

Percent of Population Working as Nonmanufacturing Employees, United States, Michigan, and East North Central States[a]

1939-1957

Year	United States	East North Central States					
		All	Ohio	Indiana	Illinois	MICHIGAN	Wisconsin
1939........................	15.5	15.5	14.4	13.6	18.8	14.0	13.1
1940........................	16.1	16.1	15.2	14.3	19.7	14.3	13.3
1941........................	17.6	17.2	16.5	15.8	21.1	15.3	14.1
1942........................	18.9	18.0	17.2	16.5	21.8	15.6	15.2
1943........................	19.4	18.3	17.6	16.6	22.3	16.0	15.0
1944........................	19.3	17.9	17.3	16.1	22.0	15.4	15.3
1945........................	19.4	18.1	17.3	16.5	22.4	15.4	15.9
1946........................	19.4	18.4	17.7	16.5	22.4	15.6	16.7
1947........................	19.8	18.9	18.5	16.9	23.0	16.0	17.0
1948........................	20.0	19.4	19.2	17.2	23.1	16.6	17.4
1949........................	19.8	18.9	18.8	16.9	22.4	16.4	17.2
1950........................	19.8	19.1	19.1	17.6	22.3	17.0	17.2
1951........................	20.6	20.0	20.1	18.1	23.2	17.8	17.8
1952........................	20.8	20.0	20.1	18.1	23.4	17.7	17.6
1953........................	20.8	19.9	19.8	18.1	23.3	18.0	17.7
1954........................	20.3	19.4	19.0	17.7	22.9	17.7	17.4
1955........................	20.6	19.7	19.4	17.9	23.1	17.9	17.6
1956........................	21.1	20.0	20.0	18.2	23.4	18.0	18.0
1957........................	21.0	19.9	19.8	18.0	23.2	17.6	18.1
Average-1919-1957[b].........	17.3	...	...	...	...	...	...
Average-1939-1957...........	19.5	18.7	18.3	16.9	22.3	16.4	16.4
Average-1939-1957, excluding war years[c].........	19.6	18.9	18.6	17.0	22.4	16.7	16.8

Source: Population—

Bureau of the Census, Current Population Reports—Population Estimates, Series P-25, Nos. 72, 139, 165, and 186.

Nonmanufacturing employees—

United States: Bureau of Labor Statistics, Employment and Earnings—Annual Supplement Issue, July 1958, p. 1.

East North Central States: Ibid., p. 101, and State Employment, 1939-1956, May 1957, various pages.

[a] Population data are for civilian population. Average percentages shown are straight arithmetic averages.

[b] Based on data not shown in table. The percentage for 1919 was 15.6 and for 1938 it was 15.2. High percentage during the period 1919-1938 was 16.8 (1929) and the low percentage was 12.9 (1933).

[c] War years excluded are 1941-1945 inclusive and 1953.

By 1957, this proportion was somewhat lower (17.6). Thus, in spite of a gain of 115,000 new jobs in nonmanufacturing since 1953, this increase was not quite large enough to match rapid population growth. Although the decline in the job-population ratio was relatively small, it should not be dismissed in view of differences between BLS and MESC data on jobs. The use of MESC data on the increase in nonfactory jobs during the four-year period would give a lower job-population ratio for 1957.

Data on nonfactory employees for the other Great Lakes states are more favorable, revealing little change in the job-population relationship during the four years after 1953. In other words, although the percentage gains in nonfactory jobs in these states were generally smaller than in Michigan, their smaller rates of population gain permitted their ratios of nonfactory jobs to population to remain steady.

Although each state's job-population percentage has remained fairly stable since 1953, the 1957 levels do show considerable variation among the states. In Illinois, 23 persons out of every 100 in the state held a nonfactory job in 1957. Ohio was also on the high side with about 20 persons. The high proportion for Illinois probably reflects Chicago's importance as a financial, distribution, and transportation center. Although Michigan had experienced the next-to-highest percentage gain in jobs from 1953 to 1957, its job-population percentage in the latter year (17.6) was the lowest of any of the five states under discussion.

Since 1939, the share of Michigan's population working for nonmanufacturing employers has advanced from 14 to almost 18 percent. This increase is below regional experience on the average, the region having moved up by 4.4 percentage points during the two decades, from 15.5 to 19.9. Moreover, the state's increase was smaller than that of any of the other states in the region.

In large part, the failure of Michigan's nonmanufacturing employment to keep pace with that of the other East North Central States during these two decades can be attributed to the abundance of factory jobs in the state through 1955. Factory jobs held a number of attractions for the average unskilled worker. In general, factory jobs paid much better wages for the work performed, frequently could be learned more quickly, offered more fringe benefits, and provided better working conditions. In the period from 1942 through 1949, it is reported that thousands of nonmanufacturing job opportunities in Michigan went without takers.

Summary

THE FOLLOWING PARAGRAPHS summarize briefly the principal findings of this chapter.

Over-All Experience

Since 1950, job opportunities in Michigan have not kept pace with the rapid growth in the state's population. From 1950 to 1957, the number of people living in Michigan increased by 20 percent. According to Michigan Employment Security Commission data, the number of jobs increased by only 7 percent during these same years.

Michigan reached a postwar employment high in 1953 when Korean-defense production attained its peak in the state. From 1953 to 1957, the state may have lost as many as 130,000 jobs. There was a loss of 180,000 factory jobs during these years. This loss was partly offset by a gain in nonfactory jobs.

Thus, Michigan's employment problem had developed before the 1958 recession aggravated the situation.

Manufacturing

Employment in Michigan's manufacturing economy is largely concentrated in durable goods industries. The decline of 180,000 manufacturing jobs in the state from 1953 to 1957 was confined almost entirely to the durable goods industries. Heaviest losses of employment were experienced in automobiles and parts, in the metal industries, and in nonelectrical machinery. The nondurable goods industries as a group provided a modest increase in jobs after 1953.

The percentage of Michigan's factory workers engaged in the durable goods industries has ranged from 82 to 85 percent since 1949. Two labor market areas in the state — Battle Creek and Kalamazoo — which have a relatively small share of their factory employment in durables experienced relatively low levels of unemployment from 1956 through 1958.

The loss of defense-related jobs not only accounted for a great share of the decline of all factory employment in Michigan after 1953, but also contributed to the decline of jobs in the automotive industry, especially during 1954. Most of the loss in defense-related employment had occurred by 1955. Following 1955, the drop in job opportunities in the automotive and other industries accounted for declining factory employment during 1956 and 1957.

Although the number of factory jobs has declined since 1953, Michigan's employment problem became crucial from the loss of such jobs after 1955. A long-range view of past relationships (factory jobs to population) indicates that factory employment in 1955 was still at or above long-time average rates, even though manufacturing employees were 75,000 fewer in number than in 1953. However, the support provided the factory jobs level in Michigan in 1955 by peak automotive production levels obscured the developing problem of the loss of factory jobs in the state.

Other data reveal that the Detroit area suffered a very much larger decline in employment after 1953 than did outstate Michigan, both in actual numbers and in the rate of percentage change. Much of Michigan's employment problem is localized in the Detroit area.

Michigan was not alone in experiencing a loss of factory jobs after 1953. All of the other Great Lakes states lost manufacturing employment during the period 1953-1957. However, the decline in Michigan was more severe.

Nonmanufacturing

On a percentage basis, the increase of over 115,000 nonfactory jobs (BLS data) in Michigan from 1953 through 1957 very nearly matched population growth. From a longer point of view, the number of nonfactory employees increased less from 1939 to 1957 (in relation to population) in Michigan than in the other East North Central States. In large part, this may reflect the relative abundance of factory jobs in the state through 1955.

The following three areas of nonmanufacturing activity — finance, insurance, and real estate; service and miscellaneous industries; and government — showed a 15 to 20 percent gain in employment in Michigan during the period 1953-1957. Although the sizable wholesale and retail trade industry recorded a more modest percentage gain during these years, it contributed over 20,000 new jobs during the period.

In general, growth trends in the individual nonfactory industries in Michigan from 1953 to 1957 were similar to those in the region. But, in wholesale and retail trade jobs, and especially in construction work, Michigan's rate of gain was well below regional experience.

Chapter IV

Recent Changes
in Automotive Employment

IN THE POSTWAR ERA, ceaseless change has been an outstanding characteristic of the automotive industry. The growth of new markets, the development and introduction of highly mechanized or automated equipment, and the Korean-defense production requirements all affected the industry. During this period there were also important style changes. Cars became larger, heavier, more powerful, more heavily ornamented, and more thoroughly equipped with accessories. For example, automatic transmissions and powered equipment, innovations early after the war, became commonplace. All of these developments contribute to the difficulty involved in attempting to analyze industry and employment trends both in Michigan and in the nation at large.

Moreover, most of the available employment data for the industry are given for the motor vehicles and equipment industry (Standard Industrial Classification 371). This industry, however, is made up of four components: motor vehicles and parts, truck and bus bodies, truck trailers, and automobile trailers. Although the motor vehicles and parts sector accounts for the bulk of employment, developments in one of the other three categories could affect somewhat total employment for the industry.

Another difficulty involved in analyzing trends in the automotive industry is that there are two types of plants: fabricating and assembly. It is the latter which is usually associated with this industry. Yet there are many more fabricating plants, those producing parts and equipment, than there are assembly plants. There are no data readily available on the volume of employment in each type of plant. Thus, if there are developments within the assembly sector of the industry, it is difficult to evaluate their impact on over-all employment levels.

Still another problem of analysis is that all of the employment associated with this industry is not likely to be included in the employment total. In a recent study of the industry, it was pointed out that under the classifications used in the *1947 Census of Manufactures* automotive products and products associated with automotive use were produced in at least 24 other industries.[1] It was suggested that there were many production workers in the metal industries in Michigan and Ohio who were making parts and equipment for the automotive industry, but who would not be counted as employees of this industry. The problem is dramatized by the fact that General Motors has 26,000 supplier firms.[2] Since General Motors manufactures a number of nonautomotive products, only part of these firms supply its automotive divisions. But this number of firms is approximately ten times the number of establishments classified in the motor vehicles and equipment industry.

Recognizing the complex character of the industry, the difficulties cited above, and the inadequacy of the available employment data, we are able, nevertheless, to point out the following trends and developments:

> Since 1929, from 4.0 to 5.5 percent of all manufacturing employees in the nation have worked in the automotive industry, the percentage for a given year depending in large part on the production level.
>
> Beginning in the 1930's, Michigan has accounted for a declining proportion of all automotive jobs. By 1956, and again in 1957, Michigan's share of these jobs amounted to just about half of the industry total. In 1958, it was below this level.
>
> As a result of this decline in automotive employment, wage and salary workers in automotive plants have accounted for an irregularly diminishing proportion of all nonagricultural employment in Michigan.
>
> Since most of Chrysler Motors' plants are located in Michigan, Chrysler's production volume noticeably affects the number of auto jobs in the state.
>
> Michigan has suffered a decline in the share of automotive productive facilities located in the state.
>
> The decentralization program which undoubtedly affected automotive employment in the state appears to have been completed in large part, except for Chrysler. Continued decentralization by Chrysler may reduce Michigan's share of all automotive jobs.
>
> In the future, the number of auto jobs will depend basically on the demand for new vehicles. Michigan's future share of all auto jobs will depend on developments in decentralization, automation, and integration. It will also be influenced by developments resulting from the introduction of the small car series of the Big Three.

We shall discuss these and other findings in greater detail.

---

1 Detroit Metropolitan Area Regional Planning Commission, *Study of Expansion Trends in the Automotive Industry with Special Reference to the Detroit Region* (Detroit: The Commission, October, 1956), p. 1.
2 General Motors Corporation, *GM Annual Report 1957*, p. 14.

The Auto Industry in Michigan's Economy

WE ALLUDED PREVIOUSLY to the "feast or famine" character of Michigan's employment record. This was explained largely in terms of the state's dependence on the durable goods industries, with their wide variations in production. And, as everyone knows, autos are Michigan's most important durable goods product. Data discussed in this chapter highlight the fact that in recent years jobs in Michigan automotive plants have accounted for about two-fifths of all factory jobs in the state, running above this level early in the 1950's and below in more recent years.

A considerable portion of the swings in the volume of job opportunities in Michigan can be attributed to the variable and largely unpredictable demand pattern of the automobile-buying public. Unlike the demand for many consumer goods, the automobile market has an extreme pattern of fluctuation, swinging from a high year to a mediocre year within 24 months.

With the exception of a home, the automobile represents the most expensive purchase that the average American wage earner will make. The purchase of a new car, if not made from available cash, usually involves a down payment which represents a fairly sizable amount of liquid funds and a balance that may be an obligation against his future earnings for periods as long as three years. Unlike most other purchases of the average family, the buying of a new automobile is usually a deferrable transaction which need not be made at a specific time. If emergencies develop, or unexpected drains on the family income occur, the purchase of an automobile can be, and usually is, postponed. This peculiar position of the automobile in the roster of consumer purchases injects a great element of risk and unpredictability in developing production schedules for the automobile industry.

Factors on the supply side serve to complicate the situation further. Because of yearly model changes and because of the large physical size of the automobile, cars cannot be stockpiled to the extent possible with many other manufactured products. As a result, the prudent auto manufacturer must direct close attention to his inventory position and may be required to make sudden changes in production schedules in order to maintain a proper balance between output and retail deliveries. The revision of production schedules may affect not only the number of workers employed but the length of the work week and the number of shifts as well.

All of these factors are reflected, singly or in combination, in sharply varying annual levels of automotive employment, both in Michigan and elsewhere. And, as noted earlier, employment levels in the metals industries in Michigan are affected to a substantial degree by production levels in the auto industry. Although some success in smoothing out the public's purchases of automobiles may be achieved in the years ahead, it seems likely that annual variations in automotive production schedules will continue to be appreciable. So long as the automotive industry remains important in the state's economy, appreciable annual variations in the number of total factory jobs in Michigan may be expected also.

Employment Trends

ALTHOUGH EMPLOYMENT data on the automotive industry have limitations, there is sufficient information available to afford a rough indication of a number of trends. Where there are gaps in the data, we shall attempt to bridge them with, at best, informed guesses.

Automotive and Total Manufacturing Employment

Workers in the nation's auto industry have accounted for from 4.0 to 5.5 percent of all manufacturing workers during the last three decades.[3] The following data indicate that the range in the

Year	Total Vehicle Production*a* (thousands)	Automotive Employees as Percent of all Manufacturing Employees
1947	4,798	5.1
1948	5,286	5.2
1949	6.254	5.4
1950	8,003	5.5
1951	6,765	5.2
1952	5,539	4.8
1953	7,323	5.4
1954	6,601	4.8
1955	9,169	5.5
1956	6,921	4.8
1957	7,214	4.7

Source: Production: Appendix Table IX.
       Employee percentage: Appendix Table VIII (BLS data)

*a*Cars, trucks, and buses. Based on factory sales.

---

3 See Appendix Table VIII for workers in the nation's auto industry as a percent of all factory employees for the period 1929-1957. The table is based on three different sources in order to provide a complete record for the period and to serve as a means of checking the consistency of the several series. It appears that, in the Department of Commerce data shown in the table, part of the workers in auto plants have been classified in other industries for the war years.

postwar period has been from 4.5 to 5.5 percent of all factory personnel. Thus it appears that during the last thirty years automotive jobs have increased at about the same rate as have all factory jobs and thus have maintained their relative importance in the nation's manufacturing work force.

The above data indicate that automotive employment, compared with total factory jobs, is most important in years of peak vehicle production. Both in 1950 and in 1955, high production years, 5.5 percent of all manufacturing jobs were held by automotive employees. For earlier peak production years, 1929 and 1937, the same situation prevailed.[4] In the former, 5.2 percent of employees in manufacturing were engaged in automotive production while in the latter year there were 5.5 percent.

This employment-production relationship is not so evident for years of lower automotive production levels. In 1949, for example, the industry accounted for 5.4 percent of all manufacturing jobs, yet the production level, while good, was below most subsequent levels. In that year, however, total manufacturing employment was at a postwar low. As is to be expected, variations in total manufacturing employment affect the percentage of all factory job holders found in the automotive industry.

Data for 1958 indicate that jobs in the automotive industry accounted for 4.1 percent of all manufacturing jobs for the year. This percentage was the lowest during the postwar period.[5] The principal explanation is the low level of automotive production during 1958. Total output of cars, trucks, and buses — about 5.1 million units — marked the lowest production record since 1947.[6]

Michigan's Share of Automotive Employment

Among informed observers, it has been known for some time that Michigan has been accounting for a steadily diminishing share of all automotive jobs. Table 10 traces the decline in Michigan's share. In 1950, the state accounted for over 56 percent of all jobs in the industry. By 1957, Michigan held only 50 percent. Preliminary data indicate that Michigan's share was about 47 percent in 1958.[7]

---

4 See Appendix Table VIII (Department of Commerce data).

5 A similarly sharp drop, to 4.0 percent, occurred in 1938, also a recession year. See Appendix Table VIII.

6 See Table 14. The preliminary production estimate shown in the table for 1958 corresponds closely with the final official figure.

7 Michigan's low share in 1958 reflects in large part the relatively low share of the market accounted for by Chrysler Motors. This point is discussed at a later point in the chapter.

Table 10

Percent of All Employees in Motor Vehicles and Equipment Industry Employed in Michigan

1949-1958

(Employees in thousands)

Year	Total Employees		Michigan as Percent of United States
	United States	Michigan	
1949....................	759.6	430.0	56.6
1950....................	825.2	468.0	56.7
1951....................	844.5	473.0	56.0
1952....................	790.2	435.0	55.0
1953....................	928.9	503.0	54.2
1954....................	775.6	417.0	53.8
1955....................	903.8	467.0	51.7
1956....................	809.9	404.0	49.9
1957....................	786.3	395.0	50.2
1958....................	627.3	a293.0	46.7

Source: United States: Bureau of Labor Statistics, *Employment and Earnings,* May, 1955, July, 1958, and February, 1959.

Michigan: Michigan Employment Security Commission, *Michigan's Labor Market,* January, 1959.

a *Unrevised basis.*

There are other data which tend to confirm this general downward trend. Appendix Table X, which is based on reports filed by employers under the old-age and survivors insurance program, indicates that Michigan's share of total jobs in the automotive industry declined from 56 percent in 1949 to 48 percent in 1956.[8] In the latter year, the state accounted for a smaller share of automotive employment in the East North Central region than earlier. It also appears that the region itself lost some of its importance from 1949 to 1956 as the center of automotive employment. A similar downward trend, dating from the thirties, can also be observed in Census of Manufactures data on production workers only.[9]

These data indicate that a progressively declining proportion of all automotive jobs has been available to Michigan workers in

8 It will be noted that Appendix Table X shows a lower percentage employed in Michigan in 1950 than in 1951 and in 1953. In large part, this situation reflects a strike in the plants of the Chrysler Corporation during the first several months of 1950. Since the data in Appendix Table X are as of mid-March, they reflect the loss of employment because of the Chrysler work stoppage to a greater extent than do the yearly averages shown in Table 10. The latter are, of course, better indicators of over-all experience.

9 See Appendix Table XI. These Census data indicate that during the 1930's Michigan accounted for from 62 to 64 percent of all production workers in the automotive industry as compared with about 54 percent in 1947 and 51 percent in 1954.

recent years. Whether this trend will continue remains to be seen. If it does, the task of providing sufficient manufacturing jobs to ameliorate Michigan's employment problem will be that much more difficult.

Automotive Employment in the Michigan Economy

As Michigan's share of automotive employment declined, the percentage of factory employees in the state holding jobs in the industry also declined. In 1949, as shown in Table 11, auto workers

Table 11

Relative Importance of Employment in Motor Vehicles and Equipment Industry in Michigan

1949-1958

(Numbers in thousands)

Year	Total Nonfarm Employment	Wage and Salary Workers			Wage and Salary Workers in Motor Vehicles and Equipment as Percent of—		
		All	Manufacturing		Nonfarm employment	All wage and salary workers	Manufacturing wage and salary workers
			All	Motor vehicles and equipm't			
1949........	2,240	2,020	976	430	19.2	21.3	44.1
1950........	2,381	2,160	1,070	468	19.7	21.7	43.7
1951........	2,489	2,267	1,122	473	19.0	20.9	42.2
1952........	2,499	2,275	1,104	435	17.4	19.1	39.4
1953........	2,694	2,466	1,230	503	18.7	20.4	40.9
1954........	2,556	2,325	1,075	417	16.3	17.9	38.8
1955........	2,646	2,413	1,155	467	17.6	19.4	40.4
1956........	2,584	2,349	1,074	404	15.6	17.2	37.6
1957........	2,576	2,335	1,050	395	15.3	16.9	37.6
1958[a]......	2,356	2,113	863	293	12.4	13.9	34.0

Source: Michigan Employment Security Commission, *Michigan's Labor Market*, January, 1959, p. 8.

[a] Unrevised basis.

held 44 percent of all factory jobs in the state. By 1957, they accounted for less than 38 percent. During the recession of 1958, jobs held by auto workers dropped still further in relative importance to 34 percent of all factory jobs, reflecting in part the sharp drop in automotive production. During this period, 1949-1958, automotive jobs as a percentage of total nonfarm employment in the state declined from a high of about 20 percent in 1950 to 12 percent in 1958.

The downward trend was irregular, with reversals in the trend occurring in 1953 and again in 1955. In 1953, the number of automotive jobs in the state reached a peak of 500,000, reflecting a good year for the industry. Not only was production fairly high (7.3 million units), but the industry was engaged in a considerable volume of defense production. Automotive production in 1955 was, of course, at its all-time peak with the production of over 9 million cars and trucks.

These data indicate that automotive employment has become relatively less important in the state's economy in recent years. A more diversified manufacturing economy for the state involves a lessening of the relative importance of auto jobs. It would have been far better, of course, if this objective could have been achieved without a reduction in the absolute number of automotive jobs, as has been our experience since 1953. The loss of these automotive jobs, if permanent, makes more difficult the restoration of Michigan's industrial economy to its former vigor.

Decline in Production Jobs

The production worker or blue-collar worker in Michigan's automotive industry has been confronted with a special problem in recent years. Since 1951, not only has total employment in the industry in Michigan declined irregularly, both in an absolute and in a relative sense, but also the share of all automotive jobs available to production workers diminished. As indicated in the data that follow, blue-collar employees in 1951 accounted for 85 percent of total employment in the industry in Michigan. By 1957, they held only 79 percent of these jobs. While these data for Michigan may be somewhat inconclusive, it is apparent that blue-collar workers have suffered more than white-collar workers in the relative decline of the industry in the state.[10]

The gradual decline in the relative importance of production workers in the automotive industry, in Michigan and in the country generally, is not an isolated phenomenon. Nonproduction workers in manufacturing industries have been increasing much more rapidly than production workers since World War II.[11] Increased

---

10 The Michigan data shown in Appendix Table XII are based on two different sources, giving rise to some element of noncomparability in the computation of the percentage figures for Michigan.

Other available data suggest a somewhat greater decline in recent years in the proportion of automotive jobs in Michigan held by production workers. Data for the transportation equipment industry group, of which the automotive industry is the chief component in Michigan, suggest that in this larger industry group production workers accounted for 87 percent of all workers in 1951 but for only 78 percent in 1957. See annual issues of the *Annual Survey of Manufactures* (Bureau of the Census).

11 For a detailed discussion of national experience, see "Nonproduction Workers in Factories, 1919-56," *Monthly Labor Review*, April 1957, pp 435-40.

Year	Production Workers as Percent of all Auto Employees	
	United States	Michigan
1950	85.0	....
1951	83.8	85.2
1952	81.5	84.4
1953	82.6	84.3
1954	80.5	78.2
1955	82.6	81.6
1956	80.1	77.2
1957	80.1	79.0

Source: Appendix Table XII.

research and development activity, increased productivity from large-scale investment in new plant and equipment, and expansion of overhead functions have all contributed to this rapid growth in the number of white-collar personnel.

If total automotive employment in the state should increase substantially in the future, it is probable that production workers would, in the short run, increase their share of all automotive jobs. But over the longer run, the persistence of the gain, either absolute or relative, by white-collar workers will probably mean a diminishing share of automotive jobs for production personnel. This likely development is not significant with regard to the total number of automotive jobs but only as an indication of the probable shift in the occupational composition of the industry's work force.

Production Trends

HAVING EXAMINED recent developments in automotive employment in Michigan, we shall consider data on automotive production trends in the state. Since production in the automotive industry consists of the production of components as well as the assembly of vehicles, there is no direct way to trace production records for a particular state. Our rather limited review of automotive production trends in Michigan reflects this problem.

Value Added by Manufacture

Comparisons among areas are often made in terms of the value added by manufacture. As indicated in Table 12, Michigan accounted for a somewhat smaller share of total value added by manufacture in the automobile industry in 1954 than in 1947. In view of the decline in the state's share of all auto jobs in the nation, a similar decline in the value added by manufacture was to be ex-

Table 12

Value Added by Manufacture in Motor Vehicles and Equipment Industry, United States, East North Central States, and Michigan

1947 and 1954

(Dollar amounts in millions)

Year	Value Added by Manufacture			Michigan as Percent of—		East North Central States as Percent of United States
	United States	East North Central States	Michigan	United States	East North Central States	
1947.........	$3,790.9	$2,883.2	$1,880.7	49.6	65.2	76.1
1954.........	6,406.6	4,513.2	3,009.9	47.0	66.7	70.4

Source: 1954 Census of Manufactures, Vol. III, Table 2-A, pp. 20-21; Table 2, p. 10-28; and Table 4, p. 121-10.

pected. Both downward trends suggest some decentralization of the industry away from Michigan.

From 1947 to 1954, Michigan's percentage of the value added by manufacture in the region as a whole increased slightly, from 65 percent to almost 67 percent. We have already seen that Michigan's automotive employment declined in relation to that of other states in the region. One possible explanation for these divergent trends is that relatively more of Michigan's production may have been concentrated on medium-priced and luxury cars in 1954 than in 1947.

It can also be seen from Table 12 that the East North Central region held a smaller share of all value added in the industry in 1954 than in 1947. From 76 percent in 1947, the region's share dropped to 70 percent in 1954. This development parallels the region's modest loss in relative importance of automotive employment, discussed earlier.

Passenger Car Assemblies in Michigan

At first glance the data in the text table below seem encouraging. For five years, 1953-1957, inclusive, Michigan maintained quite well its share of total car assemblies. About 36 percent of all cars were assembled in the state in 1953 as compared with about 35 percent in 1957. The poorest record in recent years was 1958, when only 30 percent were assembled in the state.

Year[a]	Percent of All Assemblies
1953	35.8
1954	32.1
1955	34.1
1956	33.0
1957	34.6
1958	29.9

Source: For 1953-1957, Appendix Table XIII.

For 1958, *Ward's Automotive Reports,* communication dated November 24, 1958.

[a]*Calendar year except for 1958 which is on model-year basis.*

Although Michigan accounted for a fairly steady share of the industry's assemblies during the years 1953-1957, this stability was not matched by a similar stability in the state's share of all automotive jobs. As we noted before, that share was declining during these years. In view of Michigan's stable share of car assemblies, one might assume that the state also accounted for a fairly stable share of all employment in the industry's assembly plants during the years. If this assumption is correct, then Michigan would appear to have been accounting for a progressively smaller share of jobs in fabricating plants.

The drop to 30 percent as Michigan's share of total passenger cars assembled in 1958 reflects, in part, increased penetration of the market by the Wisconsin-made Ramblers and the loss of market share by Chrysler-made cars, most of which are assembled in Michigan.

Impact of Chrysler Production on Michigan Auto Employment

As indicated above, most Chrysler cars are assembled in Michigan. In the 1957 model year, about four-fifths of all Chrysler production came off Michigan assembly lines (See Appendix Table XIV). While data on the share of Chrysler cars assembled in Michigan in other years are not readily available, it may be assumed that previous production was also concentrated in the state. Chrysler cars were assembled in only three other states during the 1957 model year. Most of the corporation's manufacturing plants are also located in Michigan. Thus, because of this heavy concentration of Chrysler operations in the state, annual variations in the number of automotive jobs in Michigan may stem, to a significant degree, from the Chrysler sales experience.

The data brought together in Table 13 can be interpreted to suggest some relationship for most years between Chrysler's share of the market and the level of automotive jobs in Michigan. In general, years in which both Chrysler and the industry as a whole enjoyed good production levels were years in which Michigan automotive jobs were also at high levels. Such years were 1950, 1951, 1953, and 1955. The high level of automotive job opportunities during these years must be assumed to reflect the high level of operations in the state by all of the Big Three.

Table 13

Relation of Production by Chrysler Corporation and Automotive Employment in Michigan

1949-1958

(Numbers in thousands)

| Year | Total Automotive Production[a] | | Percent by Chrysler | Percent of Cars Assembled in Michigan[b] | Automotive Jobs in Michigan | |
| | Number of units | | | | Number | Percent of United States |
	Total	Chrysler				
1949.........	6,250	1,266	20.3	...	430	56.6
1950.........	8,002	1,316	16.4	...	468	56.7
1951.........	6,747	1,393	20.6	...	473	56.0
1952.........	5,561	1,115	20.1	...	435	55.0
1953.........	7,345	1,352	18.4	35.8	503	54.2
1954.........	6,532	818	12.5	32.1	417	53.8
1955.........	9,188	1,457	15.9	34.1	467	51.7
1956.........	6,905	962	13.9	33.0	404	49.9
1957.........	7,199	1,299	18.0	34.6	395	50.2
1958.........	5,145	640	12.4	29.9	[c]293	46.7

Source: Automotive production: *Automotive News 1958 Almanac*, p. 25. Data for 1958 based on preliminary data from the press.

Percent of cars assembled in Michigan: *Automotive News 1958 Almanac*, and 1956 and 1955 issues, pp. 26, 31, and 32, respectively. For 1958, communication from *Ward's Automotive Reports*.

Automotive jobs in Michigan: Michigan Employment Security Commission, *Michigan's Labor Market*, January, 1959, p. 8, and Table 10 of this report.

a Covers cars, trucks, and buses.
b Covers passenger cars only.
c Unrevised basis.

The relationship for other years is less clear. Especially striking, however, is experience during 1958. During the 1958 slump, the automotive industry as a whole produced only 5.1 million cars and trucks, a decline of 29 percent from the preceding year. Chrysler produced only 640,000 cars and trucks, or half of its production during the preceding year. There were only 293,000 jobs available in Michigan's automotive industry in 1958. Chrysler's especially low production levels undoubtedly contributed to the low level of auto employment in the state in 1958.

Thus, Chrysler market levels, among other factors, appear to have an important influence on the number of auto jobs in the state. However, only in 1957 did a good production year by Chrysler contribute to a stemming of the steady decline since 1950 in Michigan's share of the nation's automotive jobs.

Trends in Plant Location

DURING RECENT YEARS, there has been considerable discussion of decentralization of the automotive industry and of its impact on the state. These discussions suggest that decentralization in the industry is a fairly recent phenomenon, having become important only in the postwar decade. Actually, the industry began its decentralization program very early in its history. The Ford Motor Company built its first assembly plant outside of Michigan in 1910 at Kansas City, Missouri.[12] Additional assembly plants were established by Ford during the next few years. By 1915, about twenty such plants, including some on the West Coast, had been constructed outside of Michigan.

In the early years of the industry, there was a large number of independent car producers. Because of the scattered locations of these firms and of the decentralized operations of Ford, Michigan accounted for only about half of the production workers in the industry from 1914 to 1931.

However, during the twenties, General Motors and Chrysler became increasingly important in the industry. Much of their early employment centered in Michigan. Moreover, the Great Depression took its toll of the independent producers still in operation. Thus, in spite of Ford's early decentralization policy and General Motors' subsequent decentralization of operations, Michigan assumed a more dominant position in the industry during the thirties. Sixty percent or more of the production workers in the industry were employed in Michigan during that decade.

Thus, the late thirties found the Big Three centered in Michigan, but with Ford and General Motors already operating on a decentralized basis, so that "the locational patterns of heavy manufacturing and assembly operations had already developed by 1938."[13] It is probable, therefore, that the capital expansion program of the industry during the postwar period has consisted largely of a modifi-

12 Detroit Metropolitan Area Regional Planning Commission, *op.cit.,* p. 4. Much of the material in the next several paragraphs is based on this study.
13 *Ibid.,* p. 9.

111

cation of the locational pattern already in existence at the end of the war. In the following pages, we shall try to determine the nature of this modification.

Recent Capital Expenditures

The Census data quoted below suggest that the automotive industry has been making the major share of its expenditures for new plant and equipment in Michigan during the postwar period. However, even though the state accounts for a large share of these capital outlays, a diminishing proportion of them appears to have been placed in the state. In 1947, 57 percent of the capital outlays of the industry were made in Michigan. The state's share dropped to 50 percent in 1956 and to 40 percent in 1957. Although these data have limitations and cover only four years in the postwar period, they do reflect the direction of capital outlays, i.e., decline in Michigan, and gains in other states.[14]

Year	Capital Outlays (millions)		Percent in Michigan
	United States	Michigan	
1947	$ 269.7	$154.3	57.2
1954	722.2	394.4	54.6
1956	1,038.3	518.5	49.9
1957	678.9	276.8	40.8

Source: 1947 and 1954: Appendix Table XV.
1956 and 1957: *Annual Survey of Manufactures,* Series MAS-56-5, p. 12; MAS-57-4, p. 12; and MAS-57-6, Table 3.

The purpose for which capital outlays are made has implications for employment in the industry. Expenditures for new structures or additions ordinarily imply more jobs. If, however, expenditures are for more efficient equipment to replace existing equipment, there may be a loss of production worker job stations.

There is no detailed information available on the breakdown of the capital outlays of the automotive industry in Michigan during the postwar period. A review of recent annual reports of the Big Three does indicate that a substantial share of their capital outlays has been made for office buildings, for engineering and technical centers, and for proving grounds. Such expenditures are signifi-

---

14 The data for 1947 and 1954 are for motor vehicles and parts, a category which accounts for the great bulk of the motor vehicles and equipment industry. The figures shown for the United States for 1956 and 1957 are for the motor vehicles and equipment industry. Capital outlays shown for Michigan for 1956 and 1957 are for transportation equipment. The amount for motor vehicles and equipment only would be smaller, so that the percentages for Michigan for 1956 and 1957 would be somewhat smaller than those shown.

cant in that they reflect Michigan's continued position as the center of the industry. They may not, however, increase job opportunities for Michigan workers in the same direct sense as expenditures for new assembly plants.

Automotive Establishments in Michigan, 1949-1956

The data shown below are of help in tracing the impact of recent plant location developments on Michigan's position in the auto industry. These data, which are based on reports filed by employers under the old-age and survivors insurance program, cover all establishments classified in the industry, including the many relatively small firms which supply parts to the Big Three and to other primary producers.

From these data, it can be seen that there was a small decline in the number of automotive establishments in the state after 1953, the year when auto jobs in Michigan were at their peak. More importantly, these figures reveal a decline since 1950 in Michigan's share of all plants in the motor vehicles and equipment industry. In 1950, Michigan accounted for almost 17 percent of these plants. By 1956, only 15 percent were located in Michigan. The same general trend is indicated for the East North Central region. In 1950, the region accounted for 43 percent of all plants in the industry, whereas in 1956 the percentage was about 41. However, the decline in the region's share reflects Michigan's decline since anaylsis reveals that the share of all plants held by the other four states in the region remained steady after 1950.

Year	All Plants	Michigan		East North Central States	
		Plants	Percent of all	Plants	Percent of all
1949	2,141	331	15.5	876	40.9
1950	2,064	345	16.7	888	43.0
1951	2,144	350	16.3	913	42.6
1953	2,314	358	15.5	956	41.3
1956	2,344	351	15.0	965	41.2

Source: Appendix Table XVI.

The above data seem to substantiate our earlier findings that the automotive industry has declined in relative importance both in Michigan and in the East North Central region. Not only did automotive employment in the state and in the region decline as a percentage of total automotive employment, but both areas experienced a drop after 1950 in the share of all establishments in the industry.

113

Postwar Plant Location Developments

As just noted, there has been a decline in the proportion of all automotive plants located in Michigan. This would suggest for one thing that most new automotive plants have been located in states other than Michigan during recent years. Data compiled by the Automobile Manufacturers Association show that this is what has happened.[15] The AMA figures reveal that motor vehicle manufacturers have built 113 new plants and plant additions since the end of World War II. Of this total, 44 were constructed in Michigan, 35 in other Great Lakes states, and the remaining 34 elsewhere in the United States. Thus Michigan received less than two-fifths of these additional automotive facilities provided by vehicle manufacturers in the postwar period.

These data do not tell the whole story, of course, but they are probably indicative of plant location developments in the industry as a whole. It is likely that independent parts suppliers have been, in fact, locating many of their new plants outside of Michigan in accordance with the decentralization pattern followed by the vehicle manufacturers themselves.

Although three-fifths of all new plants established by auto and truck manufacturers in the postwar period have been located outside Michigan, almost half of the plants of the Big Three are still located in the state. The following summary, which provides a rough count of Big Three plants in 1956, also indicates that about 70 percent of Chrysler's plants are located in Michigan while only about one-third of General Motors' plants are found in the state.

Company	Automotive Plants, 1956[a]		
	United States	Michigan	Percent in Michigan
Big Three, total	217	101	47
General Motors......................	113	39	35
Ford................................	54	26	48
Chrysler............................	50	36	72

Source: Based on tabulation of data shown in *Automotive News 1957 Almanac*, p. 17.

a Excludes plants under construction.

Since half of the Big Three plants are located in Michigan and since the state is the center of the industry's administrative, research, and engineering activities, Michigan still holds a position

---

15 Harry A. Williams, "The Future of the Automotive Industry in the Great Lakes States," presented as an address before the Great Lakes States Industrial Development Council, Ann Arbor, Michigan, January 15, 1959, p. 9, and communication from the Automobile Manufacturers Association, March 3, 1959.

of dominance in the automobile world. But its margin of leadership has been trimmed by recent plant location developments.[16] While the locational pattern of the industry, as shown by these data on the Big Three, retains the same general pattern as that of the prewar period, an appreciable drop in Michigan's relative importance is suggested.

Factors Behind Relative Decline of Michigan's Automotive Employment

Decentralization

From the statistics on capital expenditures and plant locations discussed in the preceding section, it seems clear that the decentralization of the automotive industry during the postwar period has been a primary, if not the principal, factor in the decline of the share of all auto jobs held by Michigan workers. The increasing proportion of facilities located outside of Michigan has coincided with a decline in the proportion of all auto jobs provided in Michigan factories.

The mere number of plants is not, however, a direct measure of job opportunities. Some plants employ more workers than others. It may be that those plants built in Michigan in the postwar period were larger than those constructed elsewhere. Such a situation could offset, in part, the greater number of new fabricating and assembly units located outside Michigan. But it seems very doubtful that such an offset could be more than a partial one.

Discontinuance by Independent Producers

Another explanation of Michigan's loss in auto jobs is the experience of the independent producers. The combination of Hudson, Kaiser, and Packard with other companies and their moving out of the state had some influence on the job picture.

However, the removal of these companies to other states may have had less effect on the number of auto jobs in the state than is sometimes supposed. During the last few years of their operation in Michigan, the independents accounted for successively smaller shares of production and employment. Even after moving out of the state, their market continued to shrink, with the Big Three ab-

16 The data shown for Michigan in the text table include plants taken over by the Big Three in recent years from former independents such as Briggs, Hudson, and Kaiser-Frazer. Such plants, of course, have not added to Michigan's auto plant inventory in the same way that most additional Big Three facilities provided elsewhere have represented an actual increase in plants.

sorbing it. In effect, there may have been a partial transfer of employment during this period from the independents to the Big Three. While not all former employees of the independent producers were absorbed, the cessation of operation in Michigan by the independents did not constitute a total loss of the jobs involved.

Impact of Automation

No attempt will be made here to define or explain automation. Furthermore, we shall not anticipate its ultimate effect. We shall merely use the term loosely to describe the continued introduction into American factories and offices of more highly mechanized and automatic industrial equipment and processes.

The number of jobs permanently lost as a result of automation in Michigan's auto factories or in the industry at large is not known. Dramatic examples of reductions in automotive jobs through automation have been cited. Some appraisals, however, suggest that, on an over-all plant or company basis, the loss of jobs resulting from automation itself may not be serious. As is often the case, many things are attributed to one causative factor when in reality there may be many complex, highly interrelated factors.

There are many variables, of which automation is only one, that affect employment in the automotive industry, both in Michigan and in the nation. There have been, however, attempts to measure the impact of increased mechanization on jobs in the automotive industry during the last decade. In 1948, according to one study, output per auto worker (including white-collar workers) during the year amounted to 6.7 cars and trucks.[17] By 1958, output per worker had increased to 8.1 cars and trucks, a reflection supposedly of increased productivity during the decade. The study concludes that, if productivity had remained at 1948 levels, some additional 130,000 auto workers would have been needed in 1958 to produce the 5 million cars and trucks assembled that year.

Undoubtedly there had been a steady increase in productivity in the automotive industry. But a look at the record of automotive production and job levels since 1929 suggests that the impact of technological advances upon job opportunities in the industry cannot readily be discerned.

Table 14 has been prepared to show vehicles (cars, trucks, and buses) produced per employee for the period 1929-1958, exclud-

---

17 "Why Jobs are Slow to Come Back," *U. S. News and World Report,* February 13, 1959, pp. 88-89.

Table 14

Motor Vehicles Produced per Employee in Motor Vehicles and Equipment Industry, United States, by Year

1929-1958

Year[a]	Vehicles Produced[b] (thousands)	Number of Employees (thousands)	Vehicles Produced per Worker
1929...............	5,337	540	9.9
1930...............	3,363	403	8.3
1931...............	2,380	352	6.8
1932...............	1,332	299	4.5
1933...............	1,890	300	6.3
1934...............	2,737	433	6.3
1935...............	3,971	464	8.6
1936...............	4,461	492	9.1
1937...............	4,820	580	8.3
1938...............	2,508	363	6.9
1939...............	3,589	466	7.7
1940...............	4,472	532	8.4
1941...............	4,841	654	7.4
1946...............	3,090	662	4.7
1947...............	4,798	776	6.2
1948...............	5,286	789	6.7
1949...............	6,254	760	8.2
1950...............	8,003	825	9.7
1951...............	6,765	845	8.0
1952...............	5,539	790	7.0
1953...............	7,323	929	7.9
1954...............	6,601	776	8.5
1955...............	9,169	904	10.1
1956...............	6,921	810	8.5
1957...............	7,214	786	9.2
1958...............	5,145	627	8.2

Source: Vehicles produced: *Automotive News 1958 Almanac*, p. 28. Data for 1958 based on preliminary data from the press.

Number of employees: For 1929-1938, *National Income—A Supplement to the Survey of Current Business*, 1954 Edition, Table 25.

For 1939-1941 and 1946-1957, Bureau of Labor Statistics, Individual Historical Summary Tables, *Automobiles (371)*, various dates.

For 1958, *Employment and Earnings*, February, 1959, Table A-8.

a Excludes war years, 1942-1945.

b Based on factory sales including sales of military vehicles. Includes passenger cars, trucks, and buses.

ing the World War II years. All employees (production and non-production) are reflected in the data. The increase in vehicles produced per worker from 1948 to 1958 shown in this table is about of the same magnitude as that shown in the study mentioned above.

From the data in Table 14, there does not appear to be a decided trend in vehicles per worker, either in the short run or in the long run. In 1929, there were 9.9 vehicles produced for every worker in the industry. In 1957, the figure was 9.2. In the peak production year of 1955, ten vehicles were produced per worker. Other high levels were achieved in 1936 with 9.1 and in 1950 with 9.7. In general, these high levels of vehicles per worker have tended to occur in "good" production years, as might be expected.

In the last decade, 1948-1958, the gains in vehicles per worker depend on the years taken as the base. As indicated above, the use of 1948 as the base year indicates an increase in vehicles per auto worker by 1958. If 1949 is used as the base year, there is no change by 1958. With 1950 as a base, vehicles per employee drop sharply by 1958.

There are, of course, noncomparable elements reflected in the data which affect the comparison of the vehicles-per-worker figures over the years. Some of these relate to the nature of the product, others to the count of employees. We have previously alluded to the ever-increasing complexity of the American motor car. The heavier, larger, and more complex passenger car of 1958 can hardly be compared with its 1929 predecessor or even with a 1948 model. The industry mix as between cars and trucks can change abruptly in a year's time, with a resultant impact on the vehicles-per-worker figure. Again, during the Korean period, the automotive industry was producing a substantial volume of vehicles for the armed forces. The problems attendant on the production of these special military vehicles undoubtedly are reflected in the relatively low vehicles-per-worker figures shown for 1951, 1952, and 1953.

The vehicles-per-worker figure is also affected by variation in the average length of the work week during these years. Data shown in the source documents for Table 14 indicate that average weekly hours for production workers in the industry during the thirties (1934-1940, inclusive) ranged from 33 to 39. Had employees been working a longer work week, the vehicles-per-worker figures for those years would have been larger than those shown in Table 14. During the good production years of 1950 and 1955, weekly hours averaged 41.2 and 42.7, respectively. Thus, the high vehicles-per-worker ratios experienced in those two years reflect in part a relatively long work week for production workers. On the other hand, the vehicles-per-worker figure for 1958 (8.2) would undoubtedly have been higher but for the intermittent production schedules that characterized a considerable portion of the industry's production during the year.

Another factor affecting the count of employees from year to year may be variations in the proportion of workers in supplier firms who are classified as part of the automotive industry as opposed to those who are counted in nonautomotive industries. Thus, it is possible that the movement toward integration (discussed briefly on page 121) may have bolstered the count of automotive employees in recent years, as compared with earlier years.

Thus, vehicles-per-worker data in Table 14 reflect many variables, of which technological advance is only one. The table does suggest that the growing complexity of the motor vehicle has tended to offset increasing efficiency brought about by technological advances so that vehicle production and *total* employment in the industry have tended to move upward roughly together over the years. In most years, the number of vehicles produced per employee has varied between 7 and 10, the level for any one year being influenced often by special factors pertaining to that year.

The effects of recent technological advances in the industry remain to be seen. It may well be that increases in efficiency resulting from new capital installations will be sufficient to raise the vehicle-per-worker figure above the range experienced in recent years. The historical data suggest, however, that the relation between vehicle output and *total* employment in the industry at large (including both production and nonproduction workers) may be less influenced by technological advances, including automation, than is generally assumed.

It is possible that technological advances reflected in new and modernized plants in Michigan have made the state's auto plants more efficient than those in the industry generally. In that case, automation and related technological advances may have contributed to the decline in Michigan's share of all auto jobs. Until more information is available, this possibility will have to remain an area of uncertainty.

Loss of Defense Orders

In Chapter III, the importance of defense-related employment in Michigan during the early fifties was noted. The high point of such employment was in 1952 and 1953 when from 16 to 17 percent of all factory workers in the state held defense jobs. By 1957, the percentage had dropped to 5 percent. Although the number of defense jobs in the automotive industry is not a matter of record, the loss of defense orders undoubtedly contributed to the decline of automotive employment in the state after 1953.

Future Auto Jobs in Michigan

DECENTRALIZATION has been suggested in the preceding section as the most important factor in explanation of Michigan's declining share of all auto jobs. In this section, we shall be concerned with this factor and with others that will influence the number of jobs in the automotive industry in the immediate years ahead and the state's share of this employment.

Decentralization Prospects

Michigan's relative position as the production center of the automotive industry may not deteriorate seriously in the near future as a result of further decentralization. Both General Motors and Ford have indicated that their postwar capital expansion programs have largely been completed. Although some additional new capital facilities will be provided from time to time, the money amounts involved may be relatively modest compared with amounts expended during the last decade. Thus, Ford had spent $2.6 billion on its capital expenditures program through 1957. In the latter year, Ford expenditures for expansion, modernization, and replacement amounted to $376 million. For 1958, they were expected to be "substantially lower." General Motors was also planning relatively limited amounts of future capital expenditures.[18]

This announced policy of limited volumes of capital outlays in the near future by Ford and General Motors would seem to be borne out by the current capacity of the industry. Some 9.2 million cars and trucks were turned out in 1955. Since then, additional capacity has been added. Production facilities now appear to be adequate to meet peak production schedules for some years to come.

Chrysler Corporation is, however, in a somewhat different position. In its 1957 Annual Report (p. 2), the company states, "Continued substantial expenditures for new plant and facilities in future years will be required to keep our company competitive." This statement presumably reflects the need for more modern facilities to replace some of the company's older plants. Moreover, as already indicated, Chrysler is less decentralized than its two larger

---

18 This discussion is based on material in the 1956 and 1957 annual reports of these two companies.

competitors, with over two-thirds of its plants still located in Michigan. Thus, Chrysler may be expected to continue a program of capital expenditures for some time.

The location of new plant facilities by Chrysler will undoubtedly affect the state's relative position in the industry. The company may be expected to establish some additional assembly plants in other states to fit marketing patterns. There is concern in the Detroit area that some of the company's new manufacturing facilities may also be located outside of Michigan. However, if Chrysler's capital expenditure program is carried out slowly, the adverse effect on the state's economy will be spread over time.

Automation Prospects

It is difficult to determine the impact of automation on future auto jobs in the state. With a more limited program of capital outlays in prospect, it may be the rate of introduction of additional labor-saving machinery and equipment in the industry will be relatively slow. On the other hand, the Big Three and other large-scale producers in the industry can be expected to continue to introduce new machinery and equipment if technological developments indicate savings in production costs.

The Movement toward Integration

It has been suggested that there has been some movement toward greater integration by the Big Three in recent years, that is, a movement for these companies to fabricate a larger proportion of the parts and equipment that go into the assembly of their cars. Such a movement would imply more automotive employment available in the plants of the Big Three and less employment in the factories of the suppliers. The net effect might be less total employment in the industry in view of the likely greater efficiency of the industry leaders. On the other hand, the count of employees in the industry might be bolstered, somewhat artificially, to the extent that employees in the supplier firms losing contracts to the Big Three had been classified in nonautomotive industries.

The degree of integration and its impact on automotive employment in Michigan cannot be determined. Much would depend on the location in and out of Michigan both of the supplier firms which lost Big Three contracts and of the Big Three plants which took over the manufacturing of parts. If, on balance, the net effect of this movement has been to bolster automotive employment in the state, as some observers have suggested, its beneficial effect has not been significant enough to offset the decline in Michigan's share of automotive jobs. In view of the uncertainty concerning the recent impact of integration, one can only bear this development in mind in evaluating future employment trends.

Production of Small Cars

The introduction by the Big Three of a new series of small cars for the 1960 model year market introduces new elements of uncertainty into the job prospects for Michigan auto workers. As the 1960 production year got under way, General Motors and Chrysler were assembling their small cars in Michigan while Ford was assembling its line in Ohio. It was reported that General Motors and Ford might also utilize plants in other states for small car assemblies later in the production year.

The effect of the production of the small car lines on the number of jobs in Michigan automotive plants will depend on several factors. That two of the cars will be assembled in the state, at least initially, is encouraging. But before this possibility could be regarded as a plus factor for auto jobs in Michigan, other aspects of the situation would have to be evaluated. How large will be the market for these small cars? If of substantial size, will it develop at the expense of foreign car imports, or of domestic small-car makes, or of the larger size cars of the Big Three? Where will the new parts and equipment needed for the small cars be fabricated? To what extent may production for and assembly of General Motors and Chrysler small cars in Michigan mean a shifting of production activity on larger cars elsewhere? It will be some time before the production pattern for these cars, and its implications for Michigan auto workers, become evident.

Future Market Demand

Basically, the number of jobs in the automotive industry in the future, both in Michigan and in the nation generally, will reflect the level of demand for new vehicles. Data cited earlier suggest the positive relationship between motor vehicles output and employment. In years of high demand and production levels, employment in the industry was also at high levels.[19] As will be dis-

---

19 Data for 1958 reflect very dramatically the impact of a poor automobile market on auto jobs. In the three-year span, 1955 to 1958, production of cars and trucks dropped by 44 percent, jobs in the industry declined by about 31 percent, and auto jobs in Michigan fell off by 37 percent.

cussed in a later chapter, the outlook for the decade ahead suggests that the demand for new cars should be on a rising trend through 1970. If these expectations are fulfilled, then Michigan may expect to benefit from an irregularly expanding volume of employment in the industry.

Chapter V

Other Industrial and Economic Trends

THUS FAR, this report has discussed recent changes in Michigan's population, labor force, and employment. This focus was chosen because Michigan's economic health depends in large part on the extent to which people in the state have jobs.

There are, however, other economic statistics that can be examined to see whether or not they confirm or modify the impressions that have been gained from reviewing employment trends only. These other areas include changes in the number of industrial plants, in the volume of capital expenditures, and in per capita personal income.

Manufacturing Establishments in Michigan

AN ASPECT OF Michigan's industrial situation that has commanded considerable attention during recent years is the extent to which there has been gain or loss in the number of manufacturing plants in Michigan. Statistics from various sources have been quoted to support differing views on this matter. It is true that there is no organization, public or private, that is carrying on a systematic, year-by-year reporting plan for tabulating the number of manufacturing plants in Michigan according to a standard definition. Still, there are some data which permit some comparison over time and among states. There is other information that provides an indication of the nature of changes in the industrial population of Michigan. Although these data have limitations, they do tend to indicate what has been happening to the state's industrial structure.

In view of the loss of factory jobs in the state since 1953, one may wonder whether there has been a corresponding decline in the number of factories. If so, has the loss of manufacturing plants been as great as the loss of jobs? Again, would it be likely that the number of factory units has actually increased in recent years in the face of such a substantial loss of factory employment? The following discussion treats these questions.

The Michigan Record, 1949-1956

The data in Table 15 indicate a very substantial increase in the number of factory units in Michigan during the seven-year period 1949-1956. As shown below, the number of manufacturing establishments increased from 10,900 in 1949 to 12,350 in 1956.

1949	10,914
1951	11,380
1953	12,069
1956	12,355

These figures reveal that Michigan recorded a net gain of over 1,400 new manufacturing establishments during these seven years, or an increase of 13 percent.[1] Almost half of this growth occurred from 1951 to 1953 — the period when defense production in the state was being expanded so vigorously. But what is surprising is the fact that there was a net gain in the number of factory units from 1953 to 1956 — the period when industrial jobs were being

Table 15

Manufacturing Establishments under Old-Age and Survivors Insurance Program, United States, East North Central States, and Michigan

Selected years, 1949-1956

Area	Number of Manufacturing Establishments[a]				Percentage Increase			
	1949	1951	1953	1956	1949-1956	1949-1951	1951-1953	1953-1956
United States[b]	274,202	280,678	284,980	286,064	4.3	2.4	1.5	0.4
East North Central States	55,693	56,369	58,321	58,481	5.0	1.2	3.5	.3
Ohio	13,417	13,672	14,388	14,433	7.6	1.9	5.2	.3
Indiana	5,899	6,015	6,227	6,210	5.3	2.0	3.5	− .3
Illinois	18,146	17,927	18,175	18,057	− .5	−1.2	1.4	− .6
MICHIGAN	10,914	11,380	12,069	12,355	13.2	4.3	6.1	2.4
Wisconsin	7,317	7,375	7,462	7,426	1.5	.8	1.2	− .5

Source: U. S. Department of Commerce and U. S. Department of Health, Education and Welfare, *County Business Patterns, First Quarter, 1949-1951-1953-1956,* Part 4 for 1951, 1953, and 1956, Part II for 1949.

a Based on "reporting units." "Virtually all of the reporting units shown for manufacturing industries represent single establishments." Data are as of the first quarter of the calendar year. Each establishment had at least one employee during part of the calendar quarter.

b Continental United States.

1 For a somewhat earlier period (1947-1954), Census of Manufactures data suggest a 28 percent increase in the number of manufacturing establishments in Michigan. *1954 Census of Manufactures,* Vol. I, Table 4-B, p. 47.

lost in substantial numbers in Michigan. According to these data, Michigan gained 286 active establishments during this period.[2] Something under 300 additional plants is not a large addition for a three-year period. However, in view of the decline in the number of factory jobs, one might have expected fewer factories at the end of the period.

How does one explain an increase in the number of factories but a loss in the number of jobs during the three years after 1953? A principal explanation must be that many of Michigan's large plants contracted employment after the Korean-defense peak. It is known that some other plants moved out of the state or closed their doors. Employment in the new plants was of course insufficient to match the loss of jobs elsewhere.[3]

But the very fact that Michigan's manufacturing plant population expanded during these years is encouraging. The job picture for the future is much brighter than if the number of factories had declined after 1953. While many or most of the new plants were undoubtedly small, there seems no reason to believe that all of them will remain small. Some of these small factories may, it is true, fail or voluntarily go out of business, and some will continue on a small-scale basis. But others will thrive and some of this group should "grow up" into substantial providers of jobs for Michigan residents. As long as additional factories are added to the state's industrial structure, there is that much more support for industrial job opportunities in Michigan. Even so, one must frankly recognize that it takes a large number of new, small plants to offset the loss of jobs that occurs when a large plant lays off a considerable number of its personnel, ceases operations entirely, or moves out of the state.

Michigan and the East North Central States

We noted in Chapter III that all of the Great Lakes states experienced a loss in factory jobs after 1953. In spite of this loss of factory employment, did the other states in the region build up their inventory of manufacturing establishments during the three years, 1953-1956, as Michigan did?

Table 15 reveals little change in the inventory of active factory units in the other states during these three years. Michigan's gain

2 As indicated by data shown at a later point, part of this increase represented a gain in administrative and miscellaneous units associated with manufacturing operations.
3 As will be shown somewhat later, it is apparent that the new plants were generally small in terms of employment provided.

of 286 manufacturing units from 1953 to 1956 was relatively small, amounting to a percentage gain of something over 2 percent. Still, it was a conspicuous gain, compared with the small gains or losses reported for the other states in the region and for the nation at large.

Looking at the longer period (1949-1956), one can see that Michigan's growth in number of manufacturing establishments during this entire period was clearly superior to that of its neighbor states. The 13 percent net gain in industrial units in Michigan is almost double the rate of gain in the next best state — Ohio. The percentage gain in Michigan during the seven years was more than double the regional gain and about three times that of the nation.

Why would Michigan's factory inventory increase after 1953 while that of other states in the region showed little change? One can only speculate on what has been happening in the region in recent years. Sections of all of the Great Lakes states are located in the nation's "manufacturing belt."[4] One would expect that all of these states would continually be gaining new small plants to serve as suppliers to the larger companies in these states. From the record after 1953, it would seem that the other East North Central States either were obtaining relatively few additional "feeder" factories or were suffering greater attrition in the number of existing factories than Michigan during this three-year period. In any event, it is clear that Michigan's record in adding to its industrial plant inventory during the three years after 1953 was better than that of its sister states in the region.

Changes in Plant Size

We have already speculated on the apparent contradiction between an increase in the number of factories in Michigan from 1953 to 1956 and the decrease in factory jobs. It was suggested that the explanation in part might be a substantial decline after 1953 in the number of large-size plants. Table 16 supports this view.

The most noticeable feature of Table 16 is the decline in the number of largest size factories — those employing 500 workers or more. In 1956, there were 44 fewer of these large plants than in 1953, a drop of 12 percent. On the other hand, the next size factory group — the 250-499 employee bracket — showed some gain during the three years. In all probability, some of the factories

---

4 The "manufacturing belt" is discussed in Chapter VI.

Table 16

Manufacturing Establishments under Old-Age and Survivors Insurance Program, Michigan, by Number of Employees

1953 and 1956

Employee-Size Class	Number of Manufacturing Establishments[a]		Percent Distribution		Percent Change in Number 1953-1956
	1956	1953	1956	1953	
All Classes...............	12,355	12,069	100.0	100.0	2.4
0-7 employees............	5,504	5,477	44.6	45.3	.5
8-49 employees..........	4,594	4,265	37.2	35.3	7.7
50-249 employees........	1,632	1,672	13.2	13.9	− 2.4
250-499 employees.......	312	298	2.5	2.5	4.7
500 employees and over..	313	357	2.5	3.0	−12.3

Source: U. S. Department of Commerce and U. S. Department of Health, Education and Welfare, County Business Patterns, First Quarter 1953 and First Quarter 1956, Part I, Table 2.

a Based on "reporting units." "Virtually all of the reporting units shown for manufacturing industries represent single establishments." Data are as of the first quarter of the calendar year. Each establishment had at least one employee during part of the calendar quarter.

employing 500 or more workers during the Korean-defense boom slipped down into the 250-499 employee grouping as employees were released after the loss of defense work. Morover, many of the factories still employing 500 workers or more in 1956 had undoubtedly reduced their work forces substantially after 1953.

At the bottom of the scale, the number of very small units, those with fewer than eight workers, showed little change over the three-year period.[5] The next largest size establishments, those in the 8-49 employee bracket, increased in number by about 325, or by almost eight percent during the three years.

The net effect of this general pattern of more establishments at the bottom and fewer at the top in 1956 as compared with 1953 is, of course, some increase in concentration in establishments of smaller size. However, this increase is slight. In 1953, about 81 percent of all Michigan manufacturing units employed fewer than 50 persons. By 1956, the proportion had moved up to around 82 percent. Those who may fear that Michigan is developing an undue proportion of these tiny factories should note that, in the nation at large in 1956, establishments employing less than 50 workers accounted for 82.5 percent of all industrial units.

5 The detailed data upon which Table 16 is based show two near-counteracting movements within this large group of very small industrial units. Establishments with less than four employees increased in number from 1953 to 1956 while those with four to seven workers decreased.

Change by Industry

In Chapter III, it was noted that all of the durable goods industry groups in Michigan were providing fewer jobs in 1957 than in 1953. On the other hand, nondurable goods industry lines, as a group, reported a modest increase in the number of jobs. In view of this background, it is interesting to see whether or not changes in the number of factories followed this same pattern — a decline in durables and a gain in nondurables. The following data show that both sectors of the state's industrial economy gained additional plants from 1953 to 1956.[6]

Industry Division	Number of Plants Added
All industries	286
Durables	129
Nondurables	78
Miscellaneous	41
Administrative and auxiliary	38

Source: Appendix Table XVII.

The above tabulation indicates that, even though the durable goods industries in Michigan were laying off workers after 1953, the number of establishments was still increasing. In fact, the gain in durable goods plants (129) exceeded that in nondurables (78). This fact suggests how the predominance of the durables industries in Michigan tends to attract new establishments in the durables field.

The data cited below show the more sizable gains and losses in plants from 1953 to 1956 for industry groups within durables and nondurables.

Industry Group	Number of Plants Added or Lost
Durables	
Lumber and wood products	− 69
Fabricated metal products	+154
Machinery (nonelectrical)	− 53
Electrical machinery	+ 33
Other transportation equipment	+ 42
Nondurables	
Textile mill products and apparel	− 24
Printing, publishing, and allied prod.	+ 75
Chemicals, petroleum, and coal prod.	+ 22
Rubber products	+ 18

6 It should be noted that the data on plants are for a three-year period while the employment data referred to cover a four-year span, 1953-1957.

These additional data for industry groups point up the fact that the over-all record of growth of manufacturing establishments in both the durable and the nondurable sectors is the net result of gains and losses in the various component industries. This pattern thus differs from the record on employment previously discussed, in which all the durable industry groups reported a job loss and most of the nondurable groups reported a modest job gain.

Industrial Growth after 1956

The information on the increase in the number of plants in Michigan that has been presented thus far stops with 1956. One wonders what has been happening since then. Did the total number of factories in Michigan continue to increase during 1957 and 1958?

Some idea as to what was happening during 1958 is available from internal operating records of the Michigan Department of Economic Development. The Department maintains a listing of actions involving industrial plants in the state, such as plants moving into and out of the state, plant expansions, discontinuances, etc. As noted above, the listing, called "Movement of Industry in Michigan," is intended to serve as a rough basis for operating purposes; the Department points out that there are several limitations to the data.[7]

Recognizing these limitations, we may still gain an impression of the total story that this information seems to tell. The Department's summary of the listing for 1958 carries several categories of plant actions which have been combined into three principal groupings in the following tabulation:

Type of Plant Action	Number
All actions	380
Plant gains, total	264
Plants moving into Michigan	27
Plants expanding locally	152
Plants expanding elsewhere in Michigan	31
Plants newly started	50
Plants reopened	4

---

7 The information is based largely on newspaper accounts of these plant actions. There is no assurance that all such actions are reported in the newspapers that are surveyed. This would be especially true of small plants, many of which start or discontinue without public notice. These announcements sometimes reflect planned changes; not all changes contemplated are necessarily carried out. Sometimes the newspaper stories report actions already taken. Thus, the data are not complete and are not entirely comparable from a time standpoint.

Type of Plant Action	Number
Plant losses, total	**57**
Plants closing	32
Plants moving out of state	25
Other plant actions, total	**59**
Plants relocating within Michigan	13
Plants expanding outside Michigan	33
Plants contracting operations[a]	13

[a]Includes companies moving part of their operations into other states.

However much we may qualify these data, the picture presented by them is an encouraging one. They suggest a net gain of over 200 new plants or plant additions in Michigan during 1958. Plant gains (264) were more than four times as great as plant losses (57). And this increase in Michigan's factory population occurred in 1958 — a recession year following several years of industrial decline in the state.

Nature of Industrial Growth

The Michigan Department of Economic Development data on types of plant actions occurring during 1958 suggest the major source of additional plants for the state's industrial structure. Expansions by existing companies and newly started plants were both more numerous than plant move-ins.[8] Certainly, it would have been desirable for more outside plants to have located in Michigan. But the data suggest that Michigan's highly industrialized economic structure provides substantial impetus for its own continued expansion. Such a tendency is more encouraging than if the state were heavily dependent on move-ins from other states to assure its continued industrial growth.

Statements have been made suggesting that the strength of Michigan's industrial structure is being diminished seriously by the number of plants moving out of the state. The Department's data for 1958 indicate that there were 25 move-outs important enough to be newsworthy. Although this loss could be serious in terms of the jobs that were lost, it would appear that plant move-outs were not numerous enough during 1958 to constitute a threat to continued industrial growth in Michigan.

* * *

The data cited in this section must be regarded as providing an encouraging background against which to weigh the decline in

---

8 It has been suggested that some of the expansions reflect a "split-off" of large plants into smaller plants. In these cases, there would be an increase in the number of plants without any significant increase in employment.

industrial jobs since 1953. Although Michigan lost many defense-related jobs between 1953 and 1955 and suffered an automotive-related loss of jobs after 1955, still there appears to be a continuing gain in the total number of factory units in the state. These additional manufacturing establishments, with their gradually increasing employment opportunities, should make an important, even though temporarily modest, contribution to solving Michigan's employment problem.

Capital Expenditures in Michigan

THE GROWTH in the number of factory units in Michigan in the past few years affords some justification for the belief that Michigan's basic industrial structure may continue to grow. Data on the dollar amounts spent on new factory buildings and equipment in Michigan in recent years should throw additional light on what has been happening to the state's industrial structure. For this purpose, we shall examine capital expenditure data reported in the *Census of Manufactures* and in the intercensal *Annual Survey of Manufactures*.

The Michigan Record Since 1939

The data in the tabulation below show that capital expenditures reached their peak in Michigan in 1956. In that year, over one billion dollars of new plant and equipment was put in place in Michigan. Part of these expenditures represent, of course, replacement of existing plant and equipment. Moreover, inflation accounts for a part of the dollar increase over earlier years. Still, a billion dollars of new plant and equipment is a substantial volume of capital formation.

| Year | Expenditures | |
	Amount (thousands)	Percent of United States
1939	$ 110,200	8.8
1947	427,700	7.1
1951	588,500	7.6
1952	607,800	7.6
1953	708,300	8.8
1954	897,800	10.9
1955	805,800	9.8
1956	1,014,900	9.0
1957	ᵃ694,700	5.7

Source: Appendix Table XVIII.

ᵃExcludes data for establishments under construction.

133

More meaningful, however, are the percentage figures presented above. They show that during the four years, 1953-1956 inclusive, capital expenditures in Michigan were accounting for from 9 to 11 percent of all capital expenditures being made throughout the whole country. Moreover, during this period, Michigan's share of all capital expenditures was larger, for the most part, than during the earlier years for which data are shown. Thus, it does not appear that Michigan's basic industrial foundation was deteriorating through 1956. A state that for several years was accounting for about one-tenth of the nation's new plant and equipment can be assumed to have considerable industrial vitality.

It is true that Michigan's share of the nation's total capital expenditures was somewhat smaller in 1956 than in the preceding two years. Moreover, during 1957, there was a substantial drop in the level of capital outlays in the state and in Michigan's share of all capital expenditures. The approximately $700 million spent on capital plant and equipment by Michigan manufacturers in 1957 represented a 30 percent drop from the 1956 peak level. There was likewise a decline in Michigan's share of the nation's capital expenditures, from 9 percent in 1956 to less than 6 percent in 1957.[9]

In spite of the drop from 1956 levels, the $700 million expended on new factories and equipment in Michigan during 1957 represented a very substantial investment in the state's economic future by Michigan industrialists. In dollar volume, it compared favorably with expenditures for years prior to 1954 (although price increases after 1953 would impair the comparison somewhat). But, in general, these figures for 1957 tie in with others that indicate the slowdown in the state's industrial economy that began to make itself known after Michigan's "good" year of 1955.

Michigan and the East North Central States

Does Michigan's share of all capital expenditures look good or bad in comparison with the shares accounted for by nearby states? From the text table presented below, it is clear that Michigan's record on capital expenditures during the years 1953 through 1956 was very good in comparison with outlays made in its neighbor

---

9 It should be noted that the capital expenditures data for Michigan for 1957 exclude data for establishments under construction whereas data for earlier years include such data. This results in some overstatement of the decline in capital outlays in the state during 1957. Michigan's share of all capital expenditures in 1957 is somewhat above 6 percent if expenditures for plants under construction are also excluded from capital expenditures for the nation as a whole.

states. Michigan and Ohio were the two leading states in terms of state shares of national expenditures. The two states accounted for similar shares (from 9 to 10 percent) of the nation's addition to its capital plant and equipment during these years. Since Ohio is a larger state than Michigan (both in population and in manufacturing employment), Michigan appears to have fared somewhat better than Ohio through 1956.

In 1957, as we have noted, Michigan's share of the nation's outlays for plant and equipment dropped to about six percent. Both Ohio and Illinois accounted for a larger share of all capital expenditures in 1957 than Michigan. In each of the other East North Central States, outlays increased in 1957 while in Michigan they declined.

Area	Percent of Total Capital Expenditures				
	1957	1956	1955	1954	1953
United States..................	100.0	100.0	100.0	100.0	100.0
East North Central region.......	**31.5**	**33.3**	**32.4**	**33.3**	**32.8**
Ohio.........................	10.0	9.4	8.3	9.4	9.1
Indiana......................	5.4	ᵃ5.2	5.5	ᵃ3.7	5.3
Illinois......................	7.6	7.3	6.8	7.0	7.5
MICHIGAN..................	ᵃ5.7	9.0	9.8	10.9	8.8
Wisconsin...................	ᵃ2.6	ᵃ2.0	2.1	ᵃ2.1	2.1

Source: Appendix Table XVIII.

ᵃExcludes data for establishments under construction.

An important point to note from the text table is the fact that the East North Central States as a group provided the market for one-third of the nation's new plant and equipment during these five years. (From 1953 through 1956, Michigan and Ohio together provided almost one-fifth of the national market.) The attention that has been given to industrial growth in other sections of the country should not obscure the fact that the East North Central States have been laying the foundation, through substantial outlays for plant and equipment, for their continued industrial preeminence.

We do not mean to imply that the volume of these outlays, by itself, tells the whole story. There are qualifications to these data. Broken down into their components, the figures may present a somewhat different picture. Varying interpretations can be given to some of the data. But, just as the increase in the number of plants in Michigan is encouraging, so also is the fact that capital outlays in Michigan were being maintained at a very high level

135

through 1956, and at a substantial, if reduced, level through 1957.

Through 1956, Michigan was continuing to maintain its share of national expenditures. With Ohio, it provided a leading market in the East North Central area for industrial plant and equipment.[10] In the absence of such a sustained high level of capital expenditures in recent years, the state's future would be much less promising.

Plant versus Equipment Expenditures

We suggested above that a breakdown of total capital expenditures might be helpful in interpreting these data. A percentage breakdown of these expenditures between plant and equipment is provided in Table 17.

Table 17

Percentage of Total Manufacturers' Capital Expenditures Expended for Plant and for Equipment, United States, East North Central States, and Michigan[a]

Selected years, 1939-1957

Year	United States			East North Central States			Michigan		
	Total	Plant	Equip-ment	Total	Plant	Equip-ment	Total	Plant	Equip-ment
1939.........	100.0	31.4	68.6	100.0	29.9	70.1	100.0	23.7	76.3
1947.........	100.0	35.3	64.7	100.0	35.7	64.3	100.0	27.9	72.1
1951.........	100.0	33.3	66.7	100.0	34.2	65.8	100.0	32.1	67.9
1952.........	100.0	32.4	67.6	100.0	32.6	67.4	100.0	35.9	64.1
1953.........	100.0	32.1	67.9	100.0	28.8	71.2	100.0	22.3	77.7
1954.........	100.0	30.0	70.0	100.0	28.1	71.9	100.0	20.3	79.7
1955.........	100.0	29.5	70.5	100.0	28.5	71.5	100.0	24.4	75.6
1956.........	100.0	30.9	69.1	100.0	28.7	71.3	100.0	22.9	77.1
1957.........	100.0	31.8	68.2	100.0	30.8	69.2	100.0	18.5	81.5

Source: Appendix Table XIX. Data for 1939, 1947, and 1954 based on *Census of Manufactures*. Data for other years are estimates provided in the intercensal *Annual Survey of Manufactures*.

[a] Plant expenditures cover new structures and additions to plant; equipment expenditures cover new machinery and equipment.

Let us look first at data for Michigan. The table shows that from one-fifth to one-fourth of total capital expenditures in the state were being used to provide new industrial structures during the four years, 1953-1956 inclusive. These proportions are considerably smaller than those for 1951 and 1952 when the percentages

10 Review of data for all of the states reveals that Michigan was not only a regional leader in the amount of capital expenditures in 1954 and 1955 but was also a national leader. Michigan led the nation in those two years and was a very close second to Ohio in 1956. Even in the face of a substantial decline in outlays during 1957, Michigan still ranked seventh among all states in the volume of expenditures.

amounted to about 32 and 36 percent, respectively. The higher proportions expended on additional factory space in these two years may reflect construction of new factory facilities in connection with the Korean defense build-up. Earlier, in 1947, about 28 percent of all capital expenditures had been for industrial plant. In prewar 1939, the proportion had been about 24 percent. In general, then, the proportion of total capital outlays spent on additional plant space in Michigan during the years 1953-1956 was less than that spent during the Korean-period defense build-up of 1952-1953 but was somewhat similar to the proportion spent in 1939. However, the decline in capital expenditures in Michigan during 1957 was accompanied by a smaller share of expenditures (18.5 percent) that went for factory structures.

These figures show, then, that the bulk of industrial capital spending in the state in the past few years has been for new machinery and equipment. Offhand, this heavy concentration on equipment (from 75 to 80 percent of all expenditures) might appear to provide a reason for concern for those interested in the job outlook in the state. Some of these expenditures for machinery and equipment are, of course, intended to equip newly built plants and thus would be associated with additional jobs. Many of these expenditures, however, would merely represent replacement of existing equipment which has become obsolescent or too inefficient to maintain in operation. Such replacements do not add jobs in a given factory. Actually, with the increasing development of automated and other highly specialized machinery, replacement of industrial machinery and equipment can and often does lead to the loss of job opportunities. The decline in factory jobs in Michigan after 1953 may have been intensified, therefore, by the introduction of a large volume of labor-displacing equipment into Michigan's industrial structure.

We do not know the importance of this factor. Specific examples can, of course, be cited of job losses through the introduction of new machinery. For perspective, one should note, however, that expenditures for new machinery and equipment were predominant in Michigan in 1939 and again in 1947, accounting for over 70 percent of all capital outlays in those years. The new machinery installed in those years was presumably much more efficient than the machinery that was replaced. We do not mean to say that the technologically advanced machinery of recent years may not be more labor-displacing in character than that installed earlier. We merely point out that the data in Table 17 suggest that Michigan's industrial growth has been associated for many years with a relatively high concentration of capital outlays on machinery and equipment.

How does Michigan's pattern of industrial outlays compare with the expenditure patterns in larger areas? From Table 17, it can be seen that, in the Great Lakes states as a group, expenditures for new machinery and equipment have accounted for a smaller share of all capital outlays than in Michigan during each of the years shown, except for 1952. And in most years, outlays for machinery and equipment in the United States at large have been relatively less important than in the Great Lakes region.

It seems noteworthy that in all three of these areas — the United States, the Great Lakes region, and Michigan — the share of capital outlays going for machinery during the years 1953-1957 was similar to the share in prewar 1939. These data suggest that each of these areas has a somewhat different capital expenditure pattern but that experience since 1939 has followed a somewhat similar course in all three areas. If that is so, then Michigan's heavy concentration on machinery expenditures in recent years may have no special adverse implication for the state, unless the new industrial machinery installed in recent years is, as we have speculated, much more labor-displacing in its total impact on job opportunities than in earlier years.

Expenditures by Industry Groups

The following data show the industry groups that have accounted for five percent or more of capital outlays in Michigan in at least one of four recent years for which data are available.

Industry Group	Percent of Total Capital Expenditures			
	1957	1956	1954	1947
All groups—Amount (millions)	$694.7	$983.9	$870.5	$427.7
All groups—Percent	100.0	100.0	100.0	100.0
Food and kindred products	4.5	4.3	3.7	7.0
Pulp, paper, and products	3.8	3.0	3.1	5.1
Chemicals and products	9.9	5.9	4.9	13.1
Primary metal products	13.0	9.0	14.4	10.8
Fabricated metal products	5.2	6.0	9.7	7.1
Machinery, except electrical	12.9	10.8	8.5	9.4
Transportation equipment	39.8	52.7	46.1	37.2

Source: Appendix Table XX, and *1957 Annual Survey of Manufactures*, Series MAS-57-4, June 23, 1959, p. 12.

If data for the four years shown above are representative of experience during the last decade or so, it is clear that capital outlays in the transportation equipment field have accounted for a substantial portion of capital expenditures in the state in recent years. Since the transportation equipment industry group in Michigan consists almost entirely of the automotive industry, it appears that investment in new automotive plant and equipment has been accounting for from 40 to 50 percent of all capital expenditures in Michigan in recent years.

Differing interpretations can be drawn from these data. On the one hand, the fact that the automotive industry has continued to invest heavily in Michigan should lessen some of the fears that the industry has been decentralizing rapidly. On the other hand, such heavy concentration of investment in the automotive industry may suggest that other areas of industrial investment have been neglected. In this connection, however, it should be noted that almost half a billion dollars of capital outlays were made in nonautomotive industrial categories in Michigan, both in 1954 and in 1956. In spite of the over-all decline in capital expenditures in Michigan during 1957, well over $400 million was expended in nonautomotive industries during the year. These are very sizable sums of money. For example, nonautomotive capital expenditures made in Michigan during 1956 accounted for over four percent of the nation's total capital outlays. Again, these nonautomotive capital outlays in Michigan during 1956 were larger than *total* capital expenditures in each of 39 other states. The fact that about half of the state's capital outlays may have been expended in the automotive sector of the state's industrial structure during recent years does not mean that outlays in other industrial groups have been negligible.

*   *   *

The optimism about Michigan's future economic prospects that one might derive from the capital expenditure record through 1956 must be tempered with full recognition of the decline in these expenditures revealed by data for 1957. Undoubtedly there was a further decline in capital expenditures in Michigan during 1958 in accordance with the downward trend nationally. However, there are indications that during 1959 the volume of capital outlays by Michigan industry was on the upswing again. As Census data on capital expenditures in the state become available for years after 1957, some idea can be gained as to whether Michigan's loss of position in industrial capital outlays during 1957 represents a permanent deviation from its former position.

Personal Income in Michigan

IN CHAPTER I, we pointed out that the decline in industrial activity and employment in the state during the past few years was reflected in data on per capita personal income. It was noted that during our 1953 employment peak per capita income in Michigan was very substantially above that of the nation as a whole and somewhat greater than the average of the East North Central States. By 1957, our per capita income was only moderately above that of the nation and was somewhat below that of the East North Central region. These developments reflect primarily the fact that from 1955 through 1957 per capita income in Michigan was increasing very little while in the nation and in the region it was rising appreciably.

These short-run changes in Michigan's per capita income situation are dramatic. They coincide with and are, indeed, a reflection of the state's recent decline in economic activity. But from a longer point of view, are these shifts as serious as they may seem? In keeping with our policy of taking a long look whenever possible, we shall review Michigan's personal income record for a longer period of time. In this review, we shall cover primarily the period through 1957, before the 1958 recession exerted its especially strong adverse impact.

Per Capita Personal Income Since 1929

Table 18 indicates that in 1957 the per capita income of Michigan ($2,192) was still averaging seven percent above the national average. In view, on the one hand, of the substantial loss of factory jobs after 1953, and, on the other, of the continued rapid growth of population, one might say that Michigan had done well to maintain a per capita income position that compared so well with that of the country as a whole. And this is probably true. But examination of income data for earlier years indicates that, relatively speaking, 1957 was a poor year for Michigan. In only a very few of the years since 1929 has per capita income in Michigan averaged as low as 107 percent of the national level. Only during the postwar reconversion years of 1945-1946 and during the worst depression years of the thirties had Michigan's average income level dropped

140

to such relatively low levels. It is apparent that recent developments in the state have had, as one would expect, an adverse impact on the state's income situation as compared with earlier years.

However, if attention is given to the relationship between Michigan and the nation for 1956 and 1955, a more favorable comparison is seen. In 1956, average personal income in Michigan was 111 percent of the level for the country as a whole. This level was

Table 18

Per Capita Personal Income, United States, East North Central States, and Michigan, by Year

1929-1958

Year	Per Capita Personal Income			Michigan as Percent of—	
	United States[a]	East North Central States[b]	Michigan	United States	East North Central States
1929	$ 703	$ 803	$ 793	113	99
1930	624	684	659	106	96
1931	529	568	540	102	95
1932	401	411	394	98	96
1933	375	380	349	93	92
1934	423	449	452	107	101
1935	472	518	528	112	102
1936	534	593	616	115	104
1937	573	656	682	119	104
1938	527	574	572	109	100
1939	556	621	624	112	100
1940	595	667	679	114	102
1941	719	817	827	115	101
1942	909	1,003	1,047	115	104
1943	1,102	1,237	1,347	122	109
1944	1,194	1,316	1,387	116	105
1945	1,234	1,346	1,319	107	98
1946	1,249	1,349	1,318	106	98
1947	1,316	1,457	1,454	110	100
1948	1,420	1,592	1,542	109	97
1949	1,382	1,514	1,504	109	99
1950	1,491	1,661	1,684	113	101
1951	1,649	1,869	1,855	112	99
1952	1,727	1,939	1,932	112	100
1953	1,788	2,050	2,120	119	103
1954	1,770	1,961	1,982	112	101
1955	1,866	2,083	2,146	115	103
1956	1,975	2,194	2,191	111	100
1957	2,043	2,238	2,192	107	98
1958	2,057	2,182	2,099	102	96

Source: U. S. Department of Commerce, *Personal Income by States since 1929*, Table 2, pp. 142-43, and *Survey of Current Business*, August, 1959, Table 2, p. 15

a Continental United States.
b Michigan, Ohio, Indiana, Illinois, and Wisconsin.

higher than or equal to that of several other postwar years although it was still in the lower range of the percentage relationships since 1929. The 115 percent income relationship between the state and nation in 1955 was equaled or surpassed in only a few of the other years in the three-decade period. Thus, as recently as 1955, Michigan's average income level was exceeding the nation's by a margin wider than that of most earlier years.

The last column in Table 18 compares Michigan's per capita income level with that of the East North Central region. In general, the conclusion is about the same as when we compare Michigan with the nation. The Michigan-East North Central States relationship was low in 1957, as compared with earlier years. The relationship in 1956 was more favorable to Michigan but was still a bit on the low side in relation to earlier years. In 1955, the per capita income of Michigan averaged three percent higher than that of the region; in only a few of the earlier years had Michigan enjoyed a greater advantage over the region as a whole.

These figures on per capita income through 1957 thus tie in with the data cited earlier on industrial employment. The Michigan record on income suffers by long-range comparison only after 1955, and suffers substantially during 1957 only. However, the relatively low income level experienced during 1957 provides another indication of the extent to which the state's economic situation had deteriorated after 1955.

Preliminary income figures for 1958 show a further decline in average income for the state, both in actual amount and in comparison with regional and national levels. Not since the early thirties had Michigan fared so badly in these comparisons. Even so, it is well to remember that even in Michigan's "poor" income year of 1958, per capita income in the state was still larger than in the country at large and in two neighboring states (Indiana and Wisconsin).[11]

The recent decline in per capita income does not necessarily portend a continuing loss of Michigan's relative income position. Michigan's position, relative to that of the region and of the nation, has fallen and risen in the past; it is reasonable to assume that it will rise again as industrial employment in the state recovers from the low levels of 1958.[12] But only with reasonably full employment

11 *Survey of Current Business,* August, 1959, Table 2, p. 15.

12 Some indication of the recovery in personal income levels in Michigan during 1959 is afforded by monthly data carried by *Business Week.* According to its estimates, total personal income in Michigan during June, 1959, was 17 percent higher than in June, 1958 (*Business Week,* August 29, 1959, pp. 104-07). In an earlier issue (July 25), a May-to-May gain of over 16 percent had been indicated.

may we expect Michigan's relative income position to regain its former level.

Population Growth and Per Capita Income

In the discussion above, we have referred to the decline in industrial employment as a prime cause of the relative decline in Michigan's per capita income position after 1955. Per capita income depends, however, not only on the volume of income going to the residents of a state but also on the number of persons living in the state among whom the income must be averaged. A state such as Michigan, with a rapidly growing population, must have a rapidly growing volume of employment and personal income if its per capita position is not to suffer, either when compared with its record in earlier years or when compared with the record of other areas.

Normally, of course, as population increases, so does the number of persons working. But, in Michigan, as we have pointed out previously, this has not been true during the past several years. A decreasing number of workers has been providing income for an increasing population. It is apparent that the additional people in the state's population have not been contributing proportionately to the state's income base.[13] If Michigan's population had been increasing at a slower pace, then its per capita income position would have looked less serious in 1957 and in 1958.[14]

It is, of course, pleasant to be able to say that one's state is growing by leaps and bounds. But unless such substantial population growth is accompanied by a somewhat similar growth in job opportunities, the average level of income available to the people of the state is bound to decrease, either absolutely or in relation to what is happening elsewhere, or both. The data quoted in the preceding pages indicate that the failure of job opportunities to match population growth in Michigan after 1955 resulted in a decline through 1957 in the state's income position as compared with that of the nation and of the region, a decline that was accentuated dur-

---

13 In view of the state's recent employment decline, it may seem strange that the volume of personal income in the state continued to increase through 1957 (See Appendix Table XXI).

Although wage and salary disbursements in manufacturing were lower in 1957 than in 1955, there were increases in wage and salary disbursements in certain nonmanufacturing lines, in property income (dividends, interest, and rent) and in transfer payments (pensions, unemployment benefits, direct relief, etc.). (See *Survey of Current Business*, August, 1959, Table 20, p. 18.)

14 In Chapter II, we speculated that Michigan's population may not be growing as rapidly as Bureau of the Census estimates suggest. This possibility should be borne in mind in evaluating the reported levels of per capita income in the state. If population is overstated, then per capita income is understated.

ing 1958 by the severity of the impact of that year's recession on the Michigan economy.

*   *   *

The data cited in this chapter tend to offset in part the grim picture of Michigan's economy that comes from considering solely recent labor force and employment developments. The increase in the number of manufacturing establishments through 1956, and presumably through 1958, should in time contribute to increased factory employment. The maintenance of capital expenditures in Michigan at high levels through 1956, and at a substantial level during 1957, should also have a salutary effect on industrial employment levels. Although long-range data on per capita income in Michigan reflect a decline in the state's relative income position after 1955, Michigan's average income level in 1958 still ranked above that of the nation at large. The long-range data suggest that the state's relative income position will improve as industrial employment moves to higher levels.

PART III

PROSPECTS FOR THE FUTURE

Chapter VI

Michigan and Basic Industrial Location Factors

THE EXTENT TO which Michigan will expand its volume of job opportunities in the future depends in large part on the extent to which industrial enterprisers decide to initiate or to expand operations in the state.

As we noted in Chapter III, nonmanufacturing jobs were increasing in number in the state through 1957, offsetting part of the loss of factory jobs. But in the future the volume of additional jobs available in wholesale and retail trade, construction, public utilities, service industries, and other nonfactory lines will depend primarily upon the degree to which manufacturing activity regains its former importance. In some other states, principal basic sources of income may include agriculture, tourism, mining, federal government activities, or the provision of distribution, financial, and transportation facilities. But in Michigan, the economy of the state for many years has been based on a high level of industrialization which has provided the basis for a high per capita income for a rapidly growing population.

That a foundation for the resumption of industrial growth is being laid in the state was suggested by data shown in chapter V on the number of factories and on capital expenditures. Yet there are a number of factors in Michigan's economic situation that can lead to some doubts about the expectation of an early return to its former industrial importance. Some observers appear to believe that such importance may not soon be regained. These views reflect such developments as the relative decline of the automotive industry in the state, the loss of defense-related production jobs because of a shift in the nature of defense procurement, and the faster rates of growth of industry in certain other parts of the country. Assertions have also been made that the state's progress is being retarded by a failure to obtain as many new plants from outside the state as it should. Influences deterring outside manufacturers from locating in Michigan are described as an unfavorable tax structure, the high degree of unionization of the state, and a generally unfavorable "business climate" brought about in part by the attitude of the state administration.

In this chapter, we shall look briefly at several of the basic industrial location factors and shall suggest Michigan's assets and liabilities in these areas.

Basic Industrial Location Factors

SOME YEARS AGO, the U. S. Department of Commerce developed a list of 13 basic industrial location factors which generally govern the evaluation of prospective plant locations.[1] The Department's list is as follows:

I. Location of production materials	VII. Distribution facilities
II. Labor	VIII. Power
III. Sites	IX. Water
IV. Industrial fuel	X. Living conditions
V. Transportation facilities	XI. Laws and regulations
VI. Market	XII. Tax structure
	XIII. Climate

These factors are primarily intended for use at a local or community level, since a state or region is rarely homogeneous enough to permit its evaluation as a unit according to one of these basic factors. Also, these factors are intended to be applied to specific industries and not to manufacturing in general. Despite these limitations, however, some of the basic factors can be analyzed in a general way at a state or regional level to provide some ideas as to the strengths and weaknesses of such larger areas as a location for industry.

In the following pages, Michigan's advantages and disadvantages for industry will be considered in terms of a number of these basic factors. Several of these discussions (those on taxes, labor, and transportation) will provide brief summaries of detailed analyses provided in Appendix statements to this study. The other discussions will represent relatively limited treatment of the subject matter, but enough, it is hoped, to point to the role of these factors in the future industrial development of the state.

---

1 *Basic Industrial Location Factors — Guide for Evaluating an Area's Resources for Industrial Development*, Revised June, 1947, 18 pp.

Markets

THAT MICHIGAN OFFERS an excellent location for manufacturers for whom access to markets is a top consideration should be obvious from several sets of data that have been cited thus far in this study. Yet it is very easy to take Michigan's favorable market position for granted without full realization of the importance of that market potential in influencing manufacturers to start new plants, expand present ones, or establish branch plants in the state. In order to emphasize Michigan's strategic position as a location for market-oriented firms, several sets of data are reviewed below.

Michigan and the Consumer Market

Manufacturing firms that produce consumer goods are interested, of course, in locating a plant in a strong consumer market. Michigan would appear to satisfy the requirements for such a location. The state itself provides a strong market for consumer goods. Its location in the heart of one of the nation's heaviest concentrations of population and income — the East North Central region — means that manufacturers located in Michigan are situated in one of the nation's richest and largest consumer markets.

A few figures provide a quantitative basis for this appraisal. In 1957, Michigan itself accounted for 4.5 percent of the country's population, and for 4.8 percent of the nation's personal income. In 1954, the latest year for which official state data are available, it accounted for 4.8 percent of all retail sales. The strength of the East North Central market is suggested by the fact that the region accounted for 20.5 percent of the nation's population, for 22.5 percent of its personal income, and for 21.8 percent of its retail sales.[2]

These figures highlight the strength that Michigan's economic importance, and that of its neighboring states, provides as a location factor for consideration by industries that produce for the consumer market. These five states together receive almost one-fourth of the nation's personal income and account for over one-fifth of the nation's retail trade. The $16.7 billion of personal income received by Michigan residents in 1957 was exceeded in only five other states.

---

2 Population data are based on Bureau of the Census, *Current Population Reports,* Series P-25, No. 186, October 27, 1958, Table 1. Personal income data are from *Survey of Current Business,* August, 1958, p. 10. Retail sales data are based on *Statistical Abstract of the United States* — 1958, p. 834.

Michigan and the Industrial Market

Many other market-oriented industrial firms produce for an industrial market. Some of these manufacturers produce semi-processed materials and parts and finished products that constitute the material inputs for other plants. Other manufacturers produce the industrial machinery and equipment that are used by industry in providing new productive facilities or in expanding and modernizing existing plants.

In this respect, even more impressive data can be cited to indicate the tremendous market that is afforded by the industrialized East North Central area including Michigan. Let us look first at the market available to those manufacturers who sell their products to other fabricators for further processing. Some idea as to the importance of that market in the region and in Michigan can be obtained from the share of the nation's production that is carried on in these areas. The following data for 1956, which are based on value added by manufacture, indicate the size of the market, both on an over-all basis and for several industry groups.

| Industry Group | Percent of Value Added by Manufacture Accounted for by — | |
	East North Central States	Michigan
All industries..............................	31	7
Machinery (nonelectrical).................	50	11
Transportation equipment................	44	23
Fabricated metal products...............	42	10
Primary metals..........................	41	6
Rubber products.........................	41	5
Electrical machinery.....................	38	3
Furniture and fixtures....................	32	7

Source: *1956 Annual Survey of Manufactures*, Series MAS-56-5, April 25, 1958.

From these figures, the tremendous importance of the East North Central region as a production area and therefore as an industrial market is clear. It accounts for almost one-third of the nation's production (in terms of value added). In several important industry groups, the area accounts for from 40 to 50 percent of all production value. In three of these industry groups, Michigan accounted for 10 percent or more of production value in 1956.

In Chapter V, we discussed the high level of capital expenditures in Michigan. Enough was probably said in that chapter to suggest the outstanding market that Michigan and its neighboring states provide for manufacturers of industrial machinery and equipment.

A few of these figures may be cited again to emphasize the point. During the years from 1951 through 1956, the East North Central States were accounting for around one-third of the nation's expenditures for new plant and equipment. Michigan's share of country-wide capital outlays varied from 8 to 11 percent during these years. In 1954 and 1955, manufacturers in Michigan led the nation in the volume of capital outlays. The strength of the Midwest market for producers' equipment is reflected in the fact that about half of the country's production of machinery takes place in the region. (See preceding text table.) It is only natural that much of the nation's production of industrial equipment should take place in an area that provides its primary market.

Michigan and the "Manufacturing Belt"

Michigan and the other Great Lakes states not only comprise one of the nation's most concentrated industrial markets but substantial portions of all these states are located in what has been called the "manufacturing belt." As shown by Ullman, this belt stretches from Boston and New York in the East, in a strip about 300 miles wide, to beyond Chicago and to St. Louis in the West. The southern half of Michigan's Lower Peninsula is included in the manufacturing belt. Within this area, which accounts for only 8 percent of the nation's land area, are found over two-fifths of its population, over half of its income, and about two-thirds of its manufacturing employment.[3] And to these data cited by Ullman could be added the fact that during the six-year period, 1951-1956, well over half of all expenditures for new manufacturing plant and equipment were made in this general area.[4]

It is obvious then that manufacturers located in Michigan have access not only to the strong consumer and industrial markets afforded by the immediate nearby states but also to the nation's greatest concentration of population, income, and industrial activity.

Michigan and the Canadian Market

That Michigan has in the Canadian market next door a strong potential market may be overlooked by some. Ullman quotes data indicating that the area running along the northern border of Lake Erie and on the western shores of Lake Ontario accounts for one-

---

3 Edward L. Ullman, *American Commodity Flow* (Seattle: University of Washington Press, 1957), p. 7. Reference is made to Ullman's Core Area I. The "as of" date of the data cited is not specified.

4 The data for capital expenditures cover the East North Central States and the Middle Atlantic States (New York, New Jersey, and Pennsylvania).

fifth of Canada's population and one-third of its manufacturing employment.[5]

Michigan has, in effect, another state, with an appreciable consumer and industrial market, on its eastern borders. Trade barriers, of course, prevent free access to this market. But it remains as a potential market for Michigan in the future if trade opportunities between the United States and Canada are liberalized in the years ahead.

* * *

The data cited in the preceding pages make it clear that from a market standpoint Michigan enjoys a very definite industrial location advantage. True, that advantage is shared with a number of other states. But the fact remains that, in any list of plus and minus factors that is drawn up rating Michigan as a location for manufacturing enterprise, its market position calls for a strong plus rating.

Materials

THE SCOPE OF this report does not permit an evaluation of raw materials that are available in Michigan as a factor in the state's industrial development. That the state does possess several outstanding raw material resources is obvious. One merely has to mention salt, limestone, iron, copper, and forest products to be reminded that Michigan ranks high in several important natural resources. Several of Michigan's important industries have developed in the state solely or largely because of the availability of these raw materials. Still it may be that the availability or nonavailability of raw materials is not of such paramount importance in plant location decisions as may sometimes be assumed. The following quotation indicates the basis for such a view:

> Attention needs to be directed toward manufacturing as the main source of its own materials. An industrialist searching for components for a product may not look directly to the forests, mines, or farms of the country, but rather to other factories. Four-fifths of the industries in the United States utilize materials that have already been processed by other industries.[6]

Inasmuch as manufacturing industries are so heavily dependent on processed materials, Michigan merits a plus rating on materials as an industrial location factor. The heavy degree of industrialization typical of Michigan and the other states in the manufacturing

---

5 Ullman, *op. cit.,* p. 7.
6 Chauncy D. Harris, "The Market as a Factor in the Localization of Industry in the United States," *Annals of the Association of American Geographers,* December, 1954, p. 341.

belt means that Michigan and these other states provide many of the materials that manufacturers need to have in close supply for efficient operations.

Water

THAT MICHIGAN'S ABUNDANT water supply is potentially one of the state's principal advantages in promoting industrial growth has been commonly recognized. "Michigan Is First in Water Resources" is the title of an industrial promotion brochure released by the Michigan Economic Development Department.[7] A recent study of Michigan's water resources in relation to plant location states:

> In practical terms, therefore, Michigan's water resources potential is not intermediate in the listing of states but stands at the very top.[8]

Michigan's favorable situation with regard to water supply reflects several factors. Its primary water supply (excess of precipitation over transpiration and evaporation) is fairly good in comparison with the rest of the country; stream flow is stable for the most part; and the state's geological base is such as to provide large reservoirs of ground water. And the fresh waters of the Great Lakes are no more than 85 miles distant from any point in the state.

Industrial Users of Water

There appear to be no comprehensive studies of industrial requirements for water, on either a quantitative or a qualitative basis. The detailed data in the *1954 Census of Manufactures* on industrial water use will presumably be used ultimately to make more complete analyses than appear to be available at the present.

One of the Paley Commission reports provides information on the principal industrial uses of water.[9] According to this report, it was estimated that industrial water use in 1950 amounted to 80 billion gallons per day. The percentage of this use by major industry was as follows:

All industrial uses	**100**
Steam-electric power	44
Steel	16
Petroleum refining	9
Wood pulp and paper	5
Other	26

7 *Michigan's Water Resources for Industry*, Industrial Survey Bulletin No. 3, Lansing, January, 1957.

8 Olin W. Blackett, *Water Resources and Plant Location in Michigan*, C.E.D. Executive Study Group (Ann Arbor: University of Michigan, 1957), p. 3.

9 *Resources for Freedom — A Report to the President by the President's Materials Policy Commission*, Vol. V (Washington: Government Printing Office, 1952), pp. 86-87.

The above data indicate that electrical generating plants are the principal industrial users of water. Since electrical generation is not classified as a manufacturing industry, it follows from the data cited above that steel-making is the principal manufacturing line in the usage of water.

As suggested above, the *1954 Census of Manufactures* provides statistics on the total amounts of water used by various industry groups in manufacturing. The following tabulation indicates the industry groups that were principal users in 1954:

Industry Group	Water Intake during 1954[a] Number of gallons (billions)	Percent
All industry groups	11,757	100
Food and kindred products	590	5
Textile mill products	273	2
Pulp, paper, and products	1,607	14
Chemicals and products	2,810	24
Petroleum and products	1,516	13
Stone, clay, and glass products	267	2
Primary metal industries	3,641	31
Transportation equipment	253	2
All other	800	7

Source: *1954 Census of Manufactures*, Vol. 1. Table 4, p. 209-22.

[a]Based on establishments reporting gross water intake of 20 million gallons or more.

These later data are in rough agreement with the Paley Commission data quoted above in that they confirm the high proportions of total water use in manufacturing which are accounted for by steel-making, petroleum refining, and the paper industry. They point up, however, the fact that the chemicals industry is also one that has large water requirements, outranking both the paper and petroleum refining industries in the percent of total industrial water intake.

These data indicate the general industrial groups that account for the major share of the nation's industrial water use. But some of these industry groups may account for substantial proportions of all water use, not only because their operations involve relatively heavy water requirements but also because these groups account for a relatively substantial share of total manufacturing activity. A more reliable indicator of the need for industrial water by a plant in a given industry may be the amount of water usage per employee. Such information, based on data made available in the *1953 Annual Survey of Manufactures,* is shown in Table 19.

Table 19

Water Use per Employee in Selected Manufacturing Industries, United States

1953

Industry Group[a]	Total Water Intake During Year[b]	
	Number of gallons (billions)	Gallons per employee (millions)
All industries............................	11,430	1.50
Food and kindred products..............	521	0.92
Canning, preserving, and freezing.....	47	.69
Sugar.................................	107	4.63
Beverages............................	81	.78
Textile mill products....................	299	.57
Cotton and rayon fabrics..............	120	.51
Dyeing and finishing textiles [...].....	61	.97
Lumber and wood products [...]........	c	1.58
Miscellaneous wood products.........	2	.61
Paper and allied products..............	1,256	5.20
Pulp, paper, and paperboard..........	1,231	6.41
Paper coating and glazing.............	9	.52
Chemicals and allied products..........	2,784	5.87
Industrial inorganic chemicals.........	783	11.98
Drugs and medicines..................	28	.54
Soap and related products............	22	.87
Gum and wood chemicals.............	32	5.63
Petroleum and coal products...........	1,923	9.85
Coke and byproducts..................	313	8.93
Rubber products........................	c	.55
Tires and inner tubes.................	80	.81
Stone, clay, and glass products.........	185	.86
Primary metal industries................	3,670	3.64
Blast furnaces and steel mills.........	3,357	5.61
Primary nonferrous metals............	181	3.79
Nonferrous metal rolling [...].........	55	.63

Source: Statistical Abstract of the United States—1957, Table 1023, p. 802. Based on estimates derived from 1953 Annual Survey of Manufactures.

a Industry groups shown are those in which per employee usage amounted to .5 million gallons per year or more. Brackets indicate portion of industry title not given.
b Fresh plus brackish water.
c Withheld by Bureau of Census because the estimate did not meet publication standards.

The water intake figures per employee show that, although the primary metal industries (largely blast furnaces and steel mills) took almost one-third of the nation's industrial water in 1953, their water usage per employee was well below that of some other indus-

155

try lines. The industrial inorganic chemicals group required about twice as much water per employee as blast furnaces and steel mills. Water requirements on a per worker basis were very high also for petroleum and coal products as a group. Per employee requirements for pulp, paper, and paperboard were similar to those of the steel mills. The sugar industry — a relatively small industry — was also a very heavy user of water on a per employee basis.

Blackett has suggested that two of these major industry lines, steel-making and petroleum products, are not likely to expand much in Michigan despite the state's abundant supply of water.[10] It is possible, however, that detailed analysis of these Census data on industrial water usage may point to certain industries for which the state's bountiful water supply constitutes a compelling locational advantage.

Michigan's Future Advantage from Water

The real benefits arising from Michigan's relatively abundant supplies of water should make themselves known in the years ahead. The increasing importance of water supply in plant location is suggested by the following statement from the Paley Commission report:

> Water supply has always had a significant effect on industrial location, but until recently most of this influence was exerted in an indirect manner. By 1975 water supply may be the most important factor affecting industrial location.[11]

A number of sections of the country have already experienced difficulty in providing enough water to cope with substantial population and industrial growth. Some areas are subject to considerable variation in the adequacy of their water supplies.

Referring to the rapid rate of population growth in the Southwest, a press release of a demographic research agency states: "The Bureau's Director, Robert C. Cook, predicted that some of these localities might be forced to take steps to restrict the number of new residents, and more especially of new industries in some communities."[12] Elsewhere in the release, it is stated, "In 1957, an estimated one in every four Americans felt the water shortage in some manner . . ."

To what extent do Michigan's water resources provide an industrial location advantage in the years ahead, especially in relation

---

10 Blackett, *op. cit.*, p. 43.
11 *Resources for Freedom*, *op. cit.*, p. 86.
12 Population Reference Bureau, Inc. (Washington, D. C.), press release of February 3, 1958. The press release is the source of Chart I.

to its neighboring states in the Great Lakes area? Chart I suggests a very striking answer. The top map in the chart shows that substantial population growth is anticipated through 1970 in all of the East North Central States. However, the bottom map, which indicates areas for which water supply problems may be expected by 1970, presents a different picture. The map indicates that only slight water supply problems for Michigan are likely by 1970, in spite of anticipated substantial population increase and therefore, by implication, of similarly substantial industrial growth. In contrast, two of Michigan's immediate industrial competitors — Ohio and Indiana — are expected to be experiencing critical water problems by 1970 in two-thirds of their state areas.

If these anticipations concerning future water problems in the region are reasonably correct, the implication for Michigan seems quite clear. Manufacturers using substantial quantities of water in their operations can be assured of an adequate water supply for the long-run future in Michigan. This assurance appears to be lacking for substantial areas of the region. Even those plants that require only moderate amounts of water will often want to locate in Michigan to be sure that even their moderate water requirements can be met without question and that water problems will not stunt the residential growth of the community in which their operations are carried out. Without community growth, an area's labor supply cannot increase.

Another implication seems to be suggested by Chart I. In view of the possibility that critical water problems may affect the lower two-thirds of Ohio and Indiana, additional industrial growth in these states may tend to occur increasingly in their northern areas, next to Michigan. Such a development could increase Michigan's market potential.

We should acknowledge that some authorities take a more optimistic view of the water supply situation in the future.[13] Whether or not the situation becomes as critical in nearby states within a decade or two as is suggested by Chart I, it is clear that Michigan's long-run advantage in water supply should be a very important factor in assuring the state's continued industrial growth.

Maintenance of Michigan's Advantage in Water

The fact that Michigan has an abundant water supply does not

---

13 See Gilbert F. White, "The Facts About Our Water Supply," *Harvard Business Review*, March-April, 1958, pp. 87-94. With regard to industrial use of water, the article suggests that many industries are currently wasteful in such use and will take positive steps to reduce their water requirements as the costs increase.

mean that water is freely available everywhere in the state at all times. Local shortages can develop, either from increasingly heavy withdrawals, reflecting continued residential and industrial growth, or from natural developments. Thus, Blackett, citing a study by the Detroit Metropolitan Area Regional Planning Commission of the water supply of six southeastern counties of Michigan, states, ". . . it was found that 3.6 million persons and many industries were served by water systems that could satisfy only the demands of 173,000 added people with existing water facilities."[14]

Shortages of water in various urban areas of Michigan can be expected in the future as population pressure pushes at existing facilities. But the point is that Michigan has a water supply that can be tapped to cope with these shortages as they develop. More and deeper wells can provide additional water in some instances. Streams can supply some of the additional industrial requirements. More piping of water from the Great Lakes will probably take place.

As water use in the state expands, additional facilities will have to be provided to get water to the places where it is needed. Facilities are costly and water costs will inevitably increase. Another estimate cited by Blackett indicates that in the decade 1955 to 1965 local governments in Michigan will spend almost one billion dollars for new water facilities and for sewage disposal systems.[15] Industry will need to spend substantial amounts to obtain the water it needs. But even though water becomes more costly in Michigan, the state will have a real advantage over those areas where the physical supply is less abundant.

Michigan needs to appreciate its favorable water supply situation. It needs also to look ahead to its future water requirements so that it may plan and provide adequate facilities to serve the people and the industries of Michigan with the water needed. Only by taking such positive steps can Michigan expect to enjoy the full advantage that its favorable water supply situation gives it in promoting industrial growth.

Transportation

Need for Comprehensive Study

Relatively little of a comprehensive character appears to have been written concerning transportation as a factor in Michigan's

---

14 Blackett, *op. cit.*, p. 41.
15 *Ibid.*, p. 4.

Chart I

Rate of Population Growth, 1955-1970, and Anticipated Water Problems, 1970

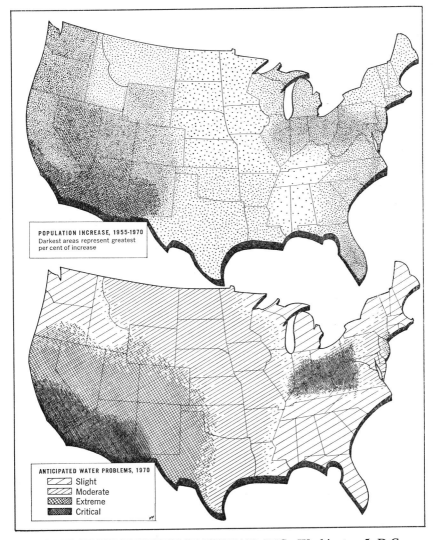

POPULATION INCREASE, 1955-1970
Darkest areas represent greatest per cent of increase

ANTICIPATED WATER PROBLEMS, 1970
Slight
Moderate
Extreme
Critical

POPULATION REFERENCE BUREAU, INC., Washington 5, D.C.

These maps show the distribution of population in 1970, as projected by the U. S. Census Bureau, and the areas of extreme and critical water shortage as projected by forecasts from the Department of Commerce and Geological Survey data.

159

industrial development. There have been a number of discussions of recent transportation developments affecting the state's future industrial growth, such as the Seaway, the Mackinac Bridge, and the Interstate Highway System. But an integration of such studies into an over-all investigation of Michigan's advantages and disadvantages in the field of transportation with respect to the state's industrial growth appears to be lacking.

Because of the obvious need for a comprehensive evaluation of Michigan's transportation situation and prospects, the Upjohn Institute engaged the services of the Fantus Factory Locating Service to develop a plan for a complete study in this important area. The outline prepared by the Fantus Service is presented as Appendix Chapter C to this report under the title, *Michigan's Transportation System and the State's Industrial Development: Some Questions Regarding These Aspects of Michigan's Economy.*

The introduction to the Fantus plan for a comprehensive transportation study provides encouragement for the view that positive, beneficial action could be taken by appropriate official groups in the state after the completion of such a study. The report states:

> If communities were aware of the fact that more frequent or lower cost rail, truck, air, or water transportation services were needed in their area and if they were aware of the role which transportation plays in economic development, they could take action to improve these services.
>
> It is no longer necessary to accept the quality and cost of transportation as "given." Aware citizens groups and government boards, by pointing out revenue opportunities and by influencing common carrier regulations which can increase the profit and quantity of these services, can encourage the improvement of transportation services.
>
> The extent to which coordinated transportation planning can influence economic growth depends upon the nature and quality of the research, the implementation philosophy (i.e., the extent to which genuine economic incentives are provided to the carriers), and the extent to which a permanent organization is willing to accept the responsibility for transportation planning.

A thorough review of the Fantus transportation study plan is recommended to the Committee on Michigan's Economic Future, to appropriate agencies of the state government, and to all other groups and individuals responsible for or interested in the future economic growth of Michigan.

General Observations

A few general observations may be made concerning transportation as a factor in plant location in Michigan. We have commented on Michigan's strong role as a market and as a source of materials for manufacturers and on its close proximity to the remainder of the manufacturing belt. This favorable location minimizes somewhat any adverse impact of such possible unfavorable factors as deficient transportation facilities and unfavorable rates. On the other hand, it is obvious that Michigan's transportation situation is less favorable than that of the states on its southern border — Ohio, Indiana, and Illinois. The northern portions of these states are on the direct east-west routes for railroads and major highways.

There has been much speculation with regard to the probable impact of the current transportation developments referred to previously. The completion of the developing Interstate Highway network should permit faster and more economical movement of goods into and out of Michigan by truck. The Mackinac Bridge is expected to be helpful in developing the Upper Peninsula. It is expected to promote tourism and to improve market access for such manufacturing as now exists, or may develop, in the Upper Peninsula. It has also been suggested that truck traffic from the East may increasingly use the Bridge and the Upper Peninsula as a transport route to the Northwest. Such increased traffic flow by heavy vehicles would, of course, give a boost to those service enterprises in northern Michigan that serve such traffic.[16]

Various economic advantages have been suggested as likely to accrue to Michigan from the enlargement of the Seaway. A study made in 1957 concludes on a less-than-optimistic note with regard to the likelihood that the Seaway may prove a substantial, immediate boon to the state's economy, as follows:

> From the mass of potential benefits, only two appear of great significance to the Michigan area. There will be definite advantages accruing from economies in the shipment of bulk materials, and in the leverage effect on shipment rates of an alternate available route.[17]

The second advantage referred to relates, of course, to the probability that the rails will lower certain of their rates to meet the competition offered by the tolls on the Seaway. Dixon's appraisal of the economic potential of the Seaway appears to concur in general with other more general analyses which suggest that the bene-

---

16 It has been suggested that lower rate schedules might be established for trucks crossing the Bridge after midnight. Such lower rates during "off-hours" could reduce transportation costs for industry located in the Upper Peninsula and could increase use of the Bridge by trucks serving the Northwest.

17 Brian Dixon, *The St. Lawrence Seaway and the Connecting Channels: Their Influence on Plant Location in Michigan*, C.E.D. Executive Study Group (Ann Arbor: University of Michigan, 1957), p. 20.

fits from the Seaway may not be as great or as immediate as may have been hoped for in earlier discussions.

However, even though the economic benefits flowing from these recent transportation developments may not turn out to be as substantial as one would wish, still they are plus factors with respect to Michigan's economic growth. And it is entirely possible that they may contribute appreciably to Michigan's future development in ways that are not foreseen at this time. Thus, one possible unanticipated development springing from the deepening of the St. Lawrence Seaway may be the contract awarded a Bay City shipbuilding firm for the construction of four destroyers. Without the deepened Seaway, these ships could not have been built on the Great Lakes.

Labor

IN APPENDIX CHAPTER A to this report, Dr. Daniel Kruger presents a detailed discussion of the topic, *The Labor Factor in Plant Location in Michigan*. In summarizing his analysis, Dr. Kruger points to several aspects of the labor factor in Michigan which industrialists may regard as advantageous in plant location decisions and to several which they may regard as disadvantageous. These advantageous and disadvantageous aspects are indicated below.

Advantageous Aspects of the Labor Factor in Michigan

Labor supply. Michigan offers an adequate supply of experienced factory labor, possessing many skills. The projected population of the state indicates an adequate future supply of manpower. That there will be continued improvement of the skills of the labor force is suggested by the strong support given to public education in the state.

Labor productivity. Data are quoted to indicate that the Michigan worker's contribution to the productive process in 1954 and 1956 was higher than that of the U. S. worker. It is pointed out, however, that Michigan's favorable record may stem largely from the fact that the state's manufacturing economy is largely composed of industries in which value added is high. In the body of the discussion, quotations from Michigan manufacturers are given, citing the production-minded character of Michigan workers.

Stability of labor force. Data on this topic are presented in terms of the quit rate and of work stoppage experience. The quit rate of production workers has been lower in the state than in the nation

162

as a whole in recent years. With regard to work stoppages, it is indicated that Michigan compares favorably with other industrial states.

Workmen's Compensation Act costs. These costs appear to be advantageous to Michigan employers in comparison with costs in other industrial states. A study of average manual rates for 45 major occupational classifications for the years 1950-1956 shows Michigan to have ranked only eleventh in costs among sixteen leading industrial states in six out of the seven years involved.

Disadvantageous Aspects of the Labor Factor in Michigan

Wage rates. Production workers in Michigan have the highest average weekly earnings in the nation. High earnings generally coincide with high wage rates. High earnings may be expected in Michigan because of its predominance in high-value-added industries and because of its relatively large percentage of skilled and semiskilled workers. Valid comparisons of earnings by industry between geographical areas are beset with difficulties. However, one set of data for 1958 is cited in which average hourly earnings were similar in Michigan and Ohio in four out of the five industries listed. In the other industry, hourly earnings were 20 percent higher in Michigan.[18]

Unemployment compensation costs. The Michigan rate for unemployment insurance was higher than that of other nearby industrial states in eight out of the nine years, 1950 through 1958. Here, again, an important reason for this higher average rate in Michigan is the industrial composition of the state, especially the predominance of the automotive industry.

The "labor situation." Reference is made to the image which many employers, in Michigan and elsewhere, have of the strong position which labor unions, especially the UAW, and labor leaders occupy in the state.

* * *

In the summary section, as well as throughout his discussion, the author points to many areas where more data, and more comparable data, are needed so that more thorough and more satisfactory research concerning these various aspects of the labor factor can be carried out.

---

18 In addition to the data cited in Appendix Chapter A, other comparisons of hourly earnings and rates in various industries between Detroit and other midwestern cities are provided in Cecil M. Birch, "Can Detroit's Economy Be Diversified?" *University of Detroit Research Bulletin*, November, 1958, 18 pp.

Taxes

IN APPENDIX CHAPTER B to this report, Dr. Harvey Brazer discusses the topic, *Taxation and Industrial Location in Michigan.*[19] We quote below conclusions contained in the summary section of Appendix Chapter B:

> First, state and local taxes do not appear, for most manufacturing firms, to represent a major element of costs. But there is now insufficient information available . . . Evidence as to the differentials in business taxes, at various locations within and among states, is not now available with sufficient reliability to warrant the suggestion that they have, in fact, been measured.
>
> Our second conclusion is that even if we had reliable measures of inter-community tax differentials, we would still need to know more than we now do about how important such differentials are as a location factor. It may well be, for example, that a small differential, relative to total costs, does serve, in many instances, as a major irritant, and therefore as a major location factor. On the other hand, even large tax differentials, *if* accompanied by commensurate differences in the quality and availability of public services, may be of little or no importance in location decisions.
>
> Finally, we must recognize that the actual moving of a plant is a very costly job and rarely occurs. Of far greater importance are decisions with respect to expansion through the construction or acquisition of new facilities and decisions forced by the obsolescence of old plants. The process of economic growth in a dynamic economy is bound to be accompanied by technological changes that make old sites or even urban sites undesirable, and give rise to new influences on location decisions. Changes in transportation costs, location of markets, and sources of supply are all likely to bring movements of industry into and out of all states. The role of taxes in this process of change must be the focus of attention of any enlightened or enlightening research in this area.

Elsewhere in his discussion, Dr. Brazer indicates that, despite the inadequacies of recent studies of interstate differentials in taxes on business firms, "there is good reason to believe that taxes paid by business firms in Michigan are in fact higher than they are in Illinois, Indiana, and Ohio . . ."

The Climate for Industry

THE "CLIMATE FOR INDUSTRY" is not one of the 13 basic industrial location factors to which we referred at the beginning of this chapter. The climate for industry, or "business climate," cuts across several of these basic factors. But the lack of a clear-cut concept or definition of the areas covered by the term has not prevented Michigan's business climate from being a widely discussed topic in

---

19 Dr. Brazer was Director of Research of the Michigan Tax Study (1958) sponsored by the Legislative Committee of the House of Representatives, Rollo G. Conlin, Chairman.

Michigan in recent years. During 1958 and 1959 especially, increased public awareness of Michigan's employment problem and the uncertainty of the state's prospects of regaining its former levels of employment made Michigan's climate for industry a timely, controversial, and important topic.

The climate for industry means different things to different economic groups. Its meaning differs somewhat at the state and at the community level. For purposes of discussing Michigan's climate for industry, we shall use the term to include a variety of governmentally influenced factors affecting the cost of conducting a business, and also a variety of factors not influenced by government.

The over-all list of matters affecting the climate for industry is almost identical with a list of the issues on which business groups and labor union groups differ. On many of these matters, action by the executive, legislative, and judicial branches of the state government is decisive. These areas include state expenditure programs for unemployment insurance and workmen's compensation, in terms of coverage, benefits, duration, and qualification rules. They include the levels of state expenditures for public assistance and other general welfare programs. On the governmental revenue side, these issues include the level and types of taxes levied by the state, and especially those levied on business and industry.

In the nongovernmental sphere, factors affecting the state's business climate include the extent of unionization and union activities, including strikes, and the general level of wage rates and fringe benefits typically provided in leading industries.

Michigan's Climate for Industry

If the factors mentioned above are some of the principal ones involved in a state's business climate, how would Michigan look to an industrialist who is thinking of locating a plant in Michigan? The review made earlier of the findings in Appendix Chapter A on the labor factor suggests that he would gain a mixed impression of the various aspects of the labor situation in Michigan. He would find some aspects favorable and others acceptable; he would find others of a character tending to deter him from locating in the state. With regard to the taxation factor, he would find that Michigan at present does appear to tax industry somewhat more heavily than some nearby industrial states. Whether or not he found Michigan state expenditures to be "high" would depend in part on his point of view and on his social philosophy, including the extent of his concern for a high level of educational and other public services in the state where he lived and carried on his business.

But the impression that the industrialist might have of Michigan's climate for industry would not be based solely on his appraisal of the various matters mentioned above. There are other factors, intangible yet real, involved in a state's climate for industry. The kind of attitude that governmental officials and agencies take toward industry, and toward labor, will influence the industrialist's thinking as to whether he should locate a new plant in Michigan. In this connection, the claims of an "alliance" between the state administration of Michigan and the leading union in the state could be a matter of concern for a prospective industrialist. Without knowing (or being in a position to ascertain) the degree to which such a charge was well-founded, he could believe that administrative decisions would favor the labor position in situations where both labor and management were involved. Likewise, the administrative branch of the state government initiates budget proposals, administers expenditure programs, and recommends legislation; and these actions are of direct importance to industry.

The preceding observations have applied primarily to the administrative branch of Michigan's state government. The other branches of government, legislative and judicial, also exert influence on Michigan's climate for industry. This is especially true of the legislature which, of course, is actually and directly responsible for the legislation concerning taxation, labor, social welfare, and other matters that affect the profitability of industry in the state. The authors of this report are not aware of any statements to the effect that the state legislature has assumed a pro-labor attitude in recent years. Thus, it would hardly be proper to say that the laws under which industry operates in Michigan reflect a pro-labor bias.

Michigan's Reputation for Business Climate

We have pointed to some of the factors that go into the determination of Michigan's business climate. It would seem extremely difficult, or impossible, to present an objective appraisal of the state's climate for industry, relative to the climate in other competitive states. However, whether such an over-all, objective appraisal might rate the state's business climate as good, bad, or average, it appears that Michigan has been acquiring a reputation in the nation's press that is generally unfavorable from the viewpoint of industrialists. The following quotations suggest the type of published references that have been made recently concerning Michigan's business climate:

> "Cold shoulder" for business? One reason frequently cited by some businessmen for this decline in jobs is that the State has an "unfavorable climate" for attracting and holding private business and industry. All through the State government, businessmen say, they run into an "attitude of hostility." ("A 'Welfare State' Runs Into Trouble," *U. S. News and World Report,* February 13, 1959, p. 51.)
>
> Politics — Tied in close to the labor climate in Michigan as to seem nearly inseparable, is the political climate. Little happens in state government that doesn't bear the stamp of approval of the UAW. ("Why Industry Shuns Michigan," *Iron Age,* December 18, 1958, p. 50)

To these quotations could be added others appearing during 1959 which reported in lurid terms Michigan's "bankrupt" condition and the factors contributing to it. Many would question the extent to which the charges contained in the above quotations and in other similar reports can be documented. But the important point is that these are the kinds of reports on Michigan's business climate that have been read by businessmen throughout the country. If reports similar to these continue to appear in national publications, it seems obvious that the state will acquire an increasingly unfavorable reputation as a location for industry, one that will be extremely difficult to offset.

Even though Michigan may have acquired a reputation among many industrialists as a state with a poor business climate, there is some evidence that this view is not universally held. Thus a *Wall Street Journal* news item of May 11, 1959, reporting on the removal of a firm's production facilities from Wisconsin to Michigan and Ohio locations, quotes a company statement to the effect that the move "will bring these products closer to their major markets and to relatively more favorable labor climates." The *Detroit Free Press* of March 21, 1959, reporting the removal of an automotive parts business from a Michigan location to one in North Carolina, quotes a company spokesman as stating, "The labor factor is not the reason for the local shutdown."

However, in general, we must report that there is a fairly widespread impression, if not conviction, that Michigan does not offer a "good" climate for industry. Many industrialists, both in Michigan and elsewhere, appear to hold this view. Whether right or wrong, this unfavorable image does influence businessmen's decisions and must be corrected.

Influence of Developments Elsewhere

There are some forces at work in other states that may tend to reduce the disadvantage that Michigan's currently poor reputation for business climate may give the state. First of all, it should be clear that the issues involved in business climate are not confined to Michigan. Almost every industrialized state is concerned with these matters. One has but to examine the situation in New York, Pennsylvania and Massachusetts — to mention the more obvious — to recognize that Michigan is not unique in this respect. Groups in these states, as well as in others, also claim that their conditions of doing business are more unfavorable than elsewhere.

We have previously noted that there is an image in the minds of many industrialists that labor is especially influential in Michigan's state government. To the extent that this is so, the elections of 1958 suggest that a number of other industrial states may be moving in the direction of experiencing greater influence in state governmental operations by labor unions. The 1958 elections in several industrial states were generally interpreted as indicating a victory for candidates, parties, and issues supported by labor unions. Thus, if Michigan has been leading the parade toward union objectives — and that has not been established — the events of November, 1958 suggest that several of her sister states in the manufacturing belt and elsewhere were moving up fast toward the head of the procession.

On a more specific note, we have observed that Michigan's tax burden on industry appears to be somewhat heavier than that imposed by several neighboring states. In that connection, however, Dr. Brazer refers in his discussion of comparative tax burdens among states (Appendix Chapter B) to the need for studying the tax situation over time. He points out that the relative tax burden in different states can change in a few years' time.

There are some indications that some of Michigan's neighboring industrial states will soon be increasing their tax loads. The *Detroit Free Press* carried stories in its issues of February 25 and March 5, 1959, to the effect that Pennsylvania and Ohio, respectively, would be needing to levy additional taxes in the near future. Whether or not expanded tax programs in these and other states do reduce the disparity existing between the tax burden on industry in Michigan and in certain other states, there is a suggestion that Michigan's relative position on the tax factor could change for the better in the next few years.   *   *   *

The observations in the preceding paragraphs suggest that Michigan's climate for industry may be improved, relatively speaking, by developments outside the state. This does not mean, however, that Michigan residents can be complacent about this matter. Since Michigan needs badly both the in-migration of industry and the industrial growth deriving from instate expansion by Michigan firms, it is vital that our reputation for business climate be improved by all means at our disposal.

Manufacturers' Geographic Preferences for Plant Location

THE REVIEW just completed of Michigan's position with respect to several basic industrial location factors makes it of interest to know how industrial executives throughout the country regard Michigan as a possible location for a new plant. A survey made by *Business Week* magazine in 1958 provides data on this point.[20]

Respondents to the survey were requested to list states, metropolitan areas, or cities that "you would consider if your company were going to select a site for a new plant." The survey data show that 108 out of the 283 respondents to the survey mentioned one or more locations within the East North Central region as possible plant locations. The region was mentioned more times than any other of the Census geographic regions. The next region in order of times mentioned (94) was the South Atlantic area. Among the states, California was mentioned the most times, with 77 mentions.

The preference by states (or state cities) within the East North Central region was as follows:

State	Number of Mentions	
	Total	First Choice
Ohio	61	31
Indiana	24	7
Illinois	39	8
MICHIGAN	19	3
Wisconsin	17	7

---

20 *The Plant-Site Preferences of Industry and the Factors of Selection,* A Business Week Research Report, August, 1958, 12 pp.

The Survey was carried out by *Business Week's* advertising research department. Results of the survey were not published in *Business Week.*

The survey questionnaire was sent to 1000 manufacturing executives in 19 cities throughout the country. Of the 283 responses, 162 were received from five cities, as follows: New York (87), Cleveland (23), Detroit (22), Milwaukee (15), and Minneapolis (15).

Executives in six industry groups accounted for over half (171) of the 283 responses, as follows: Fabricated metal products (37), Machinery, nonelectrical (34), Chemicals and allied products (30), Printing, publishing, and allied industries (27), Electrical machinery, equipment, and supplies (22), and Food and kindred products (21).

Company presidents were respondents in 103 cases.

In the Great Lakes area, only Wisconsin, the least industrialized state, was mentioned fewer times than Michigan. And Michigan was the first-choice location of only three executives of the 283 who responded to the survey. Ohio drew down 31 first-place preferences.

It is disconcerting to find that Michigan rated so low in this mail survey of manufacturers' preferences for plant sites. It is possible, of course, that a different group of respondents, or a survey undertaken at some other time, would have shown a greater preference for Michigan. Moreover, had each of the 283 companies actually been planning the location of a new plant, the pattern of location preference could have been different. Nor should overwhelming weight be given to a mail survey with a response of only 28.3 percent. But, to the extent that this survey was representative, Michigan did not seem to be an attractive location for industrialists in the summer of 1958.

Relative Importance of Industrial Location Factors

IS IT POSSIBLE, on a regional basis, to pick out several of the basic 13 locational factors that seem to be regarded as most important? A look at several sets of materials should reveal whether different surveys and analysts appear to be in agreement on which of these factors seem to be most influential in plant location decisions.

The Business Week Survey

The *Business Week* survey that was discussed earlier asked the following question of its respondents:

> What are the major factors or reasons that enter your decision when considering new plant locations?

The responses given to this question were not cross-classified with the respondent's choice of locations for plant sites. Thus, the factors that account for Michigan's relatively poor showing in the manufacturers' preferences for industrial locations cannot be identified. The responses given can, however, serve to indicate the considerations that presumably guided these industrial executives in indicating their geographical preferences.

Since many respondents obviously mentioned several considerations, the number of times that these factors were mentioned (747) considerably exceeds the 283 respondents involved in the survey. Moreover, the respondents described the factors in their own words so that the factors are not always easily identifiable in terms of the

13 basic factors mentioned earlier. We have attempted to group the forty or so considerations cited by the respondents into factors that tie into the 13 basic factors, with the following result:

Industrial Location Factor	Mentions Number	Mentions Percent
All factors	**747**	**100**
Markets	188	25
Labor	138	18
Transportation	89	12
Raw materials	80	11
Taxes	39	5
Climate	31	4
Labor climate	25	3
Distribution facilities	21	3
Living conditions	20	3
Power	15	2
Laws and regulations	11	1
Fuel	3	..
Not classifiable[a]	27	4
Less than 3 mentions[b]	60	8

[a]Includes such reported factors as "Proximity to home office," "Strategically located," and "Competition."

[b]Not identified in Business Week report. Presumably responses were not susceptible of classification under any of above headings.

A number of comments on the above tabulation are in order. First of all, it is apparent that markets were a primary consideration of the industrial executives queried in this survey. One out of every four considerations mentioned related to the market. Labor likewise was an influential factor, accounting for one-fifth of all the considerations listed by these respondents collectively. Transportation and raw materials were also relatively important in the thinking of the respondents, each of these factors accounting for around one-tenth of all considerations listed in the survey.

What may be somewhat surprising is the fact that taxes and the "labor climate" do not show up importantly in this survey. Only one out of every 20 considerations mentioned related to taxes. A somewhat smaller proportion (around 3 percent) was concerned with the labor climate.[21] Taken together, these two components

21 "Labor climate" is not one of the 13 basic location factors. But, because of the interest in this topic, we have grouped under this heading responses listed in the survey that seemed to fall in this area. Thus, the labor climate category shown in the text table includes such considerations reported in the *Business Week* tabulation as attitude of unions or general union conditions, labor climate, and non-union labor.

The "labor" category shown in the text table represents entries shown in the *Business Week* tabulation under such headings as available labor supply, available skilled or semi-skilled labor, and labor costs. It is very possible, of course, that some respondents may have intended to cover the labor climate also under the headings just listed so that "labor climate" considerations could be more important than these data suggest.

It should also be noted that if the 25 mentions of labor climate are added to the 138 mentions of labor, the latter becomes almost as important as markets in terms of number of mentions.

of business climate are mentioned about one time out of eleven. The relatively limited number of mentions of taxes and labor climate suggests that these factors may not be as influential in guiding plant location decisions as one might assume from newspaper discussions and magazine articles.

We may also compare the number of references to these factors with the number of respondents (283) to the survey. Such a comparison is provided by the following:

Industrial Location Factor	Respondents Mentioning Specified Factor —	
	Number	Percent
All factors..........................	283	a
Markets............................	188	66
Labor..............................	138	49
Transportation......................	89	31
Raw materials.......................	80	28
Taxes..............................	39	14
Labor climate.......................	25	9

*a*Percentages add to more than 100 percent because some respondents mentioned more than one factor.

On the basis indicated by the tabulation, the paramount importance of markets is suggested. About two-thirds of the industrialists involved in the survey listed markets as one of the probable determinants in their plant location decisions. Half of them listed labor. About one in seven listed the tax factor. Less than one-tenth mentioned labor climate specifically.

What implications do these responses hold for Michigan as a plant location choice? We have seen that the respondents in this survey were not kindly disposed toward Michigan as a plant location site. Yet the well-publicized factors that are assumed by many to reflect unfavorable location factors for Michigan — the tax system and the labor climate — were hardly mentioned frequently enough in the survey to account for the evident preference for location in other states. More detailed analysis would appear to be needed to account for Michigan's poor showing in the *Business Week* survey.

This survey does suggest, however, that market and labor considerations are principal factors considered by industrialists in locating a new plant. Also suggested as of major importance are transportation and raw materials.

The Dun's Review Survey

Dun's Review carried an article in March, 1959, reporting on a survey it had made of the methods used and of the factors involved in making decisions on factory locations.[22] The survey reflects responses by 107 manufacturing concerns in various industries to a 4-page questionnaire.

The information on plant location factors reported in this article is not presented in such a way as to permit statistical summarization. But the following quotations from the article do permit some appraisal of the relative importance of the different locational factors as developed by this survey.

> Although the availability of a reliable labor supply remains the No. 1 consideration with most of the surveyed companies, other factors in plant location are becoming increasingly important. More than half the companies report that transportation has increased most in importance in the last few years.

> Several are now more concerned with finding locations which provide good schools and a cultural environment that attracts high-level technical people.

> There also is a much keener awareness today of the importance of the "business climate" — the community attitude toward business.

> Some of the surveyed companies are already making plans which take into account the effect that jet air transportation will have on their plant locations.

> Only about a half dozen of the 107 surveyed companies express any firm resolution to omit any particular state or geographic area from their site selection list. In virtually every company surveyed, the site is chosen in light of the individual facts involved.

> The states and metropolitan areas that the six companies hold in disfavor are noted for large labor concentrations and union strength.

> Industry's movement to the South, Southwest, and Pacific states in recent years is likely to continue, survey respondents predict.

> The reasons given for the geographical shift include such things as good productive labor supply, lower building costs, and better business climate. But the most important reason is simply the development of new, untended markets in these areas.

From the above quoted material, it would appear that labor supply was the most important factor in making a plant location decision in the minds of the 107 respondents to this survey. It is difficult to appraise the relative importance of other locational factors to the executives who responded to the survey. But it is apparent that transportation has been increasing in relative importance in recent years. The indication that industry will often locate in the South, Southwest, and Pacific states reflects the importance of market orientation.

---

22 "New Light on Site Seeking," *Dun's Review and Modern Industry,* March, 1959, pp. 90-91, 104-11.

It is also of interest that only six respondents out of the 107 surveyed had crossed out particular states or areas as potential locations. Even though a favorable labor or business climate was suggested several times as desirable, the number of cases where this factor might be the single determinant was relatively small.

It may be noteworthy that the only specific reference to taxes that is made in the article refers to the liking of 22 respondents for plant location in rural areas. Lower taxes are among the advantages upon which such a preference is based.

In general, this survey suggests labor supply as very important in plant location decisions, with transportation and markets also important in management thinking.

Other Evaluations

The views of several discussants of industrial location factors will be helpful in indicating general appraisals of the more important factors. Several such appraisals are quoted or summarized in the following paragraphs.

Water Resources and Plant Location in Michigan. This study by Professor Blackett contains the following summary paragraph:

> Michigan industry will not develop merely because it has water supplies that place it at the top of the list. Labor supply, transportation, and a suitable tax system will be the major determinants. Failure to develop Michigan's water potential can be a deterrent, even though other factors are favorable.[23]

Where to Put Your Plant. Two key excerpts from this article in *Fortune* are as follows:

> The selection of a new plant site has become an important management decision and it is usually influenced by dozens of factors. In almost all cases, however, one or more of the following three basic considerations enter importantly into the final judgment: (1) the availability of raw materials — including fuel, power, and water; (2) proximity to markets; and (3) personnel considerations—including both the availability of labor and the preferences of management.
>
> Probably more industrial sites are finally chosen because of personnel considerations than because of raw-material availability and market considerations combined. Usually it is the availability of unskilled or semiskilled labor that is decisively important.[24]

Changing Regional Economies. This article contains the following views with respect to possible changes in the locational requirements of expanding industries:

> A next step is to become better informed on the changing location requirements of expanding industries. Here, I can suggest some of the possible future trends in location factors:

23 Blackett, *op. cit.,* p. 45.
24 Richardson Wood, "Where to Put Your Plant," *Fortune,* July, 1956, pp. 100-104, 128, 133.

a) In the past, materials and natural resources have been of top importance in attracting industry. More recently, market orientation has been emphasized even more than resource orientation. In the future, I expect to see greater freedom in the selection of location, with labor supply increasing in importance . . .

b) Another independent locational trend, related to other types of expansion, will be the increased importance of water supply for processing and cooling purposes . . .

c) Trained labor supply and training facilities will also become more important in locating new industries . . .

d) A final trend in plant location factors that I will mention is an increased pressure to reduce transportation costs. The cost of railway and truck transportation appears to have increased more rapidly than production and distribution costs as a whole. If this tendency continues, the pressure will be strong in many industries for increased use of water transportation, for new uses of pipelines and conveyor belts, and a much greater use of air cargo.[25]

* * *

In general, the materials reviewed in the preceding pages are in rough agreement as to the more important elements in plant location. Without exception, all these surveys and discussions point to labor supply as a top-ranking consideration. All but one refer to the importance of markets. Transportation and materials are commonly cited as other important considerations.

On the other hand, the tax structure does not appear to carry the importance in plant location decisions that one might assume from current discussions. Business or labor climate also receives relatively limited prominence in these surveys and discussions. However, a favorable labor climate could well be a facet of the labor supply situation that all industrialists consider in planning for a new plant location, even though not specified separately.

Comparative Operating Costs in Eleven Selected Cities

APPENDIX CHAPTER D to this report provides a summary of a special study entitled *Operating the ABC Corporation in Eleven Midwestern Cities.* This study was prepared especially for this report by the Fantus Factory Locating Service. The purpose of the study was to illustrate the cost-analysis phase of decisions about plant locations, with particular reference to location of a given plant in 11 selected cities in Kentucky, Ohio, Indiana, Illinois, and Michigan.

---

25 Stefan H. Robock, *Changing Regional Economies* (Kansas City: Midwest Research Institute, 1957) pp. 4-5. (Reprinted from *Iowa Business Digest,* December, 1957.)

The hypothetical "ABC Corporation" produces stamped metal parts used in the manufacture of other finished products. It is assumed that the Corporation sells to a national market.

This study is of special interest at this point in that it indicates for one industry the relative importance, from an operating-cost standpoint, of several of the industrial location factors that have been discussed in the preceding pages. The study highlights also the appreciable differences among cities in these several types of variable operating costs.

The operating cost pattern for two of the Michigan cities included in the study is as follows:

Variable Operating Cost	Michigan City C	Michigan City A	Difference
	(Amounts in thousands)		
Total.....................	$4,518.6	$4,172.3	$346.3
Labor.....................	3,152.6	2,836.5	316.1
Occupancy.................	122.8	114.9	7.9
Freight...................	1,025.9	1,006.3	19.6
Taxes.....................	143.4	142.6	.8
Utilities.................	73.9	72.0	1.9

A glance at these cost estimates reveals that labor costs (wages plus the costs of fringe benefits, unemployment insurance, and workmen's compensation) represent the major portion of those costs that vary from location to location. In these two Michigan cities, labor costs account for almost 70 percent of all variable costs. Freight charges are also important, accounting for around one-fourth of the variable operating costs for the ABC Corporation in these two cities. Finally, the state and local tax bill is shown as more limited in importance, accounting for somewhat over three percent of variable operating costs in both cities. (All of these cost items would be less important when measured against *total* costs of the Corporation.)

These figures point up the fact that, from the standpoint of operating costs that vary from city to city, the labor bill is the most sizable item. Freight charges are also important. Taxes are of lesser importance. In these two Michigan cities, labor costs differ by over $300,000 and account for most of the total cost difference of about $350,000. When comparisons are made of cost differences between other comparable cities of the 11 included in the study, differences in labor costs show up as most important also, although in some cases differences in other items, notably in freight charges, are also substantial.

The total cost difference of $350,000 between the two Michigan cities is striking. Reflecting primarily the difference in labor costs, this finding is in accord with an earlier study of the labor factor in plant location in Michigan which stated:

> In summary, the study group finds that . . . labor cost variations within the State are as great as labor cost variations between states.[26]

Appreciable but smaller differences in variable operating costs within the other states included in the study are also indicated. Between two Ohio cities, there is a difference of $107,000; between two Indiana cities, $184,000; between two Illinois cities, $153,000; and between two Kentucky cities, $48,000.

A study such as that of the ABC Corporation can not suggest directly the relative importance of such major location factors as raw materials and markets. It does confirm, however, that from a cost standpoint labor and transportation charges can be very important considerations for an industrialist who is evaluating different communities as a site for an operation. It serves also to suggest that the tax bill would tend to be a secondary factor, rather than a primary one.

Survey of Michigan Manufacturers

WHAT DO MICHIGAN industrialists think of Michigan as a base for their manufacturing activity? What are the state's advantages and disadvantages in their minds? There appear to be no recently published data on this point. There is, however, information available from a survey made almost a decade ago. The results of this survey may no longer typify the thinking of Michigan industrialists. Yet, there may be some carry-over of these industrial evaluations of Michigan as a plant location. And in any event, it is of interest to know what locational factors were involved in the reactions of these industrialists to their Michigan location.

The survey was carried out in 1950 by the Survey Research Center of the University of Michigan.[27] The study was intended "to illuminate the causes and extent of likely movement into and out of Michigan of manufacturing plants . . ." Information was obtained from some 200 Michigan manufacturers on the factors causing satisfaction and dissatisfaction with their Michigan location.

26 Edward D. Wickersham, *Labor as a Factor in Plant Location in Michigan,* C.E.D. Executive Study Group (Ann Arbor: University of Michigan, 1957), p. 1.
27 *Industrial Mobility in Michigan,* Survey Research Center, University of Michigan, December, 1950, 77 pp. The text tables in this section are based on Tables 6 and 11 of this study.

The following data show the various disadvantages that manufacturers found in their Michigan location in 1950 and the relative importance of these disadvantages:

Disadvantages of Michigan	Percentages of Employment Represented[a]
Labor (largely labor costs)	51
Pressures from organized labor (two-thirds of these also included under labor above)	12
Distance from materials (nearly half specified steel)	16
Distance from markets	11
Taxes	9
Power, fuel, utilities	6
Other factors (including transportation)	12
No disadvantages	25
No answer	3

[a] "Percentages of Employment" are percentages of total employment in the industries included in the sample.
Percentages add to more than 100 percent because some respondents mentioned two or three different disadvantages.

Looking at the factors that represented advantages to these Michigan industrial executives, we find the following information:

Advantages of Michigan	Percentages of Employment Represented[a]
Proximity to markets	64
Favorable labor situation	34
Proximity to materials	16
Favorable transportation facilities	9
Other advantages	9

[a] "Percentages of Employment" are percentages of total employment in the industries included in the sample.
Percentages add to more than 100 percent because some respondents mentioned two or three different advantages.

From these two sets of data, we may note that the labor and market factors were most prominent as reasons for satisfaction or dissatisfaction with a Michigan location in 1950. In terms of disadvantages, the cost of labor in Michigan was the principal disadvantage cited. Pressures from organized labor were specifically cited as a disadvantage by manufacturers representing over 10 percent of the total employment in the industries included in the survey sample. From the standpoint of advantages, Michigan rated well with these industrialists because of its proximity to markets. A favorable labor situation was also a principal advantage. Thus these data for 1950 seem to agree with recent and general information that labor and markets are primary locational factors taken into account when plant location decisions are being made.

What was the net effect on Michigan manufacturers of these advantages and disadvantages with respect to their possible migration out of the state? The following summary paragraph from the study suggests a limited impact of any net disadvantage over advantages:

> It seems clear from these results that there is not a very serious problem of loss of industry facing Michigan in the immediate future. The number and importance of plants whose executives are thinking of moving out is small, and the number with real moving plans is still smaller. Likewise, the group which is building branches and expanding elsewhere is not particularly large, and the reasons given are in many cases the serving of other market areas or getting closer to materials. Where high wages or difficulties with organized labor are mentioned as reasons for moving or expanding elsewhere, usually reference is also made to the desire to remain close to the Detroit market, or to get closer to steel. This does not mean that high wages, particularly if they are not matched by high productivity, are not a problem in Michigan, nor does it mean that union difficulties are unimportant. A few manufacturers were quite bitter about their difficulties with organized labor, one even saying that he was moving out and leaving his workers to "argue and bicker with someone else." But, in general, high wages as well as taxes seems much less important in actual migration of industry than they are as pervasive irritations.[28]

Summary

FROM THE REVIEW made in this chapter, it seems clear that labor and markets are the most important plant location considerations. Materials and transportation are also important factors. On the other hand, taxes and the business climate do not seem to be as important in actual plant location decisions as might be expected.

What do these conclusions on the outstanding importance of labor and markets mean for Michigan's future industrial growth? With regard to labor, Michigan's generally high wage structure will often serve as a deterrent to plant location in the state, even though in large part it reflects the industry-mix in Michigan. The unfavorable impression that many industrialists have of Michigan as a union-dominated state could also deter manufacturers, especially those from outside the state, from carrying on operations in Michigan. From the favorable view, the availability in Michigan of an experienced, relatively stable, generally well-educated labor force, possessing a variety of skills, will continue to be an advantage for the state.

With regard to the market factor, Michigan itself enjoys a very strong position as a market for consumer and industrial goods. Its location in the Great Lakes area means that it is located in one of the nation's greatest concentrations of population and income.

---

28 *Ibid.*, pp. 28-29.

Not enough is known about Michigan's transportation position to provide an over-all evaluation. Both advantages and disadvantages can be noted. Looking at raw materials, we can point to several found in Michigan that will continue to attract industries oriented around them. The wide range of manufacturing activity in the state provides the semi-processed materials and products that will continue to serve as raw materials for many other industries.

Although taxes and the labor and political climate do not appear to be major determinants in location decisions, this hardly means that they can be regarded as unimportant. An unfavorable business climate could prove to be the decisive element in some location decisions. To the unfavorable impression that some industrialists have of the "labor situation" in Michigan and the higher taxes that industry appears to shoulder in the state must be added the state's well-publicized fiscal problems during 1959.

Michigan's adequate water supply does not appear to be an outstanding locational advantage at present. But, as population and industrial growth press at water supplies in areas less bountifully supplied with this natural resource, Michigan's advantages in water could increasingly draw certain types of industry into the state.

On balance, the locational advantages of Michigan seem to be strong enough so that the state is unlikely to develop into one of the nation's chronic "depressed area" problems. On the other hand, the state has problems which are sufficiently serious to demand that earnest efforts be made to solve them.

Chapter VII

Growth Trends in Michigan Manufacturing Industries[1]

THE RECENT DECLINE in manufacturing employment in Michigan generally, and in motor vehicles and defense industries specifically, may present a problem for the state in the years ahead. Because of the importance of the automotive industry in Michigan, it is likely that unemployment will remain a problem in the near future. Beyond that, what happens may well depend on the trends in employment in Michigan industries not closely related to the automotive industry. For this reason we must have information on Michigan's record in nonautomotive industries in recent years. Is Michigan losing ground compared with other areas not only in automotive industries, but also in nonautomotive industries? Or is it possible that Michigan is actually gaining by comparison with other areas, especially in growth industries? The purpose of this chapter is to compare Michigan's growth in nonautomotive industries with that of other areas in order to determine whether Michigan has kept pace with other areas in recent years.

In our search for answers to the all-important questions listed above, we shall examine two sets of data. First, we shall analyze Bureau of the Census employment data in major industry groups for the United States, East North Central States, and Michigan. This will provide an over-all picture of how Michigan compares with the larger areas on an industry-by-industry basis. Then, as our major focus in this chapter, we shall analyze employment data prepared by the Office of Area Development of the U. S. Department of Commerce (from Census data) on individual growth industries within the major industry groups. It is unfortunate that these more detailed data are available only for the years 1947-1954 and thus are not as current as one would wish. However, analysis of these data will indicate whether or not Michigan was keeping pace during this

---

1 This chapter was prepared by Henry C. Thole, Industrial Project Director, The W. E. Upjohn Institute for Employment Research, with assistance from Dr. Edwin Grossnickle, Professor of General Business, School of Business, Western Michigan University.

period in the more important growth industries which are likely to provide a large share of the new jobs created in the years ahead.

Trends in Major Manufacturing Industries

IN PART II employment trends for the period 1953-1957 were reviewed and analyzed to focus on problems associated with the decline in employment for that period. Now we shall cover the period 1947-1956, a longer period for which comparable figures are available. Analysis of data for this period has the advantage of comparing Michigan and other areas over a period starting and ending in prosperous years and covering a span in which there were two recessions. This analysis should enable us to obtain a clearer perspective of growth occurring in Michigan's major industries over this period. We have not included 1957 data in the period chosen for analysis because of the drop in durable goods employment due to the recession starting in that year. Major changes occurring from 1956 to 1957 are discussed separately later in this section.

Let us first look at Michigan's performance compared with the nation and the East North Central States in major industries (two-digit Standard Industrial Classification industries). Table 20 presents statistics on total employment in the United States, East North Central States, and Michigan. When we look at total employment for all industries, we find that Michigan has grown at a much slower pace than the East North Central States and the nation. The picture changes, however, when we look at total employment for all industries exclusive of motor vehicles and equipment. In such a comparison we find that Michigan has experienced a somewhat faster rate of growth in employment than the East North Central region (14.5 compared to 11.7), but has grown at a somewhat slower pace than the United States in which employment has increased by 17.4 percent. These percentage increases are not far apart, however, and thus it appears that Michigan has kept pace with the nation and the East North Central region in employment growth rates in nonautomotive industries.

Trends in Nondurable Industries

Now let us look at what has happened in specific industries. Looking first at nondurable goods industries, we see that Michigan has experienced about the same rate of growth as the East North Central region and the United States in the pulp and paper industry and nearly the same rate of growth in the chemical industry. Both Mich-

Total Employment in Manufacturing Industries, United States, East North Central States, and Michigan[a]

1947 and 1956[b]

(Numbers in thousands)

Industry Group	United States			East North Central States			Michigan		
	1956	1947	Percent change	1956	1947	Percent change	1956	1947	Percent change
All industries...............	16,704.1	14,294.0	16.9	4,749.6	4,322.8	9.9	1,032.5	975.5	5.8
All industries except motor vehicles.........	15,965.1	13,600.2	17.4	4,220.5	3,776.8	11.7	693.2	605.4	14.5
Nondurable industries									
Food and kindred products.........	1,706.8	n.a.	n.a.	397.4	n.a.	n.a.	59.5	n.a.	n.a.
Pulp, paper and products.........	565.0	454.1	24.4	147.6	123.0	20.0	31.3	26.0	20.4
Printing and publishing.........	854.0	715.1	19.4	229.3	195.3	17.4	30.2	21.7	39.2
Chemicals and products.........	760.5	626.4	21.4	172.7	142.3	21.4	40.6	34.0	19.4
Petroleum and coal products.........	184.0	174.8	5.3	35.7	35.9	.6	2.8	3.5	— 20.0
Rubber products.........	265.0	258.2	2.6	115.6	124.4	— 7.1	13.5	15.1	— 10.6
Leather and leather goods.........	366.8	383.3	— 4.3	58.9	75.4	— 21.9	3.5	4.4	— 20.5
Durable industries									
Furniture and fixtures.........	376.4	316.3	19.0	108.0	108.9	— .8	21.8	21.5	1.4
Stone, clay and glass products.........	536.0	461.0	16.3	154.2	131.9	16.9	17.9	15.6	14.7
Primary metal industries.........	1,319.2	1,191.0	10.8	525.6	513.7	2.3	84.0	92.6	— 9.3
Fabricated metal products.........	1,101.8	973.2	13.2	439.4	407.8	7.7	102.5	92.3	11.1
Machinery (except electrical).........	1,717.7	1,552.1	10.7	812.6	764.9	6.2	173.4	150.6	15.1
Electrical machinery.........	1,081.4	796.4	35.8	396.2	328.2	20.7	25.7	22.5	14.2
Transporation equipment.........	1,791.7	1,174.5	52.6	720.9	628.1	14.8	368.0	377.3	— 2.5
Motor vehicles and equipment.........	739.0	693.8	6.5	c529.1	546.0	— 3.1	c339.3	370.1	— 8.3
Other transportation equipment.........	1,052.7	480.7	118.9	c191.8	82.1	133.6	c28.7	7.2	298.6
Instruments and related products.........	296.7	244.9	21.2	68.7	n.a.	n.a.	9.2	4.8	91.7

Source: For 1947: 1954 Census of Manufactures, Vol. III.
For 1956: 1956 Annual Survey of Manufactures, Series MAS-56-5.

a Data exclude administrative and auxiliary unit employment.
b 1956 data are Census estimates based on sample. Although information on total employment in all industries is subject to a small degree of error, industry totals are not as reliable.
c Estimate based on ratio of employment in motor vehicles and equipment to transportation equipment in 1954 made by Upjohn Institute.

igan and the East North Central region have experienced declining employment in petroleum and coal products and rubber products while the United States as a whole has made slight gains.

The decline in employment in petroleum and coal products in the East North Central region and Michigan undoubtedly reflects the lack of such resources in these areas. Employment in these industries in Michigan is, of course, relatively unimportant with fewer than 3,000 workers employed. The employment decline in the rubber products industry can not be so easily explained. It is interesting to note, however, that Ohio, which employs 64 percent of all rubber workers in the East North Central region, has experienced almost exactly the same percentage decline as Michigan (10.7 to 10.6). Apparently the same forces are at work in both areas. This may reflect decentralization such as has occurred in the motor vehicles and equipment industry.

In comparison with the larger areas, Michigan has experienced a significantly greater rate of growth in the printing and publishing industry, achieving a 39 percent increase compared with an increase of 17.4 percent for the East North Central States and of 19.4 percent for the nation. Although comparable information on food industries is not available for the period 1947-1956, it is available for the period 1947-1954, exclusive of dairy products. Census of Manufactures statistics for this period show that food industries in Michigan increased by 3.3 percent while food industries in the United States increased by 1.1 percent, and those in the East North Central region declined by 1 percent.

Michigan's over-all record in those nondurable goods industries for which information is available compares very well with the larger regions. Total employment in nondurable goods increased by 16.4 percent in Michigan compared with 14.7 percent for the nation and 9.1 percent for the East North Central region. Michigan's better over-all percentage increase in nondurable industries, however, is due almost entirely to the exceptional record made in the printing and publishing industry. The state's relative performance, industry by industry, is better only in this one industry.

The poorer showing by Michigan and the East North Central region in some nondurable industries can be explained in part by locational advantages of other areas for certain types of manufacturing, such as petroleum products and leather goods. It is significant to note that those nondurable industries in which Michigan has experienced declining employment are relatively unimportant to the

Michigan economy. The total number of jobs lost in petroleum and coal products, rubber products, and leather and leather goods industries amounts to just over 3,000.

Trends in Durable Industries

In durable industries, industries in which the East North Central region and Michigan specialize, the nation has consistently achieved greater growth rates than either the East North Central region or Michigan. In the furniture and fixtures industry, the nation has experienced a significant gain of 19 percent while the East North Central region has declined somewhat and Michigan has experienced a small gain. The nation as a whole also has outperformed the East North Central region and Michigan in primary metals, electrical machinery, and transportation equipment industries. The nation's growth rate in the fabricated metals industry is greater than either that of the East North Central region or Michigan, although Michigan's rate of growth in this industry is only slightly lower than that of the nation. Michigan has experienced a greater rate of growth than the nation in machinery (except electrical) (15.1 compared to 10.7), and in instruments and related products (91.7 compared to 21.2), although in the latter industry the total number of jobs provided in Michigan is small. Growth rates in stone, clay, and glass industries are nearly the same for all three areas.

In durable industries, Michigan has experienced better percentage increases than the East North Central region in furniture and fixtures, machinery (except electrical), and fabricated metal products. In stone, clay, and glass products, growth rates were about the same for both areas. In primary metal industries, however, Michigan employment decreased substantially (9.3 percent) while employment in the East North Central region made a slight gain. In electrical machinery, Michigan's employment gain was considerably below that of the East North Central States (14.2 compared to 20.7).

Michigan's over-all rate of growth in those durable goods industries outside of transportation equipment was 7.6 percent compared with 8.0 percent for the East North Central region. Although Michigan's over-all performance in durables was not impressive, its percentage increases in nonelectrical machinery and in fabricated metal products, its most important industries other than transportation equipment, were significantly better than percentage increases in the East North Central region. These two industries alone provided 58 percent of the new jobs (33,000 of 57,000) created in Michigan during the period 1947-1956.

185

Now let us consider reasons why the East North Central region and Michigan have grown at a slower rate than the nation in some of the important durable industries. If we look again at Table 20, we see that the highest industry growth rates for the nation were in transportation equipment and electrical machinery industries. Furthermore, these industries had the greatest increases in absolute employment for the period 1947-1956. The net gain in absolute employment in these two industries alone accounted for 37 percent of the net gain achieved in all industries. In contrast to this, growth rates in the East North Central region and Michigan were considerably less in these industries. In fact, in Michigan there were actually 9,000 fewer jobs in the transportation equipment industry in 1956 than in 1947.

The much more rapid growth of the nation in transportation equipment industries is primarily attributable to growth during this period in the aircraft and aircraft parts industries. And most of the major aircraft companies are located in the east, west, and southwest sections of the country, and therefore those areas have achieved larger employment gains than either the East North Central region or Michigan. Similar reasons account for the faster growth rate of the nation in the electrical machinery industry. Although the East North Central region has experienced a very good percentage increase (21 percent compared to 36 percent for the nation), the slower rate of growth is attributable to the fact that major companies producing radio and television sets, and transistors, as well as other dynamic growth products, are located principally in the East.

Michigan's record of growth for the period 1947-1956 is poor on an over-all basis because of the decline in motor vehicles and equipment; its record of growth for all industries exclusive of motor vehicles and equipment, however, is somewhat better than that of the East North Central region and is not much below that of the nation as a whole.

Major Employment Changes from 1956 to 1957

Manufacturing employment dropped more in the East North Central region and Michigan in 1957 than it did in the nation as a whole. For all industries, employment dropped only four-tenths of one percent in the United States while it dropped 1.5 percent in the East North Central region and 1.6 percent in Michigan. There was practically no change in over-all employment in nondurable goods industries between 1956 and 1957. The nation dropped three-tenths of one percent and the East North Central region and Michigan each dropped two-tenths of one percent in those industries for which comparable information was available.

The impact of the recession starting in 1957 was more severe in durable goods industries, especially in the East North Central region and in Michigan. Following is a tabulation showing the percentage change in employment from 1956 to 1957 in selected durable goods industries for the United States, the East North Central States, and Michigan.

Industry	United States	East North Central States	Michigan
Furniture and fixtures..................	−0.4	−3.6	−6.4
Stone, clay, and glass products.........	−1.9	−2.1	−4.5
Primary metals........................	−3.6	−4.7	−2.6
Fabricated metal products.............	1.1	.4	−.2
Machinery (except electrical)...........	−.6	−3.6	−4.7
Electrical machinery...................	.4	−2.4	−10.1
Transportation equipment.............	6.1	1.8	.1

Source: 1957 Annual Survey of Manufactures, Series MAS-57-4.

Obviously the impact of the recession in 1957 was greater on Michigan than on the other areas. Only in the primary metals industry was Michigan's decline less than the declines experienced by the nation and the East North Central region. In transportation equipment industries, Michigan employment remained stable while the East North Central region increased by 1.8 percent and the nation increased by 6.1 percent. The large increase in employment in the transportation equipment industry in the nation in 1957 reflects larger defense expenditures in the aircraft and missile industries in that year.

Trends in Growth Industries

THE BRIEF ANALYSIS of major industry groups presented earlier reveals that Michigan has obtained its share of increasing employment in all industries except motor vehicles for the period 1947-1956. There still are unanswered questions, however. First of all, what are Michigan's strengths and weaknesses within these major industry groups? In which industries are we growing faster than nearby states? In which are we declining? Are we doing as well as other areas in those industries which look most promising in the years ahead?

The Office of Area Development of the U. S. Department of Commerce has published statistics on individual growth industries in the United States. These statistics are for individual four-digit Standard Industrial Classification industries which are components of the larger two-digit industries presented above. Unfortunately, these detailed statistics are available only for the period 1947-1954. They are invaluable, however, because they show trends in the more promising industries. A growth industry is defined by the Office of Area Development as any (four-digit S.I.C.) industry in which employment increased by more than 20 percent for this seven-year period. Altogether there were 106 individual industries (out of a total of 445 four-digit S.I.C. industries) in the United States in which employment increased by 20 percent or more during this period. Now let us compare trends in these growth industries in Michigan with trends in similar industries in other areas.

Over-All Comparisons

There are many ways in which comparisons can be made to obtain a picture of Michigan's growth relative to the United States and the East North Central States. First of all we might compare Michigan, the East North Central States, and the United States on total number of growth industries. In how many of these industries has Michigan grown at a faster rate than the East North Central region and the United States? There are 63 growth industries for which comparable data are available. In the following tabulation we make a comparison of percentage increase in employment in growth industries for the United States, East North Central States, and Michigan, for the period 1947-1954.

Area	Number of Growth Industries in Which Percentage Increase Was —		
	Highest	Next Highest	Third Highest
Total..	63	63	63
United States.............................	22	22	19
East North Central States..................	9	34	20
Michigan....................................	32	7	24

Source: U. S. Department of Commerce, Office of Area Development, *Industry Trend Series,* Nos. 2-15, 1957.

We find that Michigan has achieved the highest percentage increases in significantly more growth industries than either the nation or the East North Central region. On the other hand, Michigan has obtained the lowest percentage increases in somewhat more industries. All growth industries considered, however, Michigan must be given somewhat of an edge on the basis of the significantly larger number of industries which increased at a faster rate than similar industries in the East North Central region and the nation.

Although Michigan shows up somewhat better than the East North Central region as a whole in the above comparisons, it is still possible that one or two states within the East North Central region are doing significantly better than Michigan in these growth industries. To determine how Michigan compares with other nearby states, we have compared Michigan with each of the East North Central states on the basis of percent increase in employment in 65 growth industries for which comparable data are available for the period 1947-1954. The tabulation below shows this comparison.

| State | Number of Growth Industries In Which State Ranked — | |
	First in percent increase	Second in percent increase
Totals..	°74	65
Illinois...	7	15
Indiana..	17	9
Ohio...	17	10
Michigan...	17	22
Wisconsin..	16	9

Source: U. S. Department of Commerce, Office of Area Development, *Industry Trend Series,* Nos. 2-15, 1957.

a *Totals add up to more than the total number of growth industries because ties were counted at full value.*

Michigan's better record shows up clearly. It ranked first 17 times along with Ohio and Indiana, with Wisconsin very close, ranking first 16 times. Michigan, however, ranked second significantly more times than any other state. Obviously, Michigan in comparison with nearby states was doing well and without a doubt had been increasing its share of total employment in the majority of growth industries for the period 1947-1954.

To be sure of Michigan's relative position among the East North Central States in growth industries, there is still one other comparison that we must make. Many of the growth industries are small in terms of the number of persons employed. Although many of these may be exceedingly important in a few years, it is possible that Michigan could have outgained other nearby states in many small growth industries and yet could have lost ground in some important ones in which employment is large. For this reason let us now take a closer look at some of these more important growth industries.

In the following pages we shall compare Michigan with other areas in the larger growth industries in the East North Central region.[2] In addition to these larger growth industries, we shall look at some others which seem to have special promise for Michigan. By selecting the largest growth industries in the East North Central region, we shall be obtaining information on a group for which Michigan should have locational advantages. If Michigan is not growing as fast as the region in these larger growth industries, we should attempt to find out why and correct weaknesses, if any. If the state is doing better than the region as a whole in any of these industries, we should attempt to find out why and exploit whatever advantages we may possess. By comparing Michigan and the East North Central region with other areas which provide a significant number of jobs in these industries, we shall learn whether other areas are gaining at the expense of the East North Central region and Michigan.

Chart II shows the various geographic regions of the United States as defined by the Bureau of the Census. In the following analysis we shall compare growth industries in the leading geographic regions, Michigan, and the United States on the basis of absolute employment and rate of growth. Blank spaces in the tables that follow indicate that the region is not important in the particular industry involved.

Growth Industries in the Machinery (Except Electrical) Industry

Table 21 shows information on growth industries in the machinery (except electrical) industry for selected areas and the United States. First of all, this table shows the dominance of the East North Central region in these growth industries. In each one of these industries except computers the East North Central region employs more people than any other region. In computers and related machines the Middle Atlantic region provides more jobs than any other area; in fact, it provides jobs for almost as many people as the East North Central and West North Central regions combined.

A study of this table also shows Michigan's importance within the East North Central region. Within this region Michigan provides more than half of all jobs in special dies and tools and metalworking machinery attachments (statistics of these two industries were combined by the Office of Area Development); more than one-third of all jobs in machine shops; nearly one-third of all jobs in industrial patterns and molds; and more than one-quarter of all jobs in the conveyors industry. Although information on number of workers in the computers industry is not available for the East North Central region,

---

2 In order to compare Michigan with other areas on an impartial basis, and at the same time cover industries for which Michigan should possess locational advantages, we have selected from the industries which grew 20 percent or more in the nation, 1947-1954, those 25 which were the largest in the East North Central region in 1954.

Chart II. REGIONS AND GEOGRAPHIC DIVISIONS OF THE UNITED STATES

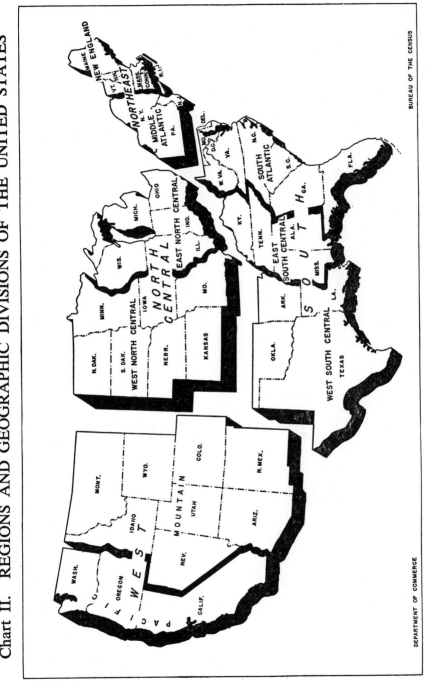

DEPARTMENT OF COMMERCE

BUREAU OF THE CENSUS

Table 21

Employment and Percent Change in Employment in 1954 from 1947 in Growth Industries in Machinery (Except Electrical) for the United States, Leading Regions, and Michigan

(Numbers in thousands)

Growth Industry	United States		New England States		Middle Atlantic States		West North Central States		East North Central States		Michigan	
	Employ-ment 1954	Percent change 1947-54	Employ-ment 1954	Percent change 1947-54	Employ-ment 1954	Percent change 1947-54	Employ-ment 1954	Percent change 1947-54	Employ-ment 1954	Percent change 1947-54	Employ-ment 1954	Percent change 1947-54
Conveyors............	32.4	32.0	...	...	5.8	64.0	2.7	105.0	19.2	16.0	5.2	62.0
Computing and related machines..........	56.7	24.0	3.4	ᵃ45.0	22.6	ᵃ45.0	...	...	ᵇ25.4	ᵇ4.0	ᶜ5.0-10.0	ᵃ0
Industrial patterns and molds..........	19.9	106.0	2.1	61.0	3.7	97.0	...	...	11.6	126.0	3.8	108.0
Machine shops..........	103.7	66.0	8.0	67.0	20.2	61.0	8.7	-3.0	39.8	53.0	13.6	36.0
Special dies and tools and metalworking machinery attachments...	122.3	38.0	18.9	5.0	18.6	50.0	...	...	74.5	36.0	41.3	71.0

Source: U. S. Department of Commerce, Office of Area Development, Growth Industries in Machinery, Industry Trend Series No. 5, October, 1957.

ᵃ Approximate figure; actual figures withheld to avoid disclosing figures of individual companies.
ᵇ Figures apply to North Central Region.
ᶜ Indicates range of employment for area; actual number not given to avoid disclosing figures of individual companies.

Michigan provides at least one-fifth of all jobs in computing and related machines for the entire North Central Region, an area including 12 states.

Not only does Michigan have an important position in all these industries, but growth rates compare favorably with other areas in most of them. In special dies and tools and metalworking machinery attachments, and conveyors industries, Michigan has grown at significantly faster rates than either the East North Central region or the United States. In industrial patterns and molds Michigan has grown at about the same pace as the East North Central States and the United States. Only in machine shop industries has Michigan grown at a significantly slower pace than these other areas.

Further evidence of Michigan's strong position in machinery industries is shown by employment increases of more than 20 percent for some industries which have not increased by this percentage rate at the national level. The following tabulation presents information on three such industries for the United States, East North Central region, and Michigan.

Industry	Employment 1954 (thousands)			Percent Change 1947-1954		
	United States	East North Central States	Michigan	United States	East North Central States	Michigan
Ball and roller bearings............	49.7	n.a.	4.1	−4.8	n.a.	29.6
Food products machinery...........	33.2	16.1	3.1	−10.0	11.0	434.2
Pumps and compressors........	60.3	23.2	4.9	7.5	6.4	86.8

Source: *1954 Census of Manufactures,* Vol. III.

First of all, we note the East North Central region's strong position in these industries. The East North Central region provides employment for nearly half of all workers in food products machinery industries and more than a third of all workers in the pumps and compressors industries. Michigan compares especially well with the larger areas, showing percentage increases much above those of the East North Central region, while the nation experienced declines in two of the three industries. Michigan's employment increase in food products machinery was remarkable, advancing from less than 600 employees to more than 3,000.

In these growth industries in the machinery (except electrical) industries, then, Michigan's record has been good. Since the future prospects for most machinery industries are bright because of the

Table 22

Employment and Percent Change in Employment in 1954 from 1947 in Growth Industries in Fabricated Metal Products for the United States, Leading Regions, and Michigan

(Numbers in thousands)

Growth Industry	United States		New England States		Middle Atlantic States		East North Central States		Michigan		South Atlantic States		Pacific States	
	Employment 1954	Percent change 1947-54	Employment 1954	Percent change 1947-54	Employment 1954	Percent change 1947-54	Employment 1954	Percent change 1947-54	Employment 1954	Percent change 1947-54	Employment 1954	Percent change 1947-54	Employment 1954	Percent change 1947-54
Structural and ornamental work..........	116.3	47.0	...	...	33.7	41.0	29.4	39.0	6.3	72.0	9.3	49.0	11.3	64.0
Metal doors, sash, and trim..............	43.3	85.0	...	...	13.2	93.0	16.9	38.0	6.0	97.0	3.9	442.0	3.2	a100.0
Plating and polishing..	36.1	26.0	4.2	23.0	8.8	40.0	15.9	6.0	4.8	-14.0	...	...	4.3	97.0
Screw machine products.............	35.0	22.0	5.8	32.0	5.7	30.0	18.7	5.0	5.1	20.0	...	...	b2.5	b124.0

Source: U. S. Department of Commerce, Office of Area Development, *Growth Industries in Fabricated Metal Products, Industry Trend Series No. 4,* September, 1957.

a Approximate figure; actual figures withheld to avoid disclosing figures of individual companies.
b California only.

increasing emphasis placed on automatic and cost reduction machinery, it appears that expansion should continue in the growth industries in machinery (except electrical) as well as in other individual industries in this group. Good long-range prospects in machinery industries enhance Michigan's future economic picture as this major group is Michigan's second largest industry.

Growth Industries in Fabricated Metal Products

Table 22 presents information on growth industries in the fabricated metal products industry for leading geographic regions. With one exception, we find that the East North Central region employs more people in each of these growth industries than any other region. The one exception is the structural and ornamental work industry in which the Middle Atlantic region employs approximately 4,000 more workers than the East North Central region. The two regions together, however, employ more than half of the total workers in this industry in the United States.

The Pacific and South Atlantic regions are among the four leading geographic areas in these metal fabricating growth industries. They are much less important than the East North Central and Middle Atlantic regions, however, and are primarily important in industries which are, to some extent, ubiquitous, such as individual industry metal doors, sash, and trim.

Table 22 also reveals the important place of Michigan factories within the East North Central region as employers in fabricated metal products growth industries. Michigan factories employ more than one-third of all workers in individual industry metal doors, sash, and trim, and nearly one-third of all workers in the plating and polishing industry, and more than one-fourth of all workers in screw machine products industries. In rates of increase Michigan compares favorably in the structural and ornamental work and in metal doors, sash, and trim industries. In screw machine products Michigan grew at about the same pace as the East North Central region. In the plating and polishing industry Michigan employment declined 14 percent, whereas there was a 6 percent increase in the East North Central region.

There are two industries in fabricated metal products which did not meet the criterion of growth industry on the national level, but which did meet this criterion in Michigan. These are bolts, nuts, washers, and rivets; and hardware, not elsewhere classified. Information on them is presented in the following table.

| Industry | Employment 1954 (thousands) | | | Percent Change 1947-1954 | | |
	United States	East North Central States	Michigan	United States	East North Central States	Michigan
Bolts, nuts, washers, and rivets...........	53.7	27.5	4.6	9.1	12.7	26.1
Hardware, n.e.c.......	88.3	45.0	21.7	13.9	24.0	29.4

Source: *1954 Census of Manufactures*, Vol. III.

Again we see that the East North Central region employs a significant percentage of total workers in these industries in the nation. It employs more than half of all workers in the United States, in both industries.

Michigan employs less than 20 percent of all workers in the bolts, nuts, washers, and rivets industry, but nearly 50 percent of all workers in the hardware, n.e.c., industry in the East North Central region (nearly 25 percent of all workers in the nation). Michigan has grown at a faster pace than the East North Central region and the nation in both industries.

Thus, we find that Michigan has more than kept pace with the East North Central region and the United States in providing new jobs in fabricated metal products growth industries. This is significant because major industry fabricated metal products constitutes Michigan's third largest industry.

Growth Industries in Transportation Equipment

Let us now compare Michigan's experience relative to other areas in the transportation equipment industries. Growth industries in this group are especially important because, nationally, they have provided more jobs and have increased at a faster rate than any other industry during the period 1947-1956, as well as 1947-1954, the period which we are considering here. Statistics on this industry are presented in Table 23. Geographic regions are combined in this table because figures for smaller areas are not available. First of all, we note that all of the larger growth industries in the transportation equipment group are in aircraft and related industries. Therefore it is not surprising to find that the West (the Mountain and Pacific regions) provides more jobs in aircraft manufacturing than any other region in the country. What is surprising, considering the location of major aircraft companies, is the large employment of the North

196

Table 23

Employment and Percent Change in Employment in 1954 from 1947 in Growth Industries in Transportation Equipment for the United States, Leading Regions, and Michigan

(Numbers in thousands)

Growth Industry	United States		North East Region		North Central Region		Michigan		South Region		West Region	
	Employment 1954	Percent change 1947-54	Employment 1954	Percent change 1947-54	Employment 1954	Percent change 1947-54	Employment 1954	Percent change 1947-54	Employment 1954	Percent change 1947-54	Employment 1954	Percent change 1947-54
Aircraft..............	457.6	212.0	62.6	159.0	74.2	474.0	[a].3-.5	n.a.	100.6	241.0	220.3	175.0
Aircraft engines............	167.4	232.0	86.5	195.5	75.9	292.0	7.9	1,650.0	[b].5-1.0	[c]1,000.0	[d]4.2	[d]135.0
Aircraft equipment, n.e.c..............	180.9	1,095.0	[a]39.4-45.1	n.a.	76.6	[c]1,000.0	over 10.0	[c]1,000.0	...	...	[d]48.7	[d]480.0
Aircraft propellers............	16.5	123.0	11.7	n.a.	4.8	n.a.	[a]1.0-2.5	n.a.	...	...	...	...

Source: U. S. Department of Commerce, Office of Area Development, *Growth Industries in Transportation Equipment, Industry Trend Series No. 7,* November, 1957.

[a] Indicates range of employment for area; actual figures withheld to avoid disclosing figures of individual companies.
[b] Texas only.
[c] Approximate figure; actual figures withheld to avoid disclosing information on individual companies.
[d] California only.

Central region in the aircraft parts industries, especially in aircraft engines, aircraft propellers, and aircraft equipment, n.e.c. The Northeast Region leads in employment in aircraft engines and aircraft propellers, while the North Central Region leads all other areas in employment in aircraft equipment, n.e.c., industries. Especially noteworthy is the rate of increase of the growth industries in the aircraft group. In general, the aircraft and aircraft engine industries have grown at a faster pace in the North Central Region than in the other areas or in the nation as a whole. An exception is the South which experienced a large percentage increase on a small amount of employment in the aircraft engines industry.

Although Michigan has a negligible number of workers in aircraft manufacturing, it has shared in the growth of employment in the other aircraft equipment industries. Michigan's growth in aircraft engines and aircraft equipment, n.e.c., has been phenomenal. In aircraft engines, employment increased from 450 workers in 1947 to approximately 8,000 workers in 1954. In aircraft equipment, n.e.c., employment increased from 500 workers to over 10,000 workers. Although these absolute increases are tremendous, Ohio and Indiana have experienced even larger absolute increases in the two industries combined.

Even though there have been substantial employment reductions in the nation and in Michigan since 1954 in certain aircraft industries such as aircraft engines, and aircraft propellers, Michigan's growth in these industries has been an important development not only because it is still an important defense industry, but also because many of the companies producing aircraft parts and controls have shifted to production of parts and controls for the missiles industry which certainly promises to be one of the important defense industries of the future. Michigan's many resources such as skilled manpower and managerial know-how in the machinery field provide an opportunity for Michigan manufacturers to share in the growth in hydraulic controls and other parts and in instruments for defense and industrial applications.

Growth Industries in Electrical Machinery

Employment in growth industries in major industry electrical machinery is concentrated in the manufacturing belt. Statistics for leading areas are presented in Table 24. The Middle Atlantic region employs more than one-third of the nation's workers in both electrical measuring instruments and radios and related products. This region

Table 24

Employment and Percent Change in Employment in 1954 from 1947 in Growth Industries in Electrical Machinery for the United States, Leading Regions, and Michigan

(Numbers in thousands)

Growth Industry	United States		New England States		Middle Atlantic States		East North Central States		Michigan		South Region		West Region	
	Employ- ment 1954	Percent change 1947-54	Employ- ment 1954	Percent change 1947-54	Employ- ment 1954	Percent change 1947-54	Employ- ment 1954	Percent change 1947-54	Employ- ment 1954	Percent change 1947-54	Employ- ment 1954	Percent change 1947-54	Employ- ment 1954	Percent change 1947-54
Radios and related products........	294.0	65.0	27.1	51.0	108.4	56.0	96.4	27.0	4.7	—7.0	24.0	178.0	25.1	627.0
Electronic tubes.........	71.0	156.0	14.9	a270.0	33.8	84.0	a10.8	a300.0	b.3-.5	a1,000.0	8.0	a300.0	2.4	a300.0
Electrical measuring instruments...........	33.0	58.0	8.7	44.0	12.0	60.0	7.8	17.0	b.5-1.0	a100.0	...	...	3.5	a700.0

Source: U. S. Department of Commerce, Office of Area Development, *Growth Industries in Electrical Machinery*, Industry Trend Series No. 3, September, 1957.

a Approximate figures; actual figures withheld to avoid disclosing information on individual companies.
b Indicates range of employment; actual figures withheld to avoid disclosing figures of individual companies.

also employs more than 48 percent of all workers in the electronic tubes industry. Not only does the Middle Atlantic region lead all other areas by a good margin in growth industries in electrical machinery in terms of absolute employment, but it also has experienced very good percentage increases considering its position of leadership in these industries.

The East North Central region is the second most important geographic region in terms of jobs provided in electrical machinery growth industries. Growth rates in these industries with the exception of electronic tubes, however, are considerably below those of the Middle Atlantic States and the nation as a whole. The East North Central region employs about 15 percent of total workers in the electronic tubes industry and its growth rate has been nearly double that of the nation.

The South and West are improving their positions in electrical machinery growth industries, but are far below other areas in number of workers employed.

Although Michigan growth rates in these industries compare favorably except in radios and related products, total employment is small in all industries. In radios and related products, Michigan has experienced a slight decline in employment while other areas have shown healthy gains.

Michigan's poor showing in electrical machinery growth industries is unfortunate because there is currently tremendous growth in these industries. Radios and related products constitute the largest growth industry in the East North Central region and the second largest in the nation. And this industry promises to be one of the fastest growing industries in the years ahead because it includes a number of products which are becoming increasingly important in military as well as civilian applications. In addition to radios and television sets, products in this industry include electronic phonographs and record players, commercial radio and television communications, radio and electronic navigation aids, radar equipment, and many others.

The electronic tubes industry is one of the larger growth industries in the nation and in the East North Central region. It, too, is growing at a fast pace as more and more uses are found for transistors.

The relatively good showing of the East North Central region in electrical machinery (both in the major industry and in specific growth industries) indicates that locational factors for the attraction of such industries may be favorable. Michigan development groups should aggressively attempt to obtain for the state a larger share of future job increases in this industry than they have obtained in the past.

Growth Industries in Chemicals

Table 25 presents information on growth industries in chemical manufacturing. Although there are ten growth industries in chemical manufacturing, there are only five which provide employment for more than 20,000 workers nationally. Although only two of these industries meet our criterion for selection here (i.e., the larger industries in the East North Central region), we shall look at all five because of the promising growth prospects of chemical industries nationally.

Table 25 reveals that the South assumes an important position in growth industries in chemical manufacturing. Chemical manufacturing plants in the South employ more than half of all workers in the inorganic chemicals, n.e.c., and organic chemicals, n.e.c., industries. In plastics materials, explosives, and chemical products, n.e.c., industries, however, the Northeast and North Central Regions dominate. These areas provide more than two-thirds of all jobs in plastics materials, four-fifths of all jobs in chemical products, n.e.c., and more than half of all jobs in the explosives industries. The Middle Atlantic region alone provides more than 40 percent of all jobs in the entire plastics materials industry for the United States.

The pattern of expansion in chemical growth industries is therefore well dispersed throughout the country. The South, Northeast, and North Central Regions are all important producers in the chemical growth industries examined here. Growth rates in the individual industries vary a good deal by geographic regions also. The South grew at the fastest pace in the inorganic chemicals, n.e.c., and chemical products, n.e.c., industries; the North Central Region grew at the fastest pace in plastics materials and explosives industries; and the Northeast section of the country grew at the fastest pace in organic chemicals, n.e.c., industry.

The North Central Region appears to be doing as well as other areas in chemical growth industries. And Michigan figures importantly in chemicals manufacturing growth industries in the North Central Region. Michigan factories employed 35 percent of all workers in plastics materials, 28 percent of all workers in organic chemicals, n.e.c., and nearly 14 percent in the inorganic chemicals, n.e.c., industry. If we look again at Table 20, we see that employment in all chemicals industries in the East North Central region and Michigan grew at about the same rate as in the nation. Although

201

Table 25

Employment and Percent Change in Employment in 1954 from 1947 in Growth Industries in
Chemicals for the United States, Leading Regions, and Michigan

(Numbers in thousands)

Growth Industry	United States		North East Region		North Central Region		Michigan		South Region	
	Employ-ment 1954	Percent change 1947-54	Employ-ment 1954	Percent change 1947-54	Employ-ment 1954	Percent change 1947-54	Employ-ment 1954	Percent change 1947-54	Employ-ment 1954	Percent change 1947-54
Inorganic chemicals, n.e.c........	97.0	146.0	9.6	-9.0	17.6	48.0	2.4	n.a.	48.9	278.0
Plastics materials..........	41.1	44.0	21.5	16.8	7.1	154.0	2.5	115.0	11.6	67.0
Explosives..........	32.5	211.0	4.9	-23.0	16.5	800.0	^{a}.1-.3	n.a.	9.5	n.a.
Organic chemicals, n.e.c.........	67.5	30.0	22.2	49.0	8.0	35.0	2.2	n.a.	35.7	n.a.
Chemical products, n.e.c.........	21.4	21.0	8.3	7.8	8.8	22.2	.6	-46.0	2.7	68.8

Source: U. S. Department of Commerce, Office of Area Development, *Growth Industries in Chemicals, Petroleum, Coal, and Rubber*, Industry Trend Series No. 10, December, 1957.

^{a} *Indicates range of employment for area; actual figures withheld to avoid disclosing figures of individual companies.*

Table 26

Employment and Percent Change in Employment in 1954 from 1947 in Growth Industries in Pulp and Paper Products for the United States, Leading Regions, and Michigan

(Numbers in thousands)

Growth Industry	United States		New England States		Middle Atlantic States		East North Central States		Michigan		South Region	
	Employ-ment 1954	Percent change 1947-54	Employ-ment 1954	Percent change 1947-54	Employ-ment 1954	Percent change 1947-54	Employ-ment 1954	Percent change 1947-54	Employ-ment 1954	Percent change 1947-54	Employ-ment 1954	Percent change 1947-54
Paper coating and glazing...........	27.7	25.0	4.2	−9.0	5.0	37.0	10.4	46.0	3.2	11.0	.6	72.0
Paperboard boxes..........	133.0	21.0	13.7	12.0	41.6	10.0	38.6	25.0	6.1	58.0	21.6	52.0

Source: U. S. Department of Commerce, Office of Area Development, *Growth Industries in Pulp and Paper Products*, Industry Trend Series No. 12, December, 1957.

Michigan may not be able to match national growth in the years ahead because of the burgeoning growth in petrochemicals in the South and West, it should continue to show healthy growth. Its natural resources such as water supply and huge reserves of salt, as well as its nearness to industrial and consumer markets, should result in continued employment expansion in this industry.

Growth Industries in Paper and Allied Products

In the larger growth industries in the pulp and paper products industry we find again that the states of the manufacturing belt, particularly the East North Central and Middle Atlantic regions, dominate in numbers of jobs provided. Table 26 shows statistics on the two larger growth industries in this group. This table reveals that the East North Central region provides nearly 38 percent of the nation's jobs in paper coating and glazing and approximately 29 percent of the nation's jobs in the paperboard boxes industry. Moreover, the East North Central region has experienced faster growth in these industries than any other area except the South, or the nation as a whole. Michigan has not grown as fast as the East North Central region in paper coating and glazing but has achieved a greater rate of growth in paperboard boxes, which is the larger of the two industries.

There are five smaller growth industries in paper and allied products which are not covered here. All five account for only 75,000 jobs nationally. In three of these, information is not available for Michigan. In the other two, Michigan compares favorably with other states both in terms of absolute employment and percentage increases.

The favorable record of the East North Central region and Michigan in paper industries suggests that there are locational advantages present for these industries. Although there has been a trend for integrated paper mills to be built in the South, the market advantages enjoyed by the East North Central region, coupled with sources of pulp available by water transportation from Canada, and waste paper from the larger cities, undoubtedly have been major factors responsible for this favorable growth. In addition, Michigan's huge reserves of hardwood forests are being increasingly utilized by pulp and paper mills, and this trend should continue.

Although the effect on growth in the paper industry of action by the Michigan Water Resources Commission to reduce pollution needs to be studied further, it appears at this time that such action

Employment and Percent Change in Employment in 1954 from 1947 in Miscellaneous Growth Industries for the United States, Leading Regions, and Michigan

(Numbers in thousands)

Growth Industry	United States		Middle Atlantic States		East North Central States		Michigan		West North Central States		South Atlantic States		Pacific States	
	Employ-ment 1954	Percent change 1947-54	Employ-ment 1954	Percent change 1947-54	Employ-ment 1954	Percent change 1947-54	Employ-ment 1954	Percent change 1947-54	Employ-ment 1954	Percent change 1947-54	Employ-ment 1954	Percent change 1947-54	Employ-ment 1954	Percent change 1947-54
Newspapers.............	281.8	20.0	61.9	9.0	63.5	25.0	11.7	30.0	28.2	15.0	31.9	29.0	33.8	28.0
Lithographing.............	77.7	48.0	23.5	33.0	24.6	63.0	2.5	75.0	6.9	−8.0	4.9	108.0	7.9	95.0
Scientific instruments...	45.3	146.0	20.2	67.0	8.4	198.0	a2.5-4.9	b2,000.0	6.9	3,800.0	n.a.	n.a.	3.4	133.0
Mechanical measuring instruments.............	69.4	14.7	22.2	3.7	19.5	12.7	3.4	54.5	7.9	n.a.	n.a.	n.a.	6.1	n.a.
Upholstered household furniture.............	56.0	25.0	10.0	22.0	13.3	10.0	2.1	−8.0	...	...	10.9	31.0	6.2	21.0
Metal household furniture.............	29.6	51.0	7.7	71.0	13.1	b20.0	1.2	72.0	...	...	2.3	b100.0	2.2	150.0
Fluid milk only and fluid milk and other dairy products.............	191.4	28.0	39.5	n.a.	43.0	n.a.	8.2	n.a.	18.7	n.a.	...	...	...	...
Food preparation, n.e.c.............	72.0	21.0	17.3	39.0	14.8	13.0	2.2	42.0	8.7	−15.0	...	...	8.2	38.0
Concrete products......	60.4	29.0	10.2	37.0	13.6	38.0	3.4	37.0	6.1	35.0	12.0	35.0	...	...
Plastics products, n.e.c.c.............	92.0	58.0	29.8	48.0	29.9	64.0	3.2	126.0	2.4	107.0	...	...	...	...
Blast furnaces and steel mills.............	518.7	−3.2	d208.2	d−7.2	d206.5	d−1.0	18.9	21.2	...	...	45.5	n.a.	n.a.	n.a.
Cereal breakfast foods..	11.5	1.8	n.a.	n.a.	7.1	6.0	6.1	27.1	2.8	21.7	n.a.	n.a.	n.a.	n.a.

Source: U. S. Department of Commerce, Office of Area Development, Growth Industries in Manufacturing. Industry Trend Series Nos. 2, 6, 8, 9, 11, and 13, 1957; and 1954 Census of Manufactures, Vol. III.

a Indicates range of employment for area; actual figures withheld to avoid disclosing figures of individual companies.
b Approximate figure; actual figure withheld to avoid disclosing figures of individual companies.
c New England is the third most important geographic region with employment of 16,400 workers.
d Figures are for three-digit industry because the four-digit industry figures are not available; three-digit industry figures are used because the two classifications are nearly the same.

will not greatly retard growth. For example, there were substantial additions to new plant in the paper industry in Michigan in 1958. This suggests that manufacturers, at least in some parts of the paper industry, can solve the pollution problem and still compete with industries located in other states. And, of course, pollution control measures would retard growth in Michigan only to the extent that the state demands more effective control of pollution than other nearby states. Although the degree of control exercised by other states has not been studied intensively in connection with the present report, it is known that other nearby states are pushing ahead with pollution control measures.

Other Growth Industries

Table 27 presents information on several important growth industries. They are grouped together here because not more than two are from any one major industry group. The first two industries listed, newspapers and lithographing, are growth industries within the printing and publishing industry. The figures again reveal the dominant position of the Middle Atlantic and East North Central regions. This no doubt reflects the large concentrations of population as well as high population growth rates in these areas and increasing advertising expenditures by manufacturers to reach these mass markets. In these industries Michigan is growing at a somewhat faster pace than either the East North Central region or the nation.

In the two industries, scientific instruments and mechanical measuring instruments, the Middle Atlantic region is most important, with the East North Central region ranking second in importance in these industries. The two regions together provide about 60 percent of all jobs in each industry. In terms of growth rates, the East North Central region and Michigan compare favorably with other regions and the nation as a whole in both industries. It is of interest to note that growth products in the scientific instruments industry were aircraft flight instruments and automatic pilots. The fastest growing products in the mechanical measuring instruments industry included aircraft engine instruments and automatic temperature controls. Thus, much of the growth in these industries was tied to the aircraft, and aircraft parts industries.

The two growth industries, metal household furniture and upholstered household furniture, are industries in which the East North Central region ranks number one among all areas in terms of the total volume of employment. Growth rates in the East North Central region, however, have been below those of many other areas and the nation in both industries. Employment in Michigan has declined in the upholstered household furniture industry, but in metal household furniture the state's employment has increased at a somewhat faster rate than the East North Central region and the United States.

Although comparable information is not available for the fluid milk only, and the fluid milk and other dairy products, growth industries, we find that Michigan employment is approximately 20 percent of East North Central employment in these industries. Of the remaining growth industries in Table 27, concrete products, food preparations, n.e.c., and plastics products, n.e.c., all show favorable growth trends in Michigan compared with other areas but are rather unimportant in Michigan, with the exception of the concrete products industry. Michigan employment in the concrete products industry is 25 percent of the total employment in this industry in the East North Central region. The plastics products, n.e.c., industry will undoubtedly grow extremely fast in the years ahead as it has in the past, and should be emphasized by area development groups. Michigan employment in this industry was only 10 percent of total employment in the East North Central region for the period 1947-1954, but increased at a much faster pace than the area as a whole.

There are two other industries which have increased by more than 20 percent in Michigan, while showing lower growth rates or declining employment in the nation. These are cereal breakfast foods, and blast furnaces and steel mills. Both look very strong in the East North Central region and Michigan compared with other areas. Michigan factories employ more than 50 percent of all workers in the nation in the cereal breakfast food industry. In blast furnaces and steel mills, Michigan showed a healthy gain in employment, while all other areas showed actual declines in employment.

To summarize Michigan's strengths and weaknesses in growth industries, we are listing in Table 28 some of the more important industries covered in the above analysis. To highlight Michigan's experience relative to that of the East North Central region we have determined Michigan's share of employment in each growth industry and its net gain or loss in employment from its share.[3] Industries were selected on the basis of largest net gain in absolute employment in the East North Central region. However, in Table 28 only those industries are shown in which Michigan's actual net gain or loss from

---

3 Michigan's experience relative to the United States was analyzed also, but results were similar, so the table is not shown here.

Table 28

Comparison of Michigan's Actual Net Gain in Employment in Growth Industries with Michigan's Theoretical Share of Net Gain in the East North Central States

1947-1954

(Numbers in thousands)

Growth Industry[a]	Net Gain in Employment, 1947-1954		Michigan's Theoretical Share[b]	Amount by Which Michigan Differed from Theoretical Share
	East North Central States	Michigan		
Special dies and tools, and metalworking machinery attachments................	19.8	17.2	4.1	13.1
Blast furnaces and steel mills.....	− 2.1	3.3	− .4	3.7
Hardware, n.e.c...................	8.7	4.9	1.8	3.1
Food products machinery........	1.6	2.5	.3	2.2
Pumps and compressors........	1.4	2.3	.3	2.0
Metal doors, sash, and trim.......	4.7	3.0	1.0	2.0
Conveyors......................	2.7	2.0	.6	1.4
Cereal breakfast foods...........	.4	1.3	.1	1.2
Scientific instruments...........	5.6	[c]2.4−4.9	1.2	1.2
Structural and ornamental work..	8.3	2.6	1.7	.9
Machine shops..................	13.8	3.6	2.9	.7
Plastics materials...............	[d]4.3	1.3	.6	.7
Mechanical measuring instruments....................	2.2	1.2	.5	.7
Screw machine products.........	.9	.9	.2	.7
Paperboard products...........	7.7	2.3	1.6	.7
Industrial patterns and molds....	6.4	1.9	1.3	.6
Plastic products, n.e.c...........	11.7	1.8	2.4	− .6
Lithographing....................	9.5	1.1	2.0	− .9
Plating and polishing............	1.0	− .8	.2	− 1.0
Aircraft equipment, n.e.c........	[c]55.0	[c]9.5	11.4	− 1.9
Aircraft engines..................	48.9	7.4	10.2	− 2.8
Radios and related products......	20.5	− .4	4.3	− 4.7

Source: U. S. Department of Commerce, Office of Area Development, *Growth Industries in Manufacturing,* Industry Trend Series, Nos. 2-15, 1957.

a *Arranged from high to low according to difference between actual gain and theoretical share (column 4).*
b *Based on ratio of Michigan population to East North Central States population in 1947.*
c *Approximate figures; actual figures withheld to avoid disclosing figures of individual firms.*
d *Figure is for North Central Region, not East North Central States, and Michigan's share is based on ratio of Michigan population to that of the North Central Region in 1947.*

its share was 600 or more workers. Michigan's share is based on the ratio of population in Michigan to population in the East North Central States in 1947. Michigan's population in 1947 was 6,076,-000 compared with 29,151,000 for the East North Central States. The ratio is thus .208.

Although this concept of Michigan's share of employment in growth industries has some obvious limitations (e.g., expansion of some growth industries may have little or nothing to do with a state's population growth), it does have the advantage of taking into account the size of the state. Thus, Michigan's share of employment in any growth industry would be greater than that of Indiana or Wisconsin, but smaller than that of Illinois or Ohio.

As we study Table 28, we notice immediately that Michigan has gained more than its share of jobs in the majority of the more important growth industries. In fact, Michigan has gained more than its share in 16 of the 22 growth industries covered in this table. Three of the six industries in which Michigan has not performed as well as the East North Central States, however, are very important ones because they are in the aircraft, aircraft parts and equipment, and electrical equipment industries in which there is currently much growth. There have been substantial employment gains in aircraft parts and equipment industries in Michigan, however, even though Michigan has not obtained its share in these industries.

There are only two of the more important growth industries in which Michigan experienced actual job losses. These are radios and related products and plating and polishing industries.

Table 28 emphasizes Michigan's strength in growth industries in machinery (except electrical) industries, and fabricated metal products industries. Of the 16 growth industries in which Michigan gained more jobs than its share, 10 were in these two industries. Michigan also showed up well in growth industries in instruments and related products. Although the major industry of instruments and related products is very small in Michigan (9,000 workers in 1956), two of the growth industries (scientific instruments and mechanical measuring instruments) in which Michigan gained more than its share of jobs are in this major industry.

It seems clear that in these larger growth industries, the East North Central region and Michigan have at least held their own compared with other regions. The East North Central region is still faring well in most of those growth industries for which it is best suited. And it is doing well in industries such as aircraft, aircraft parts, and electrical machinery for which other areas have some locational advantages. Michigan has compared very well in most growth industries except electrical machinery, aircraft, and aircraft parts industries. A poor showing in electrical machinery, aircraft, and aircraft parts industries was unfortunate, however, because four of the six largest growth industries in the East North Central region were in these industries. Therefore, a strong showing in the majority of growth industries resulted in only a mediocre over-all performance for Michigan as evidenced by total employment figures in all industries.

Declining Industries in Michigan

IN THE MATERIAL presented above, we have covered larger growth industries in which employment has increased by more than 20 percent for the period 1947-1954. In order to cover these larger growth industries (as well as some smaller ones showing exceptional growth in Michigan), we have purposely not analyzed many smaller growth industries. Also, of course, there were some industries which declined during the period 1947-1954. For purposes of locating possible weaknesses in the Michigan economy, information on a few industries showing large absolute declines is presented below for the United States, the East North Central region and Michigan. Only those industries in which there were large job declines in Michigan are covered.

Industry	Employment 1954 (thousands)			Percent Change 1947-1954		
	United States	East North Central States	Michigan	United States	East North Central States	Michigan
Motor vehicles and equipment..........	695.5	521.3	346.1	1.7	−4.5	−6.5
Gray-iron foundries....	133.9	67.3	25.7	−23.0	−24.8	−35.9
Heating and cooking apparatus, n.e.c.....	75.3	31.7	3.4	−35.5	−42.6	−62.4
Metal stampings......	128.2	70.1	17.4	−3.9	3.2	−15.9

Source: *1954 Census of Manufactures*, Vol. III.

In appraising data presented above, we must remember that 1954 was a recession year. Since all industries listed above are cyclical industries which manufacture durable goods, it is not surprising that all three areas experienced actual declines in employment in all industries listed with the exception of the motor vehicles industry in the United States and the metal stampings industry in the East North Central region. Michigan, however, experienced more severe percentage declines than either the East North Central region or the nation as a whole in all these industries.

Why has Michigan experienced more drastic declines than other areas in these industries? One answer is that these industries in Michigan are more cyclical than similar industries in the other areas because of the concentration on capital goods and consumer durables. We know, too, that some of these industries have been adversely affected by plant move-outs. The gray-iron foundries industry nationwide has been affected by changes in technology. Problems associated with the decline in automotive industries have been covered in earlier chapters; additional reasons for decline in the other industries listed above, however, should be investigated not only for evidence of possible weakness in them but also for clues which might point up possible weaknesses in other industries.

Summary and Conclusions

WE HAVE EXAMINED two basic sets of data to obtain a picture of Michigan's growth relative to other areas. Employment data in major industries (two-digit Standard Industrial Classification industries) have been analyzed to obtain an industry-by-industry comparison of employment trends in the United States, the East North Central region, and Michigan. Employment data in individual growth industries (four-digit Standard Industrial Classification industries) within major industry groups have also been analyzed to determine Michigan's relative position in those industries which are likely to provide a large share of new jobs in the years ahead.

The analysis of major industries reveals that Michigan's growth has kept pace with growth in the East North Central region and the nation in most industries exclusive of motor vehicles and equipment for the period 1947-1956. The drop in demand for automobiles to moderate levels in recent years, coupled with an unmistakable trend toward decentralization in that industry, has brought about a recent decline in manufacturing jobs which has, to some extent, obscured employment gains in other industries. A substantial decline in defense employment also has contributed significantly to this relative decline in total manufacturing jobs compared with other areas. Total employment in all industries exclusive of motor vehicles and equipment, however, has increased at nearly the same rate as in the United States, and at about the same rate as in the East North Central region. Industries which provided most of the new jobs created during the period 1947-1956 were machinery (except electrical) (23,000 new jobs), other transportation equipment (21,500 new jobs), fabricated metal products (10,000 new jobs), printing and publishing (8,500 new jobs), chemicals and products (6,500 new jobs), pulp and paper products (5,000 new jobs), and instruments and related products (4,500 new jobs).

211

Growth industries in leading geographic regions, in the United States as a whole, and in Michigan for the period 1947-1954, have been compared to obtain a picture of relative growth in the different areas. The East North Central and Middle Atlantic regions continue to provide most of the new jobs created in many of these growth industries. Notable exceptions among those industries considered here are in the aircraft, aircraft parts, electrical machinery, and chemical industries where the South and West also figure importantly.

Michigan has compared very well in the majority of growth industries, but has been out-stripped by other areas in electrical machinery, aircraft, and aircraft parts industries which have been the fastest growing industries in the nation. Michigan has shown up best in machinery (except electrical) and fabricated metals industries. The strong showing by Michigan in these industries suggests favorable location factors for firms in such industries. Possible locational advantages for these industries should be investigated and, if advantages do exist, they should be emphasized by state and area development groups. Other growth industries in which Michigan has compared as well as other areas and which should continue to show healthy growth are paper and allied products, chemicals, instruments and related products, and printing and publishing industries. Although Michigan has not done as well as other areas in aircraft and missile parts industries, their good growth prospects plus the need for accurate machining to close tolerances for many of the parts required by these industries suggest that Michigan may be able to secure a larger share of this business than it has in the past, even though most prime contractors for such business are located in the East, West, and Southwest parts of the country.

Although Michigan has kept pace with the East North Central region and the nation in nearly all growth industries examined here, absolute gains in employment have been small. The largest absolute gains in employment have been in special tools and dies, and metal-working machinery attachments in which employment increased by 17,000 workers for the period 1947-1954. Significant gains have occurred also in aircraft parts and equipment, n.e.c., (9,500 jobs) and aircraft engines (7,400 jobs). All other four-digit industries have gained less than 5,000 jobs during the period 1947-1954. During this same period the motor vehicles industry declined by nearly 24,000 jobs, and the gray-iron foundries industry declined by more than 14,000 jobs. Other significant employment declines were experienced by heating and cooking equipment (5,800 jobs) and metal stampings (3,300 jobs). Thus, many small increases in growth industries in Michigan have not been sufficient to offset losses in motor vehicles and other "nongrowth" industries and still maintain over-all growth rates comparing favorably to the East North Central region and the nation.

Keeping pace with the nation in total employment growth exclusive of motor vehicles and equipment may be more difficult for Michigan to achieve in the years ahead. For it is evident when we consider some of the fast-growing industries of today that other regions have locational advantages which are greater than those enjoyed by the East North Central region and Michigan. The petrochemicals industry, for example, is growing tremendously fast in the South and Southwest because that is where a large share of the natural resources are located. The East is also achieving a good deal of growth in some petrochemicals such as plastics materials because of the location of major chemical companies there. Location of most of the electrical machinery growth industries in the East means that that region is likely to maintain leadership in these important industries. In defense electronics the West as well as the East is also important because aircraft companies have been active in the development of missiles and other products. Although the application of atomic energy still seems far away except for a few defense and civilian products, the major growth companies in this industry are located in the East.

Michigan, therefore, will undoubtedly grow at a slower pace than the nation in some of the more promising growth industries of tomorrow. Since we do have some advantages (e.g., nearness to markets) for some of these industries such as electrical machinery, however, we may be expected to show growth. But extra effort will be required if we are to make significant gains.

The employment data presented here indicate clearly that Michigan's present problem stems largely from the decline in motor vehicles and defense industries. There is no evidence that Michigan is losing ground in the majority of growth industries examined here. Although there are no growth industries which look promising enough to alleviate our present unemployment problem in the near future, there is much evidence in the statistics on growth industries as well as in the total employment figures for all industries to suggest that the Michigan economy will continue to show growth in the years ahead.

Chapter VIII

Projections of
Michigan Population and Employment

IN CHAPTER II, we discussed Michigan's rapid rate of population increase. We noted that Michigan has been growing much more rapidly than the nation and considerably more rapidly than the Great Lakes states, taken collectively or individually. Among sizable states, only California and Florida surpassed Michigan in the rate of population growth from 1950 to 1958. People moving into the state have accounted for a substantial share of the state's remarkable growth. Up to 1955, population increase was accompanied by similar increases in the work force and in job opportunities.

However, Michigan Employment Security Commission data suggest that the labor force has not expanded significantly since 1953. During 1956 and 1957, considerable numbers of the state's workers were out of a job. During the recession of 1958, unemployment in Michigan, and especially in Detroit, ran well above national levels.

The seriousness of Michigan's recent employment problem has led a number of observers to speculate that Michigan's population is not going to increase so spectacularly in the years ahead as it has in the past. They believe that the substantial volume of unemployment still prevalent in the state in the summer of 1959, and the likelihood of a slow recovery of employment in the state, will act as a brake to further substantial population growth in Michigan. The decline of the automotive industry in the state and the shift of defense procurement away from wheeled vehicles are also mentioned as likely deterrents to rapid growth in the future. These and other influences will, it is stated, prevent industrial expansion from occurring rapidly enough to sustain population growth at a rate anywhere near that of the past. Without job opportunities, people will not move to Michigan and growth will be less rapid. With a long-continued unemployment problem, in-migration could reverse itself and become out-migration.

With this view in mind, we shall in this chapter examine and appraise some population projections that have been made for the state. Their implications for future employment levels will be explored. In the following chapter, further evaluation of the likelihood of realizing these population and employment projections will be undertaken in connection with an examination of the state's short- and long-run economic prospects.

Population Projections

IN 1957, THE BUREAU of the Census prepared population projections for all of the states for the period 1955 through 1970. The high and low projections for Michigan were as follows:

Year	High	Low
1955	7,326,000	7,326,000
1960	8,355,000	8,041,000
1965	9,380,000	8,706,000
1970	10,483,000	9,392,000

Source: Appendix Table XXII.

It will be seen that the high projections would mean an increase of over 3.1 million persons in the state during the 15 years from 1955 to 1970. The low estimate suggests a gain of something over 2 million persons during the period.

Reasonableness of Projections

Are these projections for Michigan reasonable? One's view of their reasonableness will depend in large part on the view taken as to the state's future economic prospects. But unless a very grim outlook for Michigan's future is adopted, there are considerations that appear to suggest that at least the minimum projection (a population of 9.4 million persons by 1970) should be realized.

First of all, it is significant that the national population projections, on which these Michigan projections are based, have been superseded by revised data. The revised "low" projection for the country as a whole for 1970 is 6 million greater than before while the revised "high" projection is 10 million greater.[1] Since the population projections for 1970 cited above for Michigan are based on national projections which are already obsolete because of being

---

1 Bureau of the Census, *Current Population Reports—Population Estimates,* Series P-25, No. 187, November 10, 1958, Table A, p. 2.

too conservative, it would seem that the population projections for Michigan are on a conservative basis.[2]

There are other grounds for believing that these projections for Michigan are relatively conservative, and hence that at least the minimum estimate should be realized. We refer to the fact that these projections reflect less reliance on in-migration as a factor in the state's projected growth through 1970 than one might expect on the basis of past experience.

As shown in Appendix Table XXIII, the low projection for 1970 assumes a population increase of about 2.1 million persons over 1955 levels. Of this increase, slightly over half a million would reflect net in-migration into the state. In comparison, there was a net in-migration of well over 400,000 in just the six years from 1950 to 1956. Admittedly, several of these years saw high production levels in the state which drew in large numbers of workers from other states. But the volume of in-migration associated with the low projection through 1970 assumes that net in-migration during the 15-year period involved will be little more than the net in-migration experienced in just six years of the current decade. This would appear to be a conservative assumption.

These remarks seem to add up to a reasonable conclusion that, unless Michigan were to become something of a permanently depressed state, the state's people should number 9.4 million or more by 1970, as suggested by the Bureau of the Census low projection.[3] Such a conclusion would also tend to be in agreement with the more general proposition that strong trends, such as Michigan's long-time strong rate of population growth, are not changed abruptly.[4]

Employment Projections

IF THE PEOPLE of Michigan number between 9.4 and 10.5 million persons in 1970, how many jobs are going to have to be available then to employ them? How many additional job opportunities do these job levels mean will be necessary by 1970 to afford reason-

2 Rough calculations suggest that these revised national projections would mean that the minimum population level shown for Michigan for 1970 (9.4 million persons) might be increased by 300,000 or more. The high projection might be revised upward by a half million or more.

3 A publication of Michigan State University suggests a population of 10.1 million persons for the state in 1970. See J. F. Thaden, *Population Growth Components and Potential in Michigan* (East Lansing: Institute for Community Development and Services, Michigan State University, January 16, 1959) p. 28.

4 This point is discussed in more detail in the section entitled, *The Employment Outlook, 1970*, pp. 240-42.

ably "full" employment? In what areas may these jobs be found? These are questions to which we now turn our attention.

In trying to provide rough answers to these questions, we hasten, of course, to state that we have no intention of predicting Michigan's economic future. What we shall do is to develop some illustrative data on possible employment levels that seem compatible with the population projections that have been cited and to give some approximations as to what the nature of that employment may be.

Obviously it is a risky undertaking to take a look ahead at employment possibilities. A decade ago, no analyst could have visualized the tremendous pressure that would be placed on Michigan's industry and labor force by the Korean-period defense program. Neither could there have been foreseen the ensuing problem of declining employment, culminating in the serious unemployment situation of 1958.

There are bound to be structural changes in employment in the period ahead, both in the country at large and in Michigan. We may be on the threshold of important changes in Michigan's industrial and occupational pattern. We are confronted with the realization that the automotive industry is going to be less important to the state's economy than formerly. The recent developments in transportation that have been alluded to earlier may affect our industrial structure in ways that cannot now be visualized. Increasing attention is being given to promoting Michigan as a center for scientific and technical research. Tourism may increase substantially in economic importance. Michigan will also be affected by broader forces at work such as the expected continued growth of the service industries, by the emerging importance of new areas of industrial activity, and by continuing changes in the nature of the nation's defense program. All these factors make it certain that the years between now and 1970 will be years of important changes that can hardly be anticipated.

Despite the uncertainties posed by these and related factors, one may still hope, by reference to recent trends, to provide some reasonable approximation of employment levels in 1970, and some indication of the nature of such employment.

Percent of Population Employed

There are several ways in which future employment levels may be estimated. A rather simple method involves an estimate of the proportion of the population that will be employed. Historical data suggest that it is reasonable to assume a percentage figure of 38.5 for this purpose.

Discussing the national outlook, an Upjohn Institute report of ten years ago stated:

> For the period 1900-1941, excluding the war years 1917 and 1918, the number employed, on an average, was equal to 37 per cent of the population; and for the period 1900-1929, excluding the war years, the number employed was, on an average, equal to 38.5 percent. It seems likely that employment will, on an average for the period 1949-1970, tend toward the higher of these two figures.[5]

Employment experience during the past decade appears to be in agreement with the assumption just quoted that employment after 1949 would tend to approximate something like 38.5 percent of the population. The text table below shows the record on employment levels in percentage terms since 1949, both for the nation and for Michigan.

Year	Civilian Employment as Percentage of Civilian Population	
	United States	Michigan
1949	39.8	38.2
1950	39.9	39.9
1951	40.4	41.0
1952	39.8	40.1
1953	39.7	41.8
1954	38.3	38.2
1955	38.8	38.2
1956	39.1	36.3
1957	38.6	35.5
1958	37.3	32.8

Source: *United States*: Bureau of the Census estimates of population and civilian employment. *Michigan*: Bureau of the Census estimates of population and Michigan Employment Security Commission data on total employment.

These data show that, for the most part, employment has tended to amount to more than 38.5 percent of the civilian population since 1949. This is especially true at the national level where employment fell below the 38.5 percent level only during the recession years of 1954 and 1958. The data for Michigan do not follow this pattern quite so well in that the figure shown for the state in 1955 is somewhat below the 38.5 percent level, even though the year was a "good" year for Michigan. However, if the Bureau of Labor Statistics figure on wage and salary workers in Michigan in 1955 (2,479,000) is substituted for the MESC figure (2,413,-

---

5 Julius T. Wendzel, *Perspective for Business Expansion*, August, 1949, p. 8.

000) included in the data shown, the proportion of Michigan's people working on the average during 1955 would be 39.1 percent.[6]

On the basis of past relationships, it seems reasonable to assume that about 38.5 percent of the state's people should be working in 1970 if we are to have reasonably adequate employment levels then. However, it is entirely possible that population growth to 1970 could be within the limits previously mentioned even though a smaller proportion of the state's residents held jobs in the years ahead. Such a lower percentage would imply fewer women workers, including working wives, and fewer jobs available to the younger and older groups in our population. While population could continue to grow at a substantial rate, Michigan's income situation in the future would be less favorable if the job-population percentage relationship were to run substantially below 38.5. Although real per capita and family income could increase in the state, Michigan's income position would presumably compare less favorably with that of other states as the years went by. If we are to look ahead to 1970 as a year when Michigan's employment and income levels compare as favorably with those of other states as they have in most recent years, we should set as a goal a level of job opportunities that will provide work for 38 percent or more of the state's population.[7]

Apart from their usefulness in suggesting future employment levels, the percentage figures on persons working in Michigan shown in the text table are helpful in another way. They afford another indication of the substantial degree to which defense work in Michigan had increased economic activity and the volume of

6 Reference was made in Chapter III to the fact that data issued by the Bureau of Labor Statistics and the Michigan Employment Security Commission on wage and salary employees in Michigan have occasionally shown appreciable differences. (See footnotes 1 and 10 to Chapter III.) If the BLS data on wage and salary workers for years after 1955 were reflected in the percentages shown in the text table for Michigan, the percentages for 1956 and 1957 would be 37.5 and 36.0, respectively. It will be noted that these percentages for 1956 and 1957 are somewhat larger than those shown in the text table.

7 It may be thought that, because of recent and projected changes in the age composition of the population, there could be an appreciable decline by 1970 in the proportion of the state's population that would fall in the working-age group. Such a decline could presumably lead to a job-total population relationship well below the 38.5 percent relationship mentioned in the text. A look at the age composition associated with the high and low projections of Michigan population for 1970 does not support this view. It is true, as suggested later in this chapter, that the proportion of the population expected to be found in the prime working ages of 25-44 will be smaller in the years ahead. But persons aged 18-64, an age bracket from which the labor force is ordinarily drawn, will apparently not diminish in relative importance very appreciably by 1970. In 1955, the proportion of Michigan's population in this age bracket amounted to 57.9 percent. Under the low projection (9.4 millions) for 1970, this age group is expected to account for 57.7 percent, about the same as in 1955. Under the high projection (10.5 millions), it would be 54.9 percent, somewhat lower than in 1955. These percents are based on data shown in Bureau of the Census, *Current Population Reports — Population Estimates*, Series P-25, No. 160, August 9, 1957, Table 1.

jobs in the state by 1953. They also point to the seriousness of the job decline in the state by 1957 and especially by 1958. In 1957, after four years of declining job opportunities on the one hand, and of continuing population increase on the other, less than 36 percent of the people of Michigan were working. And, during the recession year of 1958, this percentage dropped to 33. This is by far the lowest level of employment in Michigan during the decade, 1949-1958. Comparison with national data indicates that the level of employment in Michigan in 1958, measured on this percentage basis, was only slightly above the low level of employment that was experienced in the nation during the depths of the Great Depression. It is clear that 1958 was a year when jobs were extremely scarce in Michigan.

Employment Projections through 1970

The following table shows the trend of employment levels that might be expected in Michigan for the period 1960 to 1970 if, on the average, 38.5 percent of the state's projected population were to be employed. For purposes of simplifying the analysis, we have applied the 38.5 percent figure to population projections that represent an average of the high and low projections for Michigan through 1970.

Year	Employment (thousands)
1960	3,160
1965	3,480
1970	3,830

These figures suggest that, on the basis of a "medium" rate of population growth, about 3.8 million persons might be expected to be holding a job in 1970. (The low population projection previously discussed would mean about 3.6 million job-holders in 1970; the high projection would have called for employment of over 4 million persons in that year.)

If we look at the employment level in Michigan in 1958 (something under 2.6 million jobs), and bear in mind the misgivings about the state's economic prospects, the employment level of 3.8 million jobs called for by 1970 by medium-rate population growth may seem extremely unrealistic. If 3.8 million employment opportunities are to be available in 1970, an additional 1.2 million or so jobs will have to be developed in the state's factories, stores, offices, construction projects, and schoolrooms in the 12-year period, 1958-1970. This would mean almost a 50 percent gain in jobs. This is indeed a sizable increase in jobs that must be found in little more than a decade if the people of Michigan are to enjoy an adequate level of job opportunities in 1970. (If we take account of the fact that perhaps 100,000 job opportunities may develop during 1959, we would need to create 1.1 million new jobs in the remaining eleven years to 1970).

Before discussing 1970 employment levels further, let us take a look at the areas in which these additional jobs might originate.

Type of Employment, 1970

We have estimated that there might be around 3.8 million jobs needed in Michigan by 1970 if population were to increase at a medium rate of growth. In what lines of work might these jobs be found? How many of the additional jobs needed by 1970 might be provided by Michigan's factories? How many job openings may arise in the service industries or in other nonmanufacturing lines? The following paragraphs provide some tentative answers.

Our estimate would be that the jobs held in 1970 by the 38.5 percent of the population that might then be working would be distributed somewhat as follows:

Type of Employment	Number per 100 of the Population
All jobs	38.5
Wage and salary workers — manufacturing	13.0
Wage and salary workers — nonmanufacturing	21.0
All other[a]	4.5

[a]Farmers and farm workers, proprietors and self-employed, domestics and unpaid family workers.

A few words of explanation for these estimates may be helpful. The 13 percent of the population shown as working in factories in 1970 is below the long-term averages discussed in Chapter III (Table 7). There it was shown that for the 30-year period, 1929-1957, 14.5 persons out of every 100 living in Michigan worked in factories. For the shorter period, 1939-1957, exclusive of the war years, the average had been 15.4 persons.

The somewhat lower importance suggested above for manufacturing employment in the state for the years ahead reflects an assumption that manufacturing activity in Michigan will be somewhat less intense in the next decade or so than it has been in recent years. It is also assumed that automotive jobs will be relatively less important in the state's industrial economy than heretofore. Furthermore, it is unlikely that any special impetus similar to the

222

defense surge of the early fifties will be available to bolster factory employment in Michigan at the relatively high levels of those years. On the other hand, Michigan's long-time status as a leading industrial state suggests that its degree of industrialization is not going to drop materially in the next decade or so. Moreover, a recent set of projections for the nation suggests that manufacturing employment may increase substantially by 1970 and may be somewhat more important then, in relation to population, than in most recent years.[8] Setting the industrial job-population ratio for Michigan in 1970 at 13 percent may prove to be conservative.

The data shown above indicate that nonmanufacturing lines — principally the services industries — may provide jobs for about 21 percent of the state's population in 1970. This level of importance compares with a level of not quite 18 percent during the five years 1953-1957, inclusive (see Table 9). The increased importance shown for this area will not be surprising. The service industries have shown strong growth for a good many years and have increased their relative importance in the labor force, offsetting declines in farm employment and in other industries.

The estimate that 4.5 percent of the state's people may be engaged in "other" activities in 1970 reflects divergent trends. Within this relatively small group, it is assumed that farm employment will continue to be less important, both in actual numbers and in relation to other components. The other types of employment accounted for by this "other" group — proprietors and the self-employed, domestics, and unpaid family workers — are expected to increase in numbers as a group and to account for about the same share of the state's population in 1970 as in recent years — something over 3 percent. The substantial growth of service industries in the state through 1970 should mean that proprietors and the self-employed will show more growth in numbers than in recent years.

Let us apply this estimated future employment pattern to Michigan's projected 1970 population on the medium basis. The following data provide a breakdown of the estimated 3.8 million jobs

8 The National Planning Association has projected manufacturing employment of 23.1 million persons (employees and proprietors) by 1970, an increase of 35 percent over the comparable figure (17.0 million) for 1957. The projections reflect full employment conditions. See *National Economic Projections, 1962-1965, 1970* (Washington: The Association, 1959), pp. 31-32.

The figure of 17.0 million persons engaged in manufacturing in 1957 is taken from the Department of Commerce, *U. S. Income and Output — A Supplement to the Survey of Current Business* (Washington: Government Printing Office, 1958), p. 214. Manufacturing employees comprise the great bulk of all persons engaged in manufacturing.

needed in 1970 according to the pattern that we have outlined. For comparison, actual employment data for 1958 (Michigan Employment Security Commission revised estimates) are also shown.

Type of Employment	Employment (thousands)		
	1970 Projected	1958 Actual	Increase
All types....................................	**3,830**	**2,580**	**1,250**
Wage and salary workers, manufacturing.....	1,290	880	410
Wage and salary workers, nonmanufacturing..	2,090	1,300	790
All other..	450	400	50

These data suggest the nature of the 1.25 million additional jobs needed to boost employment enough over 1958 levels to reach the 3.8 million jobs necessary in 1970. According to these estimates, about 410,000 of these additional jobs could be provided by factory employment. Roughly 790,000 more jobs would develop in the service and other nonmanufacturing areas. A smaller increase of 50,000 jobs might be realized in other types of employment.

Is the 1970 Job Goal Unrealistic?

In large part, our answer to this question depends on an evaluation of the economic outlook for the nation and for the state. Such an evaluation is set forth in the next chapter. But some remarks can be made now on the basis of relating this projected goal to Michigan's past performance.

First of all, the use of the recession year of 1958 as a base for measuring the additional jobs needed by 1970 represents, of course, the most pessimistic basis possible for estimating the needed future growth in job opportunities. The extremely low level of employment in the state in 1958 reflected the successive, cumulative impact of a loss of defense-related employment, two years of a relatively moderate automotive market, and finally the general recession of 1958 during which automotive production declined by more than 40 percent from peak 1955 levels.

Thus, while the 1958 situation was a real one, reflecting several Michigan problems that must be solved in the years ahead, the additional 1.2 million jobs that should be provided between 1958 and 1970 represent an overstatement of the size of the task ahead of the state. An appreciable, even though slow, recovery in jobs in the state was occurring during 1959 as the nation was emerging from the 1958 recession. This more or less automatic recovery was providing some of the additional 1.2 million jobs needed. Thus, in May of 1959, there were 120,000 more jobholders in the state than in May of 1958.

If we narrow our focus to look just at the additional factory jobs needed by 1970, the goal for the 12-year period does not seem unattainable. The 1970 factory job level is only 60,000 over the 1953 level of 1.23 million. This means that our goal for 1970 would be just to restore industrial employment to levels that had prevailed 17 years earlier and to add 60,000 more such jobs. Such a goal, though it may seem a large one under present circumstances, is not necessarily an insurmountable one.

Recent experience also suggests a basis for believing that the state might, under favorable circumstances, find in 1970 that 3.8 million of its citizens were holding jobs. If we remember that total employment in Michigan jumped by 450,000 jobs in just four years' time — from 1949 to 1953 — then a gain of over a million jobs by 1970 seems more attainable also. We do not expect, of course, that Michigan will experience any such dramatic similar surge of growth between now and 1970. But if the state were to enjoy two or three spurts of rapid growth in the next decade or so, then the goal of 3.8 million jobs for 1970 seems more possible of attainment.

Projections of Automotive Employment

IN THE PRECEDING SECTION, we suggested that there might be around 1.29 million persons working in Michigan's factories in 1970 if the number of the state's people increased according to the medium population projection. Estimates described in this section suggest that of this industrial work force some 400,000 persons may be working in automotive manufacturing and assembly plants.

This level of automotive employment suggests that there would be about as many Michigan employees working in the automotive industry in 1970 as there were during 1956 and 1957. This level of auto jobs in Michigan may seem low to those who remember the half-million workers employed in the state's auto plants in 1953. It may seem high to those who have been concerned about the dwindling number of auto jobs in the state in recent years, culminating in employment of only 293,000 auto workers during 1958.[9]

9 The figure cited is the Michigan Employment Security Commission unrevised figure for 1958. This figure is comparable with data on automotive employment for preceding years. The MESC revised figure for automotive employment for 1958 (278,000) reflects in large part the reclassification of a number of firms out of the motor vehicles and equipment industry.

The Estimates of Future Auto Jobs

The levels of automotive employment for 1970 suggested above have been obtained by two different methods, both of which give similar results. One method assumes a 10-million unit level of car and truck production (demand) in 1970 and estimates the employment that might be associated with it on the basis of past relationships. The other method assumes that automotive employment will increase in rough proportion to the growth in total manufacturing employment, as it has in the past. Both methods assume that Michigan's share of total employment in the industry may be something like 45 percent in 1970.

As mentioned, the first method uses a demand figure of 10 million cars and trucks in 1970. It is assumed that on the average there will be 11 cars and trucks produced for every worker employed in the industry, resulting in total employment of about 900,000 workers. If Michigan's share of total industry employment is 45 percent, automotive jobs in the state would number about 410,000.

The second method of estimating involves the use of more arithmetic and we shall not spell it out here. In essence, it assumes that 9.5 percent of the nation's civilian population will work in factories in 1970, that 4.75 percent of these manufacturing employees will be auto workers, and that Michigan will account for 45 percent of them. The result is comparable with that obtained by the first method.

Some comment on the assumptions employed may be in order. Several of these assumptions are discussed in the following paragraphs.

Demand in 1970

There are some who may question the 10-million vehicle figure used as a demand trend value for 1970 under the first method discussed. There are many estimates of future motor vehicle demand. We have seen estimates that imply 1970 production levels both above and below the 10-million unit level just mentioned. We have seen one prepared by a private research agency that suggests that this volume of units could be reached as early as 1965. In any event, we assume continued, if irregular, growth of automotive production and employment in accordance with long-term trends indicated in Chapter IV and in accordance with the favorable economic outlook generally foreseen for the 1960's.

Automation and Employment

Some readers may wonder if we are allowing for the impact of automation and other technological advances upon employment in the automotive industry. The 11 vehicles-per-worker relationship used under the first method in estimating likely national employment in the industry in 1970 does make what seems to be an adequate allowance for the increasing impact of automation and other labor-saving equipment and processes. It compares with the range of 7 to 10 vehicles produced per employee in the industry during most of the last 30 years. It compares with production-employee relationships of 8.5, 9.2, and 8.2 experienced during 1956, 1957, and 1958, respectively.[10] It would seem that automation would have to exert an especially adverse impact on *total* job opportunities in the industry — an impact much stronger than exerted by any previous set of technological advances — to move the vehicle-per-worker relationship beyond 11.

One would, of course, be unwise to minimize the possible adverse impact of automation on employment in the automotive industry. Substantial reductions in manpower requirements have been reported in connection with many new plants. Moreover, it is likely that the full benefits of automation, in terms of minimizing labor requirements, were not felt until the 1958 recession resulted in a general reduction in work forces. In all probability, the productivity of the automated plants will be more clearly revealed in the next few years when full-scale production economies can be realized. It is possible, therefore, that during the next several years employment in the industry will rise less rapidly than vehicle production, as compared with past patterns.

On the other hand, one must bear in mind that Michigan's low level of automotive employment in 1958 reflected several factors of which automation was only one. The foremost factor was of course the extremely poor demand for motor vehicles in 1958. Chrysler Corporation's share of this reduced market was down, further depressing Michigan's share of total employment. It has been stated also that proportionately more of the industry's white-collar personnel were laid off in 1958 than in previous recessions. As the 1959 model year production started, late in 1958, the Big Three stepped up production by means of greater use of overtime, rather than by adding personnel. This latter step has been attrib-

---

10 These data are shown in Table 14. Preliminary data for 1959 suggest a relationship of 8.9 for the first seven months of the year.

uted both to a desire by the auto-makers to avoid the various fringe cost liabilities incurred by taking on new personnel and to a desire to avoid adverse public reaction in case workers were taken on only to be laid off again if demand did not hold up.

Thus, in view of the several factors involved, it is difficult to assess the role of automation in the recent low levels of automotive employment in the state. A further consideration is that most of the discussion on automation concerns its use by the Big Three. This may mean that it has not yet figured appreciably in the plants of the auto suppliers, which account for a sizable share of industry jobs. Many of those who have studied the possible impact of automation believe that it is too early to draw any definite conclusions on the over-all economic, including employment, consequences of automation. This conservative position seems justified by the fact that in the nation at large manufacturing employment has consistently increased as the nation's population has increased.

Michigan's Share of Automotive Employment

The estimates of 1970 employment in Michigan's auto industry reflect an assumption that Michigan will account for about 45 percent of all jobs in the industry. This assumption is based on the belief that decentralization has largely run its course, at least for a few years, now that the capital expansion programs of two of the Big Three appear to be largely completed.

On the other hand, preliminary data for 1959 suggest that Michigan's share of all automobile jobs was running under 45 percent during the first four months of the year. Developments during the next few years will indicate whether or not it is too optimistic to assume a 45 percent share of all auto jobs for Michigan in the next decade.

Implications for Nonautomotive Factory Jobs

If automotive jobs in Michigan in 1970 number something like 400,000 as suggested earlier, this would mean that there would need to be almost 900,000 jobs in other manufacturing lines in Michigan in 1970, if total industrial jobs were to number 1.29 million. Industrial workers in Michigan, other than auto workers, numbered between 650,000 and 700,000 persons in each of the years 1953 to 1957. In 1958, they numbered about 600,000. Thus a gain over 1958 levels of about 300,000 nonautomotive factory jobs would be required if the 1970 industrial job goal were to be achieved. On the average, this would mean that about 25,000 non-automotive industrial jobs would have to develop in Michigan each year between 1958 and 1970. As suggested earlier, recovery from the 1958 recession provided part of this needed increase.

Implications of the Employment Projections

WE HAVE NOTED that 3.8 million people may be working in Michigan by 1970. Some 1.29 million persons may hold factory jobs. As Michigan's working population moves toward these job levels, what changes may be expected in the age-sex composition of the work force? What kinds of skills and training are workers going to have to acquire as Michigan's labor force grows in size? The following discussion outlines some of the developments that may be expected.

Number of Production Workers

There may be no more blue-collar workers employed in Michigan's factories in 1970 than there were during several years of the 1950's. There will, of course, be more production jobs available during the next few years as Michigan works out of the low level of industrial employment prevailing in 1958. But postwar trends suggest that, as factory employment increases in the decade ahead, blue-collar jobs will grow less rapidly than total factory jobs.

In 1947, blue-collar jobs accounted for 84 percent of the nation's factory jobs; in 1958, only 75 percent. Rough data suggest a similar, perhaps somewhat higher, percentage of blue-collar employees in Michigan in 1958. In view of the steady decline in the importance of production workers in America's factories since World War II, a further decline to 70 percent in their importance between 1958 and 1970 seems possible. If 70 percent of the 1.29 million industrial jobs projected for the state by 1970 are blue-collar jobs, then there would be about 900,000 production workers in that year. This number of blue-collar jobs appears to have been exceeded in 1953 and approximated in several other recent years.

While these figures are only illustrative, they suggest the trend. The changing nature of future industrial job opportunities means that relatively fewer of Michigan's factory workers can expect to hold production jobs. The greater increase in white-collar jobs in factories means that workers will have to be better educated and better trained to secure factory employment. Without such training, many entrants to the labor force will have to seek employment in other, lower paying types of jobs.

Sources of Labor Force Growth

If Michigan's workers number 3.8 million in 1970, will the types of persons employed then — male vs. female workers, young vs. older workers — be about the same in relative importance as in recent years? To what extent will recent population and labor force trends modify the age and sex composition of Michigan's work force by 1970?

Because data on employment by age and sex are not included in the Michigan Employment Security Commission regular reports on employment we know neither the number of women currently employed in Michigan, nor the division of the work force by age groups. However, if we assume that the current composition of Michigan's work force, by sex and age, is somewhat similar to that of the nation, then we may assume that anticipated changes in the nation's work force in the years ahead may also typify what may be expected to happen to Michigan's working population.[11]

A recent Department of Labor report has taken a look ahead at the likely change in the national labor force during the decade, 1955-1965.[12] An over-all increase of more than 10 million workers in the labor force is foreseen. The striking feature of this outlook is the fact that men in the prime working age groups — those from 25 to 44 — will remain fairly constant in numbers during the decade — a reflection of the nation's low birth rate in the depressed thirties. The number of women workers in this age group is expected to increase by about a million. Thus, by 1965, there may be only a net increase of one million additional workers in the 25-44 age bracket, a segment that accounted for almost half of the work force in 1955.

These figures mean, of course, that in 1965 workers under 25 and those over 44 will be much more important in the work force than in recent years. Of the over-all increase of over 10 million workers by 1965, women are expected to account for a slightly larger share, 5.4 million compared with 5 million men.

---

11 The *1950 Census of Population* indicates that in 1950 the labor force of Michigan was fairly comparable in composition with that of the country generally. In that year, 53.5 percent of the population 14 years and over was in the nation's labor force. In Michigan, the corresponding percentage was 53.8 percent. Women were somewhat more important in the nation's work force than in Michigan's. For the nation at large, 28.9 percent of females 14 years old and over were in the labor force. In Michigan the percentage was 27.3. See *1950 Census of Population*, Vol. II, Pt. 1, Table 50, and Pt. 22, Table 25.

12 *Our Manpower Future, 1955-65* (Washington: Government Printing Office, 1957). Material quoted in this paragraph is based on Sections XI, XII, and XIII.

A somewhat similar change in the composition of Michigan's working population by 1965 may also be anticipated. These changes have important implications for the appropriate training and utilization of the work force, in Michigan as in the nation. These implications have been summarized by Ewan Clague, Commissioner of Labor Statistics, as follows:

> These trends will create a number of problems in personnel training and recruiting. Most of the additional workers in the labor force will be women and young persons, who traditionally have the highest turnover rates. A growing number of workers will be available only for part-time work, and more attention will have to be given to their training and use. Shortages of men of prime working age will sharpen the need for training and utilization of younger workers. Women must be trained for jobs formerly filled by men.[13]

These likely developments mean that Michigan employers in the mid-sixties will be employing relatively more women and young workers than in the mid-fifties. The more intensive use of these workers will require more attention to their training and proper utilization.

After 1965, the number of men in the 25-44 age bracket will start increasing again, a reflection of the high number of births in the forties. However, by 1970, the proportion of persons (male and female) in this prime age group will still be smaller than in 1955.

Changing Occupational Pattern

Michigan's growing work force will find in the decade or so ahead that additional jobs will develop much more rapidly in some occupations than in others. Again, in the absence of concrete data for Michigan, we shall look at the national occupational outlook and shall assume that it may apply in large part to Michigan.[14]

The Department of Labor provides the following data on the percentage increases anticipated nationally for various occupational groups from 1955 to 1965:[15]

---

13 Ewan Clague, "Our Changing Work Force," *The Management Review,* January, 1959, p. 64. Based on an article in *The Office,* September, 1958.

14 Appendix Table XXIV indicates that from 1940 to 1950 the percentages of Michigan workers employed in the various occupational groupings moved in the same direction as did national percents and for the most part at somewhat similar rates. The table indicates that in 1950 craftsmen and operatives were relatively more numerous in Michigan than elsewhere.

15 *Our Manpower Future, 1955-65 . . . op. cit.,* Section XIV.

Occupational Group	Percentage Increase Range
Professional and technical	35-40
Proprietors and managers	20-25
Clerical and sales	25-30
Craftsmen (skilled)	20-25
Operatives (semi-skilled)	20-25
Service workers	10-15
Laborers	0- 5 (decrease)
Farmers and farm workers	10-15 (decrease)

The Department's brief narrative comments on this occupational outlook are presented below:

PROFESSIONAL AND TECHNICAL — This highly educated group which includes the scientists, engineers, teachers, physicians and nurses will be in great demand. An increase of more than one-third by 1965 appears likely.

PROPRIETORS AND MANAGERS — The growing size and complexity of business organizations demands people skilled in management who can plan and direct the work of others. An increase of over one-fifth is indicated.

CLERICAL AND SALES — Record keeping and distribution services . . . will require a substantial increase in this group — by more than one quarter.

CRAFTSMEN AND OPERATIVES — These large groups of skilled and semi-skilled workers who man our factories, build our homes, roads, and buildings are destined to grow nearly as rapidly as clerical and sales workers, or by about one quarter.

SERVICE WORKERS — A rapidly growing population will demand many more personal and protective services — more barbers and beauty shop operators, more hotel employees, more policemen and firemen. An increase of between 10 and 15 percent appears likely.

LABORERS — Although workers with limited training will be needed in 1965, unskilled jobs will decline.

FARMERS AND FARM WORKERS — The decrease in farm population has been evident for many years and will undoubtedly continue . . .

If these occupational trends also typify Michigan during the period, as we may expect, they point to the growing importance of white-collar personnel in the state's economy and to the need for a high degree of education and training for a larger proportion of the state's growing work force.

Chapter IX

Michigan's Employment Outlook

UP TO NOW, we have traced the origins of Michigan's employment problem. We have looked briefly at related industrial and economic trends in the state. We have examined some of Michigan's industrial location advantages and disadvantages. Finally, we have suggested that 1.2 million additional jobs would be needed between 1958 and 1970 if the people of Michigan were to increase in numbers as rapidly as current projections suggest.

In the following pages, we shall make a brief evaluation of the short-run employment outlook. We shall hazard a guess as to whether or not we may expect to provide 1.2 million additional jobs by 1970. Some positive steps to enhance long-run prospects will be outlined.

The Short-Run Outlook

IT IS HARD to foresee the restoration of "full employment" in Michigan during the early 1960's. Underemployment of the population is likely to plague Michigan for some time. Thus, by May of 1959, recovery in the nation was far enough along that about 38 percent of the nation's civilian population were at work. In contrast, only about 34 percent of the people of Michigan held a job in spite of the fact that a rather good year was developing in the auto industry. In terms of unemployment, only 4.9 percent of the nation's labor force were unemployed in May of 1959 while in Michigan 8.3 percent were still seeking jobs. These statistics point to a slower recovery in Michigan and to the likelihood of a period of underemployment for some time ahead. This post-recession employment problem would parallel that of pre-recession 1956 and of generally prosperous 1957 when the unemployment rate in Michigan was considerably higher than in the nation.

This is not to deny that more and more jobs will become available to Michigan residents during 1960 and thereafter. But the point is that even as more jobs become available, more people will be looking for work. Jobs are not likely to increase in number rapidly enough to absorb both the new entrants into the labor force and the large number of workers still unemployed during 1959.

There is no indication that defense employment is increasing in the state to any significant degree. Automotive employment was at relatively low levels during the first half of 1959. Higher production levels and a possibly larger share of all auto jobs for Michigan workers in connection with the 1960 models may result in a higher automotive employment level during 1960. However, unless 1960 should prove to be an extraordinary year for the auto industry, the number of auto jobs will apparently still fall below pre-recession levels. In view of this likelihood, and of the absence of the former solid employment support afforded by defense contracts, manufacturing and total employment in Michigan during 1960 and immediately thereafter will fall short of normal employment levels.

General economic recovery will of course bolster the job level in the state. As this is written, it appears that unemployment in the country as a whole will have fallen to somewhat "normal" levels by the end of 1959. The achievement of recovery at the national level would improve job levels in Michigan also, perhaps enough so that the number of the state's unemployed would be reduced to tolerable proportions during 1960 and thereafter, even though underemployment continued to be a problem. Should another recession occur in 1961 or 1962, the achievement of reasonably satisfactory employment levels in Michigan would be correspondingly delayed.

A special problem in Michigan's unemployment situation arises from the so-called "hard core of unemployment." The term refers to the low level of skills, training, and education possessed by a large number of the state's unemployed, especially in the Detroit area. Many of these workers came into the state during the Korean-defense period. In the main, they held unskilled jobs in the auto and other industries. Now they represent marginal workers. Many are reported not to be susceptible of retraining for higher skill jobs in order to improve their chances of finding employment. They cannot be absorbed until conditions of "full employment" return. Their presence in the ranks of the unemployed may pose a continuing problem for some time.

An interesting feature of the state's labor market during the business recovery of the spring and summer of 1959 was the mismatch between this pool of surplus labor in the state and the developing demand for highly skilled and professional workers by a number of the state's industries. Many Michigan companies were reported to have carried on intensive recruiting campaigns during this period, both within and outside of the state, to obtain the highly trained personnel needed for expanded production schedules. This situation reflects the shift in occupational patterns toward higher levels of skill and training discussed in the preceding chapter.

The Nation's Long-Range Outlook

IN ITS LONG-RANGE outlook report of a decade ago, the Upjohn Institute stated: "Our studies suggest that the period 1949-1970 is likely to be characterized by rapid growth and high average levels of income, employment and effective demand."[1] In the years since, the generally optimistic tone of this long-term outlook report has been confirmed by a number of other studies. Indeed, recent studies suggest very substantial gains in the nation's output by 1970. A set of projections issued by the National Planning Association indicates that Gross National Product may amount to $790 billion (in 1958 prices) by 1970.[2] An article in *Fortune* suggests a somewhat lower level ($740 billion) for that year.[3] These projections, which assume that productivity per manhour may increase at a rate of around 3 percent a year through the sixties, compare with Gross National Product of about $450 billion in 1957. If realized, the achievement of such a high level of national output by 1970 would carry obvious implications of high-level economic activity during the next decade.

Whether or not these specific figures materialize, there can be little doubt that the nation will enjoy a generally prosperous period during the sixties. And it is not easy to believe that Michigan is going to remain on the sidelines as an envious observer of the increasing levels of production, employment, and income being developed elsewhere in the nation. Its past industrial record does not make such an idea easy to accept.

Certainly, Michigan's share of the nation's high level of economic activity in the years ahead will be influenced by what we do here in Michigan to promote industrial activity in the state. But,

---

1 Julius T. Wendzel, *Perspective for Business Expansion*, August, 1949, p. 5.
2 *National Economic Projections, 1962-1965, 1970* (Washington: The Association, 1959), p. 3.
3 Charles E. Silberman and Sanford S. Parker, "How the U. S. Can Get 50 Per Cent Richer," *Fortune*, March, 1959, p. 107.
An earlier article in the same publication (November, 1955) had analyzed the impact of increasing productivity on family incomes. It foresaw the possibility that spendable income per family might rise from around $4,400 in 1955 to $8,000 in 1980.

in any event, the state is bound to grow to some degree with the nation in the decade ahead.

Michigan's Long-Range Outlook

WHETHER OR NOT there will be 3.8 million persons working in Michigan by 1970 depends on a number of factors. Obviously both unfavorable and favorable factors will be at work as the state recovers from the 1958 recession and moves to higher employment levels. Some of these factors are reviewed briefly below.

Unfavorable Factors

The fact that we must find new industrial jobs to replace those lost in defense work and in the auto industry represents an unfavorable factor in the state's efforts to work back to full employment levels. We cannot look for all such additional factory jobs to develop in the manufacturing lines which are currently important in the state. Our discussion of "growth" industries in Chapter VII points out that, although the state had made a good showing in a number of growth industries through 1956, it had participated very little in some of the larger growth industries, such as aircraft, aircraft parts, radios and related products, and electrical machinery. Thus, our efforts to provide necessary new industrial jobs in the more job-promising growth industries will suffer because of a late start.

Another fact that we must face up to is that in a general way some of our outstanding locational factors, such as markets and quality of labor supply, are not peculiar to us but are shared by our competitive neighbor states. This situation means that it is more difficult for the state to point to advantages so strong as to influence industrialists elsewhere to regard Michigan as an obvious area in which to locate a plant. Moreover, our analysis of industrial location factors discloses some aspects which must be regarded as unfavorable to Michigan, such as its location "off the beaten path," its tax structure, and certain aspects of its labor situation.

The unfavorable publicity that the state has received in the nation's press during the past year or two must also be regarded as a disadvantage. (The dissemination of information on unemployment in Michigan has, however, undoubtedly served to slow down migration into the state and thus to minimize the number of further additions to our unemployed from this source.) Outside manufacturers contemplating the establishment of a plant in the state could only be deterred by the vivid stories emanating from Michigan concerning the state's fiscal problems, its allegedly high taxes on business and industry, its apparent industrial decline as indicated by reduced factory employment levels, the reported alliance of organized labor and the state administration, and the acrimonious tone of labor-management contract negotiations. Probably no other state has had more voluminous reporting of its internal problems. In view of all of these unfavorable reports, it is somewhat surprising that a number of new plants have come into Michigan. But the reputation that Michigan may have gained from this spate of publicity could serve as a real barrier to the efforts of all those who will be working to restore Michigan to its former industrial position.

The misgivings about the state's future that appear to characterize many Michigan observers of the state's industrial scene must also rank as an unfavorable factor in the state's recovery. A belief on the part of its citizens that the state is past its industrial prime is not conducive to strong or sustained efforts to promote industrial recovery and expansion.

We think that many people are unduly influenced by the low level of jobs in Michigan during the 1958 recession. This recession appears to have had the most severe impact on Michigan of any downturn since the Great Depression. In part, the severity of the 1958 recession reflected the fact that during 1956 and 1957 Michigan had failed to make the adjustments necessary to offset the loss of defense production. Its primary cause, however, lay in the automotive field — not especially from further decentralization, not especially from automation, but from the severe slump in automotive demand. Fewer cars and trucks were produced in 1958 than in any year since 1947. Fewer vehicles were produced than in 1929 — some 30 years earlier. Such a slump could not but affect Detroit and the state severely. Long-range pessimism based largely on the 1958 slump hardly seems justified.

Some of the current misgivings may be based on a tendency to equate Michigan's problems with those of Detroit. The Detroit area is of course more heavily weighted with the automotive industry than the rest of the state. Moreover, Detroit is faced with an industrial problem with which many metropolitan areas are being confronted. The current tendency toward one-story plants with suitable parking and loading areas often means industrial location or relocation in outlying areas. Detroit may suffer from this and related problems after the balance of the state has made substantial industrial recovery.

Favorable Factors

Fortunately, there are also some favorable factors in Michigan's long-range outlook. Foremost is Michigan's long-time industrial background. It does not seem likely that a state in which from 13 to 17 percent of the state's people held factory jobs in the postwar period through 1957 is going to remain indefinitely at the relatively low level of industrialization that prevailed during 1958 and early 1959. The state's location in the nation's "manufacturing belt" and its vast reservoir of plant and equipment, of management skills and know-how (especially in mass-production techniques), and of skilled, highly trained, and well-educated workers should be major assets in the restoration to Michigan of its position as a leading industrial state.

In Chapter V, we referred to the increase in Michigan's plant inventory during 1958 — a somewhat surprising development in view of the fairly widespread assumption that the state was losing plants, not gaining them. Such growth during 1958, a year of limited economic opportunities, can only be regarded as encouraging, especially since some of the growth reflected plant move-ins. This increase in plant inventory during 1958 marked a continuation of the increase that had been indicated for earlier years by other data. More expansion of Michigan's plant inventory may be expected. These new plants, small though they may be on the average, will provide more jobs for Michigan workers in the years ahead.

There are also other encouraging signs of recent growth in the Michigan economy. In Chapter III, we pointed out that, while employment in Michigan's heavy industries was declining sharply during the years 1953 to 1957, jobs in the nondurable industries were increasing steadily, if modestly. Michigan Employment Security Commission data (revised series) suggest that there was a further small gain in 1958. This strength in Michigan's nondurable goods employment looks especially good when it is noted that in the country as a whole workers in the nondurable lines were decreasing by about 6 percent during the same 5-year period.[4] In the same chapter, we also noted that, according to BLS data, nonmanufacturing jobs in Michigan increased by over 100,000 from

---

4 *Employment and Earnings — Annual Supplement Issue,* May, 1959, Table SA-1.

1953 to 1957, offsetting in part the sizable loss of defense and automotive jobs.

The fact that Michigan has shown up well in a number of smaller growth industries is also encouraging. Though current employment opportunities in these industries are relatively limited, Michigan's good showing in many of them, in comparison with the nation and with the other Great Lakes states, represents a potential for future growth. It is conceivable that developments now unforeseen could result in a sudden spurt of development in one of these fields. Michigan's established position could permit it to advance rapidly in the industry.

Although Michigan shares most of its principal industrial location advantages with its sister states in the region, there are some factors that are Michigan's alone. The state has several raw materials (salt, limestone, iron, copper, and forest products) that serve as an attraction to industries oriented around such materials. Its outstanding importance in several industries gives it an advantage both as a supplier of semi-processed materials for further fabrication and as a market for other suppliers. Its favorable water situation will become increasingly a strong advantage. With increased leisure time, its extensive recreational advantages will make it increasingly attractive as a state in which to work and live. Even though much of Michigan's future industrial growth will reflect internal expansion, as it has in the past, the state does have locational factors that will continue to attract firms into the state from outside. These factors should in many cases be strong enough to offset the apparent lower costs of operation of some industries elsewhere.

Another factor favorable to Michigan's long-range future was the developing awareness by its people during 1959 of the nature of the state's employment problem and their desire to do something about the situation. During 1959, there were a number of indications that the people of Michigan were realizing increasingly the importance of closing ranks and of approaching the problem constructively. Representatives of various segments of Michigan's economy urged a positive approach. Reflecting these views, an editorial appearing in the *Michigan Manufacturer and Financial Record* for April, 1959, urged:

> In May, the sixth annual "Michigan Week" will be celebrated — based on the newly adopted slogan "We're Proud of Michigan." Never has there been a more appropriate time for residents of the state, regardless of political affiliation, to get together under

that banner. Only by concerted and untiring efforts to "accent the positive" and proclaim the outstanding advantages of the state can the harm of the past few years be corrected.

The Employment Outlook, 1970

Can the state expect to provide jobs for about 3.8 million workers by 1970, as medium population projections for the state would seem to require? We think that the achievement of such an employment goal is a reasonable possibility. We think that the realization of at least the 3.6 million job level implied by the low population projection for Michigan (9.4 million persons) is a strong possibility.

If we were to look solely at the recent job situation in Michigan, it would be difficult to make these statements which undoubtedly will seem unrealistic to some. However, we are guided primarily by the "long look" which has been stressed in this report. When a choice between the long look and the short look as a guide to long-range prospects is required, we prefer to be guided by the former. It was pointed out in Chapter II that Michigan's population and labor force have for a number of decades grown more rapidly than those of the nation. As the state's population has grown, so also have job opportunities. In prosperous periods, Michigan's rate of population and employment growth has been especially rapid.

In the preceding chapter, it was noted that the population projections through 1970 shown for Michigan are essentially quite conservative. In this chapter, the high level of economic activity projected for the nation through the sixties has been indicated. Just how conservative the population projections for Michigan through 1970 are, in view of the expected high level of economic activity ahead, is suggested by the following data. They show Michigan's

Period	Rate of Population Increase (percent)		Ratio of Increase, Michigan to United States
	United States	Michigan	
1910-1920	14.9	30.5	2.05
1920-1930	16.1	32.0	1.99
1930-1940	7.2	8.5	1.18
1940-1950	14.5	21.2	1.46
1950-1958	15.0	23.5	1.57
1958-1970	21.8	[a]25.8	1.18
1958-1970	21.8	[b]19.4	.89

Source: Data for 1910-1958 from Table 2. Rate of increase 1958-1970 for the United States based on a medium population projection of 211 million persons in 1970. See Bureau of the Census, *Current Population Reports*, Series P-25, No. 187, November 10, 1958, p. 2.

[a]Based on medium projection of 9.9 million population in 1970.
[b]Based on low projection of 9.4 million population in 1970.

rate of population growth in comparison with that of the nation, both for recent decades and as projected for the period through 1970.

These data emphasize the conservative character of the population projections that have been made for the state. The medium population projection of 9.9 million persons living in Michigan in 1970 would mean that during the anticipated prosperous period ahead the state would be growing, relative to the nation, at a rate comparable to that of the depressed thirties, when Michigan was more adversely affected than the nation at large. And the low projection of 9.4 million persons in the state by 1970 would mean that Michigan would have grown less rapidly than the nation. This would be the first period in more than a half-century in which Michigan had grown at a less rapid rate than the nation and this unusual development would occur in the face of anticipated rapid growth in economic activity in the nation, a period when Michigan is ordinarily on the "feast" side of the "feast-or-famine" cycle.

It may be difficult to see jobs in Michigan numbering in the neighborhood of 3.6 to 3.8 million in 1970. It is more difficult to see the rate of population growth in the state dropping below that implied by the low projection of 9.4 million. It would mean that the rate of population growth of 1.5 times that of the nation from 1950 to 1958 would be followed by one that was well under the national rate. Such a sharp modification of long-time relationships is possible but it seems unlikely. Such modifications ordinarily occur gradually, rather than abruptly.

We are not discounting the seriousness of Michigan's employ-ment problem. But we think that a problem of a few years' dura-tion should not be used as a basis for projecting the long-run growth of population and of job opportunities in Michigan unless there is a strong presumption that the problem cannot be solved. If the problem cannot be coped with, then the full employment year of 1955 did indeed mark the end of an era in Michigan.

As already indicated, we believe that Michigan's employment problem can be solved to the extent of making it possible to meet the employment goals implied by the projections of population for 1970. The strong underlying forces that have contributed to the state's dynamic growth in the past will assist in the adjustments that are necessary. However, neither a solution to the state's em-ployment problem nor the achievement of the 1970 employment goals will develop automatically. The 3.6 to 3.8 million jobs needed by 1970 can be provided only through the cooperative effort of all those who, by virtue of holding positions of influence or responsibility in Michigan, play important roles in the state's development.

New areas of industrial activity must be developed. Michigan's favorable locational factors must be exploited to the fullest. Action must be taken to eliminate or reduce the importance of unfavorable factors. The efforts of all citizens must be enlisted to assist in making the long-range adjustments needed to provide reasonably full employment for a continually increasing population.

Suggested Lines of Action

DURING THE COURSE of this study, we have received suggestions from a number of persons concerning steps to be taken to increase job opportunities in Michigan and to promote economic growth in the state in general. Additional areas of action have been suggested by the writings of other students of the Michigan economy as well as by our own studies. We present here a brief discussion of several of these indicated lines of action. While we have not had the opportunity to explore fully the factual basis underlying all of these proposals, there seems little doubt that these are areas of activity in which positive action could enhance the state's long-range economic prospects.

Greater Diversification

Greater diversification of Michigan's industrial base has been suggested from time to time in the past. The basis for this recommendation has been that such a wider range of industrial activity was needed to mitigate the swings in production and employment in the auto industry and in certain other durable industries. Now, diversification becomes a "must" for the state in order that we may compensate for the loss of defense and auto jobs.

One may wonder why attempts at diversification have not been pushed more actively in the state before now. The answer appears to be that until 1956 there were not enough workers in the state to permit significant expansion in nonautomotive lines. During the postwar period, the state enjoyed full or more-than-full employment through 1955, except for the recession years. Indeed, during the defense period of 1951 through 1953, Michigan's problem was generally one of finding workers for jobs, not that of finding jobs for workers. During much of the postwar period, Michigan could hardly have advertised to outside industrialists that it had an abundant supply of skilled labor available to man additional plants in nonautomotive lines.

The analysis of growth industries in Michigan made earlier in this report provides an excellent take-off point for identifying industries which hold promise for Michigan. It pinpoints growth industries in which Michigan has made good advances in the postwar years. It indicates others where Michigan has failed to share in regional or national expansion. It indicates also industrial areas in which Michigan has experienced decline. More detailed studies of these industries and of Michigan's locational advantages and disadvantages for them should be carried out in order to provide useful guidelines in promoting development of those industries that seem to hold promise for the state.

Although greater stability of manufacturing employment is a goal for Michigan's future, we must recognize that most of our future additional development will likely occur in the durable industries. It is these industries that have experienced substantial employment increases in recent years. It is probable that expansion of the durable lines will continue to mark the state's industrial expansion. Like other leading industrial states, Michigan will probably have to expect substantial cyclical variations in factory jobs in the future as it has in the past.

However, the recent steady, if unspectacular, growth of Michigan factory jobs in nondurable lines does hold some promise for somewhat greater industrial job stability in the state. Efforts should be directed toward increasing the rate of growth in these nondurable industries so that the share of all industrial jobs accounted for by these more stable industries can increase somewhat and thus soften the dips and peaks in the state's factory job levels.

Increased Product Research

The profitability of many companies stems from products not even known a decade ago. The managements of large firms are generally aware of the need for continuous product research and for the more basic research that underlies new products and services. However, a need for more product research on the part of many medium-size firms in the state has been suggested. This need is represented as being especially acute for many of the firms supplying the automotive industry. Cases are cited in which such firms have concentrated their production facilities on a given part or piece of equipment. If the contract for this product is lost, then the company finds itself with its principal market gone. The closing of a number of plants from this type of problem has been mentioned.

Many of these firms are reported to be of a size sufficient to permit the research necessary for the development of new products. The fabrication of a wider range of products would enable these companies to cope more successfully with changes in the nature of their market and to smooth their employment levels. Any cooperative efforts that could be carried out by state agencies, universities, trade associations, and other groups with medium-size and smaller companies to promote more product development should pay dividends in more stabilized, continuous employment opportunities in these firms.

Greater Participation in Federal Expenditure Programs

The need for obtaining more defense contracts for Michigan is obvious. A number of groups around the state are, of course, working toward this end. In our efforts to divert more defense procurement into the state, we should not overlook, however, other areas of federal expenditures. A detailed study of all expenditure programs reflected in the federal budget may suggest some nondefense areas in which the state's industries could gain a larger market.

In view of the certainty that federal spending, both defense and nondefense, will provide the market for a substantial share of the nation's output of goods and services for the foreseeable future, continued attention to federal spending patterns would seem advisable.

Promotion of Tourism

As a means of broadening the state's economic base, efforts to promote Michigan's tourist industry should be continued. Sharply increased tourist expenditures could in the future provide a partial offset, although likely a relatively limited one, for the possible lessened importance of manufacturing activity in the state's economy.

A recent study suggests that by 1970 there might be an increase of from 20,000 to 40,000 more jobs in northern Michigan (the Upper Peninsula and the northern Lower Peninsula) in those industries that serve the tourist trade.[5] While an increase of this size is quite modest in relation to the total additional jobs needed by

---

5 W. Paul Strassmann, *Economic Growth in Northern Michigan* (East Lansing: Michigan State University, 1958), p. 15.

1970, employment considerations should not be the sole guide in evaluating the impact of tourism. Increasing tourist expenditures can provide a basis for an increasing level of per capita income for upstate Michigan even though job opportunities themselves increase less rapidly than one would wish.

A full-scale study of the tourist "industry" in Michigan, including its economic potential, seems necessary if we are to know more precisely the contribution to economic growth in Michigan that can be realized from an expanding tourist trade.

Increased Industrial Promotion

There is urgent need for an aggressive industrial promotion program by the state of Michigan. Michigan has the potential to continue to be a leading industrial state on the basis of its past and current high degree of industrialization. But the impetus provided by gaining a substantial number of additional new factories from outside the state would help to provide the additional growth needed in the years ahead to compensate for the recent loss of production and employment in defense and motor vehicles. A successful promotion program of this type could shorten the period of adjustment that lies ahead for Michigan.

Such a promotional program clearly falls within the jurisdiction of the Michigan Economic Development Commission and its operating organization, the Michigan Department of Economic Development. While the latter agency would not need to carry out all phases of such a program, it should act as the coordinating and operating agency responsible for this activity.

There are several lines of activity that such a program could entail. We have already referred to the need for more detailed studies of growth industries. There is need also for analyses of the costs of operating firms in Michigan communities versus those in nearby states.[6] Such studies could "pinpoint" promising industries for Michigan in terms of the state's locational advantages for such industries. Such studies could be supplemented by the enlightened knowledge of industrial leaders in the state. It is possible that these investigations of promising industries for Michigan could be carried out as part of the research program of the Committee on Michigan's Economic Future. In any event, knowledge of the industries for which Michigan has clear-cut advantages is necessary if indus-

---

6 In view of the appreciable range in operating costs for a company within any one state, caution must be exercised in drawing general conclusions on interstate differences in operating costs. See the discussion on this point in Appendix D to this report.

trial promotion activities are to be carried out as intelligently as possible.

We do not know the size of staff needed by the Michigan Department of Economic Development to carry out a level of promotional activity commensurate with the state's need for attracting new industry. It can be assumed to be larger than the present staff of the Department. Knowledge of promising industries for the state will be of little usefulness unless the Department has sufficient personnel to utilize such knowledge in appropriate contacts with firms in the industries involved.

A long-range program of continuing institutional advertising of Michigan as a site for industrial location also seems indicated. The value of such advertising may be questioned. At the worst, however, it could do no harm. At best, it could facilitate the industrial promotion work of the Michigan Department of Economic Development, of the Michigan Industrial Ambassadors, and of other private promotional groups. A scanning of state promotional efforts in such publications as *Fortune, Business Week,* and *Industrial Development and Manufacturer's Record* reveals that a number of states continued aggressive promotional advertising through the 1958 recession. Advertising by the state of Michigan was conspicuously absent.[7] Fortunately, the utilities and other business groups continued to advertise Michigan's locational advantages, thus giving the state some promotional publicity.

A state-sponsored advertising program could do much to dispel the unfavorable publicity that the state has received in the last few years. Publicizing the fact that more than 250 new enterprises or plant expansions were announced in Michigan during 1958 — during the state's worst postwar recession — could suggest to enterprisers elsewhere that there are advantages for carrying on operations in the state. And Michigan does have some especially strong locational factors, such as its water resources, to offer to industrialists. In this connection, it is significant that the state of Illinois early in 1959 carried an advertisement in *Business Week* pointing to its water resources as a reason for plant location in Illinois.[8] Michigan can hardly afford to stand by while other states capitalize on locational advantages in which Michigan ranks at the top.

Obviously, such a promotional program as has been outlined

7 The special advertising supplement on Michigan appearing in the January, 1958, issue of *Fortune* was made possible by the cooperation of a number of the state's manufacturing and business firms.
8 January 31, 1959, p. 100.

above is going to cost money. However, failure to provide funds for the industrial promotion of Michigan could prove to be short-sighted economy. If the drag in Michigan's industrial economy were to continue indefinitely, the state's fiscal difficulties could be compounded in the years ahead. We suggest that adequate funds be made available to the Michigan Department of Economic Development to permit a sustained full-scale program of research, industrial promotion contacts, and promotional advertising.

Increased Vocational Training and Guidance

Reference has been made to the fact that many of the Michigan workers unemployed in 1958 and 1959, especially those in the Detroit area, did not possess the skills needed to fill the jobs that developed during the recovery period. While some of these workers in the surplus labor pool may not be susceptible to retraining, many of them undoubtedly are. Since job opportunities may continue to develop relatively slowly during 1960 and thereafter, efforts should be made to provide vocational training for those unemployed workers who would benefit by it.

The changing importance of various types of occupations in Michigan in the next few years was suggested in the preceding chapter. Positions requiring higher levels of education and training — those held by professional and technical workers — are going to increase tremendously; jobs requiring little or no training — notably those filled by laborers — will actually be decreasing. Our educators, as well as citizens in general, must become aware of the continuous improvement in educational facilities and vocational training programs that must be provided if new entrants into the labor force are to be prepared to fill the higher skill jobs that are going to be available in the years ahead. A great deal more research appears to be needed in the field of the new entrant into the labor force, the extent of job counseling provided by today's high schools, and the fitness of the average high school graduate for entrance into the complex labor market.

Compared with that of many other states, Michigan's labor force is well-educated and highly skilled. However, without increased emphasis in the area of vocational training and guidance to meet changing occupational patterns, Michigan's relative position could suffer in the future. Moreover, without such emphasis, some of the new job opportunities that will develop in the state might temporarily go without takers, thus contributing to a delay in the restoration of full employment in Michigan.

Passage of the "Economic Growth Act of 1960"

In view of the paramount importance of encouraging the economic growth of Michigan, in view of the need to capitalize on factors in Michigan's economic environment that are favorable to such growth, and in view of the need to eliminate or minimize as much as possible the unfavorable aspects of the state's economic setting, an "Economic Growth Act of 1960" is recommended to the people of Michigan and to their elected officials.

The Act would be a short affirmation of the intent of the state government to concern itself with the sound economic growth of the state. It would provide for a Governor's Council of Economic Advisers. It would require the Governor to deliver to the legislature an annual or biennial report on the economic situation of the state. Finally, it would set up a Joint Committee of the House and Senate on the Economic Report. The Joint Committee would be provided with its own staff. The Committee would consider the Governor's Economic Report, would conduct its own hearings, would direct its staff to provide such additional information as it wished, and would consider needed legislation in the light of all available information.

The outstanding virtue of the Act would be its requirement of an annual or biennial, over-all, objective appraisal of the state's economic situation. Such an appraisal would provide a review of the extent to which economic growth was providing adequate job opportunities for the state's increasing population. It would provide a review of the factors — both favorable and unfavorable — that were influencing the rate of economic development. Although the structure provided by the Act would resemble that outlined in the national *Employment Act of 1946,* the focus would be on economic growth, rather than on employment as such.

The appraisal of the state's economic situation would be based on the latest available data on population growth, labor force and employment trends, income levels, plant gains and losses, capital expenditure developments, state revenues and expenditures, and related economic developments.[9] The interpretation of this integrated set of economic data on Michigan, coupled with an analysis of underlying forces, could provide a comprehensive basis for public understanding and for appropriate action, both by the ex-

---

9 An important additional advantage of the annual or biennial review of available economic data would be that it would promote an improvement in the quality and volume of economic information available on the state. The better the basic information, the better the policy decisions that can be made to promote economic growth in Michigan.

ecutive department and by the legislature. Such action could result in the promotion of economic growth in Michigan by providing the best possible business climate, using the term in its best sense to mean as favorable a setting for business and industry as is compatible with the interests of all the people of the state.

A Program of Action and Study

A CONCLUDING SECTION of the summary chapter of this book provides a suggested program of action and study for Michigan citizens, based in part on discussions in this and preceding chapters and in part on discussions carried out in the body of that chapter. The attention of the reader is directed to that program (pp. 53-56) which is intended to provide a basis for advancing the economic growth of the state of Michigan.

APPENDIX CHAPTERS

Introduction

A WORD OF COMMENT may be needed to explain why the particular documents given in these Appendix Chapters are being presented.

At a very early stage in our work on this study of the Michigan economy, the importance of labor, taxation, and transportation became apparent to us, as factors which would substantially affect the economic destiny of the state of Michigan. Either as factors of intrinsic economic importance, or as factors of public interest, these three matters deserve special treatment. But we recognized also that a definitive and complete study of any one of these three subjects would be a very large undertaking — as large, in terms of time and money, as we envisioned for our whole study of the Michigan economy. The best we could hope to do, in the case of these three subjects, would be to secure an organized presentation of what is already known concerning them, together with a statement of what additional knowledge is needed in order for the people of Michigan to be able to appraise these determinants of their economic future.

Persons or groups of known experience and competence were chosen to prepare these reports: Dr. Daniel Kruger on the labor factor; Dr. Harvey Brazer on taxation; and Fantus Factory Locating Service on transportation. These three reports are presented without any implication of either agreement or disagreement on the part of the principal authors of this study.

Appendix D presents an illustrative study of the variable operating costs of a hypothetical company in each of eleven cities. We requested Fantus Factory Locating Service to secure this information for us because of our belief that the average intelligent citizen is not familiar with the methods used by industrial firms in seeking a suitable location for their plants; and because of our belief that an appreciation of these methods would be helpful to all citizens in thinking about the attractiveness of our state as a location for additional industry. Although the results of this study are not conclusive with respect to interstate operating differences as such, they do shed considerable light on the relative importance of various industrial location factors, and on the reasons why some communities are more costly than others as a location for factory operations.

Appendix E presents in systematic fashion our thoughts as to the most important areas in which the people of Michigan need additional information in order to guide our state more surely along the path of continued economic progress.

We hope that these Appendix Chapters will be useful, as important materials supplementing the chapters of the report itself.

Appendix A

The Labor Factor in Plant Location in Michigan

LABOR AND INDUSTRIAL RELATIONS CENTER

MICHIGAN STATE UNIVERSITY

THERE ARE MANY factors affecting plant location. In choosing a new location or expanding facilities of an existing plant, management examines a complex of technological, engineering, and economic considerations. Access to materials and markets, cost of transportation, availability and cost of labor and power are among the important factors given serious consideration by management. The relative importance of each of these factors depends on the type of operation and its orientation.

There are three broad categories of industries. A firm may be market-oriented, materials-oriented, or labor-oriented. In the first instance, the firm builds a plant to serve a particular market, e.g., a tire plant in Detroit or Jackson to serve the automobile manufacturing centers. A firm which is materials-oriented must have its plants located close to sources of supplies, e.g., a cement plant located close to limestone deposits. (There are, however, exceptions in locating a plant close to sources of raw materials. The important consideration in hauling heavy bulky material is the cost of transportation. Iron ore from the Lake Superior region can be hauled cheaply to the steel manufacturing centers.) A firm may be labor-oriented in that primary emphasis is on the quantity and quality of labor available, and on its cost. While labor supply is important it is a matter not only of numbers but also of skills, age, sex, and race. A labor-oriented firm has a certain degree of mobility as determined by transportation costs. For example, such a firm can move from one location to another if the savings in labor costs are larger than the additional cost of transportation.[1]

The focus of attention in this paper is on the labor factor in plant location. This immediately raises the question of definition of the term, *labor factor*. As used here it means more than the quantity of labor willing, able, and available to work. It includes the quality of that labor and its management. Since this labor works in a particular area or environment, consideration must be given to the economic, social, and legal factors affecting that environment. Thus, the labor factor is defined as the quantity and quality of labor available in a given environment in which the work effort of individuals is both directed and expended in a particular process.

Although there is much discussion about the labor factor in plant location, there is no general agreement as to its importance. It must also be recognized that it is difficult to extract and isolate this factor from the matrix of economic, legal, and social factors affecting plant location decisions. Although there are many elements affecting the labor factor, little is known about the relative importance of each, as viewed by employers. The task is also complicated by the lack of complete data which could be used to compare the labor factor in several different areas. Recognizing the difficulties inherent in trying to isolate it and in using the available data, an effort will be made to analyze the labor factor in Michigan.

The importance of the labor factor appears to be related to the nature of the work. In labor-oriented operations, relatively large quantities of labor are required. Some of the unskilled labor can be easily trained to perform the simple repetitive operations required in textiles, apparel, and shoes. The machinery or metal fabricating industries require a labor force possessing more highly developed skills.

In non-labor-oriented industries the emphasis is on markets, materials, and other factors such as weather. The automobile, aircraft, paper, steel, and chemical industries, to mention a few, are illustrative of the non-labor-oriented type of operation. Since the automobile industry in Michigan is of prime importance, the remarks of M. E. Coyle, then Executive Vice President of General Motors, speaking before the 34th Annual Conference of American Chamber of Commerce Executives in 1948, are most significant.

---

1 C. J. Friedrich, editor and translator, Alfred Weber's *Theory of Location of Industries* (Chicago: University of Chicago Press, 1929), p. 103.

In dealing with the questions of locating new plants, automobile producers have some considerations not apparent in other industries. The size and cost of our product makes it impossible to store any substantial quantity either in buildings or on adjacent property. Cars and trucks must be shipped promptly after they are produced.

Inbound and outbound freight are important considerations . . . only four finished cars can be shipped in a single freight car or on a single haulaway. This would require 2,500[2] loads to move the daily production of General Motors and it would be impossible to move any such quantity of material into and out of a single assembly point in any day. This necessitates assembly plants in certain areas where the finished cars can be moved quickly into the hands of the dealer and customers.

We have found that an area consumption of 400 cars and trucks daily for 200 days per year justified an assembly plant. This insured an annual volume of 80,000 units.[3]

Proximity to the market for the finished product, according to Mr. Coyle, is "one of the positive factors in selecting a site for an assembly plant." While he cited other factors such as transportation, water, power, and labor, the emphasis was on market considerations. His remarks on the labor factor are noteworthy.

In locating new plants, we never give consideration to moving away from labor trouble. Organized labor is on a national basis. If you have trouble in one area you will have it in another. Moving will not cure the condition.

There is another thing you cannot do. You cannot move out of one high labor cost area into low cost areas. It used to be that the South paid subnormal wages. You cannot do that any more. The union is a national union and exchanges information, and they insist upon weekly pay within near limits.[4]

Thus it would seem that the labor factor is not always the most important element in plant location decisions. It appears to be more significant in labor-oriented than non-labor-oriented industries. Where it is important, what kinds of data do employers need to assess properly the labor factor in an area? Are employers only interested in those considerations which affect labor costs? What weight, if any, is given to noneconomic considerations, e.g., the "business climate" of the state? Having determined what pertinent data are necessary to making an intelligent decision, can we secure such data? If so, how complete or extensive are the data? What yardstick will be used to evaluate such data?

In evaluating the labor factor in plant location in Michigan, the available data on economic and legal considerations affecting labor

---

2 G. M. built 2,169,186 cars in 1958. Assuming that 200 days were worked in producing automobiles, it would require 2,710 loads to move daily production.

3 M. E. Coyle, "Factors in Factory Location," (paper read before the American Chamber of Commerce Executives, Philadelphia, October 12, 1948), p. 2 of a mimeographed copy.

4 Ibid., pp. 3-4.

costs will be examined. The former include wages, labor productivity, living costs, work stoppages, and labor stability. Although there are various types of state labor legislation, attention will be focused primarily on Workmen's Compensation and Unemployment Insurance since they both affect labor costs. Since students of plant location strongly suggest that the business climate of the state be investigated, one aspect of that climate, namely, the labor situation, will also be discussed.

Since the data must be compared, the yardstick used, where appropriate, is the data for the United States as a whole, the East North Central region, and other states in the region. The data are, in some instances, incomplete, incomparable, and limited. Therefore, in the summary of this paper, there are suggestions for further studies which would furnish additional data for a more complete analysis of the labor factor in plant location in Michigan.

Economic Considerations

Wages

The importance of wage rates on plant location varies. If labor costs are a high percentage of the total cost of a given product, the community wage structures will be a significant factor in the location of a plant. There is little information available on specific wage rates for given jobs in individual companies. Some firms and employer associations in the state conduct periodic wage surveys, but these data are not available to the public.

The Bureau of Labor Statistics, the Michigan Employment Security Commission, and similar agencies in other states, publish certain data relative to wages. The state agency in its monthly *Labor Market* publishes "average weekly earnings," "average weekly hours," and "average hourly earnings" by industry for each of the principal labor market areas in the state. It must be emphasized that the data are earnings, not wage rates. Average hourly and weekly earnings differ from hourly and weekly wage rates in that they are affected by overtime wage rates, part-time earnings, and the length of the work-week. Although the data are for average earnings, both weekly and hourly, they do give a very rough index of wage rates. Table A-1 compares the earnings data for production workers in manufacturing for the United States and the states in the East North Central region for the years 1956-1958.

From this table it is clear that average weekly earnings of production workers in manufacturing in Michigan are the highest

Table A-1

Average Weekly Earnings, Average Weekly Hours, and Average Hourly Earnings for Production Workers for Select States

1956-1958

Area	Average Weekly Earnings			Average Weekly Hours			Average Hourly Earnings		
	1958	1957	1956	1958	1957	1956	1958	1957	1956
United States.......	$83.58	$82.39	$79.99	39.1	39.8	40.4	$2.13	$2.07	$1.98
East North Central States.....	92.38	89.27	88.57	39.5	40.5	41.0	2.34	2.26	2.16
Ohio...............	93.27	93.36	90.81	38.9	40.2	41.0	2.40	2.32	2.21
Indiana............	91.89	90.56	86.66	39.3	40.2	40.7	2.34	2.25	2.13
Illinois............	89.85	88.67	86.15	39.4	40.3	41.0	2.28	2.20	2.10
MICHIGAN........	99.29	97.64	94.98	39.4	40.8	40.8	2.52	2.44	2.33
Wisconsin.........	87.62	86.10	84.25	40.4	40.9	41.7	2.17	2.10	2.02

Source: U. S. Department of Labor, *Monthly Labor Review*, March, 1959.

in the region. They are, in fact, the highest in the nation. In 1958, average weekly earnings in Michigan were $99.29 as compared with $83.58 for the United States. Michigan also led the nation in 1956 and 1957. Earnings in the state are high for several important reasons. Michigan is one of the great industrial states of the nation. In 1957, 43 percent of the employees in nonagricultural establishments were in manufacturing as compared with 32 percent for the nation. The manufacturing sector of the state's economy is composed of industries utilizing large numbers of skilled and semi-skilled workers. In 1957, roughly 45 percent of the working population were in the skilled and semi-skilled classifications as compared with 34 percent for the nation. With a large proportion of such employees in the civilian labor force, it is to be expected that earnings would be high. As Woytinsky has pointed out, wage rates for skilled workers throughout manufacturing industries in the United States average about 55 percent higher than those for unskilled; semi-skilled operations requiring considerable ability average about 35 percent more than the unskilled; semi-skilled operations largely repetitive in nature average about 15 percent more than unskilled.[5]

Another reason for the high level of earnings of workers in Michigan is that 80 percent of the employees in manufacturing are

5 W. S. Woytinsky and Associates, *Employment and Wages in the United States* (New York: Twentieth Century Fund, 1953), p. 466.

employed in high wage-paying industries, e.g., motor vehicles, primary and fabricated metals, machinery and chemicals. The auto industry is a high wage-paying industry. In a news release *(Lansing State Journal,* January 25, 1959), John S. Bugas, Vice President of the Ford Motor Company, reported that wages paid by the company in 1958 to hourly-rated workers averaged $2.739 per hour and $108.88 weekly, which in both instances were the highest in the company's history. By comparison, the average weekly earnings in 1958 for production workers in the United States were $83.58.

Since the automobile industry and the work force of the state are both highly organized, there is the tendency to ascribe high average weekly and hourly earnings to unionism. A variety of studies have been made regarding the influence of unionism on earnings. All are complex in detail and all have found it difficult to separate the influence of unionism from that of other important factors. There are many problems involved in making a valid study of this kind. These studies are not conclusive; they are subject to statistical weaknesses of various sorts, and they show disagreement among the authors. Inconclusive as these studies may be, it is recognized that unions do have bargaining power. They can and do make it expensive for an employer to reject a given demand. Wages at any particular moment are not solely determined by supply and demand. Although the evidence is not conclusive, unionization and bargaining power may play an important role.

To return to the data in Table A-1, the averages for the state are calculated on the basis of data from ten labor markets in the state —Detroit, Battle Creek, Benton Harbor-Niles, Flint, Grand Rapids, Jackson, Kalamazoo, Lansing, Muskegon, and Saginaw.[6]. There is considerable variation in average weekly earnings of production workers in these labor markets, as indicated in Table A-2. Depending on production scheduling and on the number of work stoppages, there are also variations in average weekly earnings from month to month. These differences suggest that the data be used carefully in making comparisons or drawing sweeping conclusions.

---

6 A labor market covers a geographic area consisting of a central city (or cities) and the surrounding territory within a reasonable commuting distance. It may be thought of as an economically and socially integrated, primarily urban, geographical unit within which workers may readily change their jobs without changing their places of residence. A labor market area takes its name from the central city or cities, but may have many other communities within its boundaries. Major labor market areas usually have at least one central city with a population of 50,000 or more, according to the 1950 Census. In most instances, boundaries of major labor market areas coincide with those of Standard Metropolitan Areas, as determined by a Federal interagency committee.

Average Weekly Earnings, Average Weekly Hours, and Average Hourly Earnings in Manufacturing Industries, Selected Michigan Labor Market Areas

September and October, 1958

Area	Average Weekly Earnings		Average Weekly Hours		Average Hourly Earnings	
	September	October	September	October	September	October
Michigan.....................	$101.63	$98.09	40.2	39.3	$2.53	$2.50
Detroit.....................	107.09	105.21	39.9	39.2	2.68	2.68
Battle Creek...............	97.19	96.52	39.3	39.3	2.47	2.46
Benton Harbor-Niles........	90.43	90.78	42.9	42.4	2.11	2.14
Flint.......................	105.30	66.14	39.9	25.1	2.64	2.64
Grand Rapids...............	93.37	83.14	40.7	37.1	2.29	2.24
Jackson....................	101.18	94.33	41.4	38.9	2.44	2.43
Kalamazoo.................	95.72	95.60	42.3	41.8	2.26	2.29
Lansing....................	105.27	99.73	39.8	39.7	2.65	2.51
Muskegon.................	95.77	95.04	39.3	39.0	2.44	2.44
Saginaw...................	100.98	82.36	41.2	37.1	2.45	2.22

Source: Michigan Employment Security Commission, *Michigan's Labor Market*, November, 1958, and December, 1958.

To illustrate the limitations in making interstate comparisons, using average earnings, Table A-3 presents data for five "comparable" industry classifications for Michigan and Ohio for September, 1958. At first glance, one might say that the earnings of production workers for certain industries, as shown in this table, are about the same in both Michigan and Ohio. There is, however, a difference of about twenty dollars in average weekly earnings in the metalworking machinery industry. Before any tentative conclusions can be made about the earnings in this industry, we need to know whether the industry classifications as reported by the two state agencies are composed of the same components. The BLS reports three components under this classification, whereas Michigan and Ohio publish data only for the industry. For the month of September, 1958, the BLS data on average weekly earnings for this industry classification for the nation indicate a difference of $12.82 between two of the industry's components (see Table A-4). Therefore, if the broad industry classification — metalworking machinery — for Michigan and Ohio does not include the same components, the earnings data are not comparable.

If we assume that the earnings data are comparable, one possible explanation for the higher earnings in metalworking machinery in

Table A-3

Average Weekly Earnings, Average Weekly Hours, and Average Hourly Earnings of Production Workers in Select Manufacturing Industries, Michigan and Ohio

September, 1958

Industry	Average Weekly Earnings		Average Weekly Hours		Average Hourly Earnings	
	Michigan	Ohio	Michigan	Ohio	Michigan	Ohio
Service-industry and household machinery...............	$102.30	$103.93	40.5	41.1	$2.53	$2.53
Electrical generating, transmission, distribution, and industrial apparatus..........	88.91	89.96	39.5	39.1	2.25	2.30
Fabricated structural metal products.....................	97.69	99.29	39.3	40.9	2.42	2.43
Stamping, coating, and engraving....................	105.87	106.25	40.5	42.0	2.61	2.53
Metalworking machinery........	115.48	94.76	39.0	38.5	2.96	2.46

Source: Michigan Employment Security Commission, *Michigan's Labor Market,* November, 1958, and Ohio Bureau of Unemployment Compensation, *Ohio Labor Market Information,* October, 1958.

Michigan is the wage structure in Detroit. The BLS recently conducted a survey of wages in the machinery industries in twenty-one areas in 1957-1958.[7] This study indicated that Detroit, with straight time average hourly earnings in excess of $2.75 in nearly all the skilled jobs considered, "continued to lead in pay levels for machinery workers among the 21 areas."[8] Earnings of tool and die

Table A-4

Average Weekly Earnings, Average Weekly Hours, and Average Hourly Earnings of Production Workers in Metalworking Machinery, United States

September, 1958

Industry	Average Weekly Earnings	Average Weekly Hours	Average Hourly Earnings
Metalworking machinery	$ 99.31	39.1	$2.54
Machine tools........................	91.06	38.1	2.39
Metalworking machinery except machine tools..............	98.04	38.6	2.54
Machine tool accessories............	103.88	39.8	2.61

Source: U. S. Department of Labor, *Monthly Labor Review,* January, 1959.

7 Morris H. Rice, "Wages and Related Practices in the Machinery Industries, 1957-1958," *Monthly Labor Review,* September, 1958, pp. 991-999.
8 *Ibid,* p. 991.

makers in shops producing machine-tool accessories on a job or order basis were the highest in Detroit with $3.49 an hour. Likewise, Detroit machine-tool operators who set up their own machines and perform a variety of machining operations to close tolerances had the highest earnings. The hourly earnings for the unskilled laboring jobs studied were also the highest in Detroit, with janitors and cleaners averaging $2.19 an hour and material handlers, $2.27 an hour. The study revealed that average straight time hourly earnings for over half the selected occupations were highest in Detroit. The earnings in the machinery industry for the state as a whole reflect the pay levels of Detroit machinery workers.

There are other limitations in making wage comparisons between firms in the same industry in different states. For example, are the workers of identical quality, are they working equally hard, and are the jobs identical? Although many jobs such as telephone operator, clerk-typist, and calculating machine operator are reasonably uniform for a given grade of skill in different places, many others are not. For example, a drill press operator working with one type of steel may not be comparable with another drill press operator working with another type of steel.

Consideration must also be given to the cost of fringe benefits. It is estimated that fringe benefits currently amount to about 20 percent of base pay. These benefits differ widely both in type and in value from plant to plant and are not reported along with earnings. While employer associations in the state collect information on fringe benefits, there are no data available on their costs. Even the data collected are usually presented in the form of benefits rather than as a cost estimate.

In summary, the average weekly earnings of production workers in Michigan are the highest in the nation. To a considerable degree this is attributable to the state's industrial composition and to the occupational classification of its labor force.

Productivity of Labor

In any discussion of labor costs the productivity of labor must be included. Labor productivity affects unit labor costs. A plant site where low money wages are paid to labor is not necessarily a cheap labor site if the labor is inefficient. On the other hand, a site where high money wages are paid can be a cheap labor site if the efficiency of labor more than counterbalances the high money wages. Of fundamental importance, therefore, is the productivity of labor. Employers are interested in labor productivity, yet there are no objective methods for comparing it. Labor productivity, even in the same industry, varies substantially from plant to plant and from year to year. Many factors in addition to the efficiency or application of the individual worker affect productivity. Within the plant itself improvements in productivity may be traceable to more efficient and extensive use of power, better machinery and equipment, improvement in plant layout, work flow and work techniques, better engineering of jobs, and improvements in supervision and management.

The presence of these many factors makes it difficult to arrive at any precise measurement for comparing labor productivity. This has led one authority to point out that "comparative studies of efficiency are valid only in identical industries which have identical production methods."[9] Attempts, nevertheless, are made to estimate labor productivity in different areas. This is done either through personal contact with employers operating in the area to learn the latter's experience with output per man-hour worked, or by analyzing the Bureau of Census data on value added by manufacture on a state-by-state basis, or both. Both methods have serious limitations.

The information from existing employers must be evaluated most carefully. The informant may be hesitant to admit a location error. After all, employers do make mistakes in plant location and it is difficult to admit making such a mistake when large sums of money are involved. The employer contacted may be on the community's industrial committee and will perhaps paint a rosy picture to attract a new plant. Another employer, attempting to maintain his own position and not wanting competition in the labor market, may portray a dismal picture of the area. All such statements must be critically examined. As one expert put it, "Talk to all [employers], but try to recognize men's motives when listening to opinions about an area."[10]

The value added by manufacture, as used by the Bureau of the Census, is the value of shipments of manufactured goods less the cost of materials, supplies, fuels, electric energy, and contract work.

---

9 Leonard C. Yaseen, *Plant Location* (New York: American Research Council, 1956), p. 70.

10 Ronald M. Reifler, *Plant Location Factors for Small Industry*, Management Aids for Small Manufacturers, No. 99 (Washington: Small Business Administration, November, 1958), p. 3.

At best, this is a crude basis for comparing labor productivity and its limitations should be recognized.[11].

Despite its limitations, one can secure a rough approximation of the contribution of production workers to the manufacturing process by examining such data. When the data for 1954 and 1956 in Table A-5 are examined, the value added by manufacture by the Michigan worker, viewed either on a per-production-worker basis or per-man-hour-worked, is seen to be higher than that for the nation in both years. When data for Michigan and the states in the East North Central region are compared, we see that the production workers of the state contributed more to the manufacturing process than production workers in other states in the region in both years on a per-production-worker basis, and in 1956 on a per-man-hour-worked basis.

These data, while favorable, must be viewed against the industrial composition of the state. Although all the states in the East North Central region may be classified as industrial, the output of their factories is quite varied. Michigan's record, noted above, may stem largely from the fact that the state's manufacturing economy is largely composed of industries in which value added

Table A-5

Value Added by Manufacture per Production Worker and per Man-Hour Worked, United States and Select States

1954 and 1956

Area	Value Added by Manufacture per Production Worker		Value Added by Manufacture per Man-Hour Worked	
	1954	1956	1954	1956
United States........................	$ 9,449	$10,634	$4.80	$5.39
East North Central States..............	10,459	11,804	5.24	5.83
MICHIGAN.........................	10,762	12,292	5.26	5.97
Ohio..............................	10,309	11,805	5.17	5.83
Indiana............................	10,098	11,430	5.13	5.75
Illinois...........................	10,696	11,957	5.41	5.94
Wisconsin.........................	10,042	10,790	4.98	5.17

Source: Adapted from data on manufactures, by states, *Statistical Abstract of the United States* (1958), pp. 782-83.

---

11 For a more detailed treatment of these limitations see Melvin L. Greenhut, *Plant Location in Theory and Practice* (Chapel Hill: University of North Carolina Press, 1956), p. 326, and Yaseen, *op. cit.*, p. 70.

per worker is high. Since the focus in this paper is on the productivity of the Michigan industrial worker on the whole, specific industries were not examined. If value added per worker for particular industries in Michigan were compared with that of other states in the region, one might find certain industries in the state with a low value added per worker.

While the opinions on labor productivity by employers already operating in an area must be examined critically, all plant location authorities strongly urge that an employer investigating a possible new plant site should seek such information. The senior partner of the Fantus Factory Locating Service placed greatest emphasis on this. In his words, "If there is any single factor which should receive the greatest amount of attention, it is probably the experience of other manufacturers and employers."[12] A study by the National Industrial Conference Board on plant location similarly points out that representatives of local industry "can provide opinions on such subjects as the community's attitude toward industry, *labor productivity* (my italics) and whether the town is a good place in which to work."[13]

If the opinions of employers on such matters are valued so highly, the views of employers in Michigan are worth noting. The following statements appeared in a study conducted by the Survey Research Center of the University of Michigan in 1950.[14].

Quotations from interviews are presented here in order to illustrate how Michigan manufacturers speak of the advantages of this state:

Labor Situation

A small metals plant:

Here you are in an area in which the tempo of manufacturing is more accelerated. Labor thinks and acts differently. You get more from your labor here although you pay for it.

A medium-sized furniture plant:

The greatest thing in Michigan, as an advantage, is an adequate labor supply that is production-minded. You can have a labor supply, but you have to have a labor supply that is production-minded. That's the biggest advantage. We have many visitors to our plant, and they're amazed how our men work. We run at top speed for seven hours a day. I won't say eight hours. If we were to go to Illinois, Pennsylvania or Wisconsin — the tempo isn't the same as it is in Michigan. Any place in Michigan, the tempo is faster — I see it every day.

---

12 Yaseen, *op. cit.*, p. 57. See also Reifler, *op. cit.*, p. 3.
13 National Industrial Conference Board, *Techniques of Plant Location*, Conference Board Reports, Studies in Business Policy No. 61, March, 1953, p. 6.
14 *Industrial Mobility in Michigan, A Sample of Michigan Manufacturers*, Research Center, University of Michigan, December, 1950, p. 33.

A large metals plant:
> Perhaps the only real advantage Michigan has is that Michigan is the highest production-minded state in the union. We have a concentration of highly skilled workers here. We pay high labor rates but we get high labor production. That's an asset to us. And it's an advantage to the state, too.

In summary, both the data in Table A-5 and the statements cited in the study by the Survey Research Center provide some crude evidence of the productivity of Michigan labor. They further suggest that any all-inclusive indictment of labor productivity in the state is not substantiated. Undoubtedly there are examples in Michigan of firms experiencing low labor productivity, but each situation must be examined carefully before ascribing causation.

Living Costs

Living costs exert pressure on wage rates. While workers (and their wives) may not be grounded in economic theory and the price mechanism, they do know what their pay check will buy in terms of food, shelter, and clothing. The worker's welfare, then, depends not on how much money income he receives but on the purchasing power of his income — the amount of goods and services which he can buy with it. Since purchasing power and the worker's welfare are so intertwined, one authority on plant location has said that "one of the keys to worker satisfaction is the relationship between his pay and the money he spends to feed, clothe and house his family."[15]

The quantity and quality of goods and services which the worker can purchase is related to the "cost of living" in his community. There are, however, no completely satisfactory measures of retail prices. The nearest thing to a satisfactory measure is the Consumer Price Index, commonly referred to as the cost of living index, published by the U. S. Bureau of Labor Statistics.

This retail price index is compiled on the basis of data on prices collected in 46 cities across the nation. In addition to a retail price index for the United States as a whole, the Bureau of Labor Statistics prepares separate indexes for the 20 largest cities. In Table A-6, the Consumer Price Indexes for 1956-1958 are presented. It must be pointed out that the indexes measure the average change since the period 1947-1949 in the retail prices of goods and services purchased by urban wage earner and clerical worker families. *They do not indicate whether it costs more to live in one city than in another.*

---

15 Yaseen, *op. cit.*, p. 70.

Consumer Price Index — All-Item Indexes, by Select Cities

1956-1958

(1947-1949 = 100)

City	Annual Average		
	1958	1957	1956
United States City Average[a]	123.5	120.2	116.2
Atlanta, Georgia	124.5	121.4	118.1
Baltimore, Maryland	124.5	121.0	116.9
Boston, Massachusetts	124.8	121.2	117.1
Chicago, Illinois	127.0	123.3	119.5
Cincinnati, Ohio	122.3	119.6	116.0
Cleveland, Ohio	124.8	122.1	118.0
Detroit, Michigan	123.9	122.2	118.7
Houston, Texas	123.6	121.5	117.8
Kansas City, Missouri	124.1	121.1	117.5
Los Angeles, California	125.2	121.2	117.4
Minneapolis, Minnesota	124.3	121.1	117.0
New York, New York	121.1	117.6	113.9
Philadelphia, Pennsylvania	123.1	120.8	117.0
Pittsburgh, Pennsylvania	124.0	120.2	116.5
Portland, Oregon	124.4	121.7	118.0
St. Louis, Missouri	124.7	121.2	117.2
San Francisco, California	127.5	123.1	118.4
Scranton, Pennsylvania	120.2	116.9	112.9
Seattle, Washington	125.8	123.1	118.1
Washington, D. C.	121.1	118.3	114.9

Source: U. S. Department of Labor, *Monthly Labor Review*, December, 1958, and April, 1959.

[a] Average of 46 cities. The indexes are computed monthly for five cities and once every three months on a rotating cycle for other cities. The five cities are: Chicago, Detroit, Los Angeles, New York, and Philadelphia.

If the cost of living between cities is to be calculated, data on housing, food, utility rates, personal taxes on the local and state levels, and other items normally found in a family budget, must be collected and compared. In the absence of current data, no comparisons can be made between Michigan and other states. Even within the state there are probably differences in the cost of living between large cities and small towns. Armed with such data, one may well find that wage differentials among cities do not follow the same pattern as cost of living differentials.[16]

Labor Relations

In the mid-thirties Michigan was the testing ground for large in-

16 See Alfred Kuhn, *Labor Institutions and Economics* (New York: Rinehart and Company, 1956), p. 413 and footnote 26, p. 413.

dustrial unions, especially the United Automobile Workers, seeking recognition as the bargaining agent of the employees of the large industrial concerns. The period of the thirties represents an important landmark in the history of labor relations both in Michigan and in the United States. Since the early beginnings, the negotiations over wages, hours, and conditions of employment between the automobile industry and the United Auto Workers have been equally important to the state and to the nation. In more recent years the sound and fury accompanying these negotiations, however, have been often misunderstood. The heralded meetings of company and union representatives on such occasions are analogous to a pageant surrounded by "pomp and circumstance." The leading actors are expected to issue public pronouncements through the press for the benefit of their partisan supporters and the public. If, however, the number of work stoppages and man-days lost from them is one criterion for evaluating labor relations in an important industrial state, the strike record in Michigan, as indicated in Table A-7, compares favorably with similar states.

Another way of looking at work stoppages is on a state-by-state basis as a percentage of the total for the United States. Such data on workers involved and man-days idle in work stoppages for the years 1955 to 1957 are presented in Table A-8. From it we see

Table A-7

Work Stoppages, by Select States
1955-1957

Area	Work Stoppages Beginning in			Man-Days Idle During Year (in thousands)			Percent of Estimated Working Time		
	1955	1956	1957	1955	1956	1957	1955	1956	1957
United States.......	4,320	3,825	3,673	28,200	33,100	16,500	0.26	0.29	0.14
MICHIGAN..........	327	210	208	1,740	1,190	1,280	.31	.22	.24
New Jersey.........	283	190	238	1,470	1,270	912	.35	.29	.21
Pennsylvania........	566	520	440	3,350	7,280	1,360	.40	.87	.16
Ohio...............	434	357	355	2,570	4,720	1,580	.37	.66	.22
Indiana.............	170	136	85	1,140	2,090	351	.36	.65	.11
Illinois..............	260	215	199	1,480	1,750	1,140	.19	.22	.14
Wisconsin...........	95	62	68	849	537	288	.34	.21	.11
Alabama............	111	101	81	951	1,490	396	.67	1.00	.25
Kentucky...........	94	109	71	757	239	299	.59	.18	.22
Idaho..............	18	11	10	104	30	103	.38	.10	.35

Source: U. S. Department of Labor, Bureau of Labor Statistics, *Analysis of Work Stoppages*, Bulletins 1196, 1218, and 1234.

Work Stoppages, by Select States, by Percent of Workers Involved and Percent of Man-Days Idle

1955-1957

Area	Percent of Workers Involved			Percent of Man-Days Idle		
	1955	1956	1957	1955	1956	1957
United States..........	100.0	100.0	100.0	100.0	100.0	100.0
Illinois.................	6.3	6.4	5.1	5.2	5.3	6.9
Indiana................	7.2	5.8	4.9	4.0	6.3	2.1
Ohio...................	12.4	15.2	10.9	9.1	14.3	9.6
MICHIGAN.............	11.0	5.2	9.9	6.2	3.6	7.8
Wisconsin.............	1.7	1.5	1.9	3.0	1.6	1.7
Alabama...............	3.4	3.3	2.8	3.4	4.5	2.4
California..............	5.9	4.8	7.5	6.2	3.7	9.5
New Jersey............	4.7	3.6	4.9	5.2	3.8	5.5
New York..............	8.3	8.3	8.4	8.7	9.0	10.4
Pennsylvania..........	14.6	15.7	8.3	11.9	22.0	8.2

Source: U. S. Department of Labor, Bureau of Labor Statistics, *Analysis of Work Stoppages*, Bulletins 1196, 1218, and 1234.

that Michigan's record fluctuates widely during the three-year period. Ohio in each of the three years had a higher percentage of the nation's total, both of workers involved and of man-days idle than Michigan. Wisconsin had both fewer workers involved and fewer man-days idle as a percent of the total for the country than Michigan in each of the three years.

It should be recognized that the strike is part and parcel of the collective bargaining process. Remarkable progress is being made in employer-union relations when one reflects that it was just twenty years ago when the sit-down strikes in Michigan were headline news. Even today the important strikes are headline news, but the countless negotiations conducted without a strike are relegated to a small item on the inside pages. The bitterness and violence of industrial disputes have diminished considerably. Strikes do occur, and at times, lead to grievous injury to the parties themselves or to third parties. The costs, however, are frequently exaggerated. Man-days lost through industrial disputes are far fewer than losses from unemployment or the common cold.

The data, standing alone, are insufficient for an understanding of strikes. The issue or issues surrounding the dispute are also important. Unfortunately, the Bureau of Labor Statistics data do not give a breakdown on a state-by-state basis as to major issues involved. Such data would provide better criteria for evaluating a community's or state's strike record. There are, however, data available on work stoppages by industry by states. These data point out that the strike experience in the state is not evenly divided among the important industries of the state.

Furthermore, there appears to be no definite pattern in these work stoppages from year to year. For example, from the data in Table A-9 we find that in 1955, 17 percent of the work stoppages in Michigan occurred in the transportation equipment industry, involving 49 percent of all workers and accounting for 18 percent of the man-days idle. By comparison, in 1957, 26 percent of work stoppages, involving 43 percent of the workers and comprising 24 percent of the man-days idle occurred in this industry. By actual count there were 55 and 53 work stoppages in the transportation equipment industry in 1955 and 1957 respectively. There were

Table A-9

Work Stoppages in Michigan, by Select Industries, by Percent

1955 and 1957

Industry	1955			1957		
	Number of Work Stoppages	Workers Involved	Man-Days Idle	Number of Work Stoppages	Workers Involved	Man-Days Idle
All industries................	100.0	100.0	100.0	100.0	100.0	100.0
Manufacturing.............	79.2	92.8	85.1	70.7	81.9	79.7
Primary metal industries	9.8	6.1	5.4	9.1	11.6	17.3
Fabricated metal products..............	12.8	8.2	8.9	6.7	2.4	1.9
Machinery except electrical..............	13.5	6.8	23.4	8.7	4.2	7.0
Transportation equipment.............	16.8	49.3	18.3	25.5	43.4	23.9
Chemicals and allied products..............	1.2	1.6	9.3	2.4	1.7	1.6
Rubber..................	11.9	15.9	5.7	2.4	7.5	10.5
Food and kindred products..............	1.8	.8	.9	2.9	4.0	9.5
Nonmanufacturing.........	21.1	7.3	15.1	29.8	18.5	19.9
Mining..................	.6	1.0	7.6	.5	.7	2.3
Construction............	8.9	3.7	5.9	13.9	10.1	11.6
Trade..................	7.0	.4	.7	9.1	2.8	3.7

Source: U. S. Department of Labor, Bureau of Labor Statistics, *Analysis of Work Stoppages,* Bulletins 1196 and 1234.

Note: *Percentages shown for manufacturing and nonmanufacturing do not add to 100 percent because of rounding and other factors.*

144,000 workers involved in such stoppages in 1955 compared with 59,900 in 1957; man-days idle were 318,000 in the former year and 306,000 in the latter.

In the machinery (except electrical) industry, the strike experience was more erratic. In 1955, about 14 percent of the state's strikes occurred in this industry, which involved approximately 7 percent of the workers and accounted for roughly 23 percent of idle time. By contrast in 1957, about 9 percent of the strikes, involving 4 percent of the workers and comprising 7 percent of the man-days idle, were in this industry classification. Other widely fluctuating work stoppage experience in certain industries can be noted in Table A-9.

When the strike data for some of the less industrialized states are examined, some interesting comparisons can be made. For example, man-days idle as a percent of estimated working time in Alabama was 0.67, 1.00, and 0.25 for 1955, 1956, and 1957 respectively. Kentucky's experience was 0.59, 0.18, and 0.22. Idaho had only 18, 11, and 10 work stoppages during 1955, 1956,

Table A-10

Trade Union Membership, by Select States

1953

Area	Total Membership	Membership as Percent of Nonagricultural Employment
United States..........................	**16,217,000**	**32.6**
East North Central States............	**4,572,000**	**39.9**
Ohio................................	1,163,000	38.0
Indiana.............................	570,000	40.0
Illinois..............................	1,359,000	39.7
MICHIGAN.........................	1,062,000	43.3
Wisconsin..........................	419,000	38.3
Other States		
New York...........................	2,052,000	34.4
Pennsylvania.......................	1,541,000	39.9
West Virginia.......................	224,000	44.1
Kentucky...........................	155,000	25.0
Alabama............................	168,000	24.9
Montana............................	73,000	47.0
Idaho...............................	29,000	21.5
Washington.........................	394,000	53.3
Oregon.............................	202,000	43.1
California...........................	1,393,000	35.7

Source: National Bureau of Economic Research, *Distribution of Union Membership among the States, 1939 and 1953*, Occasional Paper No. 56, 1957.

272

and 1957 respectively, but the percent of estimated working time lost for each of these years was 0.38, 0.10, and 0.35. These data suggest several things. Both the number of strikes and their duration must be considered; secondly, strikes also occur in less industrialized states.

Thus, there appears to be no relationship between the degree of unionization and the time lost through work stoppages. As indicated in Table A-10, Michigan in 1953 had a larger percentage of organized workers (43.3) than either Alabama (24.9), Kentucky (25.0), or Idaho (21.5). Numerically, New York, Pennsylvania, Ohio, Illinois, and California have more organized workers than Michigan. West Virginia, Montana, and Washington, however, have a higher percentage of union members than Michigan. Even with a high percentage of union members, the member-

Table A-11

Plant Workers in Large- and Medium-Sized Establishments Covered by Collective Bargaining Agreements, 17 Labor Markets, by Percent

1953-1954

Percent of Plant Workers Covered	Labor Market
In all industries	
Over 90..........	Detroit, St. Louis, San Francisco
80-89............	Newark-Jersey City, New York City, Philadelphia, Milwaukee, Minneapolis-St. Paul, Portland (Oregon)
70-79............	Boston, Chicago, Los Angeles
60-69............	Denver
50-59............	Memphis
40-49............	Atlanta, New Orleans, Dallas
In manufacturing industries	
Over 90..........	Detroit, Newark-Jersey City, New York City, Milwaukee, St. Louis, San Francisco-Oakland
80-89............	Boston, Philadelphia, Minneapolis-St. Paul, Portland (Oregon)
70-79............	Memphis, Chicago, Denver, Los Angeles
60-69............	New Orleans, Dallas
50-59............	Atlanta

Source: U. S. Department of Labor, *Monthly Labor Review,* January, 1955, pp. 64-68.

ship in the state is not evenly distributed. Detroit has about the same percentage of organized workers as does New York City, Newark-Jersey City, Milwaukee, St. Louis, and San Francisco-Oakland. Akron, Michigan is quite different from Akron, Ohio. Similarly, there is no comparison between Brooklyn, Michigan and Brooklyn, New York.

The Bureau of Labor Statistics made a study of plant and office workers in large and medium-sized establishments covered by collective bargaining agreements in seventeen labor markets in 1953-1954.[17] As indicated in Table A-11, the percentage of wage earners covered by union contracts in Detroit's manufacturing industries is comparable to that in five other large industrial metropolitan areas, over 90 percent of plant workers being covered by contracts in each area. When the percent of office workers in all industries is compared, as in Table A-12, Newark-Jersey City, Atlanta, and Los Angeles are in the same category as Detroit with 20-29 percent.

Table A-12

Office Workers in Large- and Medium-Sized Establishments Covered by Collective Bargaining Agreements, 17 Labor Markets, by Percent

1953-1954

Percent of Office Workers Covered	Labor Market
In all industries	
20-29............	Newark-Jersey City, Atlanta, Detroit, Los Angeles
10-19............	Boston, New York City, Philadelphia, Dallas, Chicago, Milwaukee, Minneapolis-St. Paul, St. Louis, Portland (Oregon), San Francisco-Oakland
0- 9............	Memphis, New Orleans, Denver
In manufacturing industries	
20-29............	Boston, Newark-Jersey City, New York City, Philadelphia, Detroit, Los Angeles
10-19............	Memphis, Chicago, Milwaukee, St. Louis, Denver, San Francisco-Oakland
0- 9............	Dallas, New Orleans, Minneapolis-St. Paul, Portland (Oregon)

Source: U. S. Department of Labor, *Monthly Labor Review*, January, 1955, pp. 64-68.

Note: *Data for Atlanta not included for manufacturing industries.*

17 Nelson M. Bartz and James F. Walker, "Extent of Collective Bargaining in 17 Labor Markets, 1953-1954," *Monthly Labor Review*, January, 1955, pp. 64-68.

In manufacturing industries, Boston, Newark-Jersey City, New York City, Philadelphia, and Los Angeles have about the same percentage of office workers covered by bargaining agreements as Detroit. Thus, despite the high percentage of total union membership, Detroit is comparable to Atlanta in the organization of office employees.

In summary, there is no factual support for the notion that Michigan is plagued with work stoppages. On the average, only 0.26 percent of estimated working time was lost each year through strikes for the period 1955-1957. We also have seen that there is no correlation between the percentage of nonagricultural labor force organized and the amount of time lost through strikes. When the data were examined, Michigan's strike experience compared favorably with that of other industrial states. Less time was lost in Michigan than in some of the Southern and Mountain states. It was also noted that there was no definite pattern to the work stoppages occurring in the state; there were wide fluctuations in each industry in the time period studied.

Labor Stability

Employers are interested in having a stable work force. The characteristics of such a work force would include low turnover, a reasonable absenteeism rate, and a minimum of tardiness. Although a small labor turnover is desirable in that it brings new blood and new ideas into the organization, high turnover is, in itself, a source of serious problems. High labor turnover is costly.

Employers have become more aware of the costs of labor turnover because of the state unemployment compensation programs. Under the experience of merit rating provisions of these laws, separations from the payroll may be costly because they influence the contribution rate which employers pay on their payrolls.

In addition to the unemployment compensation costs, turnover is costly in many other ways. It requires more extensive recruitment, selection, and training programs, which are expensive. Newcomers are apt to be inefficient and may damage raw materials and equipment. Waste and spoilage increase. If former employees have quit because of dissatisfaction with the job or the company, they may be a source of ill will which frequently counteracts expensive advertising campaigns and prejudices recruitment. Termination procedures also add to the costs.

The simplest measure of labor turnover is the separation rate which is generally defined as the number of separations per month per 100 of the work force. Separations include all quits, layoffs, and discharges. Of significant interest is the quit rate, which, while not perfect, is a good measure of employee stability because it is employee initiated. Layoffs and discharges are initiated by employers.

The quit rate in Michigan's manufacturing industries compares favorably with that for the United States. From Table A-13, we see that the quit rate for the United States was higher than that for Michigan in each year of the period 1955-1958. Even in 1955, a year of high employment in the state, the United States annual average was 1.6 as compared with 1.5 for Michigan. In the subsequent years Michigan's record was much better. The average rate in 1956 was 1.6 for the United States and 1.0 for Michigan. For 1957 the United States had an annual average of 1.4 while Michigan had an 0.8 average. The data for 1958 are for only eleven months. On a month-by-month basis, the United States rate was double that of Michigan in 1958.

Table A-13

Quit Rate per 100 Workers in Manufacturing Industries, United States and Michigan, by Month

1955-1958

Month	Quit Rate							
	1955		1956		1957		1958	
	United States	Michigan	United States	Michigan	United States	Michigan	United States	Michigan
January......	1.0	1.1	1.4	1.2	1.3	1.0	0.8	0.4
February.....	1.0	1.1	1.3	1.0	1.2	.8	.7	.4
March........	1.3	1.6	1.4	1.0	1.3	.8	.7	.3
April.........	1.5	1.9	1.5	1.0	1.3	.8	.7	.3
May..........	1.5	1.9	1.6	.9	1.4	.7	.8	.4
June.........	1.5	1.7	1.6	.9	1.3	.7	.8	.4
July..........	1.6	1.4	1.5	.8	1.4	.7	.9	.4
August.......	2.2	1.8	2.2	1.1	1.9	.9	1.2	.5
September..	2.8	1.9	2.6	1.3	2.2	1.1	1.5	.7
October......	1.8	1.6	1.7	1.3	1.3	.7	1.1	.5
November...	1.4	1.4	1.3	1.1	.9	.6	.8	.4
December...	1.1	1.1	1.0	.8	.7	.4	...	...
Annual average....	1.6	1.5	1.6	1.0	1.4	.8	...	...

Source: U. S. Department of Labor, *Monthly Labor Review*, February, 1959, and Michigan Employment Security Commission, Memorandum dated February 11, 1959.

The data on labor turnover, however, are subject to certain limitations. Seasonal fluctuations are not reflected in the data. The condition of the labor market affects labor turnover. In a tight labor market it is relatively easy to change jobs. This is especially true for employees with low seniority rights. But when the number of persons available, willing, and able to work far exceeds the number of job opportunities available, employees tend to hold on to their existing jobs. Despite these limitations, the quit rate is one measure of employee stability, and Michigan's rate is below the national average.

There are no available data for the United States or Michigan on the absenteeism rate or tardiness. Individual employers maintain such records, and there may be exchange of such information between them. Absenteeism from the job varies widely from time to time and from one firm to another. According to Yoder, a reasonable rate is around three percent.[18] There is no similar yardstick for the tardiness rate, except that it be at a reasonable minimum. Both the absenteeism rate and amount of tardiness are significant because they are rough indications of employee dissatisfaction and unrest.

In summary, Michigan manufacturing industries possess a stable labor force as evidenced by a low quit rate. This employee stability undoubtedly has a salutary effect on training costs.

Legal Considerations

IN PLANT LOCATION analyses, employers are interested in the legal factors affecting the cost of doing business in a given state. Zoning, taxes, and labor legislation are among the most important legal factors. In this paper we are concerned only with state legislation as it affects the labor factor in plant location. Contrary to widespread belief, state labor legislation is broader in scope than national labor legislation. It includes such matters as workmen's compensation, unemployment insurance, factory inspection, hours of work, minimum wage, labor relations acts, legislation restricting union security arrangements, and fair employment practices acts. Of these, workmen's compensation and unemployment insurance have a direct bearing on labor costs. Both of these will be treated in more detail than the other types of state labor legislation.

18 Dale Yoder, *Personnel Management and Industrial Relations,* 4th edition (New York: Prentice-Hall, Inc., 1956), p. 748.

Workmen's Compensation

The principle of workmen's compensation has become an integral part of the economic and social fabric of the nation. The legitimacy of workmen's compensation has been well established and accepted. In Michigan, as elsewhere, all employers in a given industry are subject to a manual rate (e.g., same rate per $100 of payroll) so that there is no unfair cost disadvantage in relation to their competitors within the state. But are Michigan employers placed at an unfair disadvantage in relation to their competitors in other states when their products move into interstate commerce?

The cost to an employer of workmen's compensation is largely determined by his industrial classification and the hazards of that classification as modified by experience rating. An employer's costs are also affected by the level of benefits provided by the state workmen's compensation law and the method by which he insures his compensation liability. In financing his liability, the employer may do so through a private-stock company or mutual company, through an exclusive or competitive state fund, or by carrying his own risk. In Michigan in the fiscal year October 1, 1957, to September 30, 1958, 405 employers out of 106,086 were self-insured.[19]

In 1956, the Associated Industries of New York State conducted a study of workmen's compensation costs in sixteen important industrial states of the nation as reflected in the average manual rate for each of the years 1950-1956. From the data appearing in Table A-14, Michigan ranked eleventh in six of the seven years studied. In 1951, Michigan ranked ninth with an average manual rate of $.514 per $100. The average rate was based on the rates in 45 major classifications. In comparing the compensation insurance rates for some of Michigan's leading industries with similar industries in other states, as of June, 1958, we see from Table A-15, that the cost of workmen's compensation in Michigan compares favorably with rates in other states. In many instances the rate is lower for certain industries in Michigan than in other states. This is especially noteworthy since the benefits to injured workers tend to be higher than those in other states in the midwest and New York. Ohio is not listed because that state has an exclusive State Fund whose rates are computed on a different basis.

Since costs are related to benefits, we need to examine the benefits paid by the states in the East North Central region. It should

---

19 State of Michigan Workmen's Compensation Department, *Annual Report October 1, 1957 to September 30, 1958*, p. 8. The Department informed the writer that 310 employers were currently self-insured.

Table A-14

Comparison of Workmen's Compensation Costs as Reflected by Average Manual Rates, 45 Major Classifications, 16 States

1950-1956

Rank	1950 State	1950 Average Rate	1951 State	1951 Average Rate	1952 State	1952 Average Rate	1953 State	1953 Average Rate	1954 State	1954 Average Rate	1955 State	1955 Average Rate	1956 State	1956 Average Rate
1	N.Y.	$1.280	N.Y.	$1.500	N.Y.	$1.505	N.Y.	$1.619	N.Y.	$1.490	N.Y.	$1.200	Mass.	$1.178
2	Mass.	.971	Mass.	.990	Mass.	1.103	Mass.	1.237	Mass.	1.225	Mass.	1.140	N.Y.	1.107
3	Texas	.730	Texas.	.752	N.J.	.823	Texas	.957	N.J.	.989	Conn.	.960	Conn.	.940
4	Conn.	.703	N.J.	.719	Texas	.778	N.J.	.939	Conn.	.986	N.J.	.907	Texas	.879
5	Calif.	.697	Calif.	.695	Calif.	.758	Conn.	.840	Texas	.942	Texas	.855	N.J.	.805
6	Wisc.	.644	Conn.	.660	Wisc.	.741	Calif.	.801	Calif.	.793	Calif.	.705	Calif.	.739
7	N.J.	.639	Wisc.	.653	Conn.	.720	Wisc.	.748	Wisc.	.755	Md.	.691	Md.	.702
8	Mo.	.587	Mo.	.588	Mo.	.624	Mo.	.688	Mo.	.739	Mo.	.679	Mo.	.681
9	Ill.	.575	MICH.	.514	Md.	.539	Md.	.667	Md.	.720	Wisc.	.633	Wisc.	.649
10	Md.	.532	Ill.	.489	Ill.	.482	Ill.	.552	Ill.	.600	Ill.	.562	Ill.	.599
11	MICH.	.521	Md.	.484	MICH.	.444	MICH.	.487	MICH.	.491	MICH.	.483	MICH.	.480
12	Iowa	.479	Iowa	.460	Iowa	.435	Ind.	.482	Iowa	.460	Ind.	.461	Ind.	.479
13	Ind.	.462	Ind.	.454	Ind.	.433	Iowa	.458	Ind.	.443	Iowa	.427	Iowa	.427
14	Va.	.380	Va.	.334	Va.	.390	Va.	.398	Va.	.419	Va.	.377	Va.	.387
15	Pa.	.353	Ala.	.324	Ala.	.356	Ala.	.348	Pa.	.369	Pa.	.345	Ala.	.364
16	Ala.	.338	Pa.	.321	Pa.	.320	Pa.	.324	Ala.	.365	Ala.	.328	Pa.	.342

Source: Associated Industries of New York State, August, 1956.

Note: (1) The states are ranked to facilitate comparison of standings relative to Workmen's Compensation costs.
(2) The above rates are averaged for 45 major occupational classifications in each state for each year.

Comparison of Workmen's Compensation Costs as Reflected by Current Manual Rates for Select Classifications, Select States

June, 1958

Industry	MICHIGAN	Illinois	Indiana	Wisconsin	Minnesota	New York
Breweries............	$ 0.84	$1.52	$1.02	$ 0.85	$ 1.75	$ 2.70
Logging and lumbering.........	13.76	9.94	7.38	14.08	10.20	16.90
Furniture manu-facturing...........	1.02	1.49	.96	1.36	2.47	2.30
Foundries (iron).....	3.46	2.48	1.52	2.01	ª2.54	4.20
Foundries (steel).....	3.26	2.28	1.55	1.95	ª3.78	4.00
Paper manu-facturing...........	1.46	2.30	1.69	n.a.	1.65	3.00
Department stores...	.31	.27	.26	.35	.49	.78
Machine shops......	.95	1.09	1.35	.93	1.39	6.00
Auto body manu-facturing...........	.82	.88	.87	.81	1.39	1.30

Source: National Council of Compensation Insurance, *Basic Manual of Rules, Classifications and Rates.*

ª Does not include disease element.

be borne in mind that both costs and benefits are altered periodically. In recent years the state supreme courts in Michigan and other industrial states have rendered decisions which have tended to liberalize the payment of benefits in certain injuries. Undoubtedly the casualty insurance companies seek rate adjustments to cover the liberalization of benefits. Another limitation in comparing benefits is that many states use bases other than wage loss to compute benefits, e.g., medical and rehabilitation costs.[20] Recognizing these limitations, benefits for the states in the East North Central region are tabulated in Table A-16. While it should be noted that weak administration of workmen's compensation due to inadequate administrative funds is more costly to employer, employee, and the general public than a strong administration adequately financed, discussion of administration of this act in the several states is beyond the scope of this paper.[21]

In summary, while the benefits of the Michigan Act are somewhat higher than other states in the region, the cost to employers, as measured by the average manual rate, compares favorably with

[20] In 1956, 35 percent of benefits were paid in medical and hospitalization benefits, 7.5 percent in survivor benefits, and 57.5 percent in disability benefits.
[21] For discussion of administration of workmen's compensation programs, see Herman M. Somers and Anne R. Somers, *Workmen's Compensation* (New York: John Wiley, 1954).

Table A-16

Workmen's Compensation Benefits, Select States

September 1, 1958

State	Intended Benefit as Percent of Weekly Wage	Actual Maximum Weekly	Maximum Duration in Weeks	Maximum Total Payments	Maximum Medical Care	Benefits for Reha- bilitation	Coverage of Occu- pational Diseases
Illinois	a75–97-1/2	a$30–45	bW-C	c$10,750–13,500	d	No	Full
Indiana	60	36	400	15,000	...	No	Full
Ohio	66-2/3	40.25	416	12,000	...	Yes	Full
MICHIGAN	66-2/3	a33–57	450	...	...	No	Full
Wisconsin	70	49	400	e13,000	...	Yes	Full
New York	66-2/3	45	bW-C	...	...	Yes	Full

Source: U. S. Department of Labor, State Workmen's Compensation Laws, Bulletin 161, Revised.

a Lower figure represents benefits for single worker; higher figure represents benefit maximum for all dependents.

b "W" means payment to widow until death or remarriage; "C" means payment to children until 18.

c Lower figure represents payments to widow only; higher figure represents benefit maximum for all dependents.

d Limited benefits for silicosis and asbestosis.

e Additional benefits payable from children's fund to widow for children under 16 (13 percent of widow's benefit is the weekly or monthly allowance made for each dependent child) or for children over 16 if mentally or physically incapacitated.

other states. Therefore, in terms of costs, the Act does not appear to place Michigan employers at a disadvantage.

Unemployment Compensation

Another legal factor affecting labor costs is unemployment compensation. Michigan and other states in the East North Central region have a reserve-ratio type of experience rating which tends to establish a more favorable contribution rate for the employer whose employment experience is stable. In Michigan in 1959, employers with four or more employees pay tax rates ranging from 0.5 percent to 4.0 percent of the first $3,000 of wages. The individual employer's tax rate is determined by his rating account percentage[22] and the state fund balance.[23] The former relates to the individual employer's employment experience and the latter to the employment experience of all liable employers in the state. The 1957 amendments to the Michigan Employment Security Act added a third schedule of contribution rates. Employers' contribution rates vary depending on the fund balance percentage.[24] For example, if the percentage is high, employers' contribution rates are lower. Conversely, if the fund balance percentage is low, employers pay a higher rate.[25]

While the employers' contribution rate is affected by the fund balance percentage, an employer's tax rate cannot be raised more than 1 percent over his rate for the preceding year.[26] The Michigan Act, like the Ohio and Wisconsin acts, provides for voluntary payments by an employer to his rating account at any time. Voluntary payments are credited to his account and usually result in a recomputation of the rate for that year, to a lower bracket.

Prior to 1956, any employing unit which had eight or more

---

22 In computing the rating account percentage, the employer's rating account balance must first be computed. The balance as used in the Act is the excess of credits (all contributions to his account) over charges (all benefits chargeable to the employer) as of a particular computation date. The balance is divided by the employer's total wages which were subject to contributions for the twelve-month period ending on the computation date. The resulting percentage is known as the "Employer's Rating Account Percentage."

23 The State Fund Balance is the balance in the account known as the Unemployment Compensation Fund. All contributions paid by employers are credited to this account and charges are made to this account for benefit payments. The balance in the account represents money available for payment of future benefits.

24 The Fund Balance Percentage is computed by dividing the balance in the U. C. Fund as of the June 30 computation date by the total subject wages paid by all employers in the twelve-month period ending on the same June 30. The resulting percentage is known as the Fund Balance Percentage.

25 If this percentage is less than 5.0, employers' contribution rates will range from a low of 0.5 percent to a high of 4.0 percent. A percentage of 5.0 or more, but less than 8.5, will result in employers' contribution rates of 0.1 percent to 4.0 percent, and if the percentage is 8.5 or more the rates vary from no percent to 3.9 percent.

26 In the transition from the benefit ratio to the reserve-ratio system, the Act provided for a 0.5 percent limitation on rate increase for the years 1955 and 1956.

employees performing services in employment in 20 different calendar weeks within a calendar year was classified as a liable employer. Table A-17 shows that there were 31,563 employers who were assigned contribution rates for 1956. Of this number about 84 percent were rated employers in that they had qualified through experience with employment for application of some experience rating. Forty-five percent of the taxable employers had the minimum contribution rate of 0.5 percent. Thirty-nine percent of the employers fell in one of eighteen other rates. About 16 percent of the employers did not have sufficient experience in covered employment and therefore were classified as nonrated.

In 1955 the Act was amended to include any employing unit which had four or more workers. Illinois, Indiana, and Wisconsin acts also include the same size firms. A liable employer under the Ohio Act is one employing three or more employees. The 1955 amendment to the Michigan Act brought approximately 22,000 additional employers under the Act, making a total of 54,618 taxable employers by June 30, 1957. The influx of these employers greatly increased the number of nonrated employers. As indicated in Table A-17, approximately 44 percent of all taxable employers rated for 1957 were in this classification. About 56 percent were eligible for adjusted rates. Of all employers, 25.5 percent qualified for the minimum statutory rate, while 31 percent were distributed among the eighteen other rates.

Ninety-seven percent of the subject employers in 1958 were rated and 96.4 percent had sufficient experience to qualify for adjusted rates in 1959. Beginning in 1958, an adjusted rate under 2.7 percent was assigned to employers in their third year of coverage. In that year about 85 percent of the employers qualified for rates of 2.7 percent or less. In 1959 approximately 82 percent of the employers had adjusted rates of 2.7 percent or less.

The average employer contribution rate in 1957 was 2.05 percent, which included an emergency rate of 0.5 percent. An emergency rate is assessed when the solvency account has a negative balance.[27] Each employer who has completed four consecutive years of coverage is liable, in addition to his regular contribution, to an emergency rate. Depending on the amount of the negative balance, the emergency rates range from a low of 0.1 percent to a high of 0.5 percent. For example, if the negative balance is

27 For a detailed description of the Solvency Account, see Michigan Employment Security Commission, *Employers' Handbook*, April, 1958, p. 14.

Distribution of Subject Employers in Michigan, by Contribution Rates for Unemployment Insurance Assigned for Years 1956 - 1959[a]

Item	1956		1957		1958		1959	
	Number of Employers	Percent of Total	Number of Employers	Percent of Total	Number of Employers	Percent of Total	Number of Employers	Percent of Total
Total	31,563	100.0	46,832	100.0	53,349	100.0	56,183	100.0
Nonrated employers								
Insufficient experience	4,946	15.7	20,474	43.7	1,560	2.9	1,958	3.5
Seasonal	34	0.1	31	0.1	32	0.1	31	0.1
Rated employers	26,583	84.2	26,327	56.2	51,757	97.0	54,194	96.4
Employers with effective contribution rates of:								
0.1					283	0.5		
0.2					48	0.1		
0.3					63	0.1		
0.4					91	0.2		
0.5	14,209	45.0			141	0.3		
0.6					6,160	11.5	1,324	2.4
0.7	1,976	6.3			1,490	2.8	562	1.0
0.8					1,436	2.7		
0.9	1,652	5.2			2,289	4.3	1,431	2.5
1.0			11,948	25.5	2,144	4.0	10,441	18.6
1.1	1,161	3.7			563	1.1	3,054	5.4
1.2			2,282	4.9	2,370	4.4	1,895	3.4
1.3	845	2.7			939	1.8	2,797	5.0
1.4			1,775	3.8	1,813	3.4	2,257	4.0
1.5	577	1.8			1,663	3.1	1,368	2.4
1.6			1,281	2.7	1,327	2.5	1,999	3.6
1.7	432	1.4			2,932	5.5	864	1.5
1.8			934	2.0	959	1.8	1,416	2.5
1.9	1,256	4.0			2,579	4.8	667	1.2
2.0			1,215	2.6	930	1.7	1,048	1.9
2.1	263	0.8			1,825	3.4	453	0.8

Distribution of Subject Employers in Michigan, by Contribution Rates for Unemployment Insurance Assigned for Years 1956 - 1959[a]
(Continued)

Item	1956 Number of Employers	1956 Percent of Total	1957 Number of Employers	1957 Percent of Total	1958 Number of Employers	1958 Percent of Total	1959 Number of Employers	1959 Percent of Total
Rated employers (Cont'd.)								
2.2	....	....	603	1.3	543	1.0	939	1.7
2.3	84	0.3	....	....	1,388	2.6	555	1.0
2.4	....	....	458	1.0	385	0.7	812	1.4
2.5	192	0.6	....	....	986	1.8	675	1.2
2.6	....	....	364	0.8	317	0.6	612	1.1
2.7	839	2.6	....	....	9,599	18.1	10,663	19.0
2.8	....	....	371	0.8	310	0.6	588	1.0
2.9	80	0.3	....	....	....	....	....	....
3.0	....	....	278	0.6	461	0.9	599	1.1
3.1	792	2.5	422	0.9	718	1.3	477	0.8
3.2	....	....	....	....	....	....	....	....
3.3	191	0.6	772	1.6	376	0.7	298	0.5
3.4	....	....	....	....	....	....	....	....
3.5	450	1.4	....	....	....	....	....	....
3.6	....	....	310	0.7	359	0.7	301	0.5
3.7	122	0.4	....	....	....	....	....	....
3.8	....	....	220	0.5	371	0.7	373	0.7
3.9	27	0.1	....	....	....	....	....	....
4.0	1,435	4.5	294	0.6	324	0.6	439	0.8
4.2	....	....	1,134	2.4	842	1.6	1,309	2.3
4.4	....	....	200	0.4	542	1.0	346	0.6
4.5	....	....	1,466	3.1	2,191	4.1	3,632	6.5

Source: Michigan Employment Security Commission.

[a] *Effective contribution rate schedules applicable to calendar years, as follows:*
1956 The less favorable rate schedule which corresponds to the present intermediate schedule but with a minimum rate of 0.5.
1957 Same schedule in effect as for 1956. However, applicable rates shown for all rated employers include the 0.5% emergency rate assessed on all "qualified" employers.
1958 Present intermediate rate schedule. The applicable rates include the 0.5% emergency rate assessed on all "qualified" employers (in at least the fourth year of coverage). Beginning this year, an adjusted rate under 2.7% was assigned to employers in their third year of coverage. Employers in this group are not subject to the emergency rate.
1959 Least favorable rate schedule in effect. Contribution rates shown include the 0.5% emergency rate assessed on "qualified" employers.

$24,000,000 or more, the emergency rate would be the maximum of 0.5 percent. In 1958 and 1959, qualified employers also paid an emergency rate of 0.5 percent.

The average contribution rate for covered employers in Michigan for the years 1936 to 1959 is presented in Table A-18. For the period 1936-1941, the rates shown are the statutory normal rates assigned to all employers. In 1942 the reserve-ratio plan became effective and the contribution rate was adjusted based on experience in the preceding three years. The contribution rate for the years 1957, 1958, and 1959 has been the highest since the introduction of the experience rating plan. In 1957 it was 2.05 percent, in 1958 the rate was 2.12 percent, and the estimated rate for 1959 is 2.56 percent which is the highest since 1942. The rate for the year is computed on the unemployment experience of all covered employers prior to the computation date. Thus, for example, the high rate in 1959 reflects the experience of all employers prior to the June 30, 1958, computation date. (In the second, third, and fourth consecutive years of coverage, the computation date is December 31.) The low contribution rate of .91 percent in

Table A-18

Average Contribution Rate for Unemployment Insurance for Covered Employers, Michigan

1936-1959

Year	Average Contribution Rate (Percent)	Year	Average Contribution Rate (Percent)
1936	0.90	1948	1.85
1937	2.00	1949	1.78
1938	3.00	1950	1.36
1939	3.00	1951	1.56
1940	3.00	1952	1.52
1941	3.00	1953	1.56
1942	1.69	1954	1.28
1943	1.57	1955	0.91
1944	1.17	1956	1.28
1945	1.66	1957	[a]2.05
1946	1.28	1958	[a]2.12
1947	1.68	1959	[a,b]2.56

Source: Michigan Employment Security Commission.

[a] Including emergency rate of 0.5 percent.

[b] Estimated by relating 1959 rates to taxable payrolls for the twelve months preceding the 1958 computation date.

Note: For the years 1936-1941, the rates given are the statutory normal rate assigned to all employers. Adjusted rates under the reserve ratio plan of experience rating became operative in 1942, based on experience in the preceding three years.

1955, the lowest rate since the inauguration of experience rating, does not reflect the high auto sales for that year. It reflects the unemployment experience of all covered employers prior to the June 30, 1954 computation date.

By way of comparison, as in Table A-19, the average contribution rate for the United States was higher than that for Michigan in the years 1950, 1951, 1955 and 1956. In the year 1952 the difference between the average contribution rate for the United States and Michigan was .07 percent, in 1953 it was .26 percent and in 1954 it was .16 percent. However, in the years 1957 and 1958 the difference was more pronounced. In the former year it was .74 percent and in the latter .72 percent. When Michigan is compared with other states in the East North Central region, it is seen that the average contribution rate of employers in the state was higher than in any of the other states for eight of the nine years 1950-1958. In 1955, the Wisconsin rate was 1.01 percent as compared with .91 percent for Michigan. When the average contribution rates for Pennsylvania and New York, two important industrial states, are examined, it is seen that the rate for New York employers was higher than for Michigan for the years 1950-1956. Pennsylvania had a higher rate than Michigan in both 1955 and 1956. The Michigan rate was higher than Pennsylvania in 1957, and both states had almost identical rates for 1958.

New employers under the Michigan Act are subject to the standard rate of 2.7 percent of payroll (up to $3,000 per year per employee only for the first two years of operation in the state). Prior to 1952 the standard rate for new employers was 3 percent. Congress in Public Law 767 (83rd Congress) modified the requirement of three years' experience with unemployment by authorizing the states to extend experience rating tax reductions to new and newly covered employers after they have had at least one year of such experience under the state law. The effective date of the Michigan law was January 1, 1958. Ohio is the only state in the East North Central region that requires a minimum of three years experience for newly covered employers before any experience rating can be applied.

The benefits payable under the Michigan Act do not appear to be high when compared with those provided by other states in the East North Central region. As indicated in Table A-20, Michigan provides a maximum weekly benefit of $30 for workers without dependents and as much as $55 for a worker with four or more

Table A-19

Unemployment Compensation Contributions as a Percentage of Taxable Wages, United States and Select States
1950 - 1958

Year	United States[a]	MICHIGAN	Ohio	Indiana	Illinois	Wisconsin	Pennsylvania	New York
					Average Contribution Rate			
1950	1.50	1.36	1.04	0.97	0.76	0.76	1.04	2.70
1951	1.58	1.56	1.17	1.03	1.09	0.87	1.01	2.70
1952	1.45	1.52	1.14	0.74	1.10	0.90	1.04	2.35
1953	1.30	1.56	1.05	0.72	0.90	0.88	1.08	2.06
1954	1.12	1.28	0.61	0.76	0.61	0.84	1.09	1.57
1955	1.18	0.91	0.67	0.96	0.72	1.01	1.63	1.49
1956	1.32	1.28	0.74	1.09	1.10	1.07	2.24	1.49
1957	1.31	2.05	0.72	1.02	1.00	1.10	1.55	1.77
1958 (est.)	1.40	2.12	0.70	1.10	0.80	1.10	2.10	1.60

Source: U. S. Department of Labor, Bureau of Employment Security, Key Facts as to 1948-1956 Unemployment Fund Experience under the Law of Each State, October, 1957.

1957: U. S. Department of Labor, Bureau of Employment Security, 1957 Supplement to Handbook of Unemployment Insurance Financial Data.

1958: U. S. Department of Labor, Bureau of Employment Security, The Labor Market and Employment Security, March 1959, page 31.

aIncludes 51 jurisdictions (Alaska and Hawaii and District of Columbia)

Table A-20

Summary of Benefit Provisions of Unemployment Insurance Laws — Select States, as of August 12, 1959

State	Qualifying Wages or Employment in Base Period	Weekly Benefit Amount for Total Unemployment		Total Benefits Payable in Benefit Year			
		Minimum[a]	Maximum[a]	Minimum		Maximum	
				Amount	Weeks	Amount[a]	Weeks
MICHIGAN............	14 weeks of employment at more than $15.	$10.00-12.00	$30.00-55.00	$ 95.00	9.5	$ 780-1,430	26
Illinois...............	$700; and $150 outside high quarter.	10.00	32.00-50.00	100.00 [b]150.00	10 [b]15	832-1,300 [b]1,248-1,950	26 [b]39
Indiana..............	$250 and $150 in last two quarters.	10.00	36.00	62.00	6+	936	26
Ohio.................	20 weeks of employment and $240.	10.00-13.00	42.00-53.00	240.00 [c]360.00	24 [c]36	1,092-1,378 [c]1,638-2,067	26 [c]39
Wisconsin...........	18 weeks of employment	11.00	[d]41.00	138.60	12.6	1,394	34

Source: U. S. Department of Labor, Report on State Legislation, No. XXI.

aWhen two amounts are given, the higher includes dependents' allowances.
bBenefits extended by 50% when unemployment reaches specified level.
cBenefits extended by 50% for exhaustees before December 26, 1959.
dEffective January 1, 1960, the maximum benefit amount will be computed at 52½% of the Statewide average weekly wage.

289

dependents. Illinois and Ohio also provide dependents' allowances under their unemployment insurance laws. Illinois currently pays a maximum of $50 to workers with four or more dependents. The maximum allowance for dependents in Illinois is $12. Ohio provides a maximum of $53 to workers with three or more dependents. Ohio's maximum allowance for dependents is $11. Indiana pays a maximum rate of $36 without dependents. The Wisconsin Act pays a maximum benefit of $41. Beginning January 1, 1960, the maximum benefit amount in Wisconsin will be computed at 52.5 percent of the statewide average weekly wage. Under all state unemployment insurance acts, the weekly benefit amount, i.e., the amount payable for a week of total unemployment, varies with the employee's past wages within certain minimum and maximum limits. Illinois, Indiana and Ohio use a formula which bases the weekly benefit rate on wages in that quarter of the base period. Michigan and Wisconsin base the weekly rate on average weekly wages.

In Michigan, an individual's average weekly wage is the average of his wages in the calendar weeks of his base period in which he earned wages in excess of $15, for not less than 14 weeks, nor more than the most recent 39 weeks. The weekly benefit rate is determined from the average weekly wage according to a schedule of wage classes between $15.01 and $108.01, by family classes. There are six family classes corresponding to the number of the claimant's dependents. The Act does not provide a basic benefit for a specified amount of earnings. The benefit rate schedule is arranged to show the amount which a claimant in each "family class" must earn to qualify for each weekly benefit rate. As indicated in Table A-21, the earnings required for the maximum benefit rate vary according to the family class.

Michigan pays as low a minimum benefit to a worker (without dependents) as does any other state in the region. (See Table A-20). The potential maximum weekly benefit of $55 provided by the Michigan Act is higher than the potential maximum paid by the other states in the region. As indicated in Table A-21, a claimant must have average base period earnings in excess of $108 per week to qualify for the maximum weekly benefit. In the fiscal year 1957, only about 4 percent of the claimants qualified for the maximum amount. The average weekly benefit payment for total unemployment in Michigan in 1958 was $36.54. By comparison, it was $33.05 for Ohio, $29.55 for Indiana, $30.92 for Illinois,

Table A-21

Maximum Unemployment Compensation Benefits Provided in Michigan Employment Security Act

April, 1958

Family Class[a]	Wage Class	Maximum Weekly Benefit
"A"	$ 75.51 or more	$30.00
"B"	74.01 or more	34.00
"C"	74.01 or more	38.00
"D"	84.01 or more	43.00
"E"	96.01 or more	49.00
"F"	108.01 or more	55.00

Source: Michigan Employment Security Commission, Employers' Handbook, April, 1958, p. 22.

a Each class corresponds to the number of dependents an individual has. For example, Class "A" is an individual with no dependents, Class "B" is an individual with one dependent, etc.

and $33.92 for Wisconsin. The average weekly benefit for the United States was $30.58. The difference between the average weekly benefit in Michigan and those of the other states is readily explainable by the state's higher average weekly total wages in covered employment. In 1957, the latest year for which this information is available, this figure was $99.26 for Michigan. For Ohio, it was $92.21; for Indiana, $88.19; for Illinois, $93.56; and for Wisconsin it was $85.58. The average weekly total wages in covered employment for the United States was $84.18 in 1957.

As shown in Table A-20, benefits in Michigan and Indiana have a maximum duration of 26 weeks. Illinois also has a maximum benefit duration of 26 weeks, but the benefits can be extended to 39 weeks when unemployment reaches a specified level. Likewise, Ohio has a maximum benefit duration of 26 weeks, but benefits in that state can also be extended to 39 weeks for exhaustees before December 26, 1959. In Wisconsin the benefits have a maximum duration of 34 weeks. Indiana has a variable duration of from 6 to 26 weeks, whereas Michigan has a variable duration of from 9.5 to 26 weeks. All other states in the region have a higher variable duration.

The conditions for monetary eligibility under the Michigan Act are somewhat lower than those of the other states in the East North Central region. In Michigan a claimant can qualify for minimum benefits by having 14 weeks of employment in his base period in each of which he earned $15.01 or more. In Illinois, to qualify, the claimant must earn $700 in the base period and $150 in quarters other than high-quarter. In Indiana a claimant must have at least $250 in earnings in his base period and $150 in the last two quarters. In Ohio a claimant needs 20 weeks of employment and earnings of $240 in his base period; and in Wisconsin he must have 18 weeks of employment in his base period. It should be noted that the dollar amount of qualifying wages is not of significant importance in view of the present generally high wage rates in these states.

Each state establishes its requirements which an unemployed worker must meet to receive unemployment insurance benefits. All state laws require that a claimant show attachment to the labor force; all contain disqualification provisions. The eligibility and disqualification provisions are designed to limit payments to workers unemployed primarily as a result of economic causes. Under the Michigan Act wage credits are cancelled if a claimant is disqualified for voluntarily leaving his work without good cause attributable to the employer, for discharge for misconduct connected with his work, and for refusal of suitable work when offered. Since each state establishes its own rules, the administration of the acts in the East North Central States as they relate to eligibility and disqualification is not included in this paper. These rules and their interpretation either by the state agency or by state courts affect the payment of benefits.

As we have seen, the average contribution rate for Michigan for the period 1950-1958 does not compare favorably with that for the other states in the East North Central region. The average contribution rate, however, does not represent the current costs of the program. The actual cost rate is benefit payments expressed in percent of taxable wages. The benefit cost rate for the years 1950-1958 is presented in Table A-22. From the data, Illinois had a higher benefit cost rate than Michigan in 1950 and Wisconsin was higher in 1953. Michigan had a higher cost rate for the years 1951-1952 and 1954-1958 than any other state in the region. By comparison, the benefit cost rate for the United States was higher than that for Michigan in 1950, 1953 and 1955. In five of the nine years both Pennsylvania and New York had a higher benefit cost rate than Michigan. States with heavy unemployment have been faced with high benefit cost rates.

When the average contribution rates (Table A-19) and the benefit cost rates (Table A-22) are compared for Michigan, it is

Table A-22

Unemployment Compensation Benefits as a Percentage of Taxable Wages, United States and Select States

1950 - 1958

Year	United States[a]	MICHIGAN	Ohio	Indiana	Illinois	Wisconsin	Pennsylvania	New York
1950	1.68	1.07	1.44	0.63	1.53	0.69	1.52	2.68
1951	0.93	0.95	0.45	0.52	0.86	0.35	0.83	1.59
1952	1.05	1.23	0.54	0.74	0.84	0.66	1.34	1.52
1953	0.97	0.69	0.46	0.55	0.71	0.81	1.21	1.40
1954	2.10	2.83	1.86	2.21	1.92	1.91	3.28	2.28
1955	1.33	1.19	0.85	0.82	1.08	1.01	2.21	1.72
1956	1.26	2.61	0.83	1.13	0.78	1.02	1.88	1.54
1957	1.54	2.32	1.14	1.21	1.01	1.23	2.27	1.72
1958	3.20	6.30	3.90	2.70	2.80	2.90	4.70	3.50

Source: 1950-1956: U. S. Department of Labor, Bureau of Employment Security, Key Facts as to 1948-1956 Unemployment Fund Experience under the Law of Each State, October, 1957.

1957 data: U. S. Department of Labor, Bureau of Employment Security, 1957 Supplement to Handbook of Unemployment Insurance Financial Data.

1958 data: U. S. Department of Labor, Bureau of Employment Security, The Labor Market and Employment Security, March 1959, page 31.

[a] Includes 51 jurisdictions (Alaska, Hawaii and District of Columbia)

seen that the contribution rates have taken care of only a part of the actual current benefit costs during the last five years, 1954-1958. For the period 1950-1953, the average contribution rates in Michigan were somewhat higher than the benefit cost rates. In appraising the Michigan unemployment insurance program, one must consider the nature of the state's economy. Michigan's industrial structure gives rise to high benefit costs. The periodic large-scale layoffs in the mass production industries are high cost occurrences for the state's unemployment insurance program, since a large number of the workers involved are eligible for benefit payments. The program must be paid for by contributions.

In summary, Michigan employers, in general, paid higher average contribution rates than did employers in other states in the East North Central region during the period 1950-1958. Likewise the benefit cost rates for Michigan employers were generally higher than for other states in the region. In the final analysis, the unemployment experience of the state's covered employers is the major factor which determines the cost of the unemployment insurance program.

Other State Labor Legislation

The other forms of state labor legislation have varying degrees of influence on the labor factor in plant location. Relatively little study has been given to the importance of such laws as factory inspection, hours of work, fair employment practices, right-to-work, and state mediation acts in plant location. Their effect on labor costs is difficult to determine. Acts such as fair employment practices and right-to-work reflect the milieu of the state, but may not have any effect on labor costs.

In this section we are concerned only with a brief recitation of the other pertinent labor legislation in Michigan. A comparison of such labor legislation on a state-by-state basis is beyond the scope of this paper. Further research appears to be desirable in order to ascertain the importance of state labor legislation in plant location, especially legislation involving restrictions on union security arrangements.

Michigan has a factory inspection law. Such laws are among the oldest protective labor legislation on the statute books. Employers, for the most part, recognize the advantages of compliance with safety regulations. The requirements of the Michigan law are comparable with those of most other states.

The state has no minimum wage act. There is an act prohibiting the employment of women for more than an average 9-hour day, a maximum 10-hour day, and a maximum 54-hour week. Women must also be provided with a seventh day of rest. There are no state regulations applicable to the hours of employment of adult males. Michigan, like other states, has restrictions on the employment of minors under 18 years of age. Minors are limited in the number of hours they may work and the time they may be employed. For example, minors under 18 years of age who are attending school are prohibited from working during the hours 10 p.m. to 6 a.m. There is also a comprehensive list of prohibited employments for children and restrictions on the employment of women, e.g., women cannot be employed at any occupation requiring the lifting of more than 35 pounds.

Michigan as well as Indiana, Wisconsin, and Ohio has a Fair Employment Practices Act. These acts forbid employers to discriminate against job applicants on the basis of race, color, religion, or national origin. The Act in Michigan is administered by a commission of six members which is empowered to hear complaints and to order the respondent to cease and desist from such practice. The commission can order the reinstatement with back pay of persons discriminated against by employers.

The Labor Mediation Act (Bonine-Tripp Act) established a State Mediation Board whose function is to assist in the peaceful settlement of industrial disputes. In labor disputes involving public utilities and hospitals, the Act provides for the appointment of a special fact-finding commission which is authorized to make non-binding recommendations for settlement. The Act lists unfair labor practices of employers and employees similar to those of the Taft-Hartley Act with one important exception. The state law does not contain a positive obligation on the part of employers to bargain with unions. In other words, "refusal to bargain" is not an unfair labor practice under the Labor Mediation Act.

The Labor Mediation Act is the only act Michigan has which regulates labor-management relations. There is no state right-to-work law forbidding union security arrangements. Indiana is the one state in the East North Central region which has such a law.[28] Michigan does not have a law restricting the issuance of injunctions in labor disputes.

---

28 Nineteen other states have such a law: Alabama, Arizona, Arkansas, Florida, Georgia, Iowa, Kansas, Louisiana, Mississippi, Nebraska, Nevada, North Carolina, North Dakota, South Carolina, South Dakota, Tennessee, Texas, Utah, and Virginia.

In summary, it is difficult to evaluate the influence of the types of labor legislation discussed in this section on plant location decisions. Little study has been given to their importance.

Noneconomic Considerations

IN LABOR-ORIENTED industries, as contrasted with market- and material-oriented industries, labor costs play an important role. Economic and legal considerations both affect labor costs. In this sense both considerations are economic in nature. However, when plant decisions in labor-oriented industries are made, noneconomic factors are also examined. The economic factors do not stand alone; they are analyzed within a particular frame of reference, i.e., the business climate or reputation of the state as a place in which to do business. The business climate is a composite of both economic and noneconomic factors, including taxes, wage rates, extent of government services, the labor situation, community attitudes toward business, opinions of employers, and the like. The labor situation is likewise a composite of economic and noneconomic factors. We are concerned here with the noneconomic factors relative to the labor situation.

These noneconomic factors include, among other things, the history of labor relations, past and present. The well-publicized conflicts between the large and powerful companies of Michigan and its large and powerful unions, together with the political manifestations of those conflicts, have created a particular image of the state which is held by many employers, in and out of Michigan.

Is this image of Michigan which employers have a significant factor in plant location decisions? It is difficult to say. Probably greater weight is given to this image in labor-oriented industries than in non-labor-oriented, i.e., market- and material-oriented, plants, but here again we are not sure. We do know that such location decisions are not made solely in a vacuum or by feeding the data into an electronic computer. They are made by persons who act on the basis of hunches, emotions, and prejudices as well as on economic data. Both economic and noneconomic factors play a role in the decision-making process.

All plant location authorities are in agreement that the labor history of the area be investigated, especially where a considerable labor force is to be employed in the new plant. There are employers who use the labor history of the area as a basis for selecting specific locations.[29] On the other hand there are employers who reject this historical approach. For example, the Norge Division of the Borg-Warner Corporation located a washing machine plant in Herrin, Illinois, which had a past history full of bitter labor strife and "the company to date has been completely satisfied with the labor situation in the area."[30]

Employers in Michigan are not completely satisfied with the labor situation. In a survey of 188 executives in manufacturing plants in 1950 as to the advantages and disadvantages of Michigan as a manufacturing state, employers representing 51 percent of the employment (included in the study) were dissatisfied with the labor situation in general.[31] Respondents representing 12 percent of the manufacturing workers specifically cited pressure from organized labor as a disadvantage. By comparison, managers of 34 percent of the employment found the labor situation favorable. The employer's perception of the labor situation depends to some extent upon where he is located in the state. As indicated in Table A-23, 34 percent of Detroit industry sees some advantage in the labor situation while only 18 percent of employers in small towns viewed the labor situation favorably. There is little correlation between satisfaction and dissatisfaction with the labor situation among executives of plants in towns of varying sizes. In Detroit as compared with small towns (less than 50,000 population) there was

Table A-23

The Labor Situation in Michigan as an Advantage and Disadvantage for Manufacturing, by Plant Location

1950

Item	Percentage of Employment Represented			
	Metro-politan Detroit	Other Cities	Small Towns	State Average
Advantage Favorable Labor Situation.....................	34	46	18	34
Disadvantage Labor in General............................ Pressure of Organized Labor.................	63 13	43 14	33 8	51 12

Source: Industrial Mobility in Michigan, Survey Research Center, University of Michigan, December, 1950, pp. 35 and 68.

29 Glenn E. McLaughlin and Stefan Robock, *Why Industry Moves South* (Washington: National Planning Association, 1949), p. 73.
30 *Ibid.*, p. 73.
31 *Industrial Mobility in Michigan, op. cit.*, p. 35.

about twice as much satisfaction and about twice as much dissatisfaction.

The unfavorable attitude toward the labor situation held by employers representing 51 percent of the employment may well affect the labor factor in plant location in Michigan. On the whole, there is about one and a half times as much dissatisfaction with the state's labor situation as there is satisfaction. The importance of such attitudes is difficult to measure. Whether they can be measured or not is another matter. They do, in fact, exist.

In summary, extensive publicity has been and is being given to the labor situation both in and out of the state. A United States Senator, speaking in Saginaw, declared "there is widespread belief that the State of Michigan is no longer a good place to expand or to enter with a new manufacturing business."[32] No facts were given to support this view. While the weight given by employers to this and similar views is not known, they may, nevertheless, be a factor in plant location decisions. As such, the labor situation in Michigan would be considered a disadvantage.

Summary

FROM A REVIEW of the available data, what can be said of the labor factor in plant location in Michigan? To say that it is good or bad requires a certain yardstick. The yardstick used, where data were available, was that of the United States and the states in the East North Central region. The latter were chosen because Michigan is in the same geographical area. These states are more comparable in that they are industrial states. While there are inherent limitations even in making comparisons between "similar" industrial states, it is much more difficult to compare Michigan with Mississippi. The former is an important industrial state while the latter is primarily agricultural. While there is dissatisfaction with the yardstick, it is the only one currently meaningful.

Before conclusions, tentative as they be, can be made about the labor factor in Michigan, it must be pointed out that within every large industrial state there are pronounced differences. These differences tend to become blurred when emphasis and attention are constantly focused on one aspect of the state's economy, important as that segment may be. There is more to Michigan than Detroit, the automobile industry, and the UAW. Even the composition of

32 Bureau of National Affairs, Washington, D. C., *Daily Labor Report*, February 9, 1959.

Detroit and the automobile industry is not monolithic. Urban metropolitan centers, complex industrial organizations, and large and varied unions do not lend themselves to simple generalizations. All too frequently there is a tendency to generalize either on an extremely small sample or on incomplete data.

Since we live in a dynamic society where change is ceaseless, attention must be given to the element of time. An effort was made to introduce this element by examining appropriate data for several years. Time is important because there is a tendency to compare states and regions at different stages of their industrial development. For example, as of 1953, Michigan had a high percentage of its nonagricultural labor force organized. The percentage in 1959 is not known. In five or ten years newer industrial states may have an even larger percentage of their nonagricultural employment organized than will Michigan. As industrial patterns shift, we may see the same kind of shift in patterns of unionization.

Another temporal feature to which consideration should be given is the evolving nature of employer-union relations. For more than twenty years the employers and unions in Michigan's industrial firms have been developing a set of working relationships under which each has gained experience in the negotiation of collective bargaining agreements. Some have, indeed, become real artists in enacting the drama of negotiating important collective bargaining agreements. Through time, the parties have come to know each other thoroughly, not only in terms of personalities but also in terms of the economics of particular industries. With the growing emphasis on the need for workers with particular job skills and experience it may well be that employers will give serious attention to those skills and experiences acquired through the collective bargaining processes. The increasing complexity of negotiations cannot be left to novices.

On the basis of available and limited data, Michigan's labor factor deserves a "better press" than it has been receiving. With regard to the labor factor, no state is perfect in the eyes of a hypothetical rational employer who is interested in maximizing profits. Each state, however, does possess both certain advantages and disadvantages for plant location. The critical question, therefore, is whether the net advantages outweigh the net disadvantages. If the relative weight of the pertinent considerations affecting the labor factor were known, the task of appraising would be easier. Since little is known of the significance of the several factors affecting the location of labor-oriented industries, it would seem that evaluations of employers on such matters would be a fruitful area of research.

What are the advantages which Michigan possesses? The state offers an adequate supply of experienced factory labor. The projected population of the state indicates that an adequate supply of labor will be available to meet the future manpower needs of industry, business, and commerce. Quantity, however, does not stand alone. With the growing complexity of American industry, employers must be concerned with the quality of the available labor supply. Today considerable attention is being given to improving the skills of labor forces in every country in the world. Michigan has a labor force which possesses a wide variety of skills. Furthermore, the citizens of the state recognize the importance of providing opportunities for improvement of these skills by their support of public education. The public schools and institutions of higher learning are a most important asset of Michigan.

The qualitative features of Michigan's labor force take on added significance when labor productivity and employee stability are examined. It was seen that the Michigan worker's productivity in 1954 and 1956 was higher than that of the U. S. worker. Likewise, he compared favorably on a regional basis. However, to substantiate or refute the available crude evidence, there is a need for productivity studies on an industry-by-industry and state-by-state basis. Michigan is not alone in seeking more meaningful data on productivity. Currently there are discussions at the national level on the need for better measurements of productivity.

Michigan possesses a relatively stable labor force. The quit rate for the state's production workers has been lower than that of the United States in recent years. Such information gathered by the Michigan Employment Security Commission should be made available on a regular basis. In some states a separate labor turnover bulletin is issued periodically by the appropriate state agency.

The second measure of labor stability is the work stoppage experience. When the data on work stoppages and on the estimated time lost are reviewed, Michigan compares favorably with other industrial states. There is no correlation between the degree of unionization of the nonagricultural labor force and the time loss from work stoppages. It was also seen that there is no definite pattern in strike experience among the various industries of the state. While there are data on strikes by industry in the state, there is no information on the issues involved. In this connection the

Michigan State Mediation Board could perform an important service by regularly publishing data on strikes, their number and duration, and the workers, industries, and issues involved.

Costs to Michigan employers under the Workmen's Compensation Act compare favorably with those of employers in other states. The average manual rate of 45 major classifications ranked Michigan eleventh in six out of seven years (1950-1956) when compared with fifteen other states. The manual rate for certain classifications is also lower than those in neighboring states. This is particularly significant since the benefits under the Michigan Act are, in some instances, higher than these states. Since the administration and interpretation of the law affect employer costs, more attention must be given to these aspects. For example, is the Michigan Accident Fund discharging effectively its responsibilities in keeping rates at the lowest possible minimum? Secondly, how do the recent interpretations of the law by the Michigan Supreme Court — interpretations which have served to liberalize benefits in this state — compare with rulings of similar courts in other industrial states?

From a review of the data, it appears that the labor factor in Michigan possesses three aspects which may be regarded as disadvantages by employers: the first relates to wage rates, the second to unemployment compensation costs, and the third to the labor situation in the state. It was seen that production workers in Michigan have the highest average weekly earnings in the nation. While specific wage rates were not discussed, high earnings generally coincide with high wage rates. Because of the industrial composition of the state with its predominance of high value-added-by-manufacture industries and its relatively large percentage of skilled and semiskilled workers, high earnings are to be expected. The high earnings of auto workers were noted as were the earnings of workers in the machinery industries in the Detroit area. What effect, then, do these high average weekly earnings have on plant location decisions, especially for low wage rate paying industries? We do know that in this respect Michigan has no substantial disadvantages when compared with other highly industrialized states. We also know that factory workers in the Detroit machinery industries are the highest paid in the industry. We do not know if Detroit is a high-wage city for any given occupation. For comparative purposes, information is needed on specific wage rates for specific jobs in specific industries in particular locations. Michigan is not alone in needing better data for wage comparisons. It would seem that the major data-gathering agencies, private and public, could perform a greater service by agreeing to comparable reporting systems. By so doing, interstate (and intercity) wage comparisons could be more meaningful.

Fringe benefits are becoming increasingly important in labor costs. The available studies, however, only tabulate the fringe benefits, e.g., number of holidays, length of vacations, kind of pension plans, etc. Data are also needed on the costs of these benefits in order to get a more accurate picture of labor costs in Michigan. As indicated, employer associations in the state do collect data on fringes; their efforts, however, could be better coordinated and standardized so that their data could be utilized more effectively.

More studies are needed on union wage policies. For example, how extensive is pattern bargaining by the United Auto Workers in Michigan? Once negotiations are completed in the automobile industry are similar contract terms relative to wages and other conditions of employment obtained from other employers with whom this union bargains? Are there variations from the "key bargain"? If so, under what conditions are there variations? Are they related to size of firm, to the industry, or merely to the economics of the particular situation?

Professor Harold Levinson of the University of Michigan is in the process of conducting a study of pattern bargaining by the UAW in 87 firms in the Detroit metropolitan area, excluding the "Big Three." His tentative conclusion is that the union "does not impose the key bargain on *all* (his italics) firms, regardless of their individual circumstances."[33] The union "does adjust its demands to the needs of the particular situation either through a below-pattern settlement or increases in productivity."[34] Similar studies of out-state experience would provide a basis for comparison as well as additional insight into union wage policies.

The average contribution rate paid by employers under the state unemployment insurance program may be viewed as a disadvantage. While the Michigan rate did not compare unfavorably with the average rate for the United States as a whole for the years 1950-1956, it was higher than that of all other states in the region in eight out of nine years (1950-1958). One important reason for this higher rate is the industrial composition of the state, especially

33 Harold M. Levinson, "Pattern Bargaining by the United Automobile Workers," *Labor Law Journal*, September, 1958, p. 673.
34 *Ibid.*, p. 674.

the predominance of the automotive industry. However, in order to get a more accurate picture of employer costs in this program, additional information is needed. While data on the number of rated employers paying a particular tax rate are available, their contribution rate by size of firm and by industry is not. Such data would enable employers to estimate more accurately their unemployment insurance cost. The interpretations of the act by the state supreme courts in the industrial states also provide an area for further study.

Michigan has been characterized as having an "unfavorable labor situation." Widespread publicity has been given to the labor situation with the result that *some* employers in and out of the state have a particular image of Michigan. The state is pictured as being dominated by labor, in particular by Walter Reuther and the UAW. While this stereotype is held by some employers in the state, it is not universal. Not all employers in Michigan are organized by the UAW. There are employers who have developed satisfactory working relationships with unions, both with the UAW and others.

The most recent published survey of employers' attitudes on the labor situation was in 1950. Times and conditions change. Information is therefore needed both on the current status of the labor situation as viewed by employers and on their particular reasons for such views. In addition, more detailed information on the characteristics of employers included in such a study would be most helpful in making a better appraisal. Specifically we need to have evaluations of the labor situation according to size of firm, extent of ownership, the industry, the unions bargained with, and the length of the collective bargaining relationship.

In appraising the labor situation it must be recognized that not all employers can always be satisfied. The labor situation is amorphous. All too frequently there is a tendency to make the labor situation too inclusive. All of the difficulties affecting the operation of a firm cannot be attributed to labor. It may well be that inadequate capital, changing nature of the market, and inept management, to mention a few factors, also affect operations.

Since there are so many facets to the labor situation, its proper evaluation is difficult. Noneconomic considerations, nevertheless, do affect the labor factor in plant location, especially in labor-oriented industries. If, however, there were more reliance on the available data than on emotions, newspaper headlines, and loose

303

talk, a better evaluation of the labor factor in Michigan could be made. The labor factor in the state possesses important advantages which merit serious attention by employers who are either considering expanding existing facilities or seeking new plant sites.

With interstate competition for industry increasing at an accelerated pace, closer scrutiny will be given to the labor factor. While this factor is more important in the labor-oriented industries, lower transportation costs may well affect the labor factor in market- and material-oriented industries. The economic future of Michigan is related to the degree of success in expanding job opportunities for a growing population. An important element will be the labor factor and the reputation of the state as a desirable place to live and work. The former is but one aspect of the latter. In developing and disseminating this kind of reputation, Michigan needs the collective goodwill of all its citizens.

Appendix B

Taxation and Industrial Location in Michigan

BY

HARVEY E. BRAZER

ASSOCIATE PROFESSOR OF ECONOMICS AND RESEARCH
ASSOCIATE, INSTITUTE OF PUBLIC ADMINISTRATION,
THE UNIVERSITY OF MICHIGAN

THE IMPACT of state and local taxes upon economic growth, particularly growth in the industrial or manufacturing sector of the economies of the several states, has been the subject of a great deal of controversy in recent years. Virtually no segment of the nation has been immune; in the south, southwest, and in the far west, where manufacturing employment has been growing impressively, rates of growth among the states have varied and those experiencing less rapid growth than their neighbors have sought to explain their relative lag; in the mixed agricultural-extractive-industrial states, such as Minnesota and Wisconsin, there has been much concern about the ability of growth in nonagricultural employment to absorb "surplus" farm labor; and in the older heavily industrialized states of the northeast and midwest, states such as Michigan, Pennsylvania, New York, and Massachusetts, the process of decentralization of major industrial activities, resulting in rates of employment growth below those experienced in other states, has been accompanied by a continuing barrage of charges and countercharges, affirming or denying the role of taxes in the failure of the state to retain its relative share of the nation's total industrial employment.

In this Appendix, I shall not examine the question of whether or not the Michigan economy has fared as well in recent years as it might have, nor trace again the course of developments; the latter have been the major concern of the text of this volume.[1] Rather,

---

1 See also Wolfgang F. Stolper, "Economic Development, Taxation, and Industrial Location in Michigan," in *Michigan Tax Study Staff Papers* (Lansing, 1958).

305

my objective is to cast some light on the question of the level of Michigan taxes relative to those imposed in other states and on the importance of state and local taxes as a factor in industrial location.

Tax Levels Among the States

THERE IS NO EASY way to answer the question as to whether or not state and local taxes in Michigan are "high" or "low" relative to those in other states. Moreover, as urbanization and industrialization extend into new areas or increase more rapidly in some areas than in others, we find that both inter-regional income and tax-level differences tend to diminish, so that recent trends may be at least as important as current status. A further complicating factor lies in the fact that Michigan, like any other state, is not a geographically homogeneous body of land. Thus tax collections relative to population or income may be high in Detroit, but low in Roscommon or Keweenaw counties, high in Boston, but low in the villages of the Berkshire hill country.

Can we hold that state-local tax revenues in Arkansas, at $100.40 per capita in 1957, were lower than they were in Michigan, where they amounted to $181.13, when in the former state-local tax receipts represented 8.8 percent of personal income while in the latter they took only 8.4 percent of total income received in 1957?[2] Obviously if we choose to measure relative tax loads merely by dividing total tax receipts by population, Michigan ranks among the "high" tax states. In this sense it ranked, in 1957, twelfth among the 48 states. But its $181 in per capita state and local taxes was exceeded by higher figures for all three of the rapidly growing states bordering upon the Pacific Ocean, as well as such states as Colorado, Connecticut, Massachusetts, and New York. Furthermore, in Illinois and New Jersey, frequently cited as "low-tax" states, total state-local tax receipts, at $179 and $174 per capita, respectively, were not appreciably lower than they were in Michigan. This (to some surprising) result is achieved because comparatively low state taxes in Illinois and New Jersey are accompanied by very much higher levels of local tax collections than are found in Michigan.[3]

---

2 These and other data for fiscal 1957 were drawn from U. S. Bureau of the Census, *State and Local Government Finances in 1957* (Washington, 1959), pp. 16-17.

3 The proportions of total state-local tax receipts accounted for by local governments in Illinois and New Jersey were 60 and 71 percent, compared with only 45 percent in Michigan. (Derived from *State and Local Government Finances in 1957*, pp. 39, 48, and 56.) Thus higher per capita *state* tax receipts in Michigan were almost completely offset by far higher local taxes in Illinois and New Jersey.

If we employ the alternative measure of general tax level, state-local tax receipts as a percentage of personal income received in the state, a measure that may be regarded as one that more meaningfully measures gross tax "burdens," Michigan ranked thirty-first among the 48 states. State and local taxes in Michigan amounted to 8.35 percent of personal income, compared with the median ratio of 8.85 percent and a range of 4.90 for Delaware to 11.6 for North Dakota.[4] Thus in the context of a 48-state comparison Michigan, in these terms, can hardly be classified as a high-tax state. However, the high-income states in the region that may be considered relevant for competition with Michigan for industrial plants generally levy taxes representing lower proportions of income. For example, Illinois, Indiana, Ohio, and Pennsylvania ranked fortieth, forty-fourth, forty-seventh, and thirty-eighth in this respect. Only Wisconsin and New York, with state-local taxes amounting to 9.59 and 9.04 percent of income, ranked above Michigan. But what this kind of comparison suggests is that there is a rather close inverse correlation between the level of income or wealth enjoyed by a state (which is, in turn, closely related to its degree of industrialization) and state-local tax receipts expressed as a percentage of total income received. We find, therefore, that states such as Arkansas, Florida, Georgia, and Mississippi, which appear, in per capita terms, to be "low-tax" states, are in fact, relative to income, imposing substantially heavier taxes than Michigan.

A further consideration to be taken into account for purposes of evaluating the position of Michigan relative to other states is the trend in recent years in tax receipts. Government expenditures, while tending to rise generally over time, do not rise steadily; and the action taken through tax legislation to meet budgetary requirements typically proceeds with lags in time that vary substantially from state to state. Illustrative of the latter contention is the fact that the state of Ohio, having turned a surplus of some $200 million as of 1947 into a deficit by 1959, is now being asked to increase state tax receipts by some $330 million in the next biennium. Similarly, Pennsylvania needs upwards of $400 million of additional revenue for the same period, New York's governor has asked for $277 million for one year, Minnesota will have to find in excess of $100 million, and many other states are in similar positions.[5] Moreover, if we examine the data over a period of

---

4 *Ibid.*, p. 17.

5 Information from budget messages of state governors and Commerce Clearing House, *State Tax Review*, various issues.

years, we find that differences among the states in per capita state and local tax receipts have tended to narrow markedly. The two most recent years for which data are available are 1953 and 1957. When we rank the states, from highest to lowest, in terms of their levels of state-local tax receipts per capita in 1953 and their percentage rates of growth, 1953 to 1957, we find a clear tendency for these rankings to be inversely correlated.[6] That is, the states in which tax receipts increased most were generally those which ranked lowest in 1953. Thus, for example, Alabama and Arkansas, which ranked forty-eighth and forty-seventh in 1953 ranked seventh and tenth, respectively, in terms of 1953-1957 rate of growth. On the other hand, for states such as California, Colorado, Massachusetts, Minnesota, Nevada, New York, Washington, and Wisconsin, which all ranked among the first eight states in 1953, 1953-to-1957 rates of growth lay within a range of twentieth for Massachusetts to thirty-sixth for Wisconsin and forty-third for Nevada. Michigan, which ranked eleventh in 1953, experienced a rate of growth that ranked thirty-first, whereas the corresponding rankings for Illinois and Ohio were twenty-two and eleven, and thirty-four and seventeen.

The obvious implication to be drawn from the foregoing is that all states are being subjected to increasing demands for public services and that differences in the levels at which these services are nourished are declining and are bound to continue to decline, just as differences in income levels, standards of private consumption, and so forth, are narrowing. Thus if a state is judged to be a "high" or a "low" tax state in terms of its state-local tax receipts per capita, there is every likelihood that current rankings are going to be found to be ephemeral and hardly worthy of serving as the basis for decisions of long-term importance.[7] Moreover, the level of expenditures and taxation tends to be closely associated with the economic and demographic structure of the state or area within the state. That is, variations in such factors as income, urbanization, and density of population are closely associated with per capita differences in state-local expenditures, accounting for some 70 percent of such differences.[8] Hence a state in which industrial growth is bringing with it increases in income, urbanization, and,

---

6 Data for 1953 from U. S. Bureau of the Census, *State and Local Government Revenue in 1953* (Washington, 1954) and *State and Local Government Finances in 1957* (Washington, 1959).
7 See Solomon Fabricant, *The Trend of Government Activity Since 1900* (New York, 1952), pp. 120-21, for evidence of the "leveling-out" process in government expenditures.
8 *Ibid.*, p. 124.

necessarily, population density, is very likely to be one in which per capita tax collections will be rising more or less commensurately. To bring this down to the local level, it would seem obvious that the movement into an area of new industry, whatever the existing level of taxation may be, is bound to raise that level. The relevant question then becomes, not what is the level of taxes now, but what is it likely to be once the demands imposed upon public authorities by the area's shift from rural to industrial pursuits are being met?

My general conclusion, therefore, is that general measures of the level of state-local taxation are likely to be quite limited in usefulness in any analysis of the impact of state and local taxation upon industrial growth or location. This position is buttressed by the findings of two recent studies, the first by the Business Executives Research Committee of Minnesota, and the second by Professor C. C. Bloom.

Statistical Analyses of the Influence
of Taxes on Industrial Growth

THE FORMER GROUP found that the ten states which had the highest ratios of state-local taxes to personal income in 1953 experienced a 16 percent increase in manufacturing employment from 1947 to 1952, while in the ten lowest tax states the rate of growth in manufacturing employment was only 8 percent.[9]

Professor Bloom employed simple correlation techniques in an attempt to measure the association between growth in manufacturing employment, 1939 to 1953 and 1947 to 1953, expenditure on new plant and equipment, and per capita state and local taxes, as of 1953 as well as in terms of the rate of increase in such taxes between 1941 and 1953. For each of the relations between 1953 per capita state and local tax receipts and the increase in manufacturing employment between 1939 and 1953, rate of growth in manufacturing employment for 1947 to 1953, and the rate of growth, 1939-1953, the association turned out to be positive. That is, the results simply do not support the hypothesis that a high level of state and local taxes is associated with low rates of growth in manufacturing employment; in fact, quite the opposite hypothesis might be said to be supported by the statistical analysis. When the 1941-to-1953 rate of increase in state-local taxes is related to the

---

9 *Industrial Location and the Minnesota Economy* (Minneapolis, no date), p. 49.

rate of growth in manufacturing employment, the correlation coefficient again turns out to have a positive sign. In each of these instances the coefficient is very small, and it is zero for expenditure on new plant and equipment in 1952 and 1953 and per capita state-local taxes in 1953.[10]

About all that can properly be concluded from Bloom's analysis is that the case for the contention that state-local tax differentials, measured in terms of per capita amounts, tend to retard industrial growth is not demonstrable. It is possible, of course, that the high-tax states would have grown even faster and the low-tax states more slowly if their tax positions had been interchanged, but demonstrating this would require taking into account or "keeping constant," in multiple correlation analysis, the forces that do influence manufacturing employment appreciably.

An attempt to do this, using a "refined" tax variable that takes into account only estimated state and local taxes *paid by business* per nonagricultural employee, has been carried out by Professors Wilbur R. Thompson and John M. Mattila. Their over-all finding is that "State and local tax differentials, whether expressed . . . as a percentage of state income or . . . as taxes paid by business per employee, appear to have no measurable effect on interstate differentials in employment growth . . . [1947 to 1954]."[11]

Some observers have been satisfied that statistical studies of the kind described clearly demonstate that state-local tax differentials can have little or no bearing on a state's industrial future. But even the comparatively sophisticated techniques employed by Thompson and Mattila are too crude to permit definitive conclusions. The latter do not ignore tax structure entirely, for they do attempt to consider only taxes paid by business, but their analysis does not take into account differences among the states in the *kinds* of taxes paid by business. As Professor Hoover has suggested, "The locational effect of a tax depends not only on the rate but also on the form of tax used. If there were such a thing as a tax on pure 'land' in the sense of immobile, permanent, and non-reproducible property, it would have no locational effect at all."[12] But there are no such taxes in fact, and only a very small part of business taxes may reasonably be said to be borne out of "pure rent" of location. Furthermore, when we ask about the effects of tax differentials on loca-

---

10 Clark C. Bloom, *State and Local Tax Differentials* (Iowa City, 1956), pp. 18-32.
11 *An Econometric Model of Postwar State Industrial Development* (Wayne State University Press, Detroit, 1959), p. 83.
12 Edgar M. Hoover, *The Location of Economic Activity* (New York, 1948), p. 253.

tion we must necessarily be concerned not with business in general but, rather, with that segment of business that may be described as "footloose." That is, firms which provide personal services, amusements, and so forth, retail and probably much of wholesale trade, and utilities generally have no choice but to locate where their market is. Similarly, the location of other firms will be very closely oriented toward the source of their raw materials. In general, therefore, we are concerned primarily, if not solely, with firms engaged in manufacturing products in plants from which they can serve a fairly wide market area and/or which can draw their raw materials and other supplies from a number of alternative locations. Stated more bluntly, and in extreme form, the department store serving the Detroit area can hardly do so from a Toledo location. Given the technology and transport problems associated with the steel industry, there is little reason to expect that Michigan would have been blessed with a large steel industry regardless of the level or structure of the state's taxes. Tax differentials never have been and never are likely to be large enough to offset the transport cost advantages of the Chicago and Pittsburgh areas, especially in light of the fact that so much of the bulk of iron ore and coal is lost in the steel-making process.

We must look, therefore, to manufacturing industries having a high local value-added to transport cost ratio, and to those taxes that are in fact paid by such firms in various alternative locations. The relevant questions also relate to tax differentials within broad areas of alternative choice among possible locations. These tax differentials are extremely unlikely to carry much weight with respect to Florida or California as an alternative to a Michigan location. Rather, if a firm decides that the East North Central or Middle Atlantic regions would be appropriate, then the relevant choice may lie between such sites as Toledo or Cleveland, Evansville or Indianapolis, Chicago or Milwaukee, Pittsburgh or Youngstown, as against, say, Detroit or Grand Rapids.

Thus, even when it is recognized, as Thompson and Mattila do, that it is taxes paid, at least initially, by business that are important, and that location decisions are not likely to be influenced by levies such as consumer sales and excise taxes or the typically modest state personal income taxes, we still do not have the appropriate tax measure for analysis of the location-impact of state-local taxes. Taxes paid by business per nonagricultural employee, for example, will include those taxes paid by retail and wholesale merchants, utilities, and construction and mining companies, all of which are of no immediate concern to the kind of firm that may be appreciably influenced by tax considerations in its location decision. Unfortunately, however, comparable data do not exist which would permit us to estimate the relative tax burden imposed by the various states on specific relevant segments of industry.

There are essentially two basic questions to be answered. The first asks "What is the magnitude of inter-site tax differentials for a specific plant or firm?" This question is frequently posed in terms of inter-state differentials, but there is overwhelming evidence that suggests that intra-state variations are so large that state-wide aggregation or averaging can be very misleading. Closely associated with it is the question of whether or not it is possible, with methods employed thus far, to measure the differentials in tax bills. The second major question is "How important as a location factor are the tax differentials, assuming that they are measurable or are held to be known?"

Measuring State-Local Tax Liabilities and Their Implications

IN A LITTLE more than two years three attempts have been made to measure inter-state or inter-local state-local tax differentials. These studies have each employed a different approach and each of them covers Michigan and at least some of the neighboring states.

The Relative Tax Cost to Manufacturing Industry: 1957 Revision, A New Comparison of Pennsylvania with Several Other States has enjoyed a rather wide circulation and, among other things, has been cited frequently as "evidence" of the high tax cost of doing business in Michigan.[13] In this study three "hypothetical" corporations were devised by examination of the financial statements of 50 corporations "from which were selected statements of corporations which manufacture commodities representing ten of the standard industrial classifications of business which fall within the objectivity [sic?] of this report."[14] The hypothetical corporations "A", "B", and "C" differ with respect to asset mix, as between personal

---

13 Prepared for the Regional Industrial Development Corporation, Pittsburgh, Pennsylvania, by the Pennsylvania Economy League, Inc., Western Division (Pittsburgh, November, 1957). Cited hereafter as *Pennsylvania Study*.

14 *Pennsylvania Study*, p. 8. The ten industries represented are: finished wire products; chemicals; clay products; carbon, graphite, and electronic parts; basic steel; heavy machinery; building materials; hard carbide products; hardware; and auto accessory products.

and real property, and in terms of rates of return realized on net worth and sales. They differ also in capital structure. But each of the corporations is assumed to have been in operation for only one year, thus simplifying problems of depreciation; each sells its product only in the "home" state, where all of its production facilities are located as well; and each is at least moderately profitable, yielding between 23 and 29 percent on stockholders' equity before federal taxes.

The total of state and local taxes that would be paid if the hypothetical corporations were located in each of 185 urban and suburban local jurisdictions in Delaware, Illinois, Indiana, Maryland, Michigan, New Jersey, New York, Ohio, and Pennsylvania is computed. Because the differences among the three corporations are of insufficient importance to influence tax bills appreciably, especially for Michigan corporations, our discussion of the findings will be confined to Corporation "A." Obviously it is the total state-local tax bill that is of prime importance, but because of the distinct differences in the nature of the problems encountered in developing estimates of tax liability at the state as compared with the local level, the two will, at least initially, be treated separately. A further reason for this approach is that state governments ordinarily can influence local tax costs only to a limited degree, which varies from state to state. On the other hand, particularly in the political arena, the state, its legislature and executive, are too frequently tarred with a brush dipped in the pail of local circumstances that vary widely from one community to another within its borders.

Accepting, for the moment, the validity and relevance of the assumptions employed in the study, how does Corporation A fare in Michigan, compared to the nine other states, and how "important" are the *state* tax differentials?[15] The total of state taxes paid by this corporation would range from $131,153 in Pennsylvania to $12,369 in Illinois. Michigan, with a total tax liability of $84,052, including $10,433 on presumed purchases subject to sales or use tax of $348,000,[16] $30,562 in franchise tax, $42,201

---

15 The tax data cited below are drawn from the *Pennsylvania Study*, p. 23, with adjustments only to include the 5 percent and 1.5 percent corporate income taxes enacted in Delaware and New Jersey, respectively, in 1958. Taxes do not include the costs of unemployment and workmen's compensation insurance.

16 State taxes are understated in Illinois relative to Michigan, Ohio, and Pennsylvania because Illinois applies the "physical ingredient" rule with respect to the exemption from sales tax of purchases by industrial firms, whereas the other states apply the "direct-use" rule. Thus purchases of machinery and equipment are taxable in Illinois and exempt in Michigan, Ohio, and Pennsylvania. See Denzel C. Cline, "The General Sales Tax," in *Michigan Tax Study Staff Papers*, p. 419.

for business activities tax, and $796 in intangibles tax liabilities, would rank fifth among the ten states. In addition to Pennsylvania, states which impose higher tax liabilities are Delaware, Maryland, and New York. The absolute level of state taxes in Michigan is undoubtedly less significant than the saving that might be effected if the corporation moved to the lowest tax state, Illinois. This differential amounts to $71,683. Since the corporation is assumed to be earning profits subject to the marginal federal income tax rate of 52 percent, and since state taxes are deductible in computing income for federal tax purposes, the relevant differential is not $71,683, but the net differential or saving, taking the federal offset into account. Thus the relevant figure is $34,408.[17] The latter sum is equal to approximately three-tenths of 1 percent of the total estimated cost of doing business (exclusive of taxes).

But even a net differential of this magnitude may be arrived at only because of the authors' assumption that the hypothetical corporation has all of its payroll, property, and sales in the home state. This assumption was adopted because it was believed that complexities involved in allocation problems would be best avoided and because of the view that any other assumption would necessarily be an arbitrary one.[18] However, if we are concerned with the impact of taxation on location, then surely it is not relevant to consider the case of the corporation producing only for home consumption. Rather, the type of manufacturer in which we are interested is the one who sells his product in a national or at least multi-state market — that is, one who is presented with a real choice in his location decision. It would therefore seem more reasonable to assume that the firm sells as much as 90 percent of its product to out-of-state purchasers. In this event we should find that the Michigan liabilities under the franchise and business activities taxes would have been reduced by some 30 percent, or about $21,800. On the other hand, the Illinois total liability would remain virtually unaffected, so that the gross differential would be reduced from almost $72,000 to less than $50,000, and the net (after federal offset) differential to $24,000 (from $34,408).

The foregoing is not meant to cast doubt upon the objectivity of those who prepared the tax estimates, but it does suggest that one's

---

17 $71,683 (1 - .52). Some observers insist that the federal offset should not be taken into account. If it is not, however, it seems to me that at some point in the firm's calculations it must surely recognize that its choice of site will influence its federal tax liability and that this influence will vary inversely and proportionately with the amount of state-local taxes paid at each alternative site.
18 *Pennsylvania Study*, pp. 9-10.

choice of assumptions in something as basic as the question of the proportion of the firm's sales to be allocated to the state of location can make a difference in the computed tax liability of 25 percent or more. Thus the findings, while not questioned when the assumptions are accepted as relevant, look very different when they are not and alternative assumptions are used.

Is a tax differential of the dimensions indicated, about $50,000, likely to influence appreciably, in itself, the decision to locate a plant in one state rather than another? I do not believe that an unequivocal answer to this question is possible. But the question should be placed alongside one which asks whether a 1 to 1½ percent differential in wage rates will be of any influence in this decision, for in the case of our hypothetical firm wages and salaries amount to more than $4 million. Will a firm base a location decision on a differential equal to 2½ percent of income before federal taxes? To suggest that "if all other things are equal" a differential of this size may be the determining factor is to beg the question entirely, for "other things" are never "equal," especially in the case of public services. Certainly it would seem safe to conclude that, given the very small magnitude of *state* tax differences, a whole host of other minor factors could just as well tip the balance in one direction or the other. These other factors (not all of which will be minor ones for any one firm) will include such things as climate, recreational facilities, and quality of public services in general.[19]

But, since local taxes are estimated to represent as much as 70 percent of total state-local taxes for the hypothetical corporation in a Michigan location, they must be afforded an even closer look. The city of Plymouth, Michigan, enjoys the dubious distinction of ranking second only to Bloomington, Indiana, in the array of urban and suburban places in which the Pennsylvania Economy League placed its hypothetical Corporation A. Given the property tax rate levied in Plymouth, a little arithmetic reveals that Plymouth, together with other Wayne County jurisdictions, was assumed to assess land and buildings at 50 percent of actual current value (book value of our one-year old plant) and machinery, equipment, and inventories at 90 percent of book value. In view of the fact that the U. S. Bureau of the Census has estimated that the ratio

---

19 The value attached by business to public expenditures for public schools, parks, police and fire protection, higher education, mental hospitals, health services, and so forth, may vary widely among firms, but it is difficult to believe that it is zero. If the labor force value such services and the same degree of rationality is attributed to it as we attribute to the firm, then reduced public services or higher personal taxes may lead only to higher labor costs offsetting lower business taxes.

315

of assessed to sales value of residential, commercial, farm, and vacant real property in Michigan was approximately 30 percent in 1956, the 50 percent figure for Wayne County is difficult to accept.[20] Wayne County contains about 40 percent of total assessed value of property in Michigan. Thus, if it assesses at a ratio of 50 percent and the ratio for the entire state is 30 percent, then the ratio in the rest of the state must be about 17 percent.[21] However, a similar check of the assumed assessment ratios for Flint, in Genesee County, revealed them to be equal to about 75 percent — which would require reducing even further the average rest-of-the-state ratio necessary to make the assumptions used in this study compatible with observed facts. Finally, the City Assessor of Plymouth maintains, upon inquiry of him, that industrial land and buildings have been assessed in recent years at 30 percent of current value; that machinery and equipment are being assessed at a ratio of 33 to 41 percent, and inventories within a range of 75 to 90 percent.

Suppose we accept the estimates of the City Assessor, who is currently conducting a re-appraisal of all properties in Plymouth, using the upper limits of the ranges offered. We may then arrive at estimated property tax liabilities of approximately $36,000 for land and buildings, $54,940 for inventories, and $49,700 for machinery and equipment, or a total of $140,640, as opposed to the Pennsylvania Study's figure of $223,715 (p. 34). If the difference of more than $83,000 is deducted from the estimated state-local total tax liability of $307,767 incurred by Corporation A in Plymouth, its rank falls from second to twelfth, just above Gary, Indiana. The tax liability incurred in Plymouth then falls from almost double the level for the median location, DeWitt Township, New York, to about 45 percent more ($70,000).

However, even a difference of the size suggested assumes that the average assessment ratio actually applied to our hypothetical corporation. But anyone who has observed the results of assessment-sales ratio studies is well aware of the fact that for given kinds of property the degree of variation found is always very high, even when the kind of property examined is residential real estate, which is so much more homogeneous than industrial property and for which sales prices provide the assessor so much more frequently with evidences of market value. Data are not at hand that would

---

20 U. S. Bureau of the Census, *Assessed Values and Sales Prices of Transferred Real Property* (Washington, 1958), pp. 6-13.
21 $(.50 \times .40) + (.1667 \times .60) = .30$.

permit illustration of the wide variation in assessments in Plymouth, but a recent study covering the Lansing area makes the point clearly enough.[22] In the city of Lansing, for example, the median assessment-sales ratio was found to be 30 percent, but the range extended from 10 to 167.5 percent. Even within the middle 80 percent of the sample the range was 29.9 percent.[23] If variation in assessment-sales ratios is as great in Plymouth as well as in the other 184 locations, and there is no sound reason for believing otherwise, then how useful can estimates of local property tax liability be?

To return to Plymouth, where the average assessment ratio is believed by the assessor to be 30 percent, it is certainly not unlikely that many properties are assessed at as low as 15 percent of market value, while others are assessed at as high as 45 percent of value. Again, the statistical probabilities involved cannot be ascertained, but experience elsewhere suggests this as a reasonable range within which as many as two-thirds of all assessment ratios might fall. Thus the tax that would be paid on land and buildings by our hypothetical corporation in Plymouth might be, not the $36,000 suggested above, but $18,000 or less, or, at the other extreme, $54,000 or more.

The difficulties suggested here are acknowledged by the authors of the Pennsylvania Study, who grant that "information on municipal taxation of corporations is difficult to obtain, subject to inaccuracies and opinions when it is available . . ."[24] What is surprising is that, despite the fact that, for Michigan in particular, the local estimated tax bill far outweighs the state liability, the estimates are presented as having any real reliability at all. In light of the available data on local property taxes it is extremely difficult to believe, for example, that Michigan municipalities such as Detroit, Plymouth, and Mount Clemens, impose in fact property taxes approximately twice as high as those suggested for Chicago, Danville, Lincoln, and Aurora in Illinois. First, there is the fact that per capita local property taxes collected in Illinois in fiscal 1957 amounted to $93.94, considerably more than the $78.17 collected in Michigan.[25] And second, the assessed value of industrial real

22 Raleigh Barlowe and Othmar A. Limberger, "Relationship of Tax Assessed Valuations to the Sales Values of Real Properties, Ingham County, Michigan, 1950-53," *Quarterly Bulletin*, Michigan Agricultural Experiment Station, Michigan State University of Agriculture and Applied Science, Vol. 39, No. 1 (August, 1956).
23 *Ibid.*, p. 149.
24 *Pennsylvania Study*, p. 24.
25 Derived from U. S. Bureau of the Census, *State and Local Government Finances in 1957* (Washington, 1959), pp. 39 and 48, and July 1, 1957, estimates of population.

estate represents 12.0 percent of total assessed value of nonfarm real property in Illinois, 16.8 percent in Michigan.[26] Taken in combination these figures suggest that the per capita assessed value of industrial property in Illinois must be very much higher than it is in Michigan if the Pennsylvania Study's findings are to be regarded as acceptable. In fact the estimated amounts are $247 in Illinois and $197 in Michigan, a difference that would not nearly account for the indicated differences in tax liabilities.[27]

A group of findings that provides a means of checking the results presented in the Pennsylvania Study is to be found in a volume entitled *Wisconsin vs. Other States*.[28] The authors of this study interviewed forty Wisconsin-owned or Wisconsin-headquartered corporations which were conducting manufacturing operations in Wisconsin and at least one other state. Each corporation provided detailed breakdowns on the state and local taxes paid in Wisconsin on their Wisconsin facilities and their estimates of the taxes that would be paid if the same facilities were located in cities in other states in which they operate plants. The average ratio of total property taxes in Illinois to total property taxes in Wisconsin for nineteen plants was 54 percent, the range being 7.0 to 105.0 percent. For five Michigan plants the average ratio was 77 percent, with a range of 49.5 to 117.5 percent.[29] Again, there is the suggestion that property taxes are likely to be higher in Michigan than in Illinois, but there is a vast difference between results that indicate a difference of about 100 percent and those that suggest a difference of something less than 50 percent.

Apart entirely from the impossibility of obtaining acceptable or representative results with respect to the overwhelmingly important property tax through the use of the hypothetical corporation approach, there is virtually no end to the variety of results that might be obtained if corporations were established with capital turnover and profit ratios and asset structures very different from those used in the Pennsylvania Study. As Professor Joe S. Floyd, Jr. has pointed out, and as is so clearly indicated in the Wisconsin study, although *not* in the Pennsylvania findings, "There are few states in which tax bills are uniformly high or uniformly low for all types of

---

26 *Idem., Real Estate Assessments in the United States* (Washington, 1957), p. 13.
27 *Idem., Property Tax Assessments in the United States* (Washington, 1957), p. 14, and July 1, 1957, estimates of population.
28 Prepared by Dr. C. K. Alexander of the Wisconsin Taxpayers' Alliance and Robert D. Siff of the Governor's Division of Industrial Development. (Processed and dated December 19, 1956.)
29 *Wisconsin vs. Other States,* Chart 3.

concerns under all sets of conditions."[30] Professor Floyd found, for example, that locations having tax advantages or disadvantages for his hypothetical hosiery mill bear "almost no relationship" to locations having tax advantages or disadvantages for the hypothetical furniture factory.[31]

Under date of October 24, 1958, Professor Dwight B. Yntema presented to the Michigan State Senate Tax Study Committee preliminary findings drawn from a mail questionnaire sent out to some 700 to 800 (the number is not clearly indicated in the report) business corporations with locations in Michigan and at least one of a group of states that included Wisconsin, Illinois, Indiana, Ohio, Pennsylvania, New York, and New Jersey.* Only part of the list was selected at random from files of the Michigan Corporation and Securities Commission, almost half of the corporate names were included in a list "prepared for" the Advisory Committee of the Senate group, some were drawn from Business Activities Tax returns, and 10 corporations volunteered the information without solicitation. Fortunately, Professor Yntema has presented some of his tentative results separately for the Corporations and Securities Commission sample; since we are not told precisely how the other names were selected, it is not possible to evaluate the results obtained.

Questionnaires were addressed to 333 firms having payrolls in Michigan of at least $100,000 and operations in at least one of the seven listed states. The rate of response was 36 percent. Of sixteen manufacturing firms reporting operations in Michigan and Illinois, none paid more taxes per employee or per $1,000 of payrolls in Illinois than in Michigan; only one out of ten reported higher taxes per $1,000 of payrolls in Indiana; in New Jersey two of nine reported higher taxes per employee and taxes per $1,000 of payroll; for New York five reported higher taxes per employee and three a higher tax-to-payroll ratio out of twelve responses. Ohio's slate is as clean as that of Illinois for twenty-eight manufacturing firms; for Pennsylvania, however, we find six out of thirteen reporting higher taxes per employee and seven higher taxes relative to payrolls; and for Wisconsin four out of nine reported higher taxes per employee and five higher taxes per $1,000 of payroll. Thus it would appear that from the point of view of state-local non-payroll taxes there is little to choose between Michigan, Penn-

---

30 Joe S. Floyd, Jr., *Effects of Taxation on Industrial Location* (Chapel Hill, 1952), p. 67.
31 *Ibid.,* p. 69.
* See footnote on page 327.

sylvania, and Wisconsin, while Illinois, Indiana, New Jersey, New York and Ohio all appear to offer lower taxes.

Although final tabulations had not been completed, and separate estimates for the Corporations and Securities Commission group are not presented, the report suggests (page 4) that taxes in Illinois, Indiana, and Ohio are about 42 to 45 percent of their level in Michigan for manufacturing firms. In addition, while indicating that final data had not yet been compiled, Professor Yntema intimates that taxes per employee in Michigan might run to about $300 (for retailers and "others," as well as manufacturers). With total nonfarm employment of about 2.5 million this would suggest that Michigan business firms paid about $750 million in state and local non-payroll taxes (presumably in 1957, although this is not clear). The report does not indicate precisely which state-local taxes were included in the estimates. Presumably they would include the Business Activities Tax, the Annual Corporate Privilege Fee, sales and use tax on business purchases, intangibles tax, and the property tax. The first four, according to Department of Revenue data, would total about $185 million. Professors Musgrave and Daicoff have estimated, on the basis of information obtained from the State Tax Commission, that agricultural and residential property owners pay about 45 per cent of total property taxes.[32] The local property tax levy in 1957 amounted to $622 million and utilities paid $10 million in property taxes to the state. Fifty-five per cent of the $632 million total apportioned to business would bring total state-local taxes up to about $530 million. If all highway-user taxes collected in 1957 were added to this total we should fall short of $750 million by only $20 million, certainly a tolerable margin of error. However, with approximately 3 million private passenger cars registered in the state, the nonbusiness portion of motor vehicle weight taxes may be estimated at about $35 million and the nonbusiness portion of the gasoline tax at $96 million.[33] Thus $600 million may be a generous "outside" estimate of the total of state-local non-payroll taxes paid by business in Michigan in 1957. This would suggest that taxes per employee in nonagricultural business might have been as high as $240. If we accept the result suggesting that they were about 55 percent lower in Illinois, Indiana, and Ohio, then in these states the tax bill would amount to about $108 per employee. The gross differential, therefore,

32 *Michigan Tax Study Staff Papers* (Lansing, 1958), p. 175.
33 Assuming an average of 8,000 miles per year for each passenger car, 15 miles to the gallon of gasoline, and a tax of 6 cents per gallon.

would be $132 per employee per year. But federal income taxes are payable in all states, and the availability of the federal offset would, for corporations subject to the 52 percent federal income tax rate, reduce the differential to a *net* difference of $63. Assuming a full work year to involve 2,000 hours, we are then dealing with a state-local tax differential between Michigan and its immediately neighboring states of 3 cents per hour per employee.

But how acceptable are Professor Yntema's interim findings? First, it must be recalled that the questionnaire was distributed following a period during which the subject of business taxation had become an important political and emotional issue. Organized business groups, such as the Michigan Manufacturers' Association, the Detroit Board of Commerce, and others, and leading individuals in the business community had, with much publicity, proclaimed that the Michigan "tax climate" was a major factor in slowing down the state's economic growth. The M.M.A., in July, 1956, had addressed a questionnaire to its 1,700 members. The key question was "Indicate in order of importance (1, 2, 3, 4) the *four* most vital considerations involved in your decision to expand elsewhere, reduce or terminate operation in this state." "General tax levies of state, including Franchise, B.A.T., etc.," and "Special tax burdens, including U.C. tax, W.C. rates or experience, etc." received 88 and 99 "votes," and ranked third and first, respectively, among the twelve "considerations" listed. Local tax levies ranked fifth.[34] Significantly, only 221 member firms bothered to respond at all. Irrespective, however, of the almost unbelievable manner in which the questions were loaded, and the fact that almost seven out of eight member firms did not respond, even though filling in the answers would have taken no more than a few minutes' time, on the basis of Mr. McCurry's testimony newspapers carried such headlines as "Business Tax in State Among Tops: Any More Will Hurt Firms Seriously, Probers Told."[35] "Claim Gov., Labor Driving Firms Away, MMA Replies Cited as Proof,"[36] and "Fear of State Curbs Called Threat to Industrial Might."[37]

In the spring of 1957 the President of General Motors Corporation declared, as did others, that "the level of business taxation in Michigan already has led us to locate in other states where the taxes per General Motors job are less than one-half of the present taxes

---

34 From Testimony of John C. McCurry, General Manager, Michigan Manufacturers' Association, before the Senate Interim Study Committee, July 25, 1956.
35 *The Detroit Free Press,* July 26, 1956.
36 *The Detroit Times,* July 26, 1956.
37 *The Detroit News,* July 26, 1956.

per job in Michigan. This will also be taken into consideration in the placement of additional facilities."[38] Another factor, of at least equal weight in setting the scene, was the fact that the Governor of Michigan, with vocal support from organized labor, for several years had been urging the legislature to enact a corporate profits tax. Much of the concern of business, therefore, may have been inspired as much by the threat of new taxes as by the level of existing ones. In this atmosphere it is certainly highly doubtful that research techniques employing a mail questionnaire could be expected to produce entirely reliable results.

Much more significant, however, is the fact that only 36 percent of the firms to whom questionnaires were sent responded and are included among those whose replies constitute Professor Yntema's findings. Expert opinion of members of the staff of the Survey Research Center of the Institute for Social Research at The University of Michigan holds that a response rate of 36 percent does not justify drawing any conclusions whatever. I am perfectly willing to believe that the firms which responded did so in entirely objective fashion, but I have no evidence to suggest that they represent a random sub-sample drawn from the total sample. Thus it is quite conceivable that the tax experience of the non-respondents differs substantially from that of the firms which did respond.

Given these circumstances, we certainly cannot accept the "evidence," despite the undoubted objectivity of Professor Yntema and the contributions of his respondents. However, while we may doubt the validity of the actual *size* of the tax differentials suggested by the studies that have been conducted, there is good reason to believe that taxes paid by business firms in Michigan are in fact higher than they are in Illinois, Indiana, and Ohio, where the state does not levy a major business tax comparable to Michigan's Business Activities Tax or Annual Corporate Privilege Fee, the income taxes of New York or Wisconsin or the income and franchise taxes of Pennsylvania. What remains unanswered is the question, "How much higher?" But, as we have pointed out, even if the results of these studies are accepted, they suggest that state-local tax differentials represent a very small proportion of labor costs, and, of course, a far smaller fraction of total costs.

Nor, if taxes are higher in Michigan than in immediately neighboring states and if such differentials do influence appreciably location decisions, is it at all certain that Michigan should neces-

---

38 *The Detroit News*, April 28, 1957.

sarily move to reduce business taxes. If services suffer as a consequence, as much may be lost as is gained; and if nonbusiness taxes must be increased, it remains to be demonstrated that the cost to those who pay these taxes is more than offset by the gains realized by the state as a whole as a result of the influence upon location decisions of lower state-local business taxes.

Why, then, is so much concern expressed by businessmen and others about state-local taxes as a locational factor, particularly since this concern is not typically shared by economists and plant-location experts? Among economists, we may cite Melvin L. Greenhut, who concludes that "tax incentives are at best a relatively unimportant factor of location. Given the governing factor, the tax incentive may induce a specific location within the area defined by the basic factor. If the location offering tax incentives is not within the area set by the governing factor, it is simply not considered."[39] Stefan Robock, manager of the economics division of the Midwest Research Institute, speaking before the 1958 Wisconsin governor's conference on industrial development, held that ". . . there is a widespread tendency to overstate the importance of taxes as a factor on industrial development" and that "Industry is becoming more sophisticated — it doesn't necessarily want low taxes if the low taxes mean that it will get little or nothing in governmental services."[40]. In the same vein, William D. Ross found, after an intensive survey, that of total exempted investments of more than $355 million under Louisiana's tax exemption program, all but $25 million would have been put in place without tax exemption.[41] The only attitudinal survey related to this question which has been conducted by means of field interviews in some depth was the one carried out in Michigan in 1950 by the Survey Research Center of the Institute for Social Research at The University of Michigan. The conclusion drawn was that ". . . in general, high wages as well as taxes seem much less important in actual migration of industry than they are as pervasive irritations."[42] It may also be noted that of the firms whose executives were interviewed, those representing only 9 percent of total employment provided by the sample firms mentioned taxes as a disadvantage associated with a Michigan location.

---

39 Melvin L. Greenhut, *Plant Location in Theory and Practice* (Chapel Hill, 1956), p. 139.
40 *The Milwaukee Journal*, May 16, 1958.
41 "Tax Concessions and Their Effects," *Proceedings of the National Tax Association, 1957* (Harrisburg, 1958), p. 220.
42 *Industrial Mobility in Michigan* (Ann Arbor, 1950), p. 29.

In general, then, we find a sharp cleavage between those who have attempted to study the influence of taxes on location and the frequently expressed views of businessmen. Among the reasons for the latter's views we may find the fact that state-local taxes are highly visible and, unlike power, labor, material, or transportation costs, all of which generally bulk larger, they are regarded as being subject to control. No amount of rhetoric or invective is likely to influence other costs, but taxes are the product of legislative decision and are subject to being influenced by pressure groups, including business. Apart from this, many observers claim that it is not so much present taxes but fear of new taxes that inspires much of the concern, and certainly one should expect many of those whose job it is to represent business' point of view to do everything possible to convince legislators that any new taxes should not be aimed at business costs or profits. Thus the opposition to such taxes has been vocal and persistent. Beyond this, it has been suggested that "taxes are viewed, unlike other cost elements, as a charge against profits. This is unjustified, since all costs are equally charged against income, but it seems imbedded in business psychology."[43]

Conclusions and Suggestions for Research

ON THE BASIS of observations drawn from available data and studies, we may draw some general conclusions. First, state and local taxes do not appear, for most manufacturing firms, to represent a major element of costs. But there is now insufficient information available. (It is almost never given as a separate item in financial reports of corporations and it is not provided as a separable item in reports of the Securities and Exchange Commission or the Internal Revenue Service.) Evidence as to the differentials in business taxes, at various locations within and among states, is not now available with sufficient reliability to warrant the suggestion that they have, in fact, been measured.

Our second conclusion is that even if we had reliable measures of inter-community tax differentials, we would still need to know more than we now do about how important such differentials are as a location factor. It may well be, for example, that a small differential, relative to total costs, does serve, in many instances, as a major irritant, and therefore as a major location factor. On the other hand, even large tax differentials, *if* accompanied by com-

---

43 *Industrial Location and the Minnesota Economy*, p. 52.

mensurate differences in the quality and availability of public services, may be of little or no importance in location decisions.

Finally, we must recognize that the actual moving of a plant is a very costly job and rarely occurs. Of far greater importance are decisions with respect to expansion through the construction or acquisition of new facilities and decisions forced by the obsolescence of old plants. The process of economic growth in a dynamic economy is bound to be accompanied by technological changes that make old sites or even urban sites undesirable, and give rise to new influences on location decisions. Changes in transportation costs, location of markets, and sources of supply are all likely to bring movements of industry into and out of all states. The role of taxes in this process of change must be the focus of attention of any enlightened or enlightening research in this area.

Before much can be said intelligently about the impact of state-local taxes on location, we must know a great deal more about the forces which are in fact inducing corporations that are free to locate plants within broad areas to select one community as a site rather than another. Perhaps this suggestion comes under the heading of "motivational" research. We are unlikely to find useful answers in the existing literature on "location theory," most or all of which is in general terms and predicated upon the assumption that profit maximization is the ruling criterion in site selection. What is needed is objective information, directly obtained by the researcher, on considerations, and the weights to be assigned them, that are taken into account in actual location decisions. The major obstacles to this kind of research are its high cost and the necessity for obtaining the willing cooperation of the firms involved.

Perhaps just as difficult to conduct in acceptable fashion is that research which is necessary if we are to obtain reliable information on state-local tax costs relative to other costs at various locations. Or, put somewhat differently, the magnitude of state-local tax differentials relative to differentials in other costs. But mere dollar tax costs are insufficient. Businessmen may react not only to tax levels but also to differences in tax structure. A high property tax, for example, which must be regarded largely as an element of fixed overhead charges, may weigh much more heavily in the location decision than net or gross income or value-added taxes. Or taxes that are regarded as being arbitrarily assessed may be shunned more intensively than taxes the bases of which are clear-cut and not subject to dispute. Furthermore, in measuring tax differentials one would necessarily take into account the varying extents to which services are charged for on a fee or special assessment basis, as opposed to those that are paid for out of general taxes. One community, for example, may finance sewage disposal out of tax revenues, while another will levy user charges for this service. Such differences may loom large in public service costs, but they are ordinarily ignored in the available studies.

One should also need to know much more than we now do about business attitudes toward public services. If an excellent but costly public school system is regarded as an asset to a community as a plant site, and if the same is true of police and fire protection, quality and kind of access to arterial streets and highways, and so forth, then high taxes may not be regarded as high costs — no more than good quality materials or highly efficient labor are regarded as being more costly than shoddy materials or inefficient labor.

In sum, we have had more than we need of comparisons of tax costs for hypothetical corporations based on hypothetical real or effective property tax rates and of studies which involve aggregating that which loses its meaning in the process of aggregation. The lines of research suggested here may or may not answer all of our questions, but the most useful and promising approach open to us lies in examining in detail the tax and other cost differentials involved in actual multi-plant, multi-site operations, and in learning a great deal more about the motivations that in fact lie behind plant-location decisions.

One final *caveat* should be offered. Even if we should find that we can assign a specific weight to state-local taxes in plant-location decisions, many issues still remain. As Professor Hoover has put it so well, with reference to tax inducements to location, "A judicious policy of 'lubrication' cannot disregard the cost of the grease."[44] Lower business taxes must mean either a lower level of public services or higher taxes imposed upon individuals in their capacities as consumers or income recipients. And neither of these alternatives is without cost to the community at large. Moreover, with or without further research it can be concluded that lower business taxes (services remaining the same) imposed in any one jurisdiction will certainly not repel business. What is suggested, therefore, is that, ideally, we should want to know a great deal about the impact upon the community of the location within it of new industry. It cannot simply be assumed that new industry in a

---

44 *Op. cit.*, p. 271.

community necessarily means a net fiscal or even economic and social gain. And this kind of question opens another, as yet almost untouched, area for research that is closely related to the general issue involved in the matter of the impact of state-local taxes on industrial location.

---

* Footnote referred to on page 319:

Michigan's Taxes on Business, 1956 (Holland, Michigan, 1959), the final, published draft of Professor Yntema's study, was not available until long after this volume had gone to press. The basic nature of his findings was not changed, but he found the median of state and local taxes per employee (exclusive of payroll and highway user taxes) to be $226 in Michigan (p. 4), rather than $300, as cited below. He also makes it clear that no attempt was made to determine whether or not the non-responders differed significantly in their tax experience from the responding firms (p. 19).

Michigan's Transportation System and the State's Industrial Development: Some Questions Regarding These Aspects of Michigan's Economy[1]

Introduction

ALMOST ALL OF the great cities of the world were established because of the need for a transportation hub. The great capitals of Rome, Paris, London, and Moscow were all transportation focal points. Each city grew and prospered because of its importance as a transportation center. The cities, in turn, influenced the development of the region around them. The development of transportation routes has thus become a vital causal factor in economic development.

This is reflected in the fact that the experience of Fantus Factory Locating Service over a period of thirty-seven years has indicated that almost every manufacturing firm seeking a location has required some analysis of the transportation forces affecting it at each location under consideration.

Hundreds of plant location studies have pointed to great differences between areas of the nation, between regions, and even between communities in the same states, with respect to transportation costs and transportation services for inbound raw materials as well as for the shipment of finished products to markets for a given type industry.

Today, all areas claim adequate or excellent transportation services, but the fact remains that most communities are not as well served either in terms of the variety of transportation services (rail, trucks, etc.), the quality of such services, or the costs of such services as they often imagine is the case.

---

[1] This report was prepared for the present study by Fantus Factory Locating Service, Chicago, Illinois.

If communities were aware of the fact that more frequent or lower cost rail, truck, air, or water transportation services were needed in their area and if they were aware of the role which transportation plays in economic development, they could take action to improve these services.

It is no longer necessary to accept the quality and cost of transportation as "given." Aware citizens groups and government boards, by pointing out revenue opportunities and by influencing common carrier regulations which can increase the profit and quantity of these services, can encourage the improvement of transportation services.

The extent to which coordinated transportation planning can influence economic growth depends upon the nature and quality of the research, the implementation philosophy (i.e., the extent to which genuine economic incentives are provided to the carriers), and the extent to which a permanent organization is willing to accept the responsibility for transportation planning.

Plan of This Discussion

THIS ARTICLE consists of a series of questions which need to be answered in order to:

a. Provide the kind of answers which not only describe Michigan's transportation system, but which would identify and rank the problems involved,

b. Establish the implementation philosophy which will maximize growth, and

c. Determine the best kind of central organization to facilitate transportation planning and other economic development programs in the state.

This article will consider each of the basic services: truck, rail, water, highway, air facilities. In each case, questions will be raised which will inquire into the present usefulness of these services. Further questions will suggest problems of future planning. Special aspects of transportation analysis not related to a particular type of carrier will be questioned next. This will include such things as an inquiry into existing transportation laws and regulations, tariff structure analysis, passenger service, and a special comment on Upper Peninsula transportation problems. Finally, in order to relate this study to present operating problems, questions will be raised concerning, first, present users of Michigan's transportation services, and, second, as a special case, the automobile parts industry.

This article will then conclude with some suggestions on the research and implementation required to appraise properly Michigan's transportation facilities in order to maximize future growth potential.

Trucking Services

1. Truck terminal density: To what extent are Michigan communities adequately served by trucking facilities? This is more important in terms of *originating* trucklines than in terms of *delivering* trucklines. Given a specific level of manufacturing activity in selected Michigan cities, is the number of terminals operating in such cities of a comparable quality compared to the truck service offered in manufacturing centers in competitive states?

2. Time in transit: How does time in transit of typical commodities shipped via truckload or less-than-truckload to major manufacturing or consuming centers compare with comparable non-Michigan cities? Are there any unusual delays inherent in deliveries from Michigan points which do not exist elsewhere?

What would be most helpful to this analysis would be a table of truck transit times from each major Michigan city to each of the major destination points in the Midwest, the South, and the eastern markets of the United States.

3. Single and two-line haul advantages: To what extent do Michigan cities benefit from single or two-line truck deliveries to major consuming points as contrasted with similar cities in other states?

4. Truck planning for the future:

a. Periodic appraisals: To what extent would it be feasible to prepare periodic appraisals of the potential demand for truck service in all parts of the state? Such a program would allow truck line operators to respond rapidly to changes in the demand for services throughout the state. This would then serve as a positive attraction to industry.

b. Fishy-back proposals: While passenger automobile and rail carload movements exist across Lake Michigan, is there a real void in Michigan's transportation pattern in the absence of a fishy-back or cross-lake truck facility? Presently being discussed in Muskegon, such a facility would materially reduce time in transit from central and northern Michigan communities to Wisconsin points and points west of that state.

Rail Service

1. Rail service operating characteristics: What are the specific operating characteristics of rail service afforded the various regions of the state? Has the gradual disappearance of pickup and delivery service, frequency of freight trains, etc., prevalent elsewhere in the United States, taken place in Michigan? If so, has the net result been a decline in quality, speed, or an increased cost of service?

2. Future role of rail transportation: Some estimate with respect to the future role of rail transportation in Michigan should be made. Then and only then can a long-run rail transportation policy for Michigan be worked out. Such a policy would be designed to provide the kind of incentives which would encourage the preservation, maintenance, and expansion of the best features of rail transportation.

3. Expansion or contraction: To what extent would it be feasible to expand or contract rail facilities in portions of the state?

4. Effect of rail mergers: Would the merger of any two or more railroads in or outside of Michigan result in an advantage to the state? Will any merger presently contemplated work to the disadvantage of Michigan? For instance, will the possible merger of the Great Northern, Northern Pacific, and Chicago, Burlington and Quincy railroads cause the northern transcontinental railroads to solicit traffic via Chicago even more than at present, to the detriment of the Mackinaw City and Lake Michigan ferry routes?

5. Discontinuance of LCL service: Should the railroads be allowed, or encouraged, to discontinue all LCL service, thus leaving this service to Railway Express, the Post Office, and trucks?

6. Subsidy to railroads: Should governmental assistance be given the railroads, either by tax relief, lease of facilities provided by the government, extra payment for services, or other means, to encourage their development, growth, or continuance in Michigan?

7. Piggyback opportunities: Is Michigan getting a proper share in the development of trailers-on-flat-car or "piggyback" services under all of the known plans for this service? Is it possible to determine how this development should proceed?

Water Transportation: St. Lawrence Seaway and Great Lakes Routes

IS THERE a realistic appraisal of the potential influence of the St. Lawrence Seaway upon the state as a whole, as well as upon Michigan's port cities and their hinterlands?

1. Actual potential of Michigan's port cities: What is a realistic estimate of the potential of the various port cities in terms of the benefit to be derived from the Seaway? The supporting hinterland of each of the communities engaged in or thinking of port developments should be analyzed in order to determine the probable limits of activity capable of supporting various levels of port activity at each port city.

2. Natural hinterland which now uses Michigan ports: What natural geographic areas can properly use Michigan ports? An analysis of this sort must realistically estimate the potential of competing ports in Ohio, Indiana, and Illinois. The transportation networks originating or terminating at Michigan ports in contrast with those in other states should be carefully considered.

3. Likely products for Michigan ports: What products generated in Michigan proper, or in the supporting hinterland, are likely to make use of lake and ocean shipping?

4. Probable duplication of port development: Determine whether there is any duplication of effort and expense in the development of individual port communities. To what extent is there wisdom in coordinating the efforts of the various communities in order to insure development along sound channels? This study would be designed to avoid expensive investment in facilities unlikely to receive full use because of intense competition among cities.

5. An inventory of port development plans: Consider the possibility of an inventory of all port development plans among Michigan cities with a view to establishment of a coordinator for the promotion of Michigan ports as a whole.

6. Possible additional or unique port facilities: A facility which is unique on the Great Lakes could serve to attract considerable traffic through the port possessing it. Included would be such things as extremely heavy lift cranes and especially designed equipment for particularly efficient handling of a particular commodity. Also, the possibility of developing a free port area in Michigan should be considered. There is, as yet, no free port existing on the Great Lakes. Such a facility might generate considerable tonnage of traffic, as well as numerous special services within, and outside of, the free port area. The free port area of the Port of New York might well be studied as an outstanding example of a successful free port.

7. Port access: Determine whether or not all of Michigan's ports will be served by each type of transport, both rail and truck. In the past, ports have often been designed to exclude one or more of these media from access. This should be carefully avoided.

Highway Transportation Facilities

1. Influence of toll road construction: Has industrial development in other states been influenced to a large extent by the construction of new toll highways and freeways? If industry has been attracted to locations along such major tollways or thoroughfares, has this been prejudicial to the state of Michigan where such construction has not taken place? Specifically, have the Indiana and Ohio toll roads attracted industry into the northern parts of those states which might otherwise have gone to southern Michigan?

2. Effect of highways upon industrial development: To what extent does Michigan's highway system serve present needs and future growth requirements? An over-all highway development program which was based upon its actual potential for industrial development could contribute heavily to the state's future growth.

Air Transportation Facilities

1. Inventory of airport facilities: An inventory of airport facilities is an absolute essential to a state which wishes to plan for its future economic growth.

2. Forecast of airport requirements: A forecast of airport requirements five, ten, and twenty-five years from the present would provide proper information for an expansion program.

3. Coordination of airport development: The state of Michigan should establish a firm policy of planning to coordinate all statewide air development projects. In addition a determined effort should be made to encourage the providing of air service as it is needed. Those areas which lag in airport development in the future will also suffer industrially.

Existing Transportation Laws and Regulations

AN ANALYSIS of existing laws and regulations relating to transportation in Michigan should be made. This is particularly significant in connection with trucking movements, but is quite important with respect to rail, air, and water services as well. Are Michigan regulations concerning weight limits, axle loads, etc., in any way prejudicial to the origin or routing of truck movements through the state?

Is there an attractive pattern of regulation and taxation of trucking, particularly to those shippers operating their own fleets of trucks? Is there anything in the intrastate tariffs which prejudices such movements as opposed to movements into the state from without?

Tariff-Structure Analysis

A COMPLETE tariff-structure review is another essential for growth planning. Are there any rate inequities in the tariff structures which operate to the prejudice of various areas of the state in reaching major markets or in intrastate movements? Such inequities are, of course, independent of differences in pure distance. Some of the inequities which should be looked for are as follows:

1. Increase and adjustment in tariffs: Has the Michigan Public Service Commission historically allowed increases, adjustments, and new rates at levels different from that of the Interstate Commerce Commission? Intrastate levels below interstate levels discourage the carriers from promoting or encouraging enterprises which would generate intrastate traffic. Higher intrastate levels penalize Michigan shippers in serving Michigan markets.

2. In-transit privilege development: Has Michigan's peninsular location resulted in a relatively less complete development of in-transit privileges than at competitive points not in this state? It should be noted that these privileges are usually granted to points which are on a direct line from origin to final destination. If such poorer development in fact exists, would negotiation with railroads with, or in behalf of, interested actual or prospective transit operators be fruitful? Negotiations might be directed toward securing out-of-line haul transit privileges.

3. Through routes: Do through routes from and to numerous points, outside of this state, exist which will pass through Michigan? The advantages of such routes accrue not only through the greater accrued tax obligation, but through greater shipping convenience in making Michigan cities stop-off points and transit points.

4. Inequities in the tariff structure: Do rate groupings cause any important inequities? These groupings, often preserved primarily for historical reasons, often deviate from a logical pattern. Great pressure is usually brought to bear to preserve the existing pattern. Nevertheless, attempts should be made to correct anomalies such as rate group boundaries which place major producing points in a higher rated territory than other nearby points if such situations do, in fact, exist.

5. Upper Peninsula classification problems: Does the classification of the Upper Peninsula in Western, rather than Official or Eastern Territory, make it more difficult to negotiate rate adjustments on commodities moving from the Upper Peninsula to major eastern markets? The need for dealing with two different rate jurisdictions in these cases increases the difficulties of negotiation, and nearly always increases the time required for rate adjustments.

6. Water competition with rail and truck service: Has full consideration been given in the Michigan interstate and intrastate rate structure, to such considerations as water competition? Many areas have depressed rates in such commodities as grain and petroleum in cases where water carriers can handle part or all of this traffic.

7. Export rates: Export rates will soon be established to Great Lakes ports. At present, many of these rates are being most strongly supported by western railroads. Michigan should determine whether the Eastern or Official Territory railroads will attempt, with equal vigor, to institute export rates to the Lower Peninsula ports which they serve, despite their tremendous vested interest in North Atlantic ports. All possible efforts should be made to assure treatment of Michigan ports on terms equivalent to those which will be available at ports served by Western Territory carriers, such as Chicago, Milwaukee, and Duluth.

Passenger Services

THE PASSENGER services offered by airlines, railroad lines (intercity and suburban), bus lines, and water carriers play an important part in:

a. The operating conditions of business enterprise.

b. The living conditions experienced by the employees of business enterprise.

The extent to which each of these services provides frequent, convenient, and comfortable passenger transportation will influence the extent to which individual areas of the state of Michigan will be able to provide the maximum framework for orderly industrial growth.

Accordingly, an over-all passenger transportation study should be made to determine present and future requirements. Proper incentives should be provided in order to permit the continued development and expansion of passenger transportation services in Michigan. Without an orderly program, desirable services will disappear before anyone is aware of their genuine importance to the development of the state.

Transportation Problems of the Upper Peninsula

MUCH STUDY has been devoted to the development of the Upper Peninsula without any apparently sound solution. Obviously, sheer distance from markets is a deterrent to the area's growth. Yet, there are certain other considerations which should be explored.

1. The Ebasco study of the Upper Peninsula has pointed out certain other advantages offsetting transportation penalties. Among these are high productivity, good-quality workmanship, and, in some cases, lower labor rates. A quantitative determination of costs of reaching markets with various products should be made to determine the exact extent of such penalties to individual companies and the extent of other cost savings necessary to overcome such penalties.

2. Specific locational cost analyses should be made to determine which specific products can be manufactured in the Upper Peninsula without penalty. Those product lines which are least influenced by transportation costs and most capable of manufacture in that area should be identified.

3. Any inequities in the rate structure, apart from pure distance, which militate against the area should be identified and remedied.

4. Export markets to the growing Canadian economy should be carefully explored for the Upper Peninsula.

Survey of Present Users

OF GREAT PRACTICAL value would be a survey of existing Michigan manufacturers, by industry, to determine what fields of transportation they consider most troublesome in the state of Michigan. Earlier studies have indicated very little concern with this matter. Nevertheless, attempts should be made to identify clearly the areas which offer the greatest problems. Such a survey could be physically incorporated into any other survey undertaken as part of the study by the Committee on Michigan's Economic Future. If COMEF does not make an inquiry of Michigan manufacturers in connection with any other subject, the transportation matter could be handled separately. Typical of the items to be determined by such a survey would be the following:

1. How do transportation costs from Michigan plants to markets compare with costs from competitive plants in other areas?

2. What are the major market areas to which Michigan manufacturers have definite freight advantages? What is the scope of this area and, of equal importance, are there any characteristics, or by-product lines, which afford advantages to Michigan locations?

3. What improvements, if any, are indicated in the service rendered Michigan manufacturers by trucking lines and rail lines?

4. Are there any laws and regulations which are prejudicial to present firms?

5. What general aspects of transportation require improvement?

Responses to this survey of Michigan manufacturers could place in proper rank order the transportation problems of the state. It would also provide some important clues toward solving these problems.

The Automobile Parts Industry

WHAT HAS BEEN the effect of the decentralization of the automobile assembly plants on the auto parts or components industry in the state of Michigan? Determine authoritatively whether the decentralization of the basic industry has produced transportation penalties for Michigan-based suppliers who have heretofore been serving this industry. For example, compare freight costs of auto parts from Michigan to the new assembly plants versus the old pattern in order to determine if the decentralization pattern has imposed a significant penalty upon the auto parts industry. If so, determine the extent to which any transportation inequities can be removed for this group.

Research and Implementation Program

A RESEARCH and implementation program for maximizing the growth potential inherent in an effective transportation system centers about the following steps:

1. Determine what the state already has.

2. Determine what its needs will be 10, 25, and 50 years hence.

3. Determine the potential impact of various transportation services upon economic growth.

4. Develop an implementation philosophy which will allow all common carriers an incentive to earn an adequate return on their

investment. This includes minimizing costs as well as maximizing revenue. Only in this way will the carrier be able to respond to the request of the coordinating group for proper expansion.

5. Establish goals, set a time table for the working out of these goals, periodically check progress, and finally, report results frequently to a permanent organization responsible for keeping an eye on the speed and direction of Michigan's economic growth.

Conclusion

1. Transportation development has influenced in the past, and will influence in the future, the economic growth of the state of Michigan.

2. A coordinated program aimed at orderly transportation and economic growth can maximize Michigan's competitive position.

3. The foregoing questions can form the basis for a rational and orderly approach to Michigan's transportation problems as they relate to the state's future economic development.

Operating the ABC Corporation in Eleven Midwestern Cities[1]

HOW DO WAGE COSTS in Michigan compare with those of neighboring states for firms in comparable industries? How do our transportation costs compare with those of other nearby states? Is Michigan's market position such that its industries are able to compete with similar industries in other states? How do other important costs of operating a business, such as taxes, utilities, and occupancy costs in Michigan compare with comparable costs in nearby states? Such questions are being asked every day by businessmen who are making plant location decisions. If these businessmen find that total operating costs in Michigan are appreciably greater than in neighboring states, many of them will locate their firms elsewhere. If, on the other hand, they find that total operating costs in Michigan are comparable or lower than in neighboring states, then some of them will choose Michigan as a plant location. Thus, it is of the utmost importance for those concerned with the future of Michigan to find out whether there are appreciable differences in interstate operating costs for various industries.

In the hope of obtaining information regarding interstate differences in operating costs, a study of such costs was made in eleven cities in the states of Michigan, Illinois, Ohio, Kentucky, and Indiana. In this study, operating costs as of a given date (February 1, 1959) were obtained for a hypothetical firm called the ABC Corporation. While the corporation itself is hypothetical, however, the actual data are not. The data have been acquired from each of the communities on the basis of the actual experience of operating firms within each of the communities. In all cases,

---

1 The information reported in this Appendix was secured for the Institute by Fantus Factory Locating Service. The sections providing a description of the ABC Corporation and the characteristics of the cities selected for study represent extracts from this firm's report. The remainder of Appendix D represents an analysis of the data by the authors of this report. We are indebted to Henry C. Thole of the Upjohn Institute for his help in the preparation of this Appendix.

the existing data were applied to the requirements of the hypothetical company, the ABC Corporation.

Any statistician would recognize that the task of selecting two or three communities in each of several states which would be typical of results in the average communities of these states is a formidable undertaking. Our hope was, however, that by attempting to choose communities which were roughly comparable with each other in known respects which were believed to be important, we might be able to succeed in achieving results which would be truly typical of interstate operating cost differences. With the aid of a management consulting organization we chose two cities in each of the states (three in Michigan) in the belief that we might be able to achieve our objective. Intensive analysis of the communities suggests, however, that our attempt was unsuccessful.

Although we do not believe that the results of this study can be accepted as indicative of *interstate* differences in operating costs, the results are revealing in many ways. For example, the techniques used in the study are illustrative of those commonly used by management people in arriving at plant location decisions. Moreover, the results show the relative size of various components of variable cost in any one city; and they suggest the components in which cities tend to differ most from one another.

Description of the Corporation

THE ABC CORPORATION produces stamped metal parts used in the manufacture of other finished products. These would include parts for hardware, fittings, automobiles, refrigerators, snow plows, farm tractors, etc. The manufacturing processes used include stamping, assembly, and some plating. There would be no machining except in the maintenance of production machines and in the tool room for basic tool and die making.

The raw materials required are 15,000 tons annually of sheet steel obtained via carload from the nearest mill, F.O.B. mill. Two thousand tons of copper and brass alloys, F.O.B. destination, and 3,000 tons of sheet aluminum, F.O.B. destination, are required annually. In addition, minor quantities of screw machine parts, cartons, and other miscellaneous supplies are required.

Distribution to customers throughout the country is primarily via common carrier truck. Deliveries are made to other plants engaged in metalworking. The volume of distribution to each of the other plants is based upon metalworking employment as reported by *Iron Age* in "Basic Market Data on Metalworking."

Labor requirements are approximately 500 persons which include 29 top executives and technical employees, 38 female office personnel, 264 male production personnel, and 169 female production personnel. Detailed job classifications for each of these groupings are indicated in the study. Fringe benefits include shift differentials, Sunday premiums, overtime premiums, holiday premiums, pay for holidays not worked, vacation pay, retroactive pay, pensions (where applicable), Social Security taxes paid by the employer, life insurance, medical insurance, accident insurance, hospital insurance, and company contributions to guaranteed wages for layoff periods (where applicable).

Workmen's compensation costs are based upon a metal stamping and plating classification. The experience rating of the company is assumed to be one-half of the manual (published) rate. Unemployment compensation costs are based upon an average of the three-year average employer contribution rate for the entire state.

Utility costs include power, fuel for process use and for heat, and water and sewage. Power costs for 1,000 KW, 200,000 KWH per month are computed in this study. Processing fuel costs are based upon 12,000 therms per month. The lowest cost fuel which could provide the proper type of heat control, namely oil or gas, is used in this study. Space heating costs are computed on the basis of heating a building of 150,000 square feet in each of the areas. The cheapest fuel for space heating purposes in each area is coal. Comparative water and sewage costs are based upon a usage of 1,120,000 gallons of water per month.

Occupancy costs are based upon leasing a building of 150,000 square feet plus 10,000 square feet of office space. Fifteen acres of land are required for the present operation and its ultimate expansion (approximately five times the size of the building).

The financial structure of the ABC Corporation is relatively simple. It is assumed to be a domestic corporation in the state in which it is located with no employees outside of the state.

Pertinent financial statistics are as follows:

Total paid-in capital	$ 500,000
Total capital surplus	1,000,000
Total earned surplus	5,000,000
Total sales	15,000,000
Net profit before federal income taxes	2,000,000
Net profit after federal income taxes	1,000,000

Machinery equipment...$ 2,000,000
Raw materials.. 750,000
Work in process... 1,000,000
Finished inventory..   250,000
Intangibles in cash...   250,000
Real estate..   750,000
Total property.. 5,000,000

For tax purposes, sales were estimated to be in direct proportion to manufacturing employment in a given state. This was as follows:

State	Percent of Total U.S. Sales
Illinois	9.46
Indiana	5.20
Kentucky	.87
Michigan	10.26
Ohio	11.46

Characteristics of Cities Selected for Study

THE CITIES SELECTED for study had to possess the following characteristics:

1. They must be located in the states of Michigan, Illinois, Indiana, Ohio, and Kentucky.

2. Preferably, they should be within the 30,000 to 110,000 (1950) population range.

3. The economic complexion of the cities should be similar as measured by the manufacturing ratio (the ratio of manufacturing employment to total nonagricultural employment). Manufacturing ratios, 50 to 70, were considered acceptable.

Given the requirements established here, the cities selected represent the cities most similar in size and character in each of the states. The population range is from 34,000 to 105,000. The manufacturing ratio ranges from 45 percent to 69 percent. While some attention was given to geographic location in the state, this was not considered a limiting factor.

Findings of the Study

TABLE D-1 PROVIDES detailed information on the variable operating costs of the ABC Corporation in each of the eleven Midwestern cities included in the study.[2] In each state, City "A" is the lower cost city, and City "B" is the higher cost city, while, in Michigan,

---

2 From the financial statistics cited in the preceding section, it will be seen that total costs of the corporation, including materials costs, fixed costs, etc., are expected to be around $13,000,000.

Comparison of Variable Annual Operating Costs of the ABC Corporation, by City

As of February 1, 1959

Variable Operating Costs	Michigan			Ohio		Indiana		Illinois		Kentucky	
	City A	City B	City C	City A	City B	City A	City B	City A	City B	City A	City B
Total	$4,172,322	$4,300,188	$4,518,559	$3,935,607	$4,042,617	$4,142,244	$4,326,377	$4,076,962	$4,229,603	$3,915,980	$3,963,662
Labor Costs	2,836,498	3,012,050	3,152,631	2,685,450	2,814,806	2,866,326	3,057,537	2,723,317	2,845,348	2,579,118	2,591,140
Production	2,157,688	2,251,579	2,341,685	2,026,440	2,161,661	2,206,568	2,296,632	2,071,472	2,116,504	1,981,429	2,025,504
Tech. & Clerical	183,602	187,949	211,162	162,906	182,000	176,571	191,069	189,030	197,579	178,714	158,246
Fringe Benefits	444,000	520,000	546,000	470,000	444,000	452,000	538,000	428,000	496,000	372,000	360,000
Workmen's Comp.	30,208	31,522	32,784	15,604	16,645	15,887	16,536	20,715	21,165	18,625	19,040
Unemploy. Comp.	21,000	21,000	21,000	10,500	10,500	15,300	15,300	14,100	14,100	28,350	28,350
Occupancy Costs	114,948	120,602	122,809	117,422	121,706	111,181	121,706	117,154	120,008	107,733	109,431
Freight Costs	1,006,303	976,815	1,025,884	1,015,472	969,544	1,002,065	987,698	1,089,701	1,131,165	1,104,107	1,140,047
Inbound Freight	36,400	26,600	32,200	36,400	36,400	32,200	44,800	43,400	29,400	65,800	33,600
Outbound Freight	969,903	950,215	993,684	979,072	933,144	969,865	942,898	1,046,301	1,101,765	1,038,307	1,106,447
Tax Costs	142,584	120,416	143,358	54,056	69,194	92,935	95,778	79,753	59,624	68,959	66,166
Local Tax	106,480	84,312	107,254	50,434	65,572	90,012	92,855	79,560	59,431	22,383	19,590
State Tax	36,104	36,104	36,104	3,622	3,622	2,923	2,923	193	193	46,576	46,576
Utility Costs	71,989	70,305	73,877	63,207	67,367	69,737	63,658	67,037	73,458	56,063	56,878
Process Fuel	7,459	7,675	8,208	9,115	8,222	8,554	5,818	4,176	6,912	6,552	6,480
Space Heat'g. Fuel	19,023	18,028	20,176	7,975	15,004	16,415	12,438	13,377	18,840	6,608	5,822
Water & Sewage	2,907	2,002	2,893	4,777	2,801	4,364	4,998	2,696	1,074	2,391	4,064
Power	42,600	42,600	42,600	41,340	41,340	40,404	40,404	46,788	46,632	40,512	40,512

City "C" is the highest cost city of the three. This table is the source for the cost data quoted throughout this section.

Position of the Eleven Cities

Following is a list of the eleven cities, arranged by variable operating costs of the ABC Corporation in each of them.

City	Amount
Michigan — "C"	$4,518,559
Indiana — "B"	4,326,377
Michigan — "B"	4,300,188
Illinois — "B"	4,229,603
Michigan — "A"	4,172,322
Indiana — "A"	4,142,244
Illinois — "A"	4,076,962
Ohio — "B"	4,042,617
Kentucky — "B"	3,963,662
Ohio — "A"	3,935,607
Kentucky — "A"	3,915,980

It is apparent from these data that the Michigan cities which were chosen tend to rank high in cost as locations for the operations of the ABC Corporation. There are, however, several lines of investigation which suggest that the eleven-city study does not measure *interstate* differences in operating costs. In the following pages we shall cover some of this information.

Limitations of Findings as Indicators of Interstate Differences

Let us first take the data on operating costs of the ABC Corporation in these eleven communities at face value. We may note that the rank order of the eleven cities in terms of operating costs is quite similar to the rank order of these cities in terms of the number of manufacturing employees in the counties in which they are located. Here is the information:

City	Rank in Total Operating Costs	Rank in Manufacturing Employees in County
Michigan — "C"	1	2
Indiana — "B"	2	7
Michigan — "B"	3	5
Illinois — "B"	4	1
Michigan — "A"	5	3
Indiana — "A"	6	4
Illinois — "A"	7	6
Ohio — "B"	8	8
Kentucky — "B"	9	10
Ohio — "A"	10	9
Kentucky — "A"	11	11

Source: U. S. Department of Commerce and U. S. Department of Health, Education, and Welfare, *County Business Patterns, First Quarter, 1956*, Part IV, Table 3, and Part VII, Table 3.

Thus, on the basis of data for these eleven communities, larger manufacturing centers seem to have higher operating costs. While we had hoped to get away from the influence of this factor by eliminating the very large metropolitan centers as well as the very small communities in each state, it is apparent that the reported data show, even within the size range covered by our study communities, a considerable relationship between size and costs. This important consideration would make it impossible for us to say that in our illustrative studies we had in any way succeeded in measuring interstate differentials in operating costs.

Moreover, the degree to which the wage data reported in the eleven-city study actually reflect differences in typical wage costs between the *average* Michigan community and the *average* Kentucky community — to use the generally highest and generally lowest costs as illustrative — can be questioned also on the basis of other available wage data. Our study data, for example, show wage-cost differences (production workers) between the two Kentucky cities and the two highest Michigan cities of approximately 15 percent. Statistics based on the old-age and survivors insurance program (BOASI data) suggest, on the other hand, that typical average earnings in the metal stamping, plating, and engraving industry vary by less than two percent between the *average* outstate Michigan community and the *average* outstate Kentucky community. The BOASI data furthermore show that two of the three Michigan communities that we happened to choose in our study are very markedly above the earnings level in the *average* Michigan community.

In the following data, the similarity of the outstate averages for Michigan, Ohio, and Kentucky will be noted:

Area	Average Quarterly Earnings per Employee
Michigan	**$1,310**
Detroit area	1,380
Outstate Michigan	1,150
Michigan, City "C"	1,480
City "B"	1,500
City "A"	1,150
Ohio	**1,170**
Cleveland area	1,230
Outstate Ohio	1,140
Ohio, City "B"	1,090
City "A"	NA
Kentucky	**1,190**
Louisville area	1,210
Outstate Kentucky	1,130
Kentucky, City "B"	NA
City "A"	NA

Note: Data based on *County Business Patterns*, First Quarter, 1956. Average quarterly earnings

347

Between the average outstate Michigan figure of $1,150 and the average outstate Kentucky figure of $1,130, there is a difference of only $20, or less than 2 percent. Outstate Ohio is between these two, at $1,140.

It is true, of course, that the BOASI data have certain limitations, so severe, in fact, that we would not wish to present them as illustrative of interstate differences in wage costs in the metal stamping, plating, and engraving industry. The critical point, however, is that the differences between the BOASI data and the results that we achieved in our selected community study are so marked that we are unable to set forth our study results as indicative of interstate differences.

Cost Differences between Cities of Comparable Size

It is revealing to examine cost differences among cities of comparable size. In the following table, individual cost items are shown for the ABC Corporation in Indiana City "B" and Illinois City "A". These cities are closely similar in terms of population and number of manufacturing workers.

Variable Operating Cost	High (Indiana City "B")	Low (Illinois City "A")	Difference	Difference as Percent of $2 Million Profit
Total........................	**$4,326,377**	**$4,076,962**	**$249,415**	**12.5**
Labor (Wage & Fringe)........	3,025,701	2,688,502	337,199	16.9
Workmen's Compensation....	16,536	20,715	−4,179	−.2
Unemployment Insurance.....	15,300	14,100	1,200	.1
Occupancy Costs.............	121,706	117,154	4,552	.2
Freight (In & Out)...........	987,698	1,089,701	−102,003	−5.1
State and Local Taxes........	95,778	79,753	16,025	.8
Utilities.....................	63,658	67,037	−3,379	−.2

There is much to study in these data. For example, wage costs are seen to be by far the largest of the variable costs of operation. Moreover — and most important for our present purpose — *differences* in wage costs are very large. They are even greater than differences in total operating costs. With total variable costs differing by about $249,000, wage cost differences between the two cities amount to about $337,000. No other difference is anywhere near as great as this difference. If we study the data in Table D-1, we note that there are large cost differences ($258,000 in total

348

operating costs) between Michigan City "B" and Ohio City "B", two cities which rank fairly close in number of manufacturing workers. In this case wage cost differences account for $172,000 of the total difference of $258,000 in operating costs. Thus, among cities of comparable size and industrial characteristics, there can be great differences in wage costs.

Freight costs shown in the preceding text table should be looked at carefully. It will be noted that freight costs are by far the largest item of variable cost, next to wages. Although freight cost differences are much less than wage cost differences, they are nevertheless substantial, and are far higher than any of the remaining variable costs of operation.

We must keep in mind that this hypothetical firm was assumed to have the objective of serving the national market from its chosen location. This seemed to be the only way in which a number of locations could be fairly compared. But there are many firms for which this is not the objective. If such a firm wished to serve the Detroit automobile market exclusively, for example, then a Detroit location might enable it to cut the million-dollar transportation item down to a negligible amount. In such a case, the cost advantage of a Detroit or near-by Michigan location would be quite substantial and probably conclusive. The same would be true of an Illinois location for a firm wishing to serve the farm equipment industry exclusively. The size of the transportation cost item serves to dramatize the extent to which a firm must consider nearness to its own markets as an important factor in its plant location decisions.

State and local taxes shown in the previous text table also require comment. It will be noted that the total amounts are small, relative to the very large items of labor and transportation costs. Moreover, the *tax difference* between the two cities is less than five percent of the labor-cost difference. It is surely obvious that labor costs and transportation costs to the firm's own specified markets should overshadow all other cost considerations in determining a location for this kind of manufacturer.

All other cost differences are relatively small. These include workmen's compensation, unemployment insurance, occupancy, and utilities. It may be noted that the Indiana location is slightly lower in workmen's compensation and utilities costs and slightly higher in the other two. We can safely guess that these differences would be small in the cost picture of many different kinds of industries, with the exception of the power and fuel item. For some kinds of industries, the costs of process fuel and of power are practically the sole determinants of location.

Finally, we may note that the net difference in variable operating costs ($249,000) between the Indiana and Illinois locations represents over 12 percent of the approximately $2 million profit that the ABC Corporation expects to make. (The amount of profit actually made by the company would vary, of course, with the difference in operating costs among the cities studied, other factors remaining constant.)

Cost Differences within States

The listing made earlier of the eleven cities by amount of operating costs reveals that there are some sizable cost differences among cities in the same state. Between the highest and lowest Michigan cities, the cost difference is about $346,000. Between the two Ohio cities, there is a difference of $107,000; between the Indiana cities, $184,000; between the Illinois cities, $153,000; and between the Kentucky cities, $48,000.

The following data provide a breakdown of operating costs of the ABC Corporation in the high- and low-cost cities in Michigan.

Variable Operating Cost	High (Michigan City "C")	Low (Michigan City "A")	Difference
Total.	$4,518,559	$4,172,322	$346,237
Labor.	3,152,631	2,836,498	316,133
Occupancy.	122,809	114,948	7,861
Freight.	1,025,884	1,006,303	19,581
Taxes.	143,358	142,584	774
Utilities.	73,877	71,989	1,888

From these data, it is clear that the difference in labor costs would account for most of the difference (over 90 percent) in total variable operating costs of the ABC Corporation between the high- and low-cost Michigan cities.

Limitations of the Study

THERE ARE BOUND to be limitations in any inquiry of this character. In the present study, one of these may arise from the assumption regarding the market to be served. As already noted, it was assumed that the ABC Corporation would serve the national market from its location in one of the eleven Midwestern cities surveyed. Such an assumption was presumably more or less inevitable in order to make such a study feasible. But, as previously mentioned, the use of the national market does not take into consideration the especially favorable market situation enjoyed by the Michigan communities for the products of the ABC Corporation.

Let us see how the market factor would affect the ABC Corporation in Michigan, located as it is in the manufacturing belt, and in Kentucky, a state that is on the fringe of the belt. The data (taken from statistics published by *Iron Age*) reveal that 37 percent of the national market for the ABC Corporation's products would be found in the five East North Central States. It is obvious, then, that all of the chosen states, including Kentucky, are in close proximity to a substantial share of the national market. However, ten percent of the national market is found in the state of Michigan alone. Moreover, if one adds to Michigan's ten percent the additional shares of the market provided by such nearby cities as Milwaukee, Chicago, Gary, South Bend, Toledo, and Cleveland, it turns out that Michigan and these nearby cities provide over one-fourth of the nation's market. Thus, it is obvious that the Michigan cities are more favorably located to serve the bulk of the East North Central market for metal stampings than are the Kentucky cities. (Kentucky itself appears to provide less than one percent of the national market.) In addition to the transportation cost advantages of being located in this concentrated market area, Michigan producers would enjoy the advantages of closer contact with customers and suppliers, and better access to trade information.

Thus, because of the assumption employed in the study, the data on variable operating costs do not reflect the market advantage that Michigan cities would enjoy.

Another limitation of the study may be the implicit assumption that an acceptable labor supply could be obtained in each of the eleven cities at the occupational wage rates quoted for each of them. Of the 500 employees of the ABC Corporation, 433 are production personnel. Three of the four counties in which the four low-cost cities in Ohio and Kentucky are located had fewer than this number of people working in fabricated metal products in March, 1956, according to data based on reports filed by employers under the old-age and survivors insurance program. Even fewer persons would have been working, of course, in metal stamping plants. On the other hand, all three of the Michigan counties reported from one to two thousand employees working in industries classified under fabricated metal products.

It might well be, then, that a plant as sizable as the ABC Corporation, moving into one of the four low-cost cities in Kentucky and Ohio, would run into a labor supply problem. If so, the Corporation might meet its labor supply problem only by obtaining a complement of needed skilled workers from other areas. These or other methods would add to the Corporation's labor costs.

Another limitation of the study is apparent when we look at the way in which the cities were selected. First of all, the population spread among cities compared in this study (30,000 to 110,000) has turned out to be much too wide. The spread in population for medium-size cities probably should not be more than 25,000.

Selection of cities by use of the manufacturing ratio (the ratio of manufacturing employment to total nonagricultural employment) is a related limitation of the study. Such a ratio is apparently inadequate as a means of selecting cities for comparison. Under such a method, an area of 70,000 population having 16,000 nonfarm employees over-all and 8,000 workers in manufacturing might be compared with an area of 190,000 population having 70,000 nonfarm employees over-all and 35,000 workers in manufacturing. The manufacturing ratio in each case is 50 percent, but the cities are obviously not suitable for comparison because of the great difference in size.

In selecting cities for comparison a number of economic characteristics such as population, total nonagricultural employment, employment in manufacturing, and employment in specific industries should be investigated. Care should be taken to avoid comparison among communities with widely varying economic characteristics. Thus, durable goods centers should not be compared with nondurable goods centers, and cities concentrating in the production of automobile parts and equipment should not be compared with cities concentrating in the production of electrical machinery. By carefully comparing many factors, a study group could successfully select cities which are sufficiently similar in their economic characteristics.

Conclusions

IN GENERAL, what conclusions seem to follow from our study of costs in eleven cities? First, we must note that there are some sizable cost differences among cities in the same state. Because of these sizable differences within a given state, it follows that we must not say categorically that costs in one state are higher than in another. Thus, one of the Indiana cities stands next to the top in costs, but another one only sixth. Michigan cities rank first, third, and fifth. Thus, intrastate differences are very sizable.

Although our findings on interstate differences are not conclusive because of limitations of the data, we note that there are wide cost differences among cities which are comparable in terms of their economic characteristics. Studies of many more cities and many more industries are necessary, however, before such findings can be considered conclusive.

The most obvious finding of the study appears to be that wage costs and wage-cost differences represent by far the largest item of consideration in comparing one city with another. In some cases, we noted that wage-cost differences were even greater than differences in total variable costs of operation.

We have noted, also, that freight costs can be a substantial item of cost differences among various cities. Freight costs of Illinois City "A", for example, were approximately $100,000 greater than for Indiana City "B". Table D-1 shows that the cities in Illinois and Kentucky have much higher freight costs than any of the Michigan, Ohio, or Indiana cities. In fact, total freight costs for Kentucky City "B", which is the highest freight-cost city, are about $170,000 greater than for Ohio City "B", which is the lowest freight-cost city.

It is apparent that the factors causing industrial development to occur in one place rather than in another are not simple. Thus, the consulting firm's report states in the concluding section of its study of the costs of the ABC Corporation:

> Operating costs play a part in the location decision. However, firms will tend to locate in an area which not only minimizes costs, but also maximizes sales potential and is consistent with any other objective which the firm may have. Such factors as supply of trained labor, high labor productivity, proximity to important sources of raw materials, proximity to important customers, proximity to specialty job shops which can handle unusual peaks of production, etc., all influence the location decision. Good living for employees and executives plays an important role in the location decision of a company: schools, medical facilities, parks, clubs, golf courses are all vital considerations for a firm. Finally, the ways in which a company is treated by government, by labor, by town citizens strongly influence its desire to remain or move into a given area. . . . Therefore, while costs are important, they are not the full determinants of the location decision.

The fact that we have not been able to measure interstate differentials in this study of eleven cities does not in any way invalidate the use of these methods by a study group or by a particular firm which wishes to select a location for its manufacturing operations. Indeed, the procedure described here follows closely current methods used by industry in selecting plant locations. It is the hope of the authors that some study group in the state will conduct a thorough investigation of interstate differences in operating costs, and that the present study along with the analysis of its limitations will prove helpful to such a group.

Appendix E

Areas for Research

IN THE PRECEDING chapters, there have been numerous references to the need for further research on various aspects of the Michigan economy. These references reflect the need for more information and background on a number of topics discussed in this report. Because of the need for more facts, some of the conclusions drawn in preceding pages must be considered tentative. In addition, research is desirable on some other aspects of Michigan's economic situation that have not been discussed specifically in this report. The following pages present some of the areas in which more research is needed if those who are responsible for influencing the future economic growth of the state are to have an adequate basis for intelligent action.

In some cases, the research problem is discussed in statement form. In other cases, the lines of inquiry that might be pursued are suggested by questions for which answers are needed.

Industrial Location Factors

MUCH MORE RESEARCH is needed on all of the thirteen basic industrial location factors with reference to their impact on the Michigan economy. On the basis of the discussion in this report, areas in which more detailed research findings in the near future would be especially helpful include labor, taxes, transportation, the conditions of doing business in Michigan, and the impact of these and related factors on industrial location decisions.

Labor

The summary to Appendix Chapter A points to several aspects of the labor factor about which there is an insufficient volume of factual material.

One of these areas is wage rates. Most comparisons of wage levels in Michigan with those elsewhere must be carried out in terms of average earnings, and the unsatisfactory nature of this measure has been pointed out. What is needed is a systematic review of all published studies to bring together data on wage rates by occupation within industries for cities in Michigan and in other states. Also essential is an effort to obtain access to unpublished data compiled by private groups. These two steps could make available for study such wage rate data as are already in existence. Beyond this, more studies of occupational wage rates in Michigan cities and in other midwestern cities need to be carried out to acquire more information on the extent to which Michigan wage rates do, in fact, tend to exceed those elsewhere and on the extent to which they may pose a problem for continued industrial growth in the state.

Related aspects of labor costs for Michigan manufacturers could also be the focus of additional research endeavors. More research needs to be provided on union wage policies, with special reference to the extent to which an industry-wide wage agreement is imposed on all firms, including small ones, in an industry.[1] There is a need also for converting data on fringe benefits into dollars-and-cents data that can be combined with direct wage rates to provide a better indication of total labor costs. The availability of more information on unemployment insurance costs in Michigan by industry and by size of firm would be helpful in enabling employers to estimate more accurately their own costs. In some cases, merely a matter of systematic compilation and presentation of existing data is involved. In other cases, the development of new data is required.

As has been indicated, relatively high wage rates in Michigan may not be a serious problem in attracting industry to Michigan if the productivity of Michigan industrial workers ranges on the high side. But much more knowledge is necessary if a firm statistical base is to be provided for the assumption that the productivity of Michigan workers is relatively high and if this likely labor situation advantage is to be used successfully to counter the disadvantage that generally high wage rates for Michigan workers may present.

In view of the generally unsatisfactory characteristics of existing measures of productivity, basic research to develop more satisfactory measures would seem to be in order before conclusive comparisons of the productivity of Michigan workers with that of workers elsewhere can be carried out.

---

1 Harold M. Levinson, "Pattern Bargaining by the United Automobile Workers," *Labor Law Journal*, September, 1958, pp. 669-74.

Taxes

Recent studies of the tax situation in Michigan have provided a substantial fund of knowledge concerning the Michigan tax structure and its general impact relative to tax burdens in other states. However, two further lines of detailed investigation seem to merit attention as a means of obtaining a clearer picture of the effect of Michigan taxes on industry.

One line of investigation would be to ascertain whether or not Michigan communities are saddling industry with an undue share of the tax load. For example, if total taxes on a firm in some Michigan community are, say, ten percent higher than those in some comparable community in another state, the level of services in the Michigan community may be sufficiently better so that a firm will be willing and able to pay the ten percent difference. But if the tax burden on the company in the Michigan community is 30 to 40 percent higher, there could be situations in which the decision would be different.

Studies of this type could suggest the degree to which relatively high taxes imposed on an industrial firm by a given Michigan community reflected a higher level of public services than in other communities, relatively high tax rates on industry, or other factors. Whatever the cause, findings of such studies could point to Michigan communities that appear to be out of line in their tax levies on industry, both in comparison with other communities in the state and in comparison with communities elsewhere.

A second line of inquiry could be an investigation of the tax problems of Michigan companies which have reported state and/or local taxes to be a problem for them. Other companies in the same industries could also be studied to ascertain their evaluation of the impact of the Michigan tax structure on their operations, with special reference to the reported problems. A study of the tax problems of these companies, especially in relation to the tax disadvantage of operating in Michigan that some of these companies have reported, could be helpful in suggesting ways of taxing industry on a more equitable basis in Michigan.

Transportation

A research proposal for studying the transportation situation of Michigan is provided in Appendix Chapter C.

Conditions of Doing Business in Michigan

Some industrial leaders in Michigan have asserted that the state has an unfavorable climate for industry. A study is needed to determine exhaustively all of the ways in which Michigan manufacturers believe that business really is harder or more expensive to carry on in Michigan than in other comparable states, and to determine precisely in what way and to what degree the conditions of doing business in Michigan differ from those in other surrounding states. Such a study would, in essence, involve drawing up a "bill of particulars" on trouble spots in the setting for industry in Michigan based on interviews with manufacturers in the state. Information from other states would then be collected on these matters to provide a direct comparison of Michigan and these other states on the points involved.

In large part, the study would revolve around those factors that are commonly thought of as being part of a state's business climate. But the focus would be on concrete particulars. Although such a study might be difficult to design, it could be helpful in indicating problems of operating a business in Michigan that were lacking in, or common to, other industrial states.

Industrial Mobility

The detailed studies of several industrial location factors that have been suggested would broaden our knowledge of the extent to which Michigan's rating on these factors reflected favorable and unfavorable aspects for industrial location in the state. A profitable line of further investigation would reflect studies designed to determine the way in which these and other factors have actually influenced the location of plants that have moved to new locations in recent years.

Plants moving into the East North Central States. One such study might involve research into the locational factors that influenced the location of plants established from the outside in Michigan and in other East North Central States during the past several years. Such a study could be helpful in throwing light on Michigan's assets and liabilities for industry, especially in comparison with those of its neighbor states. The study would attempt to identify those factors which were major ones, and those which were subsidiary ones, in the final location decision. The extent to which Michigan's "adverse" business climate may have influenced manufacturers to locate in one of the other East North Central States might be ascertained.

The difficulty of determining in some cases the relative importance of the various factors that actually entered into the final location decision is recognized. But an objective, research approach to such a study could provide much more information on the way in which location factors have actually guided plant location in the East North Central States in recent years than appears to be presently available.

Plants moving away from Michigan. A second study relating locational factors and industrial mobility would have as its focus Michigan plants that have relocated out of the state in recent years. Answers could be sought to such questions as:

> Of the plants that have moved from Michigan, what reasons have been given by the owners for such move-outs? On the basis of observation, do there appear to be reasons other than those advanced by the owners? What factors appear to have been the decisive ones?
>
> To what extent do these move-outs represent marginal plants? What was the record of these companies on production, sales, employment, etc., prior to the time they left this state? What has their record been along these lines in their new location? Are they prospering after having moved? Were these move-outs concentrated in any industry or industry group? Was their moving elsewhere prompted in part by financial inducements given to them by the communities into which they moved?

Industrial Starts and Expansions in Michigan

In Chapter V, it was pointed out that there were over 250 new industrial starts and in-state expansions in Michigan during 1958. It may be assumed that the location in Michigan of many of these firms did not result from an over-all evaluation of Michigan's assets and liabilities for industry. Rather, these starts may simply have reflected a belief by the enterpriser that a profit-making opportunity existed. Studies are needed of recent starts and expansions in Michigan to determine the factors that did account for their location in Michigan and to provide some information on the characteristics and experience of these firms. Such studies could attempt to provide answers to such questions as:

> What reasons are given by these enterprisers for starting new plants or expanding existing ones in Michigan? To what extent were locations in other states considered? What was the background of the persons who started these manufacturing units in Michigan? Were they for the most part former employees of Michigan firms who had struck out on their own?
>
> In what Michigan industries have these new manufacturing plants started? What was the initial size of these plants in terms of employment? What has been the survival record of these firms, especially during the 1958 recession? To what extent has there

been an increase in employment in these firms? In what industries have expansions occurred? To what extent did these expansions add to employment opportunities?

Identification of Suitable Industries for Michigan

Comparison of Locational Factors with Industries' Needs

In Chapter IX, reference was made to the need for industry-by-industry studies to identify industries which hold promise of providing industrial growth for Michigan. The most basic procedure would be to take each major industrial activity in the United States which might possibly be suitable for location in Michigan and to consider the suitability of Michigan for that industry in terms of every single one of the basic industrial location factors.

As a concluding part of each such study, it would be desirable to make cost analyses showing the extent to which typical firms in the industry under consideration could compete successfully from Michigan locations with similar firms located in cities in other suitable states. These cost analyses would be of the type illustrated in Appendix Chapter D with respect to the costs of operation of the hypothetical ABC Corporation in 11 cities. Such studies should take cognizance of the problems involved in the selection of representative cities and of the limitations of cost analyses by themselves, as discussed in Appendix Chapter D.

Recent Experience in Growth Industries

Another approach to the problem of pinpointing industries which are most likely to expand successfully in Michigan is to analyze the growth industries of the United States in order to see which ones have already shown some potential strength in the state of Michigan. This approach has been illustrated in the present study by Mr. Thole's chapter (VII) on growth industries in Michigan. Such studies as this should be carried on more intensively than they have been in the present report. As additional detailed data become available, the trends shown in Chapter VII should be carried forward to show more recent experience.

Other Approaches

In addition to the suggestions listed above, other approaches to the pinpointing of suitable industries for Michigan should be utilized. In this connection, two documents should be referred to. One is a *Proposal for a Research Project Entitled "Forecasting State*

Economic Development." This was presented to the Michigan Economic Development Commission in November, 1958, by the Commission's Advisory Committee on Industrial Expansion Research. The other is a report — sponsored by that same committee — by Wilbur R. Thompson and John M. Mattila, entitled, *An Econometric Model of Postwar State Industrial Development.*[2]

Studies of Impact of Technology

As technological changes occur in the nation's industrial economy, studies should be carried out to determine their likely or potential impact on Michigan. Technological innovations result in the actual or relative decline of existing industries and in the burgeoning expansion of new ones. Studies of the likely effect of technology in terms of new products, processes, and industries should be carried on continuously so that Michigan may share in the new industries that will be of importance a decade or so hence.

Technological developments should be studied also in connection with their possible impact on Michigan's industrial location factors. Thus, Michigan's favorable situation with regard to water supply may be diminished somewhat by progress being made in efforts to develop an economical process for obtaining fresh water from sea water. If a practical process is in sight, does the development pose any significant threat to the water advantage now enjoyed by Michigan?

An atomic energy plant is being constructed in Michigan. Others have been announced as likely. What do these developments portend as a factor in industrial development in Michigan? Do they offer hope that cheaper power from this source may promote the development in the state of certain industries currently dependent on coal as a source of power?

Prospects for Growth in Nonmanufacturing Industries

The suggestions for research provided thus far relate to research in industrial growth. However, the projection of future employment in Michigan provided in Chapter VIII indicated that expansion in the number of jobs in nonmanufacturing industries must be substantially greater than in factory jobs. Such greater expansion may be expected in view of long-time trends. But research is needed so that the full potential of jobs for Michigan workers in nonfactory

---

2 (Detroit: Wayne State University Press, 1959)

lines may be realized. Such research could seek answers to the following questions:

What has been the growth record nationally and in nearby states of the various industry groups in the nonmanufacturing sector of the economy? How does Michigan's experience in these nonindustrial lines compare with experience elsewhere? What factors account for Michigan's relatively slow growth in some of these areas? Does experience elsewhere suggest especially likely areas of growth for Michigan? What problems are there in connection with developing these nonmanufacturing lines in Michigan? What might be done to promote such growth by those responsible for encouraging economic growth in the state? Do recent developments, such as the development of the Seaway, provide a potential for substantial expansion of jobs in nonmanufacturing industries? What can be done to capitalize on them?

Research on Tourism

Among the nonmanufacturing industries, the tourist "industry" is often referred to as one that holds considerable additional promise for the state. Although several worthwhile studies in this area have already been made, a comprehensive research project on the topic would seem to be in order. Such a study could cover the following points:

What is the current importance of tourism in Michigan in terms of employment and income? How much may tourism be expected to increase in Michigan in the years ahead? Can it bring about a very substantial growth in job opportunities?

What are the special problems in developing the growth of the tourist trade in the state? Does Michigan suffer from a lack of tourist attractions in comparison with those offered by other important tourist states? If so, how may Michigan's current attractions be exploited more thoroughly? Are the facilities that cater to the tourist trade, both public and private, of a quality such as to promote continued tourist expansion?

Should the agencies responsible for promoting tourism, both state and private, expend larger amounts of money for such promotion? How much are state agencies elsewhere spending for their tourist promotion activities? What are the most effective methods of promoting tourism in the state?

Industrial Promotion

Work of Promotional Groups

Does the range of activities carried out by the Michigan Department of Economic Development appear appropriate? If not, what changes might be suggested? What areas of activity should be given more emphasis? How do the activities carried out by the Michigan Department of Economic Development compare with those of similar agencies in other states? If the

Department should receive a larger budget from the legislature, what additional types of activity would seem to be indicated and how should the larger budget be allocated among the several spheres of activity?

What private groups are carrying on promotional activity on behalf of the state? What is the nature of their work? Can suggestions for improvement in their activities be made? To what extent is there coordination between the work of private groups and that of the Michigan Department of Economic Development? If greater coordination appears to be indicated, what types of program or plan for this greater coordination seem advisable?

Need for Financial Inducements

What is the record on a country-wide basis of the value of financial inducements for industry? What has been the result in specific states of the availability of such inducements as tax inducements, financing benefits such as leasing land and buildings on a subsidized basis, low interest loans, and provision of special facilities? Which of these seem worthy of a trial in Michigan? To what extent can these financial inducements be provided in Michigan? To what extent should they be left to community action, rather than being carried out at the state level?

Industrial Parks

What is an industrial park? To what extent are industrial parks being developed elsewhere in the country? What does such experience suggest in regard to the value of industrial parks in attracting new industry or in retaining industry in an area? What are the disadvantages and advantages?

How many industrial parks are there in Michigan? What are the barriers to the provision of industrial parks by public bodies in Michigan? Should communities in Michigan push this type of community inducement? If so, what type of park seems to be best and what are the conditions under which industry should be given access to industrial parks? Should the state government take an active part in promoting the development of industrial parks in Michigan communities or should it act more in an advisory capacity?

Other Areas of Research

Impact of Automation on Michigan Job Opportunities

To what extent have automation and related technological advances resulted in a net loss of job opportunities in Michigan in recent years?

Has automation contributed appreciably to the actual and relative decline of jobs in the auto industry in the state? Has automation exerted a greater impact on automotive job opportunities in Michigan than in the nation generally?

What do current developments in automation suggest with regard to the future development of factory jobs in Michigan?

In what industries is automation most likely to be used? How important are these industries in the Michigan economy? What are the changes that may occur in the types of jobs available to Michigan workers because of the developing use of automated equipment and processes? What implications do these changes suggest for the education, training, and re-training of Michigan workers?

These are but a few of the many questions that can be raised concerning the impact of automation and technological changes on the Michigan economy. As suggested by the following, relatively little actual research is being done throughout the country in this field:

> There is great imbalance today between the billions of dollars spent for research on the development and application of new technology and the few thousands of dollars devoted to original research on the social and economic consequences of the new technology. Probably no more than 15 or 20 researchers are devoting a substantial amount of time to the latter kind of study today in the United States, despite the vast amount of speculative literature on the subject.[3]

Two sources of guidance for research on the current and possible future effect of automation on Michigan's industrial economy can be suggested. The concluding chapter of a recent National Planning Association pamphlet on automation is entitled, "Guide to a Study of Automation in the U. S. Economy."[4] The study procedure and the questions raised in this chapter could be adapted for use in connection with a study of the Michigan economy. A second source of guidance could be materials available from the Governor's Commission on Automation as well as suggestions from the Commission members themselves.

Automotive Employment

> How many jobs are provided by each of the Big Three in their automotive operations in Michigan (as distinct from total employment in all of their operations)? What proportion of total automotive employment in Michigan is afforded by the Big Three? How much employment is provided by other vehicle manufacturers in the state, such as those producing trucks? What have been recent employment trends in these several areas in recent years? What implications do these trends hold for future automotive employment in the state?
>
> What are the reasons for the decentralization that has occurred in the industry in recent years? Is it attributable almost wholly to market considerations or have taxes actually been an

---

3. Charles C. Killingsworth, "Automation in Manufacturing," *Proceedings of the Eleventh Annual Meeting of the Industrial Relations Research Association,* Chicago, December 28-29, 1958, p. 34.

4 John Diebold, *Automation: Its Impact on Business and Labor* (Washington: The Association, 1959), 64 pp.

important factor also, as might be gathered from remarks made by some automotive officials? To what extent have the Big Three taken over the manufacturing of parts for their cars from independent suppliers?

Review of Economic Base Studies in Michigan Communities

Which communities in Michigan have recently carried out studies of their economic base with a view to promoting industrial growth? What degree of applicability to other Michigan communities do the findings of these studies have? Are there certain liabilities that appear to be generally common? If so, what corrective action seems to be indicated?

Appendix Tables

Population Increase, United States, East North Central States, and Michigan, by Year
1950-1958

(Numbers in thousands)

Year[a]	Conti-nental United States	East North Central States					
		All	Ohio	Indiana	Illinois	MICHIGAN	Wisconsin
		Total Population[b]					
1950.....	150,697.4	30,399.4	7,946.6	3,934.2	8,712.2	6,371.8	3,434.6
1951.....	153,384.0	30,759.0	7,963.0	4,087.0	8,755.0	6,510.0	3,444.0
1952.....	155,761.0	31,294.0	8,120.0	4,129.0	8,904.0	6,664.0	3,477.0
1953.....	158,313.0	32,100.0	8,541.0	4,169.0	9,005.0	6,860.0	3,525.0
1954.....	161,191.0	33,089.0	8,929.0	4,244.0	9,159.0	7,126.0	3,631.0
1955.....	164,303.0	33,694.0	8,981.0	4,335.0	9,316.0	7,358.0	3,704.0
1956.....	167,261.0	34,347.0	9,070.0	4,433.0	9,484.0	7,571.0	3,789.0
1957.....	170,293.0	34,978.0	9,206.0	4,507.0	9,699.0	7,705.0	3,861.0
1958[c]....	173,260.0	35,619.0	9,345.0	4,581.0	9,889.0	7,866.0	3,938.0
		Percentage Increase					
1950-1951	1.8	1.2	0.2	3.9	0.5	2.2	0.3
1951-1952	1.5	1.7	2.0	1.0	1.7	2.4	1.0
1952-1953	1.6	2.6	5.2	1.0	1.1	2.9	1.4
1953-1954	1.8	3.1	4.5	1.8	1.7	3.9	3.0
1954-1955	1.9	1.8	.6	2.1	1.7	3.3	2.0
1955-1956	1.8	1.9	1.0	2.3	1.8	2.9	2.3
1956-1957	1.8	1.8	1.5	1.7	2.3	1.8	1.9
1957-1958	1.7	1.8	1.5	1.6	2.0	2.1	2.0
1950-1958	15.0	17.2	17.6	16.4	13.5	23.5	14.7

Source: Bureau of the Census, *Current Population Reports,* Series P-25 (No. 165, November 4, 1957; No. 186, October 27, 1958; and No. 189, November 13, 1958).

a Data for 1950 are as of April 1. Data for all other years are as of July 1.

b Excludes armed forces overseas. Data for states include persons in the armed forces stationed in state.

c Provisional estimates.

Growth of the Labor Force, United States, East North Central States, and Michigan

1900-1950

(Numbers in thousands)

Year[a]	Number in Labor Force[b]			Percentage Increase		
	United States	East North Central States[c]	Michigan	United States	East Central North States[c]	Michigan
1900.................	28,282.6	5,836.2	900.8	...	...	...
1910.................	37,271.4	7,221.7	1,109.3	31.8	23.7	23.1
1920.................	41,236.2	8,501.3	1,471.4	10.6	17.7	32.6
1930.................	48,594.6	10,100.5	1,926.0	17.8	18.8	30.9
1940.................	52,789.5	10,811.3	2,125.9	8.6	7.0	10.4
1950.................	60,054.0	12,447.1	2,540.5	13.8	15.1	19.5
1900-1950...........	...	...	...	112.3	113.3	182.0

Source: Adapted from William Haber, *How Much Does It Cost* (Michigan Employment Security Commission, 1951), Table XVIII, p. 153. Data from the Bureau of the Census. Preliminary data for 1950 shown in source table replaced by final census data.

a Month in which census was taken varies. For 1930, 1940, and 1950, data are as of April 1.
b For 1900-1930, data cover ''gainful workers.'' For 1940 and 1950, data cover total labor force.
c Includes Ohio, Indiana, Illinois, Michigan, and Wisconsin.

Employees in Nonmanufacturing Establishments, United States, East North Central States, and Michigan[a]

1939-1957

(Employees in thousands)

Year	United States Employees	United States Percent	East North Central States — All Employees	All Percent	Ohio Employees	Ohio Percent	Indiana Employees	Indiana Percent	Illinois Employees	Illinois Percent	MICHIGAN Employees	MICHIGAN Percent	Wisconsin Employees	Wisconsin Percent
1939...	20,233	100.0	4,083.6	20.2	1,004.5	5.0	463.6	2.3	1,482.7	7.3	721.7	3.6	411.1	2.0
1940...	21,278	100.0	4,281.3	20.1	1,053.0	4.9	490.4	2.3	1,558.6	7.3	761.1	3.6	418.2	2.0
1941...	23,246	100.0	4,657.2	20.0	1,149.1	4.9	548.1	2.4	1,681.8	7.2	837.2	3.6	441.0	1.9
1942...	24,728	100.0	4,838.4	19.5	1,192.4	4.8	577.8	2.3	1,738.9	7.0	865.6	3.5	463.7	1.9
1943...	24,725	100.0	4,752.5	19.2	1,203.3	4.9	559.1	2.3	1,694.8	6.8	852.2	3.4	443.1	1.8
1944...	24,423	100.0	4,659.7	19.1	1,187.1	4.9	545.2	2.2	1,647.1	6.7	831.6	3.4	448.7	1.8
1945...	24,735	100.0	4,716.7	19.1	1,187.3	4.8	559.5	2.3	1,662.5	6.7	837.0	3.4	470.4	1.9
1946...	26,826	100.0	5,178.3	19.3	1,325.5	4.9	604.6	2.3	1,806.7	6.7	915.5	3.4	526.0	2.0
1947...	28,172	100.0	5,487.6	19.5	1,421.6	5.0	637.4	2.3	1,905.2	6.8	972.0	3.4	551.4	2.0
1948...	29,127	100.0	5,751.1	19.7	1,505.8	5.2	665.7	2.3	1,968.1	6.8	1,035.6	3.5	575.9	2.0
1949...	29,137	100.0	5,719.7	19.6	1,497.6	5.1	668.6	2.3	1,935.2	6.6	1,037.7	3.6	580.6	2.0
1950...	29,771	100.0	5,847.0	19.6	1,525.0	5.1	693.2	2.3	1,944.8	6.5	1,090.7	3.7	593.3	2.0
1951...	31,243	100.0	6,108.9	19.5	1,597.6	5.1	732.7	2.3	2,018.1	6.5	1,153.6	3.7	606.9	1.9
1952...	31,969	100.0	6,225.8	19.5	1,631.4	5.1	742.2	2.3	2,063.0	6.5	1,177.9	3.7	611.3	1.9
1953...	32,443	100.0	6,381.5	19.7	1,685.8	5.2	753.9	2.3	2,087.0	6.4	1,233.5	3.8	621.3	1.9
1954...	32,436	100.0	6,410.8	19.8	1,695.3	5.2	747.3	2.3	2,078.6	6.4	1,259.4	3.9	630.2	1.9
1955...	33,493	100.0	6,615.4	19.8	1,739.6	5.2	773.0	2.3	2,134.8	6.4	1,315.0	3.9	653.0	1.9
1956...	34,863	100.0	6,855.2	19.7	1,803.6	5.2	806.0	2.3	2,207.6	6.3	1,356.9	3.9	681.1	2.0
1957...	35,380	100.0	6,918.6	19.6	1,822.9	5.2	807.9	2.3	2,238.0	6.3	1,350.5	3.8	699.3	2.0

Source: United States: *Employment and Earnings—Annual Supplement Issue*, July, 1958, Table A-1.
East North Central States: *State Employment, 1939-1956, state tables*, and *Employment and Earnings—Annual Supplement Issue*, July, 1958, Tables SA-7 and SA-10.

a Percents based on national totals.

Appendix Table IV

Employees in Nonagricultural Establishments, United States, East North Central States, and Michigan[a]

1939-1957

(Employees in thousands)

| Year | United States | | East North Central States | | | | | | | | | | | | |
| | | | All | | Ohio | | Indiana | | Illinois | | MICHIGAN | | Wisconsin | |
	Employ-ees	Percent	Employ-ees	Percent	Employ-ees	Percent	Employ-ees	Percent	Employ-ees	Percent	Employ-ees	Percent	Employ-ees	Percent
1939..	30,311	100.0	6,866.2	22.7	1,758.7	5.8	813.7	2.7	2,279.1	7.5	1,348.1	4.4	666.6	2.2
1940..	32,058	100.0	7,331.1	22.9	1,879.7	5.9	871.4	2.7	2,407.6	7.5	1,478.1	4.6	694.3	2.2
1941..	36,220	100.0	8,369.4	23.1	2,168.8	6.0	1,021.6	2.8	2,696.8	7.4	1,707.0	4.7	775.2	2.1
1942..	39,779	100.0	9,005.4	22.6	2,374.5	6.0	1,115.3	2.8	2,851.9	7.2	1,819.5	4.6	844.2	2.1
1943..	42,106	100.0	9,637.2	22.9	2,566.6	6.1	1,192.2	2.8	2,958.5	7.0	2,034.0	4.8	885.9	2.1
1944..	41,534	100.0	9,522.1	22.9	2,519.9	6.1	1,164.3	2.8	2,933.9	7.1	2,003.1	4.8	900.0	2.2
1945..	40,037	100.0	9,003.3	22.5	2,381.1	5.9	1,095.0	2.7	2,833.6	7.1	1,797.9	4.5	895.7	2.2
1946..	41,287	100.0	9,345.6	22.6	2,492.4	6.0	1,103.1	2.7	2,968.2	7.2	1,853.8	4.5	928.1	2.2
1947..	43,462	100.0	9,999.2	23.0	2,666.7	6.1	1,188.6	2.7	3,145.4	7.2	2,013.7	4.6	984.8	2.3
1948..	44,448	100.0	10,256.4	23.1	2,743.6	6.2	1,221.0	2.7	3,184.3	7.2	2,093.9	4.7	1,013.6	2.3
1949..	43,315	100.0	9,867.2	22.8	2,617.8	6.0	1,181.7	2.7	3,063.1	7.1	2,018.9	4.7	985.7	2.3
1950..	44,738	100.0	10,293.2	23.0	2,723.7	6.1	1,266.1	2.8	3,128.5	7.0	2,153.9	4.8	1,021.0	2.3
1951..	47,347	100.0	10,862.6	22.9	2,912.5	6.2	1,349.7	2.9	3,264.8	6.9	2,265.6	4.8	1,070.0	2.3
1952..	48,303	100.0	10,998.0	22.8	2,966.1	6.1	1,360.3	2.8	3,318.8	6.9	2,274.8	4.7	1,078.0	2.2
1953..	49,681	100.0	11,497.4	23.1	3,109.5	6.3	1,427.2	2.9	3,411.4	6.9	2,455.5	4.9	1,093.8	2.2
1954..	48,431	100.0	10,991.4	22.7	2,986.6	6.2	1,329.3	2.7	3,290.3	6.8	2,320.6	4.8	1,064.6	2.2
1955..	50,056	100.0	11,455.0	22.9	3,086.4	6.2	1,393.2	2.8	3,392.7	6.8	2,479.2	5.0	1,103.5	2.2
1956..	51,766	100.0	11,675.5	22.6	3,174.0	6.1	1,420.2	2.7	3,498.8	6.8	2,437.9	4.7	1,144.6	2.2
1957..	52,162	100.0	11,605.1	22.2	3,162.8	6.1	1,415.1	2.7	3,497.5	6.7	2,376.0	4.6	1,153.7	2.2

Source: United States: *Employment and Earnings—Annual Supplement Issue*, July, 1958, Table A-1.
East North Central States: *State Employment, 1939-1956*, state tables, and *Employment and Earnings—Annual Supplement Issue*, July, 1958, Table SA-7.

a Covers both manufacturing and nonmanufacturing establishments. Percents are based on national totals.

Comparison of Total Employment Levels, Detroit and Outstate Michigan[a]

1949-1957

(Employment in thousands)

Year	Total Nonfarm Employment[b]						Total Wage and Salary Workers (nonfarm)					
	Amount			Percent			Number			Percent		
	Michigan	Detroit	Outstate Michigan	Michigan	Detroit	Outstate Michigan	Michigan	Detroit	Outstate Michigan	Michigan	Detroit	Outstate Michigan
1949.......	2,240	1,260	980	100.0	56.2	43.8	2,020	1,148	872	100.0	56.8	43.2
1950.......	2,381	1,329	1,052	100.0	55.8	44.2	2,160	1,217	943	100.0	56.3	43.7
1951.......	2,489	1,391	1,098	100.0	55.9	44.1	2,267	1,278	989	100.0	56.4	43.6
1952.......	2,499	1,387	1,112	100.0	55.5	44.5	2,275	1,273	1,002	100.0	56.0	44.0
1953.......	2,694	1,508	1,186	100.0	56.0	44.0	2,466	1,393	1,073	100.0	56.5	43.5
1954.......	2,556	1,394	1,162	100.0	54.5	45.5	2,325	1,278	1,047	100.0	55.0	45.0
1955.......	2,646	1,442	1,204	100.0	54.5	45.5	2,413	1,325	1,088	100.0	54.9	45.1
1956.......	2,584	1,394	1,190	100.0	53.9	46.1	2,349	1,275	1,074	100.0	54.3	45.7
1957.......	2,576	1,408	1,168	100.0	54.7	45.3	2,335	1,286	1,049	100.0	55.1	44.9

Source: Michigan: *Michigan's Labor Market,* January, 1958, p. 8.

Detroit: *Detroit Labor Market Letter,* January, 1958, p. 7.

a *Data for Detroit cover Detroit Metropolitan Area, consisting of Wayne, Oakland, and Macomb counties*
b *Includes wage and salary workers, self-employed, domestics, and unpaid family workers.*

Comparison of Employment in Durable and Nondurable Goods Industries, Detroit and Outstate Michigan
1949-1957

Year	Michigan			Detroit[a]			Outstate Michigan		
	All manufacturing industries	Durables	Non-durables	All manufacturing industries	Durables	Non-durables	All manufacturing industries	Durables	Non-durables
Number of wage and salary workers (thousands)									
1949	976	807	169	589	512	77	387	295	92
1950	1,070	896	174	633	556	77	437	340	97
1951	1,122	943	179	665	586	79	457	357	100
1952	1,104	924	180	646	566	80	458	358	100
1953	1,230	1,045	185	727	645	82	503	400	103
1954	1,075	893	182	604	525	79	471	368	103
1955	1,155	968	187	652	572	80	503	396	107
1956	1,074	886	188	590	511	79	484	375	109
1957	1,050	861	189	587	508	79	463	353	110
Percent distribution									
1949	100.0	82.7	17.3	100.0	86.9	13.1	100.0	76.2	23.8
1950	100.0	83.7	16.3	100.0	87.8	12.2	100.0	77.8	22.2
1951	100.0	84.0	16.0	100.0	88.1	11.9	100.0	78.1	21.9
1952	100.0	83.7	16.3	100.0	87.6	12.4	100.0	78.2	21.8
1953	100.0	85.0	15.0	100.0	88.7	11.3	100.0	79.5	20.5
1954	100.0	83.1	16.9	100.0	86.9	13.1	100.0	78.1	21.9
1955	100.0	83.8	16.2	100.0	87.7	12.3	100.0	78.7	21.3
1956	100.0	82.5	17.5	100.0	86.6	13.4	100.0	77.5	22.5
1957	100.0	82.0	18.0	100.0	86.5	13.5	100.0	76.2	23.8

Source: Michigan: *Michigan's Labor Market*, January, 1958, p. 8.

Detroit: *Detroit Labor Market Letter*, January, 1958, p. 7.

[a] Data for Detroit cover Detroit Metropolitan Area, consisting of Wayne, Oakland, and Macomb counties.

Employees in Manufacturing Establishments, United States, East North Central States, and Michigan[a]

1939-1957

(Employees in thousands)

| Year | United States | | East North Central States | | | | | | | | | | | |
| | | | All | | Ohio | | Indiana | | Illinois | | MICHIGAN | | Wisconsin | |
	Employ-ees	Percent	Employ-ees	Percent	Employ-ees	Percent	Employ-ees	Percent	Employ-ees	Percent	Employ-ees	Percent	Employ-ees	Percent
1939...	10,078	100.0	2,782.6	27.6	754.2	7.5	350.1	3.5	796.4	7.9	626.4	6.2	255.5	2.5
1940...	10,780	100.0	3,049.8	28.3	826.7	7.7	381.0	3.5	849.0	7.9	717.0	6.7	276.1	2.6
1941...	12,974	100.0	3,712.2	28.6	1,019.7	7.9	473.5	3.6	1,015.0	7.8	869.8	6.7	334.2	2.6
1942...	15,051	100.0	4,167.0	27.7	1,182.1	7.9	537.5	3.6	1,113.0	7.4	953.9	6.3	380.5	2.5
1943...	17,381	100.0	4,884.7	28.1	1,363.3	7.8	633.1	3.6	1,263.7	7.3	1,181.8	6.8	442.8	2.5
1944...	17,111	100.0	4,862.4	28.4	1,332.8	7.8	619.1	3.6	1,286.8	7.5	1,171.5	6.8	452.2	2.6
1945...	15,302	100.0	4,286.6	28.0	1,193.8	7.8	535.5	3.5	1,171.1	7.7	960.9	6.3	425.3	2.8
1946...	14,461	100.0	4,167.3	28.8	1,166.9	8.1	498.5	3.4	1,161.5	8.0	938.3	6.5	402.1	2.8
1947...	15,290	100.0	4,511.6	29.5	1,245.1	8.1	551.2	3.6	1,240.2	8.1	1,041.7	6.8	433.4	2.8
1948...	15,321	100.0	4,505.3	29.4	1,237.8	8.1	555.3	3.6	1,216.2	7.9	1,058.3	6.9	437.7	2.9
1949...	14,178	100.0	4,147.5	29.3	1,120.2	7.9	513.1	3.6	1,127.9	8.0	981.2	6.9	405.1	2.9
1950...	14,967	100.0	4,446.2	29.7	1,198.7	8.0	572.9	3.8	1,183.7	7.9	1,063.2	7.1	427.7	2.9
1951...	16,104	100.0	4,753.7	29.5	1,314.9	8.2	617.0	3.8	1,246.7	7.7	1,112.0	6.9	463.1	2.9
1952...	16,334	100.0	4,772.2	29.2	1,334.7	8.2	618.1	3.8	1,255.8	7.7	1,096.9	6.7	466.7	2.9
1953...	17,238	100.0	5,115.9	29.7	1,423.7	8.3	673.3	3.9	1,324.4	7.7	1,222.0	7.1	472.5	2.7
1954...	15,995	100.0	4,580.6	28.6	1,291.3	8.1	582.0	3.6	1,211.7	7.6	1,061.2	6.1	434.4	2.7
1955...	16,563	100.0	4,839.6	29.2	1,346.8	8.1	620.2	3.7	1,257.9	7.6	1,164.2	7.0	450.5	2.7
1956...	16,903	100.0	4,820.3	28.5	1,370.4	8.1	614.2	3.6	1,291.2	7.6	1,081.0	6.4	463.5	2.7
1957...	16,782	100.0	4,686.5	27.9	1,339.9	8.0	607.2	3.6	1,259.5	7.5	1,025.5	6.1	454.4	2.7

Source: United States: *Employment and Earnings—Annual Supplement Issue*, July, 1958, Table A-1.
East North Central States: *State Employment, 1939-1956*, state tables, and *Employment and Earnings—Annual Supplement Issue*, July, 1958, Table SA-10.

a Percents are based on national totals.

Selected Series on All Employees in the Motor Vehicles and Equipment Industry as a Percent of All Manufacturing Employees, United States
1929-1957

(Employees in thousands)

Year	Bureau of Labor Statistics			Census of Manufactures			U. S. Department of Commerce		
	Employees in all mfg.	Employees in motor vehicles[a]		Employees in all mfg.[b]	Employees in motor vehicles[a]		Employees in all mfg.	Employees in motor vehicles[a]	
		Number	Percent of all mfg.		Number	Percent of all mfg.		Number	Percent of all mfg.
1929..	...	...	...	9,660	494.5	5.1	10,428	540	5.2
1930..	...	...	...	...	...	...	9,309	403	4.3
1931..	...	...	...	...	...	...	7,895	352	4.5
1932..	...	...	...	...	...	...	6,678	299	4.5
1933..	...	...	...	6,558	272.3	4.2	7,204	300	4.2
1934..	...	...	...	...	...	...	8,364	433	5.2
1935..	...	...	...	8,262	425.0	5.1	8,904	464	5.2
1936..	...	...	...	...	...	...	9,645	492	5.1
1937..	...	...	...	9,786	c	...	10,591	580	5.5
1938..	...	...	...	...	...	...	9,131	363	4.0
1939..	10,078	466.0	4.6	9,527	c	...	9,967	467	4.7
1940..	10,780	532.0	4.9	...	...	...	10,882	543	5.0
1941..	12,974	654.0	5.0	...	...	...	13,137	655	5.0
1942..	15,051	576.0	3.8	...	...	...	15,284	575	3.8
1943..	17,381	756.0	4.3	...	...	...	17,402	325	1.9
1944..	17,111	793.0	4.6	...	...	...	17,050	341	2.0
1945..	15,302	663.0	4.3	...	...	...	15,186	308	2.0
1946..	14,461	662.0	4.6	...	...	...	14,493	667	4.6
1947..	15,290	776.2	5.1	14,294	693.8	4.9	15,215	749	4.9
1948..	15,321	789.3	5.2	...	...	...	15,285	766	5.0
1949..	14,178	759.6	5.4	13,567	679.9	5.0	14,183	743	5.2
1950..	14,967	825.2	5.5	14,467	756.9	5.2	14,969	810	5.4
1951..	16,104	844.5	5.2	15,310	772.6	5.0	16,122	851	5.3
1952..	16,334	790.2	4.8	15,733	717.3	4.6	16,413	799	4.9
1953..	17,238	928.9	5.4	16,693	860.4	5.2	17,231	921	5.3
1954..	15,995	775.6	4.8	15,652	695.5	4.4	16,024	786	4.9
1955..	16,563	903.8	5.5	16,344	831.9	5.1	16,579	902	5.4
1956..	16,903	809.9	4.8	16,704	738.7	4.4	16,944	817	4.8
1957..	16,782	786.3	4.7	...	...	...	...	...	...

Source: BLS series—

Employees in all manufacturing: *Employment and Earnings—Annual Supplement Issue,* July, 1958, Table A-1.

Employees in motor vehicles and equipment: Individual Historical Summary Tables, *Automobiles (371),* various dates.

Census of Manufactures series—

For 1929-1954: *1954 Census of Manufactures,* Vol. II, Pt. 1, p. 3, and Pt. 2, p. 37A-3. Data for 1949-1953 based on *Annual Survey of Manufactures.*

For 1955-1956: *1956 Annual Survey of Manufactures,* Series MAS-56-1-Rev., March 28, 1958, Table 1, pp. 2-3, 14-15.

Department of Commerce series—

National Income—A Supplement to the Survey of Current Business, 1954 Edition, Table 25, pp. 196-97, and *Survey of Current Business,* July, 1957, Table 25, p. 19.

a Employees in motor vehicles and equipment.

b Excludes employees in separate administrative and auxiliary units.

c Not available.

Number of Motor Vehicles Produced, United States, by Year[a]

1919-1957

(Numbers in thousands)

Year	Total[b]	Passenger Cars	Trucks and Buses
1919	1,876.4	1,651.6	224.7
1920	2,227.3	1,905.6	321.8
1921	1,616.2	1,468.1	148.1
1922	2,544.2	2,274.2	270.0
1923	4,034.0	3,624.7	409.3
1924	3,602.5	3,185.9	416.7
1925	4,254.8	3,735.2	530.7
1926	4,300.9	3,692.3	608.6
1927	3,401.3	2,936.5	464.8
1928	4,358.8	3,775.4	583.3
1929	5,337.1	4,455.2	881.9
1930	3,362.8	2,787.5	575.4
1931	2,380.4	1,948.2	432.3
1932	1,331.9	1,103.6	228.3
1933	1,889.8	1,560.6	329.2
1934	2,737.1	2,160.9	576.2
1935	3,971.2	3,273.9	697.4
1936	4,461.5	3,679.2	782.2
1937	4,820.2	3,929.2	891.0
1938	2,508.4	2,019.6	488.8
1939	3,588.9	2,888.5	700.4
1940	4,472.3	3,717.4	754.9
1941	4,840.5	3,779.7	1,060.8
1942	1,041.5	222.9	818.7
1943	699.8	.1	699.7
1944	738.1	.6	737.5
1945	725.2	69.5	655.7
1946	3,089.6	2,148.7	940.9
1947	4,797.6	3,558.2	1,239.4
1948	5,285.5	3,909.3	1,376.3
1949	6,253.7	5,119.5	1,134.2
1950	8,003.1	6,665.9	1,337.2
1951	6,765.3	5,338.4	1,426.8
1952	5,539.0	4,320.8	1,218.2
1953	7,323.2	6,116.9	1,206.3
1954	6,601.1	5,558.9	1,042.2
1955	9,169.3	7,920.2	1,249.1
1956	6,920.6	5,816.1	1,104.5
1957	7,214.2	6,113.3	1,100.8

Source: *Automotive News 1958 Almanac,* p. 28.

a *Based on factory sales.*

b *Detail may not add to totals because of rounding.*

Employees in Motor Vehicles and Equipment Industry, United States, East North Central States, and Michigan[a]

Selected years, 1947-1956

| Year | United States | Employees | | | | | | Michigan as Percent of— | | East North Central States as Percent of United States |
| | | East North Central States | | | | | | | | |
		All	Ohio	Indiana	Illinois	MICHIGAN	Wisconsin	United States	East North Central	
1947...........	765,700	620,100	85,700	60,600	20,600	421,700	31,500	55.1	68.0	81.0
1948...........	785,600	639,700	89,300	65,800	21,200	433,000	30,400	55.1	67.7	81.4
1949...........	682,000	541,500	57,200	63,900	14,300	380,100	26,000	55.7	70.2	79.4
1950...........	621,000	465,400	66,000	59,800	13,100	299,600	26,900	48.2	64.4	74.9
1951...........	846,900	663,200	87,300	76,200	18,600	449,300	31,800	53.1	67.7	78.3
1953...........	890,300	688,300	96,400	82,600	21,900	454,900	32,500	51.1	66.1	77.3
1956...........	802,200	591,900	89,100	64,500	20,900	387,900	29,500	48.4	65.5	73.8

Source: U. S. Department of Commerce and U. S. Department of Health, Education, and Welfare, *County Business Patterns, First Quarter* for years shown, Part 1.

a Starting with 1949, data exclude employees in administrative and auxiliary units. Data as of mid-March.

Production Workers in Motor Vehicles and Equipment Industry, United States, East North Central States, and Michigan[a]

Selected Years, 1899-1954

(Employees in thousands)

Year	United States		All[b]		Ohio		Indiana		Illinois		MICHIGAN		Wisconsin	
	Number	Percent	Number	Percent	Number	Percent	Number	Percent	Number	Percent	Number	Percent	Number	Percent
									East North Central States					
1899...	2.2	100.0	0.4	18.2	0.3	13.6	...	...	...	...	0.1	4.5	...	...
1904...	12.0	100.0	6.9	57.5	2.7	22.5	0.8	6.7	0.2	1.7	2.7	22.5	0.5	4.2
1909...	75.7	100.0	51.0	67.4	12.1	16.0	6.8	9.0	2.4	3.2	25.4	33.6	4.3	5.7
1914...	127.1	100.0	100.9	79.4	18.8	14.8	7.2	5.7	2.5	2.0	67.5	53.1	4.9	3.9
1919...	343.1	100.0	270.1	78.7	45.9	13.4	25.8	7.5	8.8	2.6	176.0	51.3	13.6	4.0
1921...	212.8	100.0	164.9	77.5	23.7	11.1	17.6	8.3	6.0	2.8	110.4	51.9	7.2	3.4
1923...	404.9	100.0	316.5	78.2	46.8	11.6	26.0	6.4	9.9	2.4	219.5	54.2	14.3	3.5
1925...	426.1	100.0	335.0	78.6	43.8	10.3	28.0	6.6	10.6	2.5	234.5	55.0	18.1	4.2
1927...	369.4	100.0	301.0	81.5	38.9	10.5	26.2	7.1	6.5	1.8	209.4	56.7	20.0	5.4
1929...	447.4	100.0	338.4	75.6	57.7	12.9	34.2	7.6	8.5	1.9	214.4	47.9	23.6	5.3
1931...	285.5	100.0	226.6	79.4	32.8	11.5	20.9	7.3	5.6	2.0	153.0	53.6	14.3	5.0
1933...	243.6	100.0	204.1	83.8	23.2	9.5	15.2	6.2	6.1	2.5	151.2	62.1	8.4	3.4
1935...	387.8	100.0	320.1	82.5	34.9	9.0	22.9	5.9	7.9	2.0	238.8	61.6	15.6	4.0
1937...	479.3	100.0	394.2	82.2	36.2	7.6	32.6	6.8	8.9	1.9	297.5	62.1	19.0	4.0
1939...	393.6	100.0	329.6	83.7	28.1	7.1	27.2	6.9	8.0	2.0	252.0	64.0	14.3	3.6
1947...	c599.3	100.0	471.7	78.7	58.6	9.8	49.8	8.3	15.9	2.7	325.8	54.4	21.6	3.6
1954...	583.0	100.0	439.2	75.3	66.5	11.4	45.6	7.8	15.0	2.6	295.3	50.7	16.8	2.9

Source: U. S. Bureau of the Census—

1899-1937: Census of Manufactures for years shown, as reported in Table XXXVII of William Haber, *How Much Does It Cost?* (Michigan Employment Security Commission, 1951).

1939-1947: Census of Manufactures, 1947, Vol. III.

1954: 1954 Census of Manufactures, Vol. III.

a Percents based on national totals.

b Detail may not add to totals due to rounding.

c Revised figure of 593,200 shown for 1947 in 1954 Census. Revised state data not available.

Production Workers as Percent of All Employees in Motor Vehicles and Equipment Industry, United States and Michigan

1947-1957

(Numbers in thousands)

| Year | United States | | | Michigan | | |
| | All employees | Production workers | | All employees | Production workers | |
		Number	Percent of all		Number	Percent of all
1947........	776.2	648.8	83.6	...	...	...
1948........	789.3	654.6	82.9	...	...	...
1949........	759.6	635.3	83.6	...	...	...
1950........	825.2	701.6	85.0	...	...	...
1951........	844.5	707.9	83.8	473	403	85.2
1952........	790.2	644.4	81.5	435	367	84.4
1953........	928.9	767.1	82.6	503	424	84.3
1954........	775.6	624.4	80.5	417	326	78.2
1955........	903.8	746.4	82.6	467	381	81.6
1956........	809.9	648.5	80.1	404	312	77.2
1957........	786.3	630.1	80.1	395	312	79.0

Source: United States—

Bureau of Labor Statistics, *Employment and Earnings—Annual Supplement Issue*, July, 1958, and *Employment and Payrolls—Annual Supplement Issue*, April, 1953.

Michigan—

All employees: Michigan Employment Security Commission, *Michigan's Labor Market*, January, 1958, p. 8.

Production workers: Based on BLS data available in office of Michigan Employment Security Commission.

Percentage Distribution of Passenger Car Assemblies, by State[a]

1953-1957

State	1957	1956	1955	1954	1953
United States.....................	100.0	100.0	100.0	100.0	100.0
MICHIGAN........................	34.6	33.0	34.1	32.1	35.8
California.........................	10.4	10.2	10.1	8.7	9.4
Missouri..........................	7.7	8.0	8.1	9.5	9.7
New Jersey.......................	6.8	6.9	6.3	6.2	5.0
Georgia..........................	5.1	5.3	5.2	4.8	4.3
Wisconsin........................	5.0	5.2	4.7	3.5	4.1
New York.........................	4.4	4.9	4.4	4.7	4.2
Indiana..........................	3.8	3.1	3.2	2.7	5.1
Texas............................	3.3	3.4	3.6	3.2	1.5
Maryland.........................	2.7	3.0	2.7	3.4	3.2
Other............................	16.2	17.0	17.6	21.2	17.7

Source: *Automotive News Almanac,* 1958, 1956, and 1955 issues, pp. 26, 31, and 32, respectively.

[a] States listed are ten states leading in assemblies in 1957. Data are for calendar year.

Passenger Car Production in the United States, by State and Manufacturer

1957 Model Year

(Numbers in thousands)

State	Production					Percent Distribution				
	All manufac-turers	General Motors	Ford	Chrysler	Other	All manufac-turers	General Motors	Ford	Chrysler	Other
United States	6,202.6	2,816.4	2,002.5	1,211.7	172.0	100.0	100.0	100.0	100.0	100.0
East North Central States	2,923.5	1,131.8	510.5	1,109.2	172.0	47.1	40.2	25.5	91.5	100.0
Ohio	149.7	149.7	...	...	...	2.4	5.3	...	...	...
Indiana	225.2	...	...	152.4	b72.8	3.6	...	...	12.6	b42.3
Illinois	103.5	...	103.5	...	...	1.7	...	5.2	...	...
MICHIGAN	2,151.2	787.4	407.0	956.8	...	34.7	28.0	20.3	78.9	...
Wisconsin	293.9	194.7	...	...	c99.2	4.7	6.9	...	...	c57.7
California	630.2	289.0	252.1	89.1	...	10.2	10.3	12.6	7.4	...
Missouri	479.6	318.5	161.1	...	...	7.7	11.3	8.0	...	...
New Jersey	415.4	135.5	279.9	...	...	6.7	4.8	14.0	...	...
Georgia	317.1	226.2	90.9	...	...	5.1	8.0	4.5	...	...
New York	288.5	208.0	80.5	...	...	4.7	7.4	4.0	...	...
Texas	213.2	67.7	145.5	...	...	3.4	2.4	7.3	...	...
Maryland	166.3	166.3	...	...	...	2.7	5.9	...	...	...
Kansas	118.9	118.9	...	...	...	1.9	4.2	...	...	...
Delaware	116.2	102.8	...	13.4	...	1.9	3.7	...	1.1	...
Massachusetts	99.3	51.7	47.6	...	...	1.6	1.8	2.4	...	...
Kentucky	99.0	...	99.0	...	...	1.6	...	4.9	...	...
Minnesota	92.3	...	92.3	...	...	1.5	...	4.6	...	...
Tennessee	85.3	...	85.3	...	...	1.4	...	4.3	...	...
Pennsylvania	82.0	...	82.0	...	...	1.3	...	4.1	...	...
Virginia	75.8	...	75.8	...	...	1.2	...	3.8	...	...

Source: Ward's *1958 Automotive Yearbook*, p. 57.

a Excludes some knocked-down export units.
b Studebaker-Packard.
c American Motors.

Expenditures for New Plant and Equipment in Motor Vehicles and Parts Industry, United States, Michigan, and Selected Other States[a]

1947 and 1954

(Amounts in thousands)

Area	Expenditures		Percent of United States	
	1954	1947	1954	1947
United States[b]......................	$722,199	$269,720	100.0	100.0
East North Central States..............	594,565	212,973	82.3	79.0
Ohio................................	106,088	29,960	14.7	11.1
Indiana.............................	[c]35,215	16,051	4.9	6.0
Illinois..............................	49,664	d	6.9	...
MICHIGAN.........................	394,354	154,300	54.6	57.2
Wisconsin..........................	9,244	d	1.3	...
Other states				
Massachusetts......................	1,448	4,592	.2	1.7
New York...........................	75,657	8,566	10.5	3.2
New Jersey.........................	5,566	1,598	.8	.6
Pennsylvania.......................	12,537	5,880	1.7	2.2
Missouri............................	9,068	d	1.3	...
California...........................	12,025	14,408	1.7	5.3

Source: 1954 Census of Manufactures, Vol. II, Pt. 2, Table 2, p. 37A-5 and Vol. III, Table 4, p. 113-10.

Census of Manufactures, 1947, Vol. II, Table 2, p. 753.

[a] This table covers motor vehicles and parts, which accounts for the great bulk of the motor vehicles and equipment industry.

[b] Includes data for states not listed.

[c] Estimated amount based on data shown for "Transportation equipment" group.

[d] Data not reported.

Establishments in Motor Vehicles and Equipment Industry, by Area[a]

Selected years, 1947-1956

| Year | Number of Establishments (reporting units)[b] | | | | | | | | Percent of All Establishments Located in— | | |
| | United States | East North Central States | | | | | | All other states[c] | Michigan | East North Central | All other states[c] |
		All	Ohio	Indiana	Illinois	MICHIGAN	Wisconsin				
1947........	1,871	817	172	126	159	308	52	1,054	16.5	43.7	56.3
1948........	2,088	902	177	138	177	351	59	1,186	16.8	43.2	56.8
1949........	2,141	876	176	133	177	331	59	1,265	15.5	40.9	59.1
1950........	2,064	888	173	138	178	345	54	1,176	16.7	43.0	57.0
1951........	2,144	913	173	136	188	350	66	1,231	16.3	42.6	57.4
1953........	2,314	956	176	159	188	358	75	1,358	15.5	41.3	58.7
1956........	2,344	965	209	152	182	351	71	1,379	15.0	41.2	58.8

Source: U. S. Department of Commerce and U. S. Department of Health, Education, and Welfare, County Business Patterns, First Quarter, for years shown, Part 1.

a Starting with 1949, data exclude administrative and auxiliary units.
b "Virtually all of the reporting units shown for manufacturing industries represent single establishments." Data are as of the first quarter of the calendar year. Each establishment had at least one employee during part of the calendar quarter.
c Other than East North Central States.

Number of Manufacturing Establishments in Michigan, by Industry Group

1953 and 1956

Industry Group	Manufacturing Establishments[a]			
	Number		Change, 1953-1956	
	1953	1956	Number	Percent
All manufacturing industries..........................	12,069	12,355	286	2.4
Durable goods industries............................	7,732	7,861	129	1.7
Lumber and wood products......................	1,242	1,173	− 69	− 5.6
Furniture..	393	401	8	2.0
Stone, clay, and glass products..................	503	516	13	2.6
Metal industries..................................	2,075	2,239	164	7.9
Primary metal products........................	492	502	10	2.0
Fabricated metal products.....................	1,583	1,737	154	9.7
Machinery, except electrical......................	2,631	2,578	− 53	− 2.0
Electrical machinery..............................	206	239	33	16.0
Transportation equipment........................	497	532	35	7.0
Motor vehicles and equipment.................	358	351	− 7	− 2.0
Other transportation equipment................	139	181	42	30.2
Instruments and related products...............	145	143	− 2	− 1.4
Other durable goods manufacturing..............	40	40	0	0
Nondurable goods industries.......................	3,514	3,592	78	2.2
Food and kindred products.......................	1,249	1,257	8	.6
Textile mill products and apparel.................	332	308	− 24	− 7.2
Paper and allied products........................	180	175	− 5	− 2.8
Printing, publishing, and allied products.........	1,196	1,271	75	6.3
Chemical, petroleum, and coal products.........	449	471	22	4.9
Rubber products.................................	37	55	18	48.6
Other nondurable goods manufacturing..........	71	55	− 16	−22.5
Miscellaneous manufacturing industries...........	690	731	41	5.9
Administrative and auxiliary.......................	133	171	38	28.6

Source: U. S. Department of Commerce and U. S. Department of Health, Education and Welfare, *County Business Patterns, First Quarter, 1953,* Part 4, pp. 119-20, and *First Quarter, 1956,* Part 4, pp. 190-91.

[a] *Based on "reporting units." "Virtually all of the reporting units shown for manufacturing industries re esent single establishments." Data are as of the first quarter of the calendar year. Each establishment had at least one employee during part of the calendar quarter.*

Manufacturers' Expenditures for New Plant and Equipment, United States, East North Central States, and Michigan

Selected years, 1939-1957

(Amounts in thousands)

Year	United States Amount	United States Per-cent	East North Central States — All Amount	All Per-cent[a]	Ohio Amount	Ohio Per-cent	Indiana Amount	Indiana Per-cent	Illinois Amount	Illinois Per-cent	MICHIGAN Amount	MICHIGAN Per-cent	Wisconsin Amount	Wisconsin Per-cent
1939...	$ 1,248,078	100.0	$ 421,071	33.7	$ 106,957	8.6	$ 69,515	5.6	$ 103,652	8.3	$ 110,197	8.8	$ 30,750	2.5
1947...	6,003,873	100.0	1,869,322	31.1	498,254	8.3	302,104	5.0	478,431	8.0	427,746	7.1	162,787	2.7
1951...	7,781,731	100.0	2,456,896	31.6	806,752	10.4	357,554	4.6	509,046	6.5	588,487	7.6	195,057	2.5
1952...	7,953,429	100.0	2,536,513	31.9	747,744	9.4	379,394	4.8	618,411	7.8	607,846	7.6	183,118	2.3
1953...	8,047,892	100.0	2,642,571	32.8	735,425	9.1	426,047	5.3	602,058	7.5	708,306	8.8	170,735	2.1
1954...	8,202,142	100.0	2,727,458	33.3	770,606	9.4	b301,247	3.7	575,233	7.0	897,842	10.9	b169,422	2.1
1955...	8,234,542	100.0	2,670,025	32.4	679,536	8.3	b448,807	5.5	562,349	6.8	805,804	9.8	173,529	2.1
1956...	11,234,581	100.0	3,742,254	33.3	1,053,550	9.4	b586,102	5.2	822,330	7.3	1,014,855	9.0	b224,031	2.0
1957...	12,145,052	100.0	3,824,763	31.5	1,208,534	10.0	651,572	5.4	923,428	7.6	b694,703	5.7	b310,713	2.6

Source: U. S. Department of Commerce, Statistical Abstract of the United States, various issues, chapter on "Manufactures." Data based on Census of Manufactures and Annual Survey of Manufactures.

a Percentages for states may not add to regional total because of rounding and exclusion of data for establishments under construction in some states.

b Excludes figures for establishments under construction. Latter included in totals for East North Central States and for the United States.

Manufacturers' Expenditures for New Plant and Equipment, by Object of Expenditure, United States, East North Central States, and Michigan[a]

Selected years, 1939-1957

Year	United States			East North Central States			Michigan		
	Total	Structures	Equipment	Total	Structures	Equipment	Total	Structures	Equipment
				Amount (in Thousands)					
1939	$ 1,248,078	$ 391,285	$ 856,793	$ 421,071	$ 125,749	$ 295,322	$ 110,197	$ 26,142	$ 84,055
1947	6,003,873	2,122,143	3,881,730	1,869,322	667,526	1,201,796	427,746	119,254	308,492
1951	7,781,731	2,593,220	5,188,511	2,456,896	839,136	1,617,760	588,487	188,792	399,695
1952	7,953,429	2,579,117	5,374,312	2,536,513	827,941	1,708,572	607,846	218,259	389,587
1953	8,047,892	2,585,339	5,462,553	2,642,571	760,788	1,881,783	708,306	158,085	550,221
1954	8,202,142	2,458,962	5,743,180	2,727,458	765,596	1,961,862	897,842	182,241	715,601
1955	8,234,542	2,425,493	5,809,049	2,670,025	761,903	1,908,122	805,804	196,513	609,291
1956	11,234,581	3,471,488	7,763,093	3,742,254	1,073,796	2,668,458	1,014,855	232,298	782,557
1957	12,145,052	3,864,793	8,280,259	3,824,763	1,178,683	2,646,080	b694,703	128,678	566,025
				Percent Distribution					
1939	100.0	31.4	68.6	100.0	29.9	70.1	100.0	23.7	76.3
1947	100.0	35.3	64.7	100.0	35.7	64.3	100.0	27.9	72.1
1951	100.0	33.3	66.7	100.0	34.2	65.8	100.0	32.1	67.9
1952	100.0	32.4	67.6	100.0	32.6	67.4	100.0	35.9	64.1
1953	100.0	32.1	67.9	100.0	28.8	71.2	100.0	22.3	77.7
1954	100.0	30.0	70.0	100.0	28.1	71.9	100.0	20.3	79.7
1955	100.0	29.5	70.5	100.0	28.5	71.5	100.0	24.4	75.6
1956	100.0	30.9	69.1	100.0	28.7	71.3	100.0	22.9	77.1
1957	100.0	31.8	68.2	100.0	30.8	69.2	100.0	18.5	81.5

Source: U. S. Department of Commerce, *Statistical Abstract of the United States*, various issues, chapter on "Manufactures." Data based on *Census of Manufactures* and *Annual Survey of Manufactures.*

a "Structures" include new structures and addition to plant. "Equipment" includes new machinery and equipment.

b Excludes data for establishments under construction.

Manufacturers' Expenditures for New Plant and Equipment, Michigan, by Industry Group[a]

1947, 1954, and 1956

(Amounts in thousands)

Industry Group	1956		1954						1947					
	Total Amount	Per-cent	Total		Structures		Equipment		Total		Structures		Equipment	
			Amount	Per-cent	Amount	Per-cent	Amount	Per-cent	Amount	Per-cent	Amount	Per-cent	Amount	Per-cent
All groups[b]	$983,928	100.0	$870,465	100.0	$167,825	100.0	$702,640	100.0	$427,746	100.0	$119,254	100.0	$308,492	100.0
Food and kindred products	41,981	4.3	31,789	3.7	9,831	5.9	21,958	3.1	29,985	7.0	10,900	9.1	19,085	6.2
Lumber and wood products	c	......	3,918	.5	905	.5	3,013	.4	4,485	1.0	2,221	1.9	2,264	.7
Furniture and fixtures	5,589	.6	4,478	.5	1,055	.6	3,423	.5	4,072	1.0	1,307	1.1	2,765	.9
Pulp, paper, and products	29,144	3.0	26,705	3.1	5,367	3.2	21,338	3.0	21,765	5.1	6,136	5.1	15,629	5.1
Printing and publishing	12,769	1.3	11,900	1.4	2,569	1.5	9,331	1.3	4,801	1.1	995	.8	3,806	1.2
Chemicals and products	58,093	5.9	42,912	4.9	9,935	5.9	32,977	4.7	56,005	13.1	20,556	17.2	35,449	11.5
Petroleum and coal products	9,374	1.0	11,767	1.4	5,759	3.4	6,008	.9	2,984	.7	1,680	1.4	1,304	.4
Rubber products	9,665	1.0	7,098	.8	c		6,745	1.0	6,675	1.6	1,280	1.1	5,395	1.7
Stone, clay & glass prod.	27,022	2.7	17,761	2.0	4,435	2.6	13,326	1.9	8,874	2.1	2,163	1.8	6,711	2.2
Primary metal products	88,196	9.0	124,913	14.4	26,318	15.7	98,595	14.0	46,091	10.8	17,171	14.4	28,920	9.4
Fabricated metal products	59,079	6.0	84,535	9.7	31,616	18.8	52,919	7.5	30,491	7.1	9,004	7.5	21,487	7.0
Machinery, except electrical	105,854	10.8	73,765	8.5	14,856	8.9	58,909	8.4	40,259	9.4	11,549	9.7	28,710	9.3
Electrical machinery	c	......	13,274	1.5	3,229	1.9	10,045	1.4	5,783	1.4	1,883	1.6	3,900	1.3
Transportation equipment	518,542	52.7	400,972	46.1	45,092	26.9	355,880	50.6	158,979	37.2	30,523	25.6	128,456	41.6

385

Source: Bureau of the Census

1956: 1956 Annual Survey of Manufactures, Series MAS-56-5 (April 25, 1958), p. 12.
1954: 1954 Census of Manufactures, Vol. I, Table 6, p. 206-15.
1947: 1947 Census of Manufactures, Vol. III, Table 3, p. 302.

a Excludes expenditures for plants under construction. "Structures" include new structures and addition to plant. "Equipment" includes new machinery and equipment.
b Includes data for industry groups not listed and for groups for which data are not available or negligible in amount.
c Not available or negligible.

Total Personal Income, United States, East North Central States, and Michigan, by Year

1929-1958

(Amounts in millions)

Year	Personal Income			Michigan as Percent of—	
	United States[a]	East North Central States	Michigan	United States	East North Central States
1929............	$ 85,661	$20,235	$ 3,803	4.4	18.8
1930............	76,780	17,328	3,186	4.1	18.4
1931............	65,597	14,431	2,593	4.0	18.0
1932............	50,022	10,501	1,882	3.8	17.9
1933............	47,122	9,737	1,668	3.5	17.1
1934............	53,482	11,544	2,167	4.1	18.8
1935............	60,104	13,378	2,554	4.2	19.1
1936............	68,363	15,394	3,014	4.4	19.6
1937............	73,803	17,109	3,389	4.6	19.8
1938............	68,433	15,060	2,891	4.2	19.2
1939............	72,753	16,428	3,215	4.4	19.6
1940............	78,522	17,818	3,610	4.6	20.3
1941............	99,953	22,084	4,522	4.5	20.5
1942............	122,417	27,227	5,812	4.7	21.3
1943............	148,409	32,748	7,269	4.9	22.2
1944............	160,118	34,901	7,570	4.7	21.7
1945............	164,549	35,511	7,215	4.4	20.3
1946............	175,701	38,332	7,743	4.4	20.2
1947............	189,077	42,488	8,832	4.7	20.8
1948............	207,414	47,505	9,579	4.6	20.2
1949............	205,452	45,924	9,522	4.6	20.7
1950............	225,473	50,744	10,803	4.8	21.3
1951............	252,960	57,557	12,103	4.8	21.0
1952............	269,050	60,768	12,902	4.8	21.2
1953............	283,140	65,761	14,516	5.1	22.1
1954............	285,339	64,894	14,127	5.0	21.8
1955............	306,598	70,208	15,785	5.1	22.5
1956............	330,380	75,341	16,587	5.0	22.0
1957............	347,911	78,283	16,893	4.9	21.6
1958............	356,328	77,734	16,507	4.6	21.2

Source: U. S. Department of Commerce, *Personal Income by States since 1929*, Table 1, pp. 140-41 and *Survey of Current Business*, August, 1959, Table 1, p. 15.

[a] Continental United States.

Projected Michigan Population as Percent of Projected United States Population[a]

1955-1970

(Numbers in thousands)

Year (July 1)	United States Population			Michigan Population							
	Series 1	Series 2-3	Series 4	Number				Percent of United States			
				Series 1	Series 2	Series 3	Series 4	Series 1	Series 2	Series 3	Series 4
				Total population							
1955	164,303	164,303	164,303	7,326	7,326	7,326	7,326	4.46	4.46	4.46	4.46
1960	178,479	176,908	175,520	8,355	8,183	8,108	8,041	4.68	4.63	4.58	4.58
1965	192,595	189,364	185,359	9,380	9,057	8,901	8,706	4.87	4.78	4.70	4.70
1970	208,346	203,688	195,438	10,483	10,043	9,799	9,392	5.03	4.93	4.81	4.81
				Population 14 years old and over							
1955	117,897	117,897	117,897	5,189	5,189	5,189	5,189	4.40	4.40	4.40	4.40
1960	125,441	125,405	125,405	5,796	5,725	5,660	5,660	4.62	4.57	4.51	4.51
1965	136,723	136,256	136,256	6,563	6,427	6,293	6,293	4.80	4.72	4.62	4.62
1970	148,973	147,620	147,426	7,406	7,188	6,986	6,977	4.97	4.87	4.73	4.73

Source: Bureau of the Census, Current Population Reports, Series P-25, No. 160, August 9, 1957, Tables 1 and 2.

a Represents "resident" population, i. e., the civilian population and the armed forces stationed in the area. For assumptions with respect to migration, fertility, and mortality underlying different series, see source document.

Appendix Table XXIII

Components of Population Increase in Michigan

Actual, 1950-1956, and Projected, 1955-1970

(Numbers in thousands)

Period[a]	Population[b]					Percentage Distribution		
	Total increase[c]	Natural increase			Net migration	Total increase	Natural increase	Net migration
		Net	Births	Deaths				
1950-1956..........	1,208	772	1,154	382	435	100.0	64.0	36.0
1955-1960								
High estimate.........	1,029	681	1,002	321	348	100.0	66.2	33.8
Low estimate.........	715	531	849	318	184	100.0	74.3	25.7
1955-1970								
High estimate.........	3,157	2,230	3,280	1,050	927	100.0	70.6	29.4
Low estimate.........	2,066	1,537	2,614	1,077	529	100.0	74.4	25.6

Source: 1950-1956: *Current Population Reports,* Series P-25, No. 165, November 4, 1957, Table 4.
1955-1960, 1955-1970: *Current Population Reports,* Series P-25, No. 160, August 9, 1957, Table 3, Series 1 and 4.

a All data as of July 1 except for 1950 which are as of April 1.
b Represents "resident" population, i. e., civilian population plus armed forces stationed in the state.
c Increases shown in this column for 1955-1960 and 1955-1970 are based on population projections (Series 1 and Series 4) shown in Appendix Table XXII.

Percentage Distribution of Employed Persons, by Major Occupation Group, United States and Michigan

1940 and 1950

Occupation Group	United States		Michigan	
	1940	1950	1940	1950
Number employed.........................	44,888,083	56,239,449	1,821,403	2,393,574
Percentage distribution				
All occupations^a........................	*100.0*	*100.0*	*100.0*	*100.0*
Professional, technical, and kindred workers.................................	7.9	8.7	7.8	8.5
Farmers and farm managers..............	11.5	7.7	7.9	4.7
Managers, officials, and proprietors, except farm.............................	8.1	8.9	7.5	7.9
Clerical and kindred workers..............	9.7	12.3	9.9	12.3
Sales workers.............................	6.8	7.0	6.8	7.0
Craftsmen, foremen, and kindred workers	11.5	13.8	15.5	16.4
Operatives and kindred workers...........	17.9	19.8	22.6	25.9
Private household workers................	4.6	2.5	3.3	1.7
Service workers, except private households.............................	7.1	7.6	7.1	7.6
Farm laborers, unpaid family workers.....	2.6	1.6	1.4	.7
Farm laborers, except unpaid, and farm foremen.................................	4.3	2.6	2.2	1.1
Laborers, except farm and mine...........	7.0	6.1	6.9	5.0
Occupation not reported..................	.9	1.3	1.0	1.3

Source: U. S. Bureau of the Census, *1950 Census of Population,* Vol. II, Pt. 1, Table 54 and Pt. 22, Table 29.

^a *Detail will not necessarily add to totals because of rounding.*

Index

Index

Index

Index

Massachusetts, 70, 168, 305, 306, 308
Mattila, John M., 310, 361
McCurry, John C., 321, 321n.
McLaughlin, Glenn E., 297n.
Michigan Corporation and Securities Commission, 319
Michigan Department of Economic Development, 131, 132, 153, 245, 246, 247, 362-63
Michigan Economic Development Commission, 245, 361
Michigan Employment Security Act, 282
Michigan Employment Security Commission, 76, 77, 80n., 86n., 90, 92n., 95, 97, 215, 219, 220n., 224, 225n., 230, 238, 258
Michigan's employment outlook, 233-49
 long-range outlook for nation, 235-36
 Michigan's long-range outlook, 236-42
 short-run outlook for Michigan, 233-35
 suggested lines of action, 242-49
Michigan Industrial Ambassadors, 246
Michigan Manufacturer and Financial Record, quoted 239-40
Michigan Manufacturers' Association, 321
Michigan State Mediation Board, 301
Michigan State University, 217n.
Michigan Supreme Court, 301
Michigan's transportation system, 158-62, 329-39
 and the state's industrial development, 329-39
 air transportation facilities, 334
 automobile parts industry, 338
 conclusion, 339
 existing transportation laws and regulations, 334-35
 highway transportation facilities, 334
 introduction, 329-31
 passenger service, 332
 research and implementation program, 338-39
 survey of present users, 337-38
 tariff structure analysis, 336-37
 transportation problems of the Upper Peninsula, 337
 trucking services, 331
 water transportation, 332-34
Midwest Research Institute, 323
Milwaukee, Wisconsin, 169n., 274, 311
Minneapolis, Minnesota, 169n.
Minnesota, 305, 307, 308
Mississippi, 295n., 307
Missouri, 70
Montana, 273
Motor vehicles and equipment;
 See Automotive industry
Mount Clemens, Michigan, 317
"Movement of Industry in Michigan," 131
Muskegon, Michigan, 260, 331

National Industrial Conference Board, 266
National Planning Association, 223n., 235
Nebraska, 295n.
Nevada, 295n., 308
Newark, New Jersey, 274, 275
New Hampshire, 67
New Jersey, 306, 313
New York, 70, 168, 273, 278, 305, 306, 307, 308, 313, 314, 319
New York City, 151, 169n., 274, 275
North Carolina, 70, 295n.
North Dakota, 295n., 307

Oakland, California, 274
Occupational patterns, 231-32, 247
Office of Area Development; *See* U. S. Department of Commerce
Ohio, 69-96 passim, 126-89 passim, 261-98 passim, 307, 308, 313, 341-54 passim
Operating the ABC Corporation, 341-54
 characteristics of cities selected for study, 344
 conclusions, 352-54
 cost differences between cities of comparable size, 348-50
 cost differences within states, 350
 description of the Corporation, 342-44
 findings of the study, 344-50
 limitations of the study, 350-52

Packard Motors, 115
Paley Commission, 153, quoted 156
Parker, Sanford S., 235n.
Passenger service, 336
Pennsylvania, 70, 168, 269-98 passim, 305, 307, 313, 314, 319
Pennsylvania Economy League, Inc., 315
"Pennsylvania Study" (*The Relative Tax Cost to Manufacturing Industry*), 312, 317, 318
Personal income, 140-44
Philadelphia, Pennsylvania, 275
Pittsburgh, Pennsylvania, 311
Plymouth, Michigan, 315, 316, 317
Population, 67-73
 areas of concentration, 71
 growth, 67
 and per capita income, 143-44
 industrial expansion and, 72
 in-migration and, 72-73
 Michigan compared, 67, 69-71
 projections of, 216-17
Product research, 243-44
Publicity, 236-37

Rail service, 332
Rambler automobile, 109
Raw materials, 152-53, 171-80 passim, 255, 256

Index